WILD VISIONARY

Stanford Studies in Jewish History and Culture

WILD VISIONARY

Maurice Sendak in Queer Jewish Context

GOLAN Y. MOSKOWITZ

STANFORD UNIVERSITY PRESS
Stanford, California

STANFORD UNIVERSITY PRESS
Stanford, California

Printed in the United States of America on acid-free, archival-quality paper

Library of Congress Cataloging-in-Publication Data

Names: Moskowitz, Golan, author.

Title: Wild visionary : Maurice Sendak in queer Jewish context / Golan Moskowitz.

Other titles: Stanford studies in Jewish history and culture.

Description: Stanford, California : Stanford University Press, 2020. | Series: Stanford studies in Jewish history and culture | Includes bibliographical references and index.

Identifiers: LCCN 2020020052 (print) | LCCN 2020020053 (ebook) | ISBN 9781503613812 (cloth) | ISBN 9781503614086 (paperback) | ISBN 9781503614093 (epub)

Subjects: LCSH: Sendak, Maurice—Criticism and interpretation. | Illustrators—United States—Biography. | Authors, American—20th century—Biography. | Jewish gay men—United States—Biography. | Children's stories, American—Authorship.

Classification: LCC NC975.5.S44 M67 2020 (print) | LCC NC975.5.S44 (ebook) | DDC 741.6092 [B]—dc23

LC record available at https://lccn.loc.gov/2020020052

LC ebook record available at https://lccn.loc.gov/2020020053

Book design: Kevin Barrett Kane

Photographic credit: Patrick Downs/*Los Angeles Times* via Getty Images

CONTENTS

ACKNOWLEDGMENTS

This book would not exist without the steadfast support and mentorship of ChaeRan Y. Freeze, who, since my time as a graduate student, invested in my work and offered critical attention and sensitive encouragement. I cannot thank her enough for the countless hours she spent reading and discussing drafts, connecting me to thought partners, and championing this project. I am grateful, also, to Sylvia Fuks Fried for challenging me to clarify my voice, and for extending solidarity and invaluable insights about editing and publishing. In addition, I express my wholehearted thanks to the many other mentors and colleagues who discussed ideas with me, read work in progress, shared sources, and offered feedback at various stages, including Jonathan D. Sarna, Ellen Kellman (with whom I also consulted on Yiddish transliterations), Kenneth Kidd, Susan Mizruchi, Noam Sienna (who commented on a final draft of the manuscript), Allyson Gonzalez, Sara Shostak, Gregory Freeze, Jeffrey Shandler, Eugene Sheppard, Mark Davila, Ellen Smith, Ilana Szobel, Laura Jockusch, Anna Shternshis, Doris Bergen, Naomi Seidman, Jonathan Krasner, John Plotz, Paul Morrison, Marc Michael Epstein, Joshua Lambert, Jodi Eichler-Levine, Lara Silberklang, Defne Çizakça, Sylvia Barack Fishman, Shulamit Reinharz, Celine Ibrahim, Jennifer Thomas, Alexandra Herzog, Elizabeth Anthony, Dienke Hondius, and Samantha Baskind. Further gratitude is due to Jonathan Weinberg, Eric Pederson, Edmund Newman, Kate Glynn, Judith Goldman, Christopher Mattaliano, James Bohlman, Loring Vogel, Glenn Dickson, Benjamin Ross, Philip Nel, Justin Cammy, and Deborah Belford de Furia for corresponding with me about their personal recollections or inherited stories about Sendak and his late partner, Eugene Glynn. In addition, I thank the librarians, archivists, and curators who lent patient assistance and crucial knowledge in support of my research, including Patrick Rodgers, Clara Nguyen, Melissa Watterworth Batt, Kristin Eshelman, Rachel Federman (who also located and facilitated usage of this book's cover image), Linnea Anderson, and Lyudmila Sholokhova. Gratitude is also owed to Margo Irvin, David Biale, Sarah Abrevaya Stein, Cindy Lim, Gigi Mark, David Horne, and their colleagues at Stanford University Press for the careful attention and expertise offered throughout the editorial and publication processes. A number of organizations and awards helped to fund this project, completed over a period that spanned from my doctoral program through appointments as a resident scholar at the Hadassah-Brandeis Institute, as Ray D. Wolfe Postdoctoral Fellow at the University of Toronto's Anne Tanenbaum Centre for Jewish Studies, and as Assistant Professor of Jewish Studies and Catherine and Henry J. Gaisman Faculty Fellow at Tulane University. Support for research, related conference travel, and publication came from the Memorial Foundation for Jewish Culture, the Andrew W. Mellon Foundation, the Hadassah-Brandeis Institute, the Tauber Institute for the Study of European Jewry, Brandeis University's Graduate School of Arts and Sciences, the Brandeis Department of Near Eastern & Judaic Studies, the Anne Tanenbaum Centre for Jewish Studies at the University of Toronto, YIVO, the Association for the Social Scientific Study of Jewry, and a Billie M. Levy Travel and Research Grant at the University of Connecticut. Manuscript preparation was supported in part through the Catherine and Henry J. Gaisman Faculty Fellowship in the School of Liberal Arts at Tulane University. Finally, and on a more personal note, I thank my parents, Sarit and Mark Moskowitz, my sisters, Tamar Jacobson (who also read proofs) and Elior Moskowitz, my grandparents, Esther and Moshe Signer and Marilyn and Herb Moskowitz, and my partner, Trey Pratt. What all of you have taught me through example, patience, and generosity of spirit has urged this book into being.

WILD VISIONARY

FROM LIMBO TO CHILDHOOD

"I DON'T LIKE ALL KIDS," the late Maurice Sendak (1928–2012) once infamously declared. "Some of them are as awful as their parents."[1] Very young people, he believed, are not categorically alike. Sendak rejected the Enlightenment-based notion that children are "blank slates," shapeable matter born to serve an enfranchised status quo by playing the socially desired role—in the case of modern childhood, that role was usually "the innocent." Ideals of childhood innocence, he felt, reflected adults' demands that children not *know* or *feel*, but instead primarily *behave*, submitting to dictation from an exclusionary society. Children, the artist asserted, were tragically socialized out of the fierce honesty and emotional transparency with which they are born and which few adults manage to maintain.[2] He believed in children's inherent capacity to differ from each other, to question, to know, to preserve endangered parts of the self, and to resist sanctioned injustices. In the artist's own words, his work explores "how a child deals with revolutionary, tumultuous feelings that have no place in a given setting, like the classroom or his mother's apartment."[3] Situated in broader cultural and historical contexts, the present study shines new light on Sendak's own displaced "revolutionary, tumultuous feelings" as they drove his sensitive inner life and his work.

During his own early years, Sendak was markedly "different" from other children. He occupied an ethereal, self-constituted realm between his Yiddish-speaking immigrant parents' Old World memories, wild fantasies inspired by the American popular arts, and the laws of an establishment culture he perceived as vapid, assimilatory, and even dangerous. Disillusioned by school and social surroundings in the 1930s through the 1950s, he thrived instead on the gruesome and sensual thrills of folklore and mass culture and on Romantic sensibilities that envisioned young people as primal vessels of nature, rather than pliable citizens-in-the-making. Like a Renaissance-era artist, he favored models of apprenticeship and practical immersion over formal schooling. The latter, he felt, subdued one's greatest passions.[4] Many refer to Sendak as the Picasso of children's literature. This likely stems from his alignment with Picasso's famous adage that every child is an artist but most do not remain so in adulthood. An autodidact and voracious reader, Sendak admired writers such as Charles Dickens, William Blake, George MacDonald, and Henry James, noting that underneath their sophisticated social and political depictions was the intensity of an observant child who survives and suffers within the artist's adult self, peering out at the world and taking it all to heart.[5] In their sensitivity to emotional possibilities forgotten or ignored, Sendak's protagonists blur the line between childhood and adulthood, perceiving harmonies and connections that surprise, comfort, and challenge. Like artists, they follow emotional and physiological rhythms that expose the limits of socially constructed boundaries and modes of being.

Sendak struggled to maintain access to the feelings of his own childhood as the root of his art. Childhood, for him, was a time of navigating terror, sensual awakening, and solitary emotional fogs while clarifying perceptions of self and surroundings. It was as a child that he'd grappled most directly with the problem of creating and socializing himself while surviving urban dangers and the normalizing coercion of teachers, peers, and media. As he repeatedly stated, he believed that the success of his work depended "almost entirely on an uninhibited intercourse with this primitive, uncensored self." Sendak claimed that he experienced his life as being in a constant state of emotional "limbo" as a professional "diver," in and out of deep memory. As he understood it, the chaos of his internal limbo state denoted childhood, and childhood thereby became the framework underlying his career.[6] He once shared that the reason he preferred creating books for younger children was their appreciation of the playful possibility of moving between worlds, of traversing the thin line between reality and fantasy.[7]

But Sendak wrote *through* the child more than he wrote *for* the child, and this is significant to why children love his work—it tackles constructions of childhood, rather than reinforcing them. As he told one interviewer in 1973, "Children were never consciously in my mind. I never think of them as an audience."[8] Although he knew that his largest and most responsive readership was below the age of eight, he resisted the label of children's book artist, as well as the notion that children's books existed as any coherent genre or category. Rather, he felt that his books addressed questions and ideas that interested sensitive individuals engrossed in particular concerns, and that most of those such individuals happened to be children. His Harper editor, Ursula Nordstrom, supported this mentality, stating plainly that the best children's book creators made their work not for children, but for *themselves*.[9] Sendak pointedly distinguished between what he termed "child view" and "creative view," tempering his fresh, child-like emotional honesty and ingenuity with his mature aesthetic restraint and erudition.[10] His sensitive, passionate, and socially liminal position was one to which most children happen to relate, along with other insider-outsiders, regardless of age. *Outside Over There* (1981), for example, featured in both children's and adult catalogs, and some critics wrote that the book was suited more to adults interested in their own "inner child" than it was to actual children.[11] Three years after its publication, a *Los Angeles Times* book review noted that a third of Sendak's sales were to "childless people in their 20s and 30s."[12] As a creative, then, Sendak honed his memory of childhood feelings into a mature sensibility all his own.

Ultimately, Sendak worked for the concerns of his own childhood feelings—his need to make meaning of an existence positioned between conflicting realities and multiple forms of endangerment. He was open about the inherently narcissistic nature of his work, claiming, "You also have to be interested in yourself to write. . . . [T]he business of being an artist is indulging oneself. My work points in no direction other than to me."[13] His art functioned, in part, to offer care for his earlier self, who had felt forbidden and unable to grow up without becoming "someone else." He claimed to have created *Where the Wild Things Are* (1963), for example, as a means of exorcising "a feeling" of his own, one he described as "the terror not so much of childhood, but of being alive."[14] As he saw it, his child self was cut off, awaiting rescue through the adult's art. Indeed, the artist claimed, "I don't really believe that the kid I was has grown up into me. He still exists somewhere, in the most graphic, plastic, physical way for me. I have a tremendous concern for, and interest in, him. I try to communicate with him all the time."[15] He would convey this feeling of a split self through various mechanisms, perhaps most blatantly in *Outside Over There*, depicting an infant replaced with a changeling ice baby with which he identified. He sublimated this childhood dissociation, allowing the wild, queer boy that he was to play and experiment in his picture books. In doing so, Sendak offered alienated readers a sensitive and bold commentary on the nature of modern social reality and modeled how to survive its emotional tribulations. His depictions of childhood's universal queerness—its wild, sensual, and irreverent oddness—resonates with those adults who most remember, or continue to experience, feelings of emotional marginalization and a yearning for liberation.

As an embodied testament to a complex historical and cultural experience, his work opens fascinating opportunities for social historians and cultural theorists alike. This book seizes some of these opportunities, taking queer Jewish Sendak by the hand, so to speak, to concentrate on the feelings that propelled his inner life and creative output in dialogue with the histories, memories, and surrounding cultural shifts that marked his inner depths. Offering historical empathy, I situate Sendak's emotional world within broader cultural narratives, drawing on insights from Jewish, American, and queer studies. Ultimately, I demonstrate how Sendak made foundational contributions from his emotional "limbo" as a queer "Old World" American Jew and as a nonconformist artist responding to a life that spanned the Depression, World War II, and the AIDS epidemic. Sendak cultivated his ability to play, suffer, and create within his culturally fraught fantasy realms, engaging in make-believe in written correspondences, retreating to the colorful beach towns of Fire Island, and drawing in a stream-of-consciousness style to classical music. His decidedly introspective and sophisticated use of "child's play" and fantasy—sometimes so sensual, homoerotic, or grotesque in content as to elicit public controversy—sat in tension in the late twentieth century with misguided characterizations of social outsiders, as well as with the public's willful ignorance about his sexuality.

Where Is Sendak Within Children's Literature?

In the early twentieth century, a culture of children's reading emerged in the United States with increases in library funding and an optimistic new generation of editors. Previously, libraries had warded off children with the policy of "No dogs or children allowed."[16] But American children's reading expanded with the establishment of children's rooms in public libraries, the creation in 1922 of the American Library Association's John Newbery Medal for best children's book, and in 1938 the Caldecott Medal for best illustration.[17] In 1924 in Boston, *The Horn Book Magazine* became the nation's first periodical review of children's literature. Growing demand for quality children's books also led publishers to create children's book departments and to hire specialist editors; Harper's children's department originated, for example, in 1926.[18] Two years later, Sendak was born, and Wanda Gág authored the first American picture book to fully integrate text and image: *Millions of Cats*, published by G. P. Putnam's Sons.[19] Nine years later, in 1937, Dr. Seuss published his first picture book: *And to Think I Saw It on Mulberry Street*.[20] Unlike Seuss, who based his work on the quirky recollections of adolescence, Sendak would draw his greatest inspiration from early childhood.[21]

Though children's reading expanded in these decades, the quality of available picture books suffered from widespread conservatism through the 1950s, which policed the category of childhood and limited the aesthetic representations available to children. In 1939, Simon & Schuster published Ludwig Bemelmans's first *Madeline* book, following its rejection by Viking Press, which perceived the heroine as "a tad *too* naughty."[22] Jewish Anglophone literature for children similarly suffered from didacticism and simplification in these years. Though standards rose somewhat after the publication of Sadie Rose Weilerstein's *The Adventures of K'tonton* (1935), a Jewish "Tom Thumb" story, Jewish picture books in English generally remained instruments of social acculturation or religious education.[23] The creation in 1954 of the Comics Magazine Association of America and its code of criteria—which forbade profanity; obscenity; ridicule of police, parents, racial, and religious groups; and exaggerations of the female anatomy—further mitigated American youths' exposure to concerns of the wider world. Dr. Fredric Wertham, a German Jewish American psychiatrist and author of *Seduction of the Innocent* (1954), argued that comic books blunted conscience, made children less susceptible to art and education, and obscured children's understanding of relations between the sexes, causing homosexuality and juvenile delinquency. Although comic strips, cartoons, and films of the previous decades had already acknowledged some of the darker, frightening aspects of childhood, "[t]he American assumption" at mid-century was, as David Michaelis writes, that children were always happy, that childhood was a "golden time."[24] American adults were eager to see children as symbols of their personal and collective futures, even at the expense of recognizing actual children's feelings.

Combined with uninspired books that failed to engage children, censorship and attendant discourses of childhood innocence prevented minority children from seeing themselves in the world. Most starkly, minutes from the 1950 White House Conference on Children condemned popular media forms and warned about the possibility of "the standards of the lowest class" infecting "the boys and girls of other social groups" through the intermixing of children. Historian Joseph Illick reads in such words a race-infused antagonism against "the spread of lower-class culture."[25] Speaking to the Jewish community, Jacob Golub of the *Jewish Book Annual* complained that same year, "We are neglecting our children. . . . [A]lmost as many books go out of print every year as are added. Thus we are barely holding our own in a land and at a time when we are supposed to become the cultural leaders of world

Jewry. It must become someone's duty to see to it that ... our children's literature expands."[26] Golub's call for books of quality for Jewish children was especially relevant given that, until the second half of the twentieth century, mainstream American children's books generally excluded Jewish and other minority youth, conveying a world centered almost exclusively on angelic, Anglo-Saxon Protestant children. Boys were boys, girls were girls, and the occasional depictions of Jewish and other ethnically or racial minority children were highly curated and sanitized for general audiences.

The content and tone of children's media began to shift with playful realists such as Charles Schulz (1922–2000), whose *Peanuts* comic strip began in 1950 to humanize childhood by coloring it with the dissatisfaction, existential gloom, philosophical musing, and complexity of adulthood.[27] More playfulness and critical thinking emerged in children's books by Ruth Krauss, William Steig, Tomi Ungerer, and others. But Sendak broke new ground by channeling an even deeper sensitivity to children's private, painful, and darker moments, also setting much of his work within the perilous landscape of the city. By presenting children in danger and obstructed from their most basic needs and desires, he awakened perhaps the most meaningful depictions of courage and creative transformation through fantasy. Expanding on Schulz's existentially frustrated but well-mannered caricatures and Dr. Seuss's zany, whimsical cartoons, Sendak reached into the universal and highly untidy dramas of infancy—the nonverbal rage, sensuality, and animal drives of forming subjects who loudly negotiate their self-worth and survival. Sendak believed that children needed stories not only for optimism but also for self-preservation, in order to "confront the incomprehensible in their lives—bullies, school, and the vagaries of the adult world."[28]

Why Focus on Jewishness?

Sendak related to multiple forms of Jewish difference in America vis-à-vis the "Old World," the Holocaust and its belated mainstream memorialization, late twentieth-century "ethnic revival," and perennial Jewish concerns around particularism and universalism. Properly situating Sendak as, in part, an "Old World" Jew helps add nuance to the

often generalized narrative of American Jewish assimilation and com-
placence. Sendak carved a markedly solitary path, insisting on a vision
of himself as an ethnically "other," atheist, Old World Jew. Despite his
atheism, he identified strongly with Jewish ethnicity, shared his adult
life with a secular Jewish partner, surrounded himself with Jewish confidantes, and connected his Orthodox upbringing with a lingering drive
to constantly make life "purposeful."[29] His conception of childhood
draws generously from a heritage located beyond dominant Protestant
American norms. While much of the interwar Jewish American establishment had arrived before 1880 and identified with acculturated
Central and Western European Reform Judaism, most Yiddish-speaking immigrants, including the Sendaks, arrived later, often fleeing
poverty or antisemitism; they stood closer to histories of traditional
Jewish community and physical endangerment as Jews. Even in the
immediate postwar decades, generally characterized by Jewish acculturation, affluence, and migration to the suburbs, the Sendaks remained
urban, Yiddish-speaking, and lower-middle class. Children like Sendak
internalized their parents' feelings of endangerment, learning to focus
on survival and in-group loyalty, even as their parents pushed them
to achieve American success. As Sendak's work conveys, the domestic
space of the home—with its special foods, songs, and rituals—remained
a site for cultivating particular cultural values and emotional investments for families like his, even as the household uneasily balanced Old
World traditions and contemporary American bourgeois expectations.[30]
Not least among these negotiations of the Jewish American home was
the reconceptualization of childhood as a pathway into modernity and
the middle class.

Yiddish-speaking Jews like the Sendaks participated in a culture
that resisted fetishistic idealizations of childhood. Generations of their
family were raised in Yiddish-speaking communities and educated in
the *kheyder* system, which, according to Gennady Estraikh, did not view
children as essentially different from adults.[31] As Estraikh notes, Yiddish
writer Shmuel Charney described the traditional conception of a Jewish
child in 1935 through the words of Mendele Moykher-Sforim's *Dos vint-
shfingerl* (the wishing ring) of 1865: this child was "a miniature adult:

distracted, depressed, with a careworn face and all the mannerism of the adult Jew with a family to support. All he needed was the beard."[32] This conception of the Jewish child as prematurely aged corresponded with a societal reality for certain Jewish populations, especially in parts of Eastern Europe—the difficulties of being poor and persecuted left little freedom for indulging in the protected, cherished pastimes and mentalities associated with modern childhood and the cultivation of children's optimal physical health. Traditional practices like early marriage and the *kest* system (in which young newlyweds lived with or were otherwise financially supported by the bride's parents) had lent to the latter image of Jews as prematurely aged, stunted adults. As Jews gained civil rights in Europe in the eighteenth and nineteenth centuries, intellectuals of the *Haskalah* (Jewish Enlightenment) advocated for cultural reforms that would reshape Jewish families, gender roles, and childhood in ways that better suited secular-Christian bourgeois ideals.[33] As David Biale writes, the Haskalah sought to relocate social power from the hands of pragmatic, traditional parents to those of their children, who were to look to their own individual emotions and physiological desires for guidance, rather than to their parents or religious leaders.[34] Such approaches to Jewish youth, though empowering for those who desired to acculturate within secular-Christian modernity, worked explicitly to "queer" Jewish traditions and to "normalize" future generations of young people by gentile standards rooted in emotional individuality. Sendak's complex relationship with this cultural legacy would, however, insist on a childhood emotional reality that was decidedly queer and that straddled both the freedoms of a secular majority culture and his parents' traditional worlds and memories.

At least since the dawn of the twentieth century, certain Jewish individuals set precedents for complicating the normalizing efforts of the Haskalah by applying painstaking scientific research and unyielding sensitivity to the emotional and bodily truths of queer outliers. For example, the sexologist Magnus Hirschfeld, a German Jewish physician, pioneered the gay rights movement and fought for positive recognition for queer and trans people. He also wrote on the complexity of queer childhood in his 1907 preface to *Aus eines Mannes Mädchenjahren*

(Memoirs of a Man's Maiden Years), a trans Jewish memoir by Karl M. Baer—director of Berlin's B'nai B'rith through 1938 and among the first documented individuals to undergo sexual reassignment surgery. Like Sendak, Hirschfeld was gay and stemmed from an Eastern European Jewish family. In his preface to Baer's memoir, Hirschfeld noted that "far-reaching conflicts may occur already in the souls of children. . . . For far too long, adults have underestimated not only the importance of childhood for life, but also of children and their significance as human beings."[35] Sendak grew to share Hirschfeld's investment in the seriousness of childhood feelings and the dignity of queer children. Like his Yiddish literary forebears, the artist would depict burdened, resilient children struggling to survive, as well as infants with strained, adult countenances. He described babies as "enormous kvetches" who were also so "vulnerable, poignant and lovable."[36] His Jewish roots, in other words, deeply informed the alternative depictions of childhood that he would offer the world.

Why Focus on Queerness?

A biographical study of Sendak cannot be separated from the effects of internalized social stigma and cultural homophobia that characterize most of the twentieth century. As Ellen Handler Spitz declares, "When an artist's sexuality, or indeed any other core aspect of his identity, is denied public acceptance and affirmation, that denial cannot but find its way into his work."[37] Critiques of a 2017 book-length study of Sendak, Jonathan Cott's There's a Mystery There, foreground a missed opportunity to examine the artist's sexuality in greater depth.[38] While a handful of scholars have briefly considered Sendak's experience as a queer artist, there has not been a sustained, extended study until now.[39] Sendak was a prolific gay man who spent most of his life in a century that pathologized, criminalized, and neglected LGBTQ people. Beyond the necessity of processing this assertion, a study of Sendak's queerness also contributes to the little-known, actively denied history of queer innovation in the field and canon of classic children's literature. While LGBTQ media have long noted that Sendak and other "gay writers" were at the forefront of children's literature, it is only in the last several years that this subject has entered mainstream discourse.[40] In 2011, literary scholar Philip Nel noted that in the field of children's literature a silenced queer history still awaited discovery.[41] Eight years later, *The New York Times* published its surprising "Gay History of America's Classic Children's Books."[42]

Despite wider cultural discomfort around recognizing queer or gay children, some of the most profound shapers of children's books have been queer, whether discreetly or avowedly so. Ursula Nordstrom, the lesbian editor-in-chief of juvenile books at Harper & Row from 1940 to 1973, discovered Sendak and almost single-handedly championed his career. Margaret Wise Brown (1910–1952), a bisexual woman, helped establish picture books as an art form through such Harper publications as *Goodnight Moon* (1947).[43] Brown got her start at the Bank Street School, from which Krauss would also collect children's notecards for *A Hole Is To Dig* (1952), which Sendak illustrated as a young man.[44] Clement Hurd, the illustrator for *Goodnight Moon*, was also involved in a gay artistic circle in Manhattan whose members photographed and painted male nudes.[45] Arnold Lobel, creator of the *Frog and Toad* series, first published by Harper & Row from 1970 through 1979, was raised by his German Jewish immigrant grandparents and lived most of his life as a closeted gay man married to a woman before dying of AIDS in 1987. His daughter Adrianne Lobel told a journalist in 2016 that she believed *Frog and Toad* was the beginning of his coming out.[46] Nordstrom also published other "confirmed bachelors" such as Edward Gorey, a friend of Sendak's who dressed flamboyantly in furs and drew gothic, subversive illustrations of domestic scenes.[47] And then, of course, there was Sendak himself, who became Nordstrom's most renowned prodigy at Harper.

What creator of children's books has been more iconic as a queer curmudgeon and social recluse than Mr. Sendak? "I think the whole world stinks," he barked in one of his final interviews. "[T]he lack of culture depresses me. . . . I don't want to be part of anything."[48] The artist was, throughout his life, an antimodernist who hated school, condemned capitalist greed, and privileged the bravery of engaging one's spontaneous eruptions of emotion. "Queer" in many respects, Sendak came of age as a Romantic nonconformist in an age of mechanical reason and restraint. A physically frail man attracted to other men but critical of hegemonic American masculinity, he also described himself as queerly haunted by family memories. He used pregnancy and birthing metaphors to describe his own processes of artistic inspiration and production and, in his later years, depicted himself as a female baby in works such as *Higglety Pigglety Pop!* and *Outside Over There*.[49] Recalling his childhood, he would admit, "I couldn't play stoopball terrific, I couldn't skate great. I stayed home and drew pictures. You know what they all thought of me: sissy Maurice Sendak."[50] Things were not much better within his family, in this regard. He claimed, "I had to hide every feeling I had from my parents, and every normal feeling was condemned by *me* as abnormal and inappropriate. . . . [Y]ou're riddled with lies and questions that never got answered about yourself—your body, your mind, your penis, whatever."[51]

Regardless of the extent to which Sendak was aware of being gay as a child, he was aware of being socially queer—a sickly boy whom others called "sissy" and a dramatic storyteller who struggled to make friends and spent much of his time with his family indoors. He was, in his own words, "a terrified child, growing into a withdrawn, stammering boy who became an isolated, untrusting young man."[52] Coming of age in the homophobic 1940s and 1950s, Sendak, like most gay men of his generation, learned to be contextually discreet and cultivated an ability to "pass" in order to avoid persecution. Aware of his same-sex attractions by his teenage years, he was exuberantly "out" to his friends and colleagues throughout his adult life, but he would not come out as gay to the mainstream press until 2008 at the ripe age of eighty.[53] He felt pressure to participate in the wider society's desire *not* to see this truth about their favorite children's book artist. Warding off the potential discomfort of readers who would prefer not to know about Sendak's sexuality or about the shared life he built with another man, countless articles and books refer to Sendak as a lifelong bachelor and to his male partner as his "friend," a euphemism Sendak admittedly also used at times, protecting his career.[54]

The artistic form of the picture book enabled Sendak to powerfully articulate his liminal subjectivity. Children's literature, like comic books and other "low art" forms, offered a way to hide "in plain sight," a place from which to be loud and passionate and emotionally honest, even when the adult public deemed the contents of one's imagination "queer" or excessive. In a later interview, he reflected on why he worked in the picture-book form. He concluded that he "picked a modest form" that allowed him to "explode emotionally" in the freest way possible: "I didn't have much confidence in myself—never—and so I hid inside . . . this modest form called the children's book and expressed myself *entirely*. . . . I'm like a guerrilla warfarer in my best books" (Sendak's emphasis).[55] Children's literature, as a realm of historically minimal interest to political watchdogs, has long operated as a sort of hidden, alternative universe, perceived as safer for queer or dissident expression, somewhat beyond the radar of broader societal concerns.[56] Mikhail Krutikov, for example, describes how in the context of the Soviet regime controversial writers such as Kornei Chukovskii found children's literature an oasis that offered more creative freedom within Soviet cultural politics.[57] Left-wing Yiddish organizations sometimes turned to children as a means to link generations and transmit messages below the radar of political censorship.[58] For example, Daniela Mantovan argues that writers like Der Nister "smuggled" disguised protests of the Soviet regime and political barbarism into their symbolist children's stories in the 1930s.[59] Gennady Estraikh understands children's literature to have benefited from its marginalized position, becoming the most vigorous and international branch of Yiddish cultural production in the interwar years, which saw both the wider political denigration of Yiddish culture and the "golden age" of Yiddish children's literature.[60] Thus, in some cases, the lack of respect or attention paid to children's literature has allowed the field to subvert restrictive political movements from a place of limited visibility. Perhaps precisely for the reason that children's literature was not seriously considered by social authorities in the interwar and immediate postwar decades, it became an outlet and refuge for political outcasts and dissenters. In the 1930s, for example, writers in Nazi Germany such as Rudolf Wilhelm Friedrich Ditzen, who used the pseudonym "Hans Fallada," and Erich Kästner, who disagreed with Hitler's politics, turned to the genres of "light literature" (*unterhaltungsliteratur*) and children's books in order to express frustrations and alternative dreams. These less-studied genres could serve as an outlet for a creative phenomenon described as "inner emigration," a tactic of psychological survival by detaching oneself from the sociopolitical context of the dominant rhetoric, disassociating from one's surroundings.[61] Sendak practiced his own form of inner emigration by cultivating a hermetic, queer world beyond the masculinized surveillance of the public sphere.

Children's publishing, as a field, was "queer" in the midcentury public's imagination, which perceived it as a feminine, marginal realm of peculiarities not worthy of serious attention. As Sendak recalled, children's books were the bottom of the cultural totem pole in the 1940s and 1950s.[62] Despite appreciating the liberties of the field's liminality, the artist would also resent the diminutive and disrespectful attitudes expressed toward children's publishing. He once exclaimed, "What is a children's-book artist? A moron! Some ugly fat pipsqueak of a person who can't be bothered to grow up. That's the way we're treated in the adult world of publishing."[63] Even when he won the Caldecott award for *Where the Wild Things Are*, his father, Philip, joked, "Well, now, maybe they'll give you a grown-up book to do." Sendak was, consequentially, a warrior for the cause of dignifying children's literature. Critical writings almost always fell short of his expectations. In 1966 he complained to the Library Services Coordinator of Highline Public Schools in Seattle, for example, about the lack of seriousness surrounding the field of children's books, which too many critics and editors treated condescendingly and exploited as a money-making enterprise. Sendak yearned to have respect and academic status granted to the field. Critics, he felt, needed to recognize that the best books for children were full of wisdom and created by highly dedicated and talented writers and artists.[64] He longed to see the end of critics' sentimental, uninformed approaches.[65] Considering the inherently queer nature of childhood against the adult public sphere, his drive to dignify children's literature was, however indirectly, a drive to earn respect in the public sphere for queer perspectives, as naturalized in the universality of childhood queerness vis-à-vis the adult world. Like the field of queer studies, Sendak's best work explores how subjects occupy alternate realms of affect, embodiment, and social formations, states of "limbo" beyond hegemonic or coercive structures. The Sendakian child uses fantasy realms as a means to survive a turbulent and unjust society, refusing emotional erasure by the rules of that society.

As Kathryn Bond Stockton has theorized, queer children who grow up in cultures that will not recognize them tend to claim their queerness only through the ghostly retrospect of adulthood—as grownups who may belatedly assert, "I *was* a queer child."[66] Literary and cultural studies scholars have recently employed queer theory to understand childhood itself as a "queer" realm, inherently estranged from adult social norms and perspectives.[67] Children, as human subjects varyingly excluded from mainstream, public society, fluctuate between embracing the boundless possibilities of play and wanting to "grow up" to gain inclusion within the rules of the wider culture. Thus, even beyond the categories of gender and sexuality, children's literature has a history of beckoning to "queer" adults whose social identities are forbidden from manifesting in the culture—adults whose endangered emotional worlds propel them toward intimate familiarity with "the void," so to speak, and toward languages that approximate what it means to exist beyond, between, or prior to the laws of society. Born of tormented beginnings, painful exclusions, and belated self-actualizations, the field of modern children's literature conveys an urgency and emotional vitality that speaks to the queerness and cherished peculiarity of *all* children vis-à-vis the adult public sphere. The present study contributes to a wider project of uncovering a growing history of queer understandings of childhood in general, and dignified representations of queer childhood specifically.

Why Focus on Feelings?

Sendak knew that for young children the world brims with possibility and anxiety. What obsessed him about his own childhood, he claimed, were "the sounds and feelings and images . . . of particular moments."[68] His talent was, as he put it, the ability to remember "the emotional quality of childhood. Not the specific, visual scenes, but the qualities, the feelings."[69] As a child who developed in contexts that failed to see him, he had learned to grapple intently in the dark. His talent for grasping onto an interesting or personally meaningful feeling before even understanding the intellectual or symbolic meanings associated with it may reflect the particular psychology cultivated in states of hermeneutical marginalization, a phrase used by Miranda Fricker to describe the experience of "growing up in a fog," separated from the processes of meaning-making and removed from the systems necessary for earning political credibility and social status.[70] Though not talented at stoopball or making friends, as Sendak often recalled, he was well exercised at navigating important sensory data and pieces of information that he did not fully understand, creatively organizing fragments of elusive meaning, and responding with emotion and intuition. He described his artistic quest as an exorcism of certain childhood-based feelings in himself, conducted to help him survive and function in the world.

The artist's movement between visual styles facilitated his aesthetic handling of elusive sensations and feelings. Playing with time and space through alternating temporal and spatial languages supported his struggle to remain "himself" against the limits of those social identities available to him in his time. Sentimental Victorian crosshatching conveyed the equally melancholic and nostalgic recollections evoked for him in Minarik's *Little Bear* series; a flatly colored, heavily contoured comic-book style best captured the fantasies of his own interwar childhood in *In the Night Kitchen* (1970) and *Hector Protector* (1965); a playful mixture of vibrant crayon and paint animated the operatic exuberance of *Brundibar* (2003) and *Bumble-Ardy* (2011), setting their horrific backstories in ironic relief; and a masterfully executed German Romanticist watercolor style for *Outside Over There* and *Dear Mili* (1988) articulated the transcendental feeling of examining his own life within the vastness of literature and history.[71] By repeatedly shifting styles, Sendak also spoke to the timeless quality of early childhood, a life stage rooted in emotion and physiology, and preceding one's initiation into collective schedules and systems. He sublimated his socially marginalized childhood feelings of emotional "excess," personal confusion and terror, irreverent *Yiddishkeit*, and queer shame by channeling them into his art. Alongside Sendak's poetic depiction and exorcism of his stifled feelings, his partner of half a century, the psychiatrist and art critic Eugene Glynn (1926–2007), published writing on the psychology of artists, their ability to evacuate the mature ego for the child's fluid and meaningfully fraught ways of thinking and feeling.[72] Spending the greater portion of their lives in an era that painted LGBTQ people as pathological and criminal, Sendak and Glynn studied and conveyed the undeniable humanity of misunderstood and neglected people's minds and hearts—an investment that surely colored their relationship. As Jonathan Weinberg notes, "Gene never wrote directly about Maurice's art, but, in a sense, he was always writing about it as he tried to come to terms with the origins of the creative act."[73] The present study thus considers insights from Glynn's writing in dialogue with the artist's feelings, as Sendak articulated them.

Picture books, as tools of emotional education and objects of sublimation, present an ideal context in which to examine questions raised by the "emotional" or "affective turn" in history.[74] Midcentury picture books, for example, reflect a coterminous popularization of psychoanalysis in everyday life. Sendak recalled, "[M]ost of us were baptized into adulthood and psychoanalysis and everywhere was an exciting and revived interest in children—their language—the state of their minds and hearts."[75] The artist made direct use of psychoanalytic concepts in his work, balancing drives of id and superego and working through the inflated, fragile narcissism that characterizes early childhood. Especially by the early 1960s, the Sendak child battled dangers of entrapment, suppression, boredom, and insignificance, and sang songs of wild triumph, of sensual awakenings and powers tasted for the first time. The artist invited both controversy and admiration for his radical departure from a Victorian-influenced, American children's book tradition of depicting Anglo-Saxon children in a rose-colored world of adult norms. His ethnic-looking children were among the first in children's literature to exhibit rage and emotional excess, as well as to demand love.[76] Ursula Nordstrom called Sendak's *Wild Things* "the first picture book to recognize the fact that children have *powerful* emotions, anger and love and hate and only after all that passion, the wanting to be 'where someone loved him best of all.'"[77]

Theorists such as Lauren Berlant, Sara Ahmed, and Ann Cvetkovitch have drawn attention to ways in which feelings have an impact on and reflect broader societal forces and expectations, such as governmental power, historical trauma, tensions between public and familial memory, rhythms and rules of the domestic sphere, various forms of intimacy, and the sociopolitical dimensions of everyday life.[78] Sendak's obsession with the feelings of his own frustrated childhood and transcendent fantasies fueled his work. His emotional creations reveal and push against positions infused by intergenerational struggles, cultural intersections, and recent historical ruptures.[79] His tendency to choose *child* protagonists draws attention to the universality of social dangers—we all begin "at risk," as children. His tendency to depict *awkward, queer,* and *ethnically marginal* children signals the humanity of social outsiders—even the most neglected or "othered" among us deserve love and safety and may become heroic archetypes in demanding those basic needs.

One of the artist's primary cultural contributions has been a subversive valuation of expressive fantasy, despite what William Reddy has termed the dominant "emotional regimes," the constellation of normalized emotions, as well as their inculcation and coercion through official rituals and practices—"emotives"—that underpin most political structures.[80] In the American context, as John Cech evaluates it, such regimes traditionally privilege "masculine logos, the law-giving, reality-accepting, reason-seeking aspects" against "creative, feminine, feeling aspects of the psyche."[81] Perry Nodelman wrote that fantasy is even perceived as "an un-American activity, an indulgence in impractical foolishness that interferes with the serious business of getting ahead by means of hard work and discipline."[82] In the first few decades of the twentieth century, these emotional regimes reared their heads in the so-called "fairy-tale wars." This episode comprised disagreements between traditionalist librarians like Anne Carroll Moore who valued fantasy and those championed by Lucy Sprague Mitchell of New York's Bank Street School who saw fairy tales as harmful to children's development.[83] By the time Sendak began his career, popular "child experts" such as pediatrician Dr. Spock had warned the midcentury American mother not to "overfill" her child "with stories," lest they both "live for hours in fairyland."[84] While the neo-Freudian value of releasing and mastering difficult feelings did help to defend the place of fantasy in children's lives, the modern American context remained skeptical of the

European Romantic, which it deemed "hysterical" or beyond "reason." As late as the 1990s, impassioned and aggressive opponents of fantasy pressured teachers, librarians, editors, and media to extract from library shelves and curricula any work that promoted imagination or fantasy, including the works of Sendak.[85] Against such conservative ideas about children's socialization, Sendak insisted on the necessity of fantasy as a means for surviving impossible social positions and maintaining personal vitality. Against an emotional regime of restrained pragmatism that stifled folk wisdom, passionate expression, and embodied self-discovery, the protagonists of Sendak's picture books exhibit theatrical bouts of uninhibited feeling through fantasy. In his own life, the artist also continuously harnessed the creative potential of modern childhood, making meaning from the sidelines of mainstream culture and its social norms by excavating transcendental feelings.

Sendak's greatest books have become modern fairy tales for at least two reasons relating to affect. First, they offer contemporary but timeless examples of projecting and resolving universal psychic challenges within the uncanny realm of the magic tale. These are the central characteristics of the fairy tale in *The Uses of Enchantment* (1976), an influential treatise by Bruno Bettelheim, the Austrian-born American psychologist who survived Dachau and Buchenwald and became known for his treatment of emotionally disturbed children and his application of the fairy-tale genre to theories of child development.[86] Kenneth Kidd understands Bettelheim's study of the fairy tale to reflect affective connections made between at least two different sorts of traumatized but resilient children—those victimized in the Holocaust and those autistic "wolf-children" of Bettelheim's clinical research. United by the universal trope of the "feral" tale, the figure of the unruly child marks the places where nature and culture intersect or diverge. Sendak's Max, in his archetypal wolf suit among the Wild Things, most effectively introduces this symbolic child stand-in to the realm of modern children's literature.[87] In a Sendak book, as in fairy tales for Bettelheim, those seemingly impossible feelings that tend to surround or obstruct developmental growth, early socialization, and spiritual reckoning take fantastical or extreme forms and invite momentous quests of resolution.

The artist works through a complex inner life through metaphor, hybridity, transformation, and other tools of the fairy-tale form.

Second, Sendak studied master illustrators of centuries past and placed them in direct dialogue with the images and feelings of his own life in the present. His emotional quests skillfully collapse conventional notions of time by interweaving the influences of German Romantic painting, Victorian picture books, black-and-white *shtetl* photographs of his murdered relatives in Poland, Walt Disney's early animation, popular comic-book art, and more. By successfully integrating the visual languages of his own twentieth-century childhood with those of classical art, folklore, and family memory, he accomplished the feat of processing his own life as a fairy tale—a feat that has vicariously entranced and empowered readers and artists of all ages. In other words, Sendak stands out among his contemporaries for having elevated picture books to serious works of art through a blend of personal and art historical excavation—his work plumbs the depths of a contemporary artist's development and situates itself within visual traditions, even as it rebels against restrictive conventions.

Layout

Sendak offers a rich example of self-searching through creative work and interpretation; describing the illustrator's occupation, he once stated, "The fun is in finding out something about yourself as you do it. It's a form of miraculous self-indulgence: in everything you do you are looking for yourself. What better way of spending your life?"[88] To study an artist's creative vision in dialogue with a search for self within and against wider historical and cultural forces requires a multiplicity of analysis. Inherent to this project is the notion that literature, art, history, and critical theory are interwoven matters—that art and life are strands in a single thread, informing and altering each other in complex, uneven ways. The circumstances of Sendak's life affected his art, and making art repeatedly interacted with his life, as well as with wider social conceptions about childhood, ethnic minorities, and queer people.

Each chapter of this book is thematic with loose chronological parameters, applying historical analyses, critical theory, and original readings of Sendak's work to illuminate a central and contextualized motif or set of tensions tackled by the artist. In some places I read Sendak's art and writings through the flux and structure of his subjectivity within his particular biographical and sociohistorical contexts. In other sections I analyze his life and surrounding contexts through literary and aesthetic considerations of his creative output. I contextualize the analysis of Sendak's life and work in Jewish American social and cultural history, as well as in changing conceptions of childhood and queerness, and in the critical reception of children's book journals and librarians. I ask how the artist's multiple perspectives as a queer, Holocaust-conscious, American-born son of Yiddish-speaking Jewish immigrants informed his life and work and interacted with the wider culture of his time.

Chapter 1 situates Sendak's artistic vision within intertwined histories of immigrant acculturation and the emergence of modern childhood during his earliest years. Early twentieth-century immigrants' children were in some ways socialized out of their own families of origin in order to join American society. Sendak was born into a zeitgeist of speed and mobility in a culture that celebrated mechanical innovation, the fresh power of youth, capitalist dreams, and superhero fantasies. Mass culture exploded in unprecedented ways alongside the solidification of child psychology, the growth of global antisemitism, and rising anxieties about fascism. As notions of modern childhood evolved in the latter interwar years, children's relationships to the public sphere were increasingly regulated through specific media channels, enforcing a dominant vision of their emotional development. Sensitive to his parents' anxieties as Jews and immigrants but also mesmerized by the wild energy of popular film and comics, Sendak felt his reality misrepresented by conceptions of childhood as a rose-colored time of angelic innocence cultivated in the service of embourgeoisement. Gritty "adult" realities, he felt, were important, pressing parts of a child's life, especially when that child struggled to exist socially and to maintain belonging within a minority group that lacked favor in the adult world—such a child especially needed to understand social obstacles, anticipate dangers, and learn how to survive. His emerging take on early childhood thus drew from culturally fraught separation anxieties experienced between immigrant parents and American children of these years.

Focusing mainly on the years of World War II, Chapter 2 examines the emotional climate within the Sendak household in relation to Sendak's use of metaphoric fusions and queer conceptions of kinship in his work. Sendak spent the war years as a young adolescent, aware of the fact that his relatives were being murdered in Nazi-occupied Poland. Tumultuous relationships within his mourning family elucidate the almost divine significance his work would attribute to ruptured parent-child boundaries, creative sibling bonds, and queerly vicarious yearnings. His artistic vision took elements characteristic, if sometimes stereotypic, of twentieth-century Yiddish-speaking Jewish families and transformed them into nursery-rhyme and fairy-tale archetypes. Overbearing, erratic mothers become divine moons who descend from the heavens to save children. Spiritually exhausted, crumbling fathers become sailors whose disembodied calls from across the ocean save their children's lives. Siblings who bind together to survive parents' intrusiveness or absence become companions who pool their resources in unions colored with mythical, even erotic undertones. And, of course, unacculturated immigrant relatives become "Wild Things," feared but also humanized and celebrated. This chapter examines Sendak's creative handling of his familial relationships in dialogue with literature on the Jewish family in contexts of migration, collective mourning, and survival. The location of his childhood within a milieu repeatedly targeted for violent destruction and shrouded in traumatic losses reverberates in his work. The artist's mythical and cosmic fusions convey feelings about growing up with precarious identifications and emotional investment in familial pasts that he did not directly experience.

Chapter 3 positions Sendak's sexual maturation and emergent career between Manhattan's creative cultural and queer subcultural scenes and his parents' Jewish Brooklyn community. In the immediate postwar years, the young artist's life stretched across competing and sometimes contradictory realities: the dominant, forward-looking "American Dream" idealized childhood innocence, heterosexual marriage, and the suburban nuclear family; his parents' traumatized Jewish

Brooklyn community looked to the past, mourning murdered families and the destroyed communities of Europe; and his own new beginning as a gay man in Manhattan offered personally liberating, if sometimes dangerous, realms of discreet exploration. I examine how the artist related to his budding sexuality as a gay man in a homophobic context and how aligning with queerness, even if reluctantly at times, preserved his sense of self apart from a mainstream culture that devalued ethnically and sexually atypical people. This personal stance primed him to relate to children's literature as a space of potential freedom and expression that, at midcentury, remained beyond the surveillance of dominant social powers. Sendak's beginnings as an illustrator and picture-book artist reflect an unassimilable subjectivity that separated him from dominant social meanings and encouraged his investment in excavating his early childhood self. With the help of queer and Jewish mentors, including picture-book author Ruth Krauss and a gay Jewish therapist named Bertram Slaff, Sendak's creative vision solidified and began to incorporate queer and ethnically marginal elements, even in a society that had preferred a more "wholesome" child ideal to stand in for the American dream.

Focusing on the social liberation era of the 1960s and 1970s, Chapter 4 connects Sendak's flamboyant and fantasy-oriented use of child's play to the challenges and triumphs of socially excluded and stigmatized outsiders of the late twentieth century. Children, as beings evacuated of all sensuality and deviance by the puritanism of the wider culture, were the natural allies of a stigmatized artist. Sendak participated in a long tradition employed by endangered insider-outsider minorities in hegemonic conformist cultures, including Jews and queer people throughout history, whose difference could be selectively hidden in order "to pass" in the mainstream. This chapter studies Sendak's relationship to costume, to the dramatic arts, and to spaces of social liberation, including Fire Island, as well as his use of child's play, theatricality, and "Camp" sensibilities in his personal correspondences and in picture books such as *The Sign on Rosie's Door* (1960) and *Bumble-Ardy* to work through feelings of queer shame and social incoherence. I read his creative process in dialogue with sociological writing on the creativity of stigmatized individuals, queer theories of time and space, and psychoanalytic writings on the "creative personality" by Sendak's late therapist and by Glynn. Sendak harnessed a stigmatized subjectivity to create messages that spoke universally to the wider culture, which by the 1960s and 1970s increasingly rejected the homogenous, middle-class ideals of midcentury America.

Chapter 5 focuses on Sendak's life and work in the years following his move to Ridgefield, Connecticut, in 1972, examining specifically how notions of "inside'" and "outside" intensified within his creative vision. As late twentieth-century Jews became, generally speaking, more enfranchised in middle-class America and were increasingly essentialized as complacent beneficiaries of "White privilege," anxiety about the need to preserve Jewish distinctiveness increased; meanwhile, America institutionalized Holocaust memory and became more comfortable with Old World nostalgia. Mainstream culture by the 1980s also retreated from social liberation movements, empowering intensified homophobia and social conservatism. Considering these contextual shifts, I examine the aging Sendak's creative handling of boundary violations and "unnatural," death-infused relations, including his visual mergers of the Holocaust with the AIDS crisis. I ask how the artist reconciled a political calling he felt during that crisis, which took many of his loved ones, with an impulse to turn inward and follow emotional intuition in private.

A Word on Sources

Sendak's will instructed his Foundation to destroy his personal letters, journals, and diaries immediately upon his death. The present study examines a representative selection of his picture books, as well as those original materials that survive in other archives, including artwork and select notes, book typescripts and dummies, correspondences, speeches, interviews, researcher notes, and other writings.[89] Among those archives surveyed were the Thomas J. Dodd Research Center, the Rosenbach Museum & Library, the New York Public Library, the Elmer L. Andersen Library of Minneapolis, the Harry Ransom Center in Austin, the Smithsonian Libraries and National Portrait Gallery Library, the NYU Fales Library, and the Library of Congress. I also draw from personal conversations and correspondences with Sendak's past colleague

Christopher Mattaliano; with Jonathan Weinberg, who was a dear family friend of Sendak's and Glynn's and now serves as Curator and Director of Research at the Sendak Foundation; with Eric Pederson, who was Sendak's personal assistant for over seven years through Harper; with Judith Goldman, a writer and curator and distant cousin of Eugene Glynn's, who as editor of *The Print Collector's Newsletter* and *Artnews* commissioned essays and reviews from him; with a niece and a nephew of Glynn's; with Glenn Dickson, who collaborated with Sendak on *Pincus and the Pig* (2004); with Loring Vogel, Amos Vogel's son, whose parents socialized often with Sendak and Glynn during Loring's childhood; with children's literature scholar Philip Nel, who corresponded directly with Sendak; with Deborah Belford de Furia, whose family purchased the Seaview home in which Sendak vacationed on Fire Island; and with Benjamin Ross, a grandson of Philip Sendak's second cousin who recalled family stories and a childhood visit by the artist.

CHAPTER 1

WHERE THE WILD
THINGS ACCULTURATE

Roots and Wings in Interwar Brooklyn

IT IS NO GREAT WONDER that the children of Sendak's picture books appear burdened and world-weary. The artist creatively obsessed over how children survive. He would write, "People used to comment continually on the fact that the children in my books looked homely—Eastern European Jewish as opposed to the flat, oilcloth look considered normal in children's books. They were just Brooklyn kids, old-looking before their time."[1] American-born, Sendak nevertheless described himself as an Old World Jew. As he once put it, "[W]hen you live with immigrant parents, you're always an immigrant. You grow up inside a ghetto, self-imposed by parents, in America."[2] Explaining why he never used his fireplace, for example, he would tell Tony Kushner, "You, you're an *emancipated* Jew, you don't know fire will kill you! *I* will *never* unlearn that!"[3] More than an Old World childhood, Sendak described his younger years as a hybrid, "conglomerate fantasy life," of "feeling as though I lived in the Old Country—the fabulous village world of my parents—and, on the other, of being bombarded with the full intoxicating gush of America in that convulsed decade called the thirties. . . . "[4] Sendak's childhood hybridity reflects a history of American immigrant family life and, more specifically, shifting ideas about American childhood.

By the end of the nineteenth century, industrialization had separated public and domestic spheres, and, to varying extents, the idea of domestic children's innocence and malleable potential transcended divisions of class, gender, religion, and race. With sufficient resources and cultural capital, a child could be molded to support the ambitions of family or nation. Modernizing Jews faced new opportunities and pressures to join—and conform to—wider secular-Christian society. For European and American Jews, modernization happened unevenly, negotiated between models of childhood developed in self-governing Jewish communal structures, *maskilic* intellectual circles, and wider non-Jewish societies. The predominant *kheyder* system—in which a *melamed* (teacher) paid by parents and the Jewish community taught male children Hebrew and Torah, often in Yiddish—gave way for most non-Orthodox American Jews to coeducational secular schooling that, in addition to teaching mathematics, English, physical education, and sciences, instilled American-Protestant ideals of order, work ethic, high standards of cleanliness, self-discipline, and patriotism.[5] Shifting family structures, acculturation, and conceptions of romantic love in secular modern societies promoted emotional individualism and painted attachments to the Old World as outdated, condemning such communal-based Jewish Eastern European social practices as arranged marriages and *kest*.[6] Urban immigrant parents of the early twentieth century saw their children participate in developing a fluid, commercially inspired popular youth culture that broke with established traditions.[7] Commercial markets and mass media developed against these stark intergenerational differences in the immigrant family and exerted both regulatory and liberating influences on first-generation American children. Parents' lack of control during the economic hardship of the Depression further exacerbated generational tensions.[8]

Meanwhile, dominant child "experts" of the 1930s and 1940s believed that a healthy child needed more time and energy for social training than was available in families of paid laborers. Because the majority of paid laborers in early twentieth-century America were ethnic minorities and immigrants, to raise modern children—by such experts' standards—required acceptance in middle-class White culture.[9] What did it mean to be a child of an acculturating family in an era that advocated for assimilation and revised its perceptions of childhood, more broadly? Sendak's forming sense of self and subsequent picture books drew explicitly from the cultural attitudes and fast-paced rhythms of his interwar childhood in an ethnically marginal immigrant household, during which government, school, and media strove to loosen parent-child bonds in order to cultivate pliable citizens and consumers. His work would convey the emotional storms of urban children of this "hinge" generation whose experiences wavered between liberation, neglect, and endangerment. He would applaud childhood resourcefulness, creativity, and resilience, encouraging direct engagement with hard realities both "inside" and "outside" as one struggled, in elastic in-betweenness, to survive and reach one's potential.

Born in Transition

I begin with a story. It is the first decade of the twentieth century in Zakroczym, a small Polish town traversed by the flowing Vistula River. The image emerges of a poor Talmudic scholar, Jacob Schindler, a rabbi and talented visual artist who, along with his wife, Minnie, runs a dry goods store. Shortly before World War I, Schindler shocks his family by passing away suddenly at about the age of forty. His teenage daughter, Sarah, blames her mother. What had Minnie done to see her husband pass at such a young age? Minnie quickly tires of Sarah's accusations. By 1911, she makes arrangements for her daughter to travel far away. Perhaps Sarah's earnings in New York, the land of opportunity, will someday afford passage for Minnie and the rest of the Schindlers to join her. Sarah is to meet a pushcart dealer in Manhattan who will rent her a room and help her find work. Upon arrival, however, what she meets is a rude awakening: the pushcart dealer has been recently struck dead by an automobile. With this would-be father figure gone, sixteen-year-old Sarah is on her own. She speaks no English and has no relations in this city, which swarms with storefronts and fast-talking dealers, as well as powerful men who think she and her kind should go back to wherever they came from. Like many other Eastern European Jewish immigrants of her time, she finds work in a sweatshop, changes her name (to "Sadie") and eventually affords passage for her mother and some of her siblings to join her.

Some time later on the Lower East Side, Sadie becomes involved in a public reading of work by Sholem Aleichem (1859–1916), a popular Yiddish writer.[10] Philip, a handsome young man who attends the event, makes her acquaintance over a shared love of the author, and the two soon learn that they have more than Sholem Aleichem in common. Like Sadie, Philip is a rabbi's child who immigrated alone as a teenager from a *shtetl* near Warsaw shortly before the war. Philip too has overcome tragedy, having journeyed from Poland to follow a young woman who ultimately rejected him. Though Philip is not fatherless like Sadie, he is virtually disowned by his father, a prominent rabbi and lumber merchant in Zambrow, who never forgives him for leaving Poland.[11] Marrying and moving to Brooklyn, Philip and Sadie associate with Jewish immigrants from their towns of origin. Philip creates a successful tailoring company, Lucky Stitching, with two *landslayt* friends, where he sews blouses and pleated skirts and dresses.[12] Sadie, who does piecework at home, gives birth to all three children on the dining room table: a daughter comes first in 1920, followed by a son two years later, and then an accidental pregnancy six years afterward, when Sadie is thirty-one.[13] Fearing the stigma a pregnancy might bring for a woman over thirty in her traditional community, Sadie attempts, with Philip's help, to abort this last child.[14] Nevertheless, she gives birth to Moishe on a Sunday in June 1928. Moishe turns out to be a sickly infant who teeters on death's threshold. Minnie, who lives periodically with Sadie and Philip upon arrival to America, superstitiously sews her infant grandson a white suit, dressing him in white stockings and white shoes to match. She sits with him on the apartment stoop to confuse Death—the infant is already a ghost, an angel, and so Death should not take him.[15] Moishe survives. As he grows, American mass media grows with him, exploding with unprecedented speed and new tools of seduction, especially in New York—an emerald city of cinematic wizards and agile superheroes. Glorious urban spectacles of youth and freedom converge unsettlingly with the tone of the Sendak household during the Depression and World War II, as Philip and Sadie Sendak's worlds crumble around them.

Maurice (Moishe) Bernard Sendak, a sickly "angel" who had cheated death, recalled his own Brooklyn childhood as "a mess of missed signals, missed cues."[16] The artist claimed that his earliest memory of his parents was of them openly fretting over the possibility of him dying from early childhood diseases, including measles and double pneumonia at age two and scarlet fever at age five, in an era predating the use of penicillin. Often harried and exhausted, Philip and Sadie were inconsistently available to their children, as Sendak painted it, fluctuating between emotional neglect and intrusiveness.[17] The artist would later identify himself with the changeling "ice baby" in his *Outside Over There* (1981), switched and replaced by some false or vacant version of himself without his mother noticing.[18] An excess of emotional and physical energy built up within this ghostly boy often forbidden from going outside, from being "wild," from being a child. He would describe *Outside Over There* as a story about the "hell of growing up" without knowing who to talk to, who to trust, and how to function.[19] In his words, he was a miserable boy and felt that "being young was such a gross waste of time."[20] Needing a great deal of attention from his struggling caretakers, he internalized a perception of himself as overly demanding, spoiled, and cranky.[21] Before Sendak had turned two, the Wall Street crash had impoverished Philip. Accordingly, Sendak would later insist that Philip connected him with the stock market crash, that "it was part of the guilt of having me."[22] The Sendaks struggled to stay afloat financially and could not afford college for the artist's older siblings, Natalie (Nettie, b. 1920) and Jack (Jacob, b. 1922). To avoid rent hikes and the chaos that came when buildings were repainted, Sadie repeatedly uprooted the family, moving between bedbug-infested apartments in Bensonhurst and Gravesend, neighborhoods Sendak recalled as tree-lined ghettos composed of Jews and Sicilians. Repeatedly switching districts complicated his ability to make lasting friendships but heightened his reliance on inventive interiority. Observing his social surroundings, for example, he imagined to himself that a Sicilian was a type of Jew who drank wine and laughed more often.

Like that of the young David Schearl of Henry Roth's *Call It Sleep* (1934), the infant Sendak's mind ignited with creative pathways gleaned between the cracks of urban immigrant life. As Selma Lanes writes, he developed an early talent for observing and venerating, rather than actively partaking in, the world around him.[23] Sometimes his imagination took on the stylization of the surrounding popular media. Watching his siblings build a snowman through the sporadic opening and closing of a window curtain, he conceptualized a comic-like series of panels dividing the motion into sequential images.[24] "We sat in front of a window," he recalled, "and my grandmother pulled the shade up and down to amuse me. . . . I was thrilled by the sudden reappearance of the backyard, the falling snow, and my brother and sister busy constructing a sooty snowman. Down came the shade—I waited. Up went the shade—the children had moved, the snowman had grown eyes."[25]

As a child Sendak wavered between competing linguistic and social realities. He claimed to speak only Yiddish at home until learning English for school. In the years of his schooling, he usually spoke a mix of Yiddish and English with his family, but he switched to mostly Yiddish during Minnie's extended stays at their home, because Minnie spoke no English.[26] In this regard he was not unusual. In acculturating twentieth-century immigrant families, children formed bridges between public and private spheres. Those immigrant parents who depended on their offspring for such basic tasks as translating their bills and letters from English and mediating American culture, more generally, needed their children to gain American cultural capital for their families' survival.[27] This may have been true, to an extent, for Philip, who did not learn to read or write English until later in life, as well as for Sadie, who never learned.[28] Irving Howe writes that those immigrant parents who staked all future success on their sons—via education and Americanization—twisted the Jewish family into new shapes.[29]

Such shifts came at emotional costs, creating tensions between parents and children, as well as shame and embarrassment around parents' loss of authority in some cases. Psychotherapist Alice Miller's 1981 study illuminates connections between parental stress and children's chameleon-like, shape-shifting talents in immigrant families. She described how some children of immigrants felt a threatened sense of autonomy if the parent, as cultural outsider, placed excessive expectations on the child, as cultural insider, to redeem the family's social disenfranchisement via special abilities, good looks, or accomplishments.[30] Objectified in these ways, immigrants' children might develop feelings of grandiosity or of having personal worth only to the extent of meeting family needs and performing extraordinary feats. Alfred Kazin, the son of immigrants in Brownsville, described the role he filled for his parents, who expected him to redeem their perpetual anxiety and social alienation by shining as an American child, as "their offering to the strange new God" of American idealism, a "monument of their liberation."[31] Chameleon-like shape-shifting, the ability to embody the role most needed for survival at a given moment, Sendak knew, was a universal talent of most children. Immigrants' children were especially pressed to cultivate this skill, forced to live between the sometimes contradictory emotions of caretakers and American authority figures.[32]

The artist's sensibilities emerged on a tightrope between pressures of acculturation and the consuming emotional needs of his family. Social expectations placed on immigrants' children to become upbeat, self-sufficient American individuals sometimes clashed with in-group expectations that they preserve a minority cultural heritage. Sendak grew fascinated with the question of how children survive development across multiple emotional contexts that often clash with each other: reverence for parental authority and inherited traditions, inclusion in the fast-changing popular culture of peers, and privately cultivated self-awareness. Powerful public agendas to "socialize" the disenfranchised competed with the need for self-preservation and meaningful embeddedness within legacies of catastrophe. Drawing on feelings from his own youth, Sendak's creative output would highlight interior struggles that remain relevant to contemporary children. How does one preserve vitality and emotional authenticity while navigating between private and public restrictions and dangers, especially when peers do not understand and when caretakers are detained or cannot see?

"Rough, Rough, Rough"

Sendak was ashamed of his mother and ashamed of being ashamed of her. As a child, when his friend Martin visited and witnessed Sadie's alarmingly frantic demeanor, Sendak instinctively pretended that she was a hired housecleaner. Recalling this, he would confess "that shame has lasted all my life. That I didn't have the nerve to say, 'That's my mother; that's how she is.'" He painted a picture of insecure, ambivalent attachment with Sadie, describing her as "so bewildering and strange," living "in another world."[33] The child artist saw his mother as awkward and distressed, imposing herself on him without offering the sort of emotional availability he desired as a sensitive child, or that he felt she should exhibit by American social standards: "She was always worried. She also had a gruff, abrupt manner. . . . " Sadie would startle Sendak by running into his room and shouting "Whooot," or by roughly tickling his feet, making him scream for her to stop. He believed, "It was her constant pain not to understand why I didn't realize she was being affectionate."[34] He sensed that she was always angry with him, calling him *vilde khaye* (Yiddish for "wild beast") and chasing him through the house. "I used to hide in the street," he would remember, "and hope she forgot before I crept up in the evening."[35] With greater perspective, Sendak would later conclude, "My mother was depressed and had trouble embracing us literally and figuratively. We were unkind to her as a form of revenge."[36] On the other hand, he was also painfully attuned to her feelings in those years. Thus he would also claim, "Feeling sorry for her was my childhood."[37]

Even beyond Sadie, Sendak would characterize *most* adults in his family as "rough." "It was all natural that your father took swipes at you that you dodged . . . *rough, rough, rough*."[38] He would remember his maternal grandmother, Minnie, as a "bitter and sharp" woman who held him on her lap while she *davened* (prayed) by the window. His more distant "greenhorn" relatives were perhaps the most frightening of the adults in his familial orbit. He would famously recall a typical Sunday afternoon in the late 1930s in which

the relatives have come to our house, as usual, to eat everything they can sink their teeth into. And that, in my feverish child's imagination, meant me too possibly! It seems, in retrospect, they even left with the furniture. They were a huge bunch who would roughly snatch you up at any moment. They'd jabber loudly in a foreign tongue—kiss, pinch, maul, and hug you breathless, all in the name of love. Their dread faces loomed—flushed, jagged teeth flaring, eyes inflamed, and great nose

hairs cascading, all oddly smelly and breathy, all dangerous, all growl-
ing, all relatives. We obeyed. We respected them. It would take a long
time to learn to love them.[39]

Despite the alleged wildness of Sendak's relatives, the artist also
consistently valued aspects of his family's emotional style. Minnie
modeled a resilient stance, serving as a most direct link to his Polish Jewish heritage, "like the bridge from the old country to the new
country," as he once stated.[40] Sadie and Philip were generally frank and
honest with their children, and thus ultimately more respectful than
those adults who, Sendak felt, condescended to young people. In this
sense, an acculturating immigrant parent's lack of social refinement by
public standards could lend to a respectful emotional solidarity with
one's children, in contrast to mainstream ideals of parenting that emphasized emotional restraint and mannered calculation.[41] As Sendak
once mused, "My parents were immigrants, and they didn't know that
they should clean [their] stories up for us, so we heard *horrible, horrible*
stories, and we *loved* them! We absolutely loved them."[42] For example,
as Sendak recalled, Philip's version of Adam and Eve was "soft porn,"
and he "didn't censor anything."[43] Repeating details of these stories in
school, the artist would be sent home by teachers to have his mouth
washed with soap.[44] Much later, for the opera version of *Wild Things*,
Sendak would in 1979 design a scene in which Max's mother, dressed
in a 1930s smock and kerchief, merges with her noisy vacuum cleaner
to transform into a grisly creature who inspires her son's fearsome
imagination.[45] He would also officially name his cast of Wild Things:
Tzippy, Moishe (Sendak's own Yiddish name), Aaron, Emile, and Bernard; he would have them mutter "terrible things in Yiddish, the kind
of things my parents said to me, and what you say to children, what you
should never say to children." Max was to start his wolf call—a string
of exclamatory phrases—with the words *vilde khaye*.[46] Thus, while
parent-child relations in families like Sendak's might have challenged
social laws of propriety, they also elicited strong emotional bonds
and inspired wild fantasies in the service of humor and truth-seeking
within an othered family unit.

More concretely, the Yiddish language and its subversive cultural attitude toward the bourgeois establishment was an essential means by which Polish Jewish immigrants like Philip and Sadie imbued their children with critical perspectives and liberal politics. Yiddish was not only a particularity of Jewish difference and of the Old World; in proletarian cultural production, writes Jennifer Young, it functioned as an international weapon against bourgeois influences that threatened to obstruct class consciousness among the Jewish working class, and this meant treating children more as competent "small adults" than as the angelic innocents reflected in the cultural depictions of bourgeois children.[47] Sendak absorbed his father's leftist ideas to some extent through Philip's Yiddish bedtime stories, which offered messages at odds with middle-class ideals—including those of ruthless competition, capitalism, and individualism. As Sendak recalled, even the happiest of Philip's bedtime stories were "always on the darker side of irony," reflecting the sensibilities of Yiddish writers, even for children.[48] In one of those stories, a boy meets a fish that warns him to differentiate between those fish who live with their families and those solitary fish who are evil, have no family, and devour other fish without remorse.[49] Tony Kushner associates this message with the pamphlets of the Workers' Bund, which advocated for strength in numbers against capitalist giants.[50] Philip drew on his Polish boyhood and Jewish folk wisdom to condemn animalistic systems in which the big eat the little, as well as the materialistic greed that turns people into monsters. He recalled his own grandfather's bedtime stories about wild animals communicating with humans. In a typescript draft of his *In Grandpa's House*, Philip would have David, the boy protagonist, ponder the blurry line between animal and human—after David plays with a lion cub and his friends in the forest, hunters strike and kill some of the animals; the hunters are then killed by other wild creatures.[51] Kushner calls *In Grandpa's House* Philip's "Socialist primer."[52] Though such influences resisted certain middle-class norms within Sendak's upbringing, middle-class culture became increasingly pervasive, even among political agitators. By July of 1935, shortly after the artist turned seven, even Communists sought to cooperate with bourgeois society to fight the greater enemy of emergent fascism in Europe. Seeking to unite against a common enemy, Socialists and Communists culturally appeased modern capitalists, playing into the middle class's starker distinctions between childhood and adulthood, characterizing the former as a realm of protected innocence in tandem with a growing commercial market.[53]

In the interwar years, traditional Jews like Philip and Sadie found themselves torn between the desire to give their children the opportunity to succeed in a culture of bourgeois values and capitalist individualism and the desire to protect the future of their repeatedly endangered minority group, for which they had suffered and survived persecution.[54] Unlike most Reform and Conservative American Jews of the 1920s and 1930s, who more willingly embraced the wider contemporary culture, Orthodox and other more traditional Jews focused on preserving an all-encompassing style of Jewish living that dictated everyday social norms and behaviors and often set them apart from other Americans. Orthodox Judaism, comprising an interconnected matrix of ethnicity, culture, history, and sensibility, resisted pressures to fashion itself as a "modern religious faith" in the image of American Protestantism. Though the Sendaks only attended synagogue on rare occasions, sending Moishe to a Polish immigrant's apartment for his Hebrew-school lessons, they saw Judaism not only as a religious faith but as an all-encompassing way of life to which any upstanding Jew was obligated.[55] During Sendak's Hebrew-school days, the family lived about a mile from Sons of Israel, a thriving Orthodox congregation and Talmud Torah, which condemned Reform Judaism and attracted Jewish European immigrants to the area, some of them survivors of antisemitic persecution and the world wars. Philip too came from a family in which even a nonbeliever felt that if one was to pray, one should pray in Hebrew and according to the traditions of the Old Country.[56] The Sendaks' Jewishness revolved around daily practices, ritual cleanliness, folk superstitions, and traditional norms that rested on togetherness of the family and the Jewish community. Sadie dutifully maintained a kosher home, family purity laws, and Sabbath restrictions, taking the children to the library most Fridays in search of books to occupy them while they observed the Sabbath.[57] Sendak loved Yom Kippur best of all holidays, as he was permitted to stay up late reading by candlelight. Sadie brought the young Sendak on trips back to the dense, traditional streets of the Jewish Lower East Side where she had first encountered America as a youth; the artist would later reminisce about the pickle barrels there and their delightful smell of brine. Much later, in his picture book *Bumble-Ardy* (2011), a decidedly nonkosher pig protagonist would express Sendak's sense of himself as somehow *treyf* (nonkosher) but still immersed in Jewish tradition. Ardy breaks the rules of his household when his caretaker is away, throwing a colorful party to guzzle bottles of brine with his friends. Like Ardy's restrictive caretaker, Sendak would recall his parents' constant preoccupation with regulating his behavior, describing Sadie and Philip as "too anxious. Everything was hard, everything was a problem, everything was a scolding. Everything was you-did-something-wrong. You went around the block, you did something wrong. You spoke to a strange person, you did something wrong." The artist internalized the message, for example, that he was "not supposed to like" a certain older cousin, because she was a Communist. Still he idolized her sophistication, later deeming her his "only superior relative." She had encouraged the young Sendak's art and spoke to him directly. He would later gush, "How romantic being loved, being respected, being *looked at* by a Communist!"[58]

Beyond the reaches of Sendak's immediate family and community, the city as a whole could also be a rough place for children of the 1930s. Brooklyn youth collided with harsh realities in the claustrophobic quarters and dangerous streets. Sendak's New York, as his Bronx-born contemporary Irving Howe recalled it, was a "brutal, ugly, frightening [and] foul-smelling jungle . . . the embodiment of that alien world which every boy raised in a Jewish immigrant home had been taught, whether he realized it or not, to look upon with suspicion."[59] Not surprisingly, middle-class Americans came to consider cities undesirable places to raise "the American child." Interwar social commentators painted the city as physically dangerous; antithetical to domestic ideals; and rife with deviance and social "others," including Eastern European Jews, Black migrants from the South, bohemians, political radicals, and queer youth fleeing intolerant families and hometowns—in other words, the cultural avant-garde of the twentieth century. The children of Sendak's neighborhood were strictly confined to their block so as not to endanger themselves by crossing the trafficked urban streets. He described how mothers' heads would appear from the windows and scream "that you would die" if you crossed the street, making you "a prisoner" of the block. One of Sendak's friends, Freddy, lived across the street, and their only interaction with each other was waving from a distance.[60] Sendak would claim that he and Natalie regularly heard the sounds of a girl suffering domestic abuse in a neighboring building. During an outdoor game of catch, Sendak even saw his friend Lloyd fatally hit by a car, thrown into the air before his eyes.[61] To make matters worse, the media-sensationalized March 1932 kidnapping and murder of Charles and Anne Lindbergh's infant son burned into the young artist's consciousness and haunted his thinking. Passing a newspaper stand, a four-year-old Sendak saw images of the kidnapped infant's remains on a front-page story. The words "Lindbergh Baby Found Dead" accompanied a large black arrow pointing to a photograph of the baby's corpse in the woods—a sordid spectacle that caused Colonel Lindbergh to sue the newspaper and force those copies off the stands. The papers were promptly replaced with alternates that displayed a more discreet front page, sans photograph.[62] Sendak would recall synthesizing his perceptions as a four-year-old of his own illnesses, the Lindbergh scandal, his family's ethnic difference, and the visual language of comic books, making

> the queer association that, since I was not meant to live long—I had been told that—if the Lindbergh baby is kidnapped, it can't die, because it's a rich, gentile baby. It has blue eyes and blonde hair. The father is Captain Marvel and the mother is the Princess of the Universe, and they live in a house in a place called Hopewell, New Jersey where there are German Shepherds, and where there are nannies, and where there are police . . . how defenseless could babies be, even among the rich? I could not bear the thought that that baby was dead . . . because if that baby died, I had no chance. I was only a poor kid. . . . And when the baby was found dead, I think something really fundamental died in me.[63]

Fearing a similar fate, the child Sendak referred to the Lindbergh infant as "the mush baby," later noting the phonetic similarity between the word "mush" and his own Yiddish name, Moishe.[64] Sendak would describe this publicized kidnapping as "the major event of my childhood, and probably the source of my conviction that it's impossible to shield children from frightening truths."[65] Following the Lindbergh kidnapping scandal, Sendak's fearful parents bought and installed new, extra-tight screens in their children's bedroom.[66] Philip even slept on the floor of the children's room in his underwear "armed with a fly swatter or bat, to ward off potential kidnappers."[67] Sendak recalled that one of his uncles joked, "Philip, who would even want your children?" Wounded by this remark, the artist would later claim to have drawn this uncle as the ugliest monster in *Where the Wild Things Are* (1963). After admitting this to his uncle in a letter, the latter never spoke to his famous nephew again.[68] Sendak, for his part, never forgot his early fear of kidnappers or the terrible internalization of potential worthlessness as a poor, unacculturated Jewish child in comparison to rich, gentile children. Never completely sure of his safety or of his parents' ability to protect him, he once confessed, "being kidnapped was always the lingering nightmare of my life."[69]

On the other hand, the most dangerous aspects of urban life also elicited some of Sendak's most pleasurable childhood memories. He recalled that in the 1930s it was still unusual in his family's Brooklyn circles to own an automobile; only one of his relatives possessed one, offering him a ride on rare occasions. The young artist would excitedly rush into the car, but, much to his disappointment, the motion of the vehicle would put him to sleep. He remembered his father reaching in to lift him, and being awake enough to know that Philip was carrying him up the stairs to bed—a warm and happy memory.[70] The popularization of the automobile and the expansion of the subway system suited modern urban culture's celebration of human elasticity and social mobility in ways increasingly focused on the individual, independent of the family structure. From Brooklyn, glimpses of Manhattan offered the young Sendak a fantasy world of bright lights and spectacles, a place of creative possibilities for the bold and the imaginative. Getting lost in a crowd at the 1939 New

York World's Fair as an eleven-year-old, for example, led to the thrilling experience of riding home to Brooklyn in a police car, the driver indulging the boy's request to put the siren on "for a grand entrance."[71]

The dynamic urban landscape of New York also offered an inspiring canvas on which to project personal negotiations of individuality in relation to immigrant cultures of origin. Accordingly, some of Sendak's most celebrated books were the first to depict children in bustling cities, despite the postwar suburban dream of a white-picket-fence childhood. New York City, specifically, pervades his creative articulations of early feelings of pleasure and danger in works such as *Kenny's Window* (1956), *Very Far Away* (1957), *The Sign on Rosie's Door* (1960), the *Nutshell Library* series (1962), and *In the Night Kitchen* (1970). The city offered models for how to transform Old World pasts and queer difference, so often suppressed in twentieth-century life, through an ever-changing culture of self-made identities in direct relation to vibrant communities of immigrants. Seth Lerer argues that Sendak's contribution to modern children's literature was turning away from the Puritan, pastoral simplicity of the rural countryside to face the dangerous city landscape—the site of modernist art, the wilderness of the interior self.[72] With its ethos of empowered, youth-driven energy, the city into which Sendak was born invited one to carve out one's independence, to experiment socially, and to try on different potential selves. Works like *Very Far Away* and *The Sign on Rosie's Door* depict children either ignored or "dumped on the sidewalk to play" in the claustrophobic but intimate atmosphere of Brooklyn, where children were captive on a single-block radius, neighbors visible to each other from the stoops of their apartment buildings. These children don disguises, distract themselves with animals, play make-believe, count automobiles, and return home to their parents.

Acculturating Through the American Child

Sendak's childhood ambivalence toward the "roughness" of his family's emotional style and their Brooklyn surroundings reflected the mixed feelings of the wider society in which he grew. The American public varied intensely in its opinions of racialized "outsiders," Jews occupying a racially ambiguous position in interwar discourse. The immigration quotas instated four years before Sendak's birth severely restricted the entry of certain peoples, including Eastern Europeans, even refugees of Nazi Europe.[73] And a rise in perceived antisemitism in the 1930s prompted the formation of the Brooklyn Jewish Community Council by the end of that decade.[74] The emergent visibility and affluence of some Jewish Americans led to restrictive quotas on Jewish admissions to universities, as well as new social policies excluding Jews from certain professions, residential areas, country clubs, resorts, and associations. Powerful figures like Henry Ford and radio priest Charles Coughlin also widely condemned Jews as capitalist exploiters, Communists, and inciters of war. Social agitators characterized Jews as lusty, predatory, and anarchistic.[75] Popular opinion polls of the late 1930s revealed that a startling percentage of Americans viewed Jews as too powerful, greedy, and at least partially to blame for their own persecution under Hitler.[76] At the same time, however, Jews were disproportionately represented in the most beloved, if sometimes illicit, forms of mass culture, including radio, comic books, popular sheet music, and "talking pictures." These cultural products were both widely consumed and condemned by an establishment culture that associated them with the urban lower classes and with ethnic and racial minorities. Classified by the U.S. government as a "race" in those years, Jews in America, writes historian Eric L. Goldstein, were perplexed and ambivalent about their place in the nation's racial system.[77] Families like Sendak's sought to prove themselves worthy of the emerging middle class's standards while struggling to survive financially and to maintain endangered cultural legacies. As Jewish communal organization grew significantly during the artist's childhood, responding both to emergent Nazism overseas and antisemitism at home, children remained a primary collective concern. Objects of ambivalence for their parents, children could represent both the cherished fruit of the successfully acculturated Jewish family and the potential shame of assimilation—rotten fruit off an already-threatened lineage.

Against the rough and perplexing elements of childhood in a harried immigrant family, interwar youth media were appealingly bright, cheerful, and direct in their message: Enjoy! Compete! Consume! Sendak would later parody this commercialized landscape in illustrations for such works as Amos Vogel's *How Little Lori Visited Times Square* (1963), in which a single storefront features the word "EAT" six times, another storefront instructs, "BUY NOW!," and a billboard unceremoniously declares, "EAT FOOD!"[78] Interwar American families spent increasing amounts of emotional energy on desiring and enjoying material objects, which child psychologists and advertisers had linked to children's emotional training. Dolls, argued the experts, helped children prepare for grief and cultivate empathy, and toys generally became consolations for older siblings jealous of newborn babies or young children learning to comfort themselves in their parents' absence.[79] A rapidly growing advertising industry spoke directly to children, ushering them into consumerism through grand spectacles and manufactured dreams. Sendak participated in this cultural moment from within the spaces available to him in Brooklyn and during occasional family ventures into Manhattan. Once during a movie matinee, for example, he was called onstage to perform yo-yo tricks, winning a tommy-gun, a badge, and a Mickey Mouse wristwatch for his performance.[80] Sendak was also mesmerized by the 1939 New York World's Fair in Queens, which marketed wonders of a "better future," publishing exhibition guides geared toward children. The Fair featured military and civilian airplanes, smoking robots, and buildings shaped as giant hats and cash registers, as well as what was then the largest built-to-scale model exhibit, depicting over thirty-five thousand feet of American land, including over five hundred thousand buildings. Sendak's visit would inspire much of his later *Night Kitchen* project. He and Jack so loved the World's Fair that they built a model of it together out of wax.[81]

Heightened by class-consciousness and social exclusions, twentieth-century Americanization and the creation of modern childhood were intertwined matters centered on securing the safety of a middle-class status and standards of American cultural "normalcy."[82] Both were facilitated in part by an emotional rift between generations, solidified by adolescence through commercial appeals to an erotically charged, peer-driven youth culture beyond the comfort zone of parents. This was not lost on communal leaders in the Jewish community. Reform rabbi

Stephen S. Wise, for example, bemoaned the "pleasure-madness of our children" in the 1920s, commenting on their hunger for crude films and sexually exciting theatrics on the stage.[83] Critiques extended to perceived failings of the Jewish religious community to maintain sufficient moral influence over its children. Jacob Kohn's 1932 study on Jewish parenting, for example, warned against turning Bar and Bat Mitzvahs into sites of "tragic spiritual ineptitude." He condemned those Bar and Bat Mitzvahs in which lavish *treyf* meals were served to a crowd of the father's business associates, and the child of honor was made to drink not only *kiddush* wine but also strong alcohol, as well as to witness his older siblings and friends intoxicate themselves "to enjoy the puerile vulgarisms" of vaudeville artists hired for the climax of the celebration.[84]

Some commentators blamed the perceived vices of youth culture on the influences of allegedly corrosive immigrants, including Eastern European Jews; others blamed the erosion of emotional solidarity between immigrant parents and their adolescent offspring, suggesting that the wildness of urban youth came from intergenerational tension, rather than from children's proximity to immigrant cultures of origin.[85] The emerging cultural norms of modern childhood—of prioritizing a specific emotional education and protecting children and adolescents from perceived social and psychological dangers—helped acculturate immigrant families by insisting that their children have an "innocent" and "safe" childhood shielded from paid labor and the adult public, in which working-class immigrant families' cultures were imagined to exist, more broadly. Beginning in 1930, for example, the Motion Picture Production Code ("Hays Code"), a censorship campaign instated to protect the impressionable minds of children, targeted what was perceived as immigrant-oriented representations of violence and sexuality in popular films. The Hays Code even limited some of the "barnyard humor" of Mickey Mouse, who was fashioned to look increasingly soft, wholesome, middle class, and child-like over the years. Sendak would call this revised Mickey Mouse a "schmuck," preferring the older, wilier version, who better mirrored the mannerisms and look of an urban, working-class child, more befitting the "roughness" of the artist's own younger years.[86]

The years of Sendak's upbringing saw unprecedented scientific, cultural, and commercial attention applied to the shaping of America's future through its children, including and perhaps especially those children born to immigrants, who readily consumed inexpensive popular media.[87] As Sendak would recall, the 1930s became a "decade of babies," including such notable portrayals as Fanny Brice's "Baby Snooks" and Eddie Cantor's performance as a baby, as well as the prevalent cultural symbols of high chairs and rattles. The birth of the identical Dionne quintuplets in 1934 created a commercialized media sensation, the young Sendak and his siblings cherishing and fighting over their set of "quint" spoons.[88] The five baby goblins in *Outside Over There* would also gesture to those five babies, whose early years were widely publicized in 1930s popular media, as a sort of modern fairy tale.[89] Public coverage of children increased, and professional "child wonders" like Shirley Temple and Bobby Breen rose to fame, transforming themselves through captivating performance.[90] Emotionally validated children of the 1930s gained more authority to determine and insist on their feelings during childhood—a phenomenon parodied in such representations as Hal Roach's *Our Gang*, later known as *The Little Rascals*.[91] They were also encouraged to comfort themselves with dime novels, pulp magazines, movies, radio, and television, to imagine achieving a glamorous adulthood, epitomized by their beloved superheroes and movie stars.[92]

Accompanying and propelling these cultural trends, child psychology shifted away from behaviorist "child-training" approaches by the 1930s, associating them with the dangers of an impersonal "age of machines," as well as with youth conformism overseas in Nazi Germany, which produced authoritarian "automatons."[93] Caretakers were instead pressured by "child experts" to adopt a child-centered approach that focused more on children's emotional development and shielded children from the potential threats of the adult public. This child-centered, neo-Freudian approach expected modern parents to abandon autocratic or "primitive" parenting styles. Implicit in this more liberal model, however, was the expectation that parents also allow their children to prioritize middle-class American culture and dismiss parents' foreign behaviors and mentalities. An emotionally "healthy" American child was a freed *individual*, suited to the public sphere and emotionally receptive to the nation's future goals. Accordingly, twentieth-century reformers repeatedly chastised Jewish parents for holding their children too closely through guilt and smothering, thus preventing them from becoming liberated American individuals.[94] "In the new order," writes Riv-Ellen Prell, "children's needs would come first. Children were to be liberated from the family."[95] Social workers and communal leaders struggled against Jewish parenting styles, argues Prell, to grant children the liberties of an individualist life, requesting that parents give up the collectivist notion that children's desires should be trumped by the family unit's economic needs or that children were links in a long, unbreakable family chain. Jewish communal leaders such as Stephen S. Wise had acknowledged the necessity of such changes in the family with empathy and notes of regret: "It is not easy for the Jewish mother to surrender that sense of possession which grows out of undivided preoccupation with child or children, that sense of possession fostered as much by a child's sense of dutifulness as by parental concern."[96] Wise warned, however, that a parent's "invasion of [the child's] personality" by nagging, busy-bodying, and ceaseless fault-finding was "an obtrusion of self into the life of another" that ultimately negates the child's sense of individuality.[97]

If freedom meant less time at home and more time spent under the surveillance and influence of the public sphere, such freedom was especially threatening to the preservation of a minority heritage. Youth culture, which emerged, by definition, beyond the influence of parents and the existing family structure, pressured immigrant parents and their children to loosen their attachments to each other. Popular parenting manuals warned against the harms of sentimental, Victorian, and otherwise "backward" or "un-American" styles of childrearing. Instead they advocated a cooler, capitalist approach that spotlighted consumerism and openness to future change, denigrating the emotional burdens of nostalgia. As cultural scholar Agnieszka Bedingfield writes, European immigrants were quick to realize that the United States "does not like to dwell on memories but prefers to create a 'usable past' convertible into building blocks for the future."[98] Advice manuals and magazines even encouraged parents to mimic consumerist tactics of coercive advertising as a way to keep a handle on their children's desires. One article from the year of Sendak's birth entreated parents to use sales techniques to enforce desired behaviors: "Do you really know your child?" the article asked. "[T]he corner store . . . is just about putting the average parent out of business."[99] Jonathan Crary connects the spectacles of interwar advertising, comic books, and amusement parks, as "a technology of *separation*" that helped shape Americans into "docile subjects" through speed and distraction (my emphasis).[100] As a 1922 newspaper article had noted, "[T]he boy of today . . . loves speed and . . . wants to move fast[,] looks forward to 300 miles an hour with confidence[,] is not interested so much in parents' old stories but in those involving modern methods of speed, of wireless, flying, even mental telepathy."[101] Even popular boys' fashion of the 1930s reflected children's interest in speed, flight, and exploration: sailor suits and caps, as well as aviator helmets of strapped leather with cheap goggles attached became popular in that decade.[102] As Bob Batchelor notes, Hollywood in those years favored the "fast-talking, wisecracking reporter" the "busy newsroom, the harried editor, the race to make a deadline, and the constant chatter of all involved."[103] If parents were to get the outcomes they desired in their children's development, they needed to keep up with the rhythms and techniques of the future-oriented popular culture that so captivated their children.

Competing with popular youth culture, parents like Philip and Sadie Sendak found themselves on uphill battles to maintain some level of investment from their children in their heritage and roots of origin. In his later years, Sendak would insist that the only joy Philip had from his son's highly celebrated career was that he illustrated a book for the Yiddish writer Isaac Bashevis Singer.[104] Evaluating his parents' position, Sendak once stated, "They came from little [*shtetlakh*] and they were living in America. . . . You don't speak English, you haven't been to school. *Your kids are being drawn away from you by society.* Their lives were unspeakable" (my emphasis).[105] But the reality of interwar immigrant parenting was also more complex than a tug-of-war between parents' traditions and American culture. Acculturating American immigrants also generally wanted to see their children succeed *as Americans*. In this regard, they sometimes even sided with middle-class authorities against their own children.[106] Whenever Sendak's unusual energies caused a teacher stress at school, he would claim, his parents took the side of the teacher, "out of a deep respect for educated people."[107] Like other Jewish families, the Sendaks grew up with inherited memories of Jewish persecution and political exclusion in Europe connected to "queer" perceptions of Jews as feminine men and aggressive women. Combatting such perceptions, acculturating Jews sought to prove their compatibility with American norms. Sendak recalled that Philip criticized not only blind assimilation but also the failure to properly perform American manhood. Philip saw Sendak and his older brother, Jack, as "duds," indoor bookworm artists with green complexions, inferior to his sister, Natalie, the smart and good-looking, "normal" one.[108] He used to scold Jack in Yiddish, "[H]unchback! stand up straight! Pull your shoulders back."[109] Philip felt like his children were his "punishment" for running away from home to chase a woman, because they were "the kind of children he could have had 'back there'" in the Old Country, because they "were not healthy and sound."[110]

Philip and Sadie likely felt pressure from both directions—for their children to meet normative American standards and for them to maintain a threatened Jewish heritage. Traditional cultural authorities like Sholem Aleichem, whose writing had first brought Philip and Sadie together, satirized immigrant parents who allowed the Jewish disengagement of their American children. His parody of the four questions traditionally asked at the Passover Seder has a child confront his elders with an alternate set of questions related to assimilation: "Why did we memorize the history of all peoples, the old ones and the new ones, but omit the history of one people—our own Jewish people?" and "Why did you send us to a school to learn only English, and forget to teach us Yiddish, our own language, or Hebrew?" and "Why do we know when it's Christmas . . . but we don't know when it's *khanike*?"[111] Children of Sendak's generation, for their part, sought to meet Jewish communal expectations but also prove themselves "American enough." Accordingly, the child Sendak juggled feelings of reverence and embarrassment toward his relatives and felt self-conscious about the name "Maurice" on a street filled with Bills, Johns, and Harrys.[112]

It is no wonder that Sendak loved comic books, which mirrored the psychological and emotional dilemmas of first-generation Americans torn between identities. Like Superman and other heroes managing a dual-identity, he negotiated sometimes conflicting spheres of belonging. The visual language of the comic book is especially suited to negotiating and reworking entangled relationships and personal hybridity. Historians note that the comics form, developed largely by first-generation Jewish Americans in interwar New York and other cities, has always been infatuated with secret identities, social justice, multiple realities, and ethical heroes. Comics scholars describe the form as prone to addressing duality and ambivalence—its protagonists fly between panels and pages in order to manage the pressures of being in multiple places at once.[113] Comic books had offered children like Sendak flights into forbidden freedom and agency. Accordingly, Sendak's pictures for *A Very Special House* (1953), *Hector Protector* (1965), *Lullabies and Night Songs* (1965), *In the Night Kitchen* (1970), and *Some Swell Pup* (1976) would all draw from comics conventions, using word bubbles, sound effects written out in capitalized letters, wild pacing, separated panels, and flat color planes.

While new approaches to childrearing and children's media placed special pressure on immigrant families, they also encouraged children's independence, flexibility, and energetic self-making. The expansion of mass entertainment in the interwar decades characterized a zeitgeist of speed, play, and dynamic self-invention. The popular arts of that time, Sendak wrote, were "liberating, socially equalizing, and aesthetically avant-garde . . . in lively communication with the fine [arts], and a kind of give and take refreshed and deepened both."[114] In comic books, cartoons, popular films, and Manhattan store windows, the boy Sendak learned about a world of expression that transcended the laws of family life and, in some cases, even subverted the public social order. Social historian George Chauncey notes, for example, that Laurel and Hardy films of the 1930s "destabilized gender categories and implied that any man might sexually desire another man" by regularly depicting "one of

the duo goosing the other, pulling down his pants, or engaging in obscene poses," such as in the film *Their First Mistake* (1932), in which
Laurel sucks a baby's bottle from Hardy's hands, Hardy stroking the
bottle "so hard that milk spurts out of it."[115] Sendak was four years old at
the time of that film's release, the same year as the dreaded Lindbergh
kidnapping. Later, for his *In the Night Kitchen*, a book that confronted
his 1930s childhood and his emergent sexuality, the artist would draw
three bumbling Oliver Hardy lookalikes as bakers who dance and physically cling to each other. The book centers around a sensually awakened
boy protagonist who floats naked through the air to pour milk down
to these bakers. Sendak would proclaim that *Night Kitchen* contained
"everything I loved: New York, immigrants, Jews, Laurel and Hardy,
Mickey Mouse, King Kong, movies."[116] With a decidedly queer spin,
Night Kitchen emphasizes the growing commercial and child-centered
ethos of Sendak's childhood with its giant brand-name products, like
the baby food containers and "Mickey oven," the enormous milk bottle,
and the console model radio set—the greatest household wellspring of
commercials and advertisements.[117]

   If older children of the interwar decades idolized Hollywood movie
stars, comic-book superheroes, famous athletes, and explorers, younger
ones absorbed cartoons and the "Sunday funnies," colorful shop signs,
ads, and radio programs, which colored their imagination. American
comics drew from cultural excitement about new, fast-paced technolo-
gies, jazz music and the speed of film, automobiles, and aviation. And by
the time of Sendak's birth, children's picture books had become more like
comic books due to improvements in color lithography and the evolution
of child psychology. Artists such as William Nicholson moved away from
illustrating wordy or didactic stories to focus instead on what became the
children's book as we know it today: a horizontal layout with individual
frames that paid more attention to the fusion of text and image, including
more entertaining, meaningful pictures and a running text that was more
fluid, spare, and suspenseful. Oversize print and exciting, often cartoonish imagery made the picture book, like the comic book, seem deceptively
simple, and both shared a low cultural status.[118] Children's literature also
reflected alienation between traditional parents and a young generation

mesmerized by larger-than-life spectacles. Theodor Seuss Geisel (Dr. Seuss), drew on his experience as an illustrator for major advertisers during the Depression when he created his first children's book in 1937, *And to Think I Saw It on Mulberry Street.* It followed a boy named Marco who envisions a fantastical parade of wild creatures and bizarre vehicles, as well as the humorous gulf between Marco and the adults who cannot understand or appreciate his imagined fantasy.[119] Sendak was nine years old when this book first appeared.

Two years later, Sendak reacted sensitively to MGM's *The Wizard of Oz,* which he saw on the big screen in 1939, likely within weeks of Germany's invasion of Poland, where most of Philip's relatives and some of Sadie's remained and ultimately perished. The artist would later recall this cinematic experience as a formative one of traumatic recognition. Two particular moments in the film initially caused him to cry and scream so much, he would claim, that he was escorted out of the theater, returning to see the film several times afterward.[120] In the first scene, Dorothy Gale, captured by the wicked witch, sees her distraught Auntie Em in Kansas crying out to her from within the witch's crystal ball. Dorothy, even more desperate, calls back in tears—"Auntie Em! Here I am!"—but Auntie Em can neither see nor hear her. Second was the scene in which Dorothy awakens in her bed in Kansas. None of the adults care to listen to her dream about Oz, focusing only on the fact that she is alive, having emerged from her trance and returned to *their* version of reality. At the film's end, Dorothy is still, in some respects, as far away from her caretakers as she was when calling to them through the crystal ball in the witch's tower. Sendak would assert that these scenes flooded his work and "broke his heart," because Dorothy and Auntie Em were, like Seuss's Marco and his parents, in the same space yet still unable to reach each other. This dynamic mirrored Sendak's own feelings as a child who, despite his investment in his parents' stories, felt so emotionally distant from them, forced to fend for himself, sometimes even in their company. The scenario also recalled Philip's and Sadie's separations from their own parents as teenagers, unable to save them from Nazi invasion, and as parents who also felt far away from their own offspring, in some respects, as the latter acculturated.

Sendak was doubly struck by the tragedy of Dorothy's "happy" ending, which conveyed how adults miss important pieces of their children's lives, even life-changing pieces; children must learn that their intensely felt and imagined experiences are theirs alone, and no parent or aunt or uncle can save them from, or fully share with them in, their own life-altering fantasies. All it takes is one moment of her caretaking sister Ida's distraction in Sendak's *Outside Over There* for the infant to find herself in the clutches of goblin intruders, whom the artist draws like the guards of the wicked witch's castle from the MGM film, marching solemnly with spears. Ida ultimately melts those goblins into a "dancing stream," as Dorothy does to the evil witch. Ida's blue dress is also an homage to Dorothy's, and her act of stretching a yellow cloak across the sky at the start of her frightening journey draws from the symbolic yellow brick road.[121] Like Dorothy Gale, whose name and storyline, Kenneth Kidd notes, link her with the flight of birds, wind, and tornados, Ida also goes unnoticed by her distracted caretaker when she takes flight beyond the safety of home into "outside over there."[122] In one of his page spreads, Sendak even mirrors the composition of the traumatic scene from *Wizard of Oz*, whether consciously or not; Ida, the child protagonist, hovers above her distraught mother, who appears in a globe-like section of the bottom right of the page, as though trapped in a crystal ball. The final words of *Wizard of Oz*, "There's no place like home," speak to the dynamic tightrope that reminded Sendak of his own childhood, torn between the drive, on the one hand, to artistically express his unusual imagination, his "Oz," alienating his parents, and on the other hand, the ingrained survivalist mentality of "these people are all I got." To be an artist was a terrifying and lonely risk for a child struggling to survive and to belong, but it was also an irrepressible calling. Some of Sendak's most powerful works would depict moments in which a child and parent are, like Dorothy and Auntie Em in the witch's crystal ball, physically proximal but emotionally worlds apart.

The year following *Wizard of Oz*, Sendak eagerly attended a showing of Disney's *Pinocchio* (1940), later citing it as formative in his creative development. The film dramatized both the tendency of twentieth-century popular culture to separate parents from children as the latter developed emotional independence and the potential dangers inherent within that popular culture. In this film, mass consumption is imagined as "other" to American cultural norms. In order to become "a real boy," the puppet protagonist must resist the advances of ethnically marked deviants—from the flamboyant, Italian Stromboli, who hoards his money and imprisons Pinocchio, to the competitive, unfeeling Lampwick, an Irish youth who smokes, drinks, and gambles on Pleasure Island, a sort of Coney Island spectacle dotted with Native American caricatures. On Pleasure Island, boys are transformed by vice into donkeys, crying for mothers they will never see again. Early Disney films like *Pinocchio* helped normalize the ideal of a wholesome, middle-class American child and helped naturalize harmful ideas about race, gender, and class through that symbolic child.[123] As Nicholas Sammond claims, these films also "played upon separation anxiety in both parent and child," following a narrative formula in which a youthful protagonist is separated from caretakers, survives dangers, and belatedly returns to family and community "as a more independent and self-sufficient individual."[124]

Witnessing wider social negations of parents' religious, linguistic, and cultural norms in the mainstream public led Jewish American children like Sendak to internalize the potential limitations of fully identifying with their Jewish immigrant caretakers. Irving Howe's *World of Our Fathers* illustrates the Pinocchio-esque dilemma of Jewish children of immigrants: "The struggle is strong because . . . [h]e is aware, and rather ashamed, of the limitations of his parents. He feels that the trend and weight of things are against them, that they are in a minority; but yet in a real way the old people remain his conscience, the visible representatives of a moral and religious tradition by which the boy may regulate his inner life."[125] Deborah Dash Moore argues that public school, charged with unifying children into a common belief system, was a potential arena of conflict between gentile teachers and Jewish students, teachers denigrating Yiddish as lower-class and un-American. Children learned to judge their parents' poor English and follow their teachers' lead in order to achieve social mobility, a feat that would ultimately allow them to best assist their parents.[126] Ethnic and racial minorities were increasingly pressured to adopt White Anglo-Saxon

Protestant social norms quickly. Public school thus offered guidance to the majority of first-generation American children as they negotiated the sharp disparities between increasingly private middle-class households, where emotional worlds were shaped, and the public world in which one was expected to take a useful, collectively defined social role, often beyond immigrant parents' full comprehension.[127] Moore writes that some second-generation New York Jews treated the public school like an "ethnic institution," in this regard.[128] Disney's *Pinocchio* extolled public-school virtues of restraint, rationalism, and education, endangering the protagonist only after he allows a seductive fox and cat to sway him from his route to school—here the animal realm is imagined as purely immoral, a less nuanced space than that which Sendak would offer on the island of Wild Things who would empower Max's clarifying emotional catharsis. For Pinocchio, straying from the path to school leads to a life of evil and danger, painted with abundant visual references to Irish, Italian, and Native American ethnicities and thereby denigrating cultures of origin out of which American school children were pressed to transition. Without school, children in *Pinocchio* perform for money, gamble, use drugs, and literally become donkeys. Acculturating Americans, on the other hand, often dissociated from ethnic particularities in order to secure their social belonging, and public education offered a clear pathway for this pursuit.

Sendak's lived experience, however, dramatized the emotional dangers of public school itself as an assimilationist and spiritually depleting institution, which he despised.[129] "School fundamentally destroys," he would later assert, "Life, living, and working at your art are the only answer for artists."[130] Feeling like herded cattle, he would lament, "I couldn't stand being cloistered with other children, and I was usually so embarrassed that I stammered."[131] He found most of his peers overly competitive and felt "very alone."[132] Perhaps reflecting this discomfort around school, an earlier draft of his first authored book, *Kenny's Window*, would open with the interruption of Kenny's dream by the noise of children outside on their way to class.[133] In school, the sensitive Sendak was repeatedly hit with a ruler in order to stop writing with his left hand, in order to become right-handed.[134] He also recalled reading assemblies that, he felt, were utterly "anti-reading," even "anti-life." In these assemblies, "you sat, row by row, class by class . . . with your hands folded in your lap. . . . [M]onitors walked up and down to see if your hands indeed were clasped tightly . . . all you thought about were your hands. . . . "[135] Preserving his emotional integrity as a loner in a sterile atmosphere, the artist focused on the physicality of the books themselves, to which he related as companions, as "holy objects to be caressed and sniffed and treasured."[136]

Parent-Child Bonds Reimagined

If popular culture and public schooling enforced separations between immigrant children and their parents, literature and reading, Sendak felt, helped sustain, or at least reimagine, parent-child bonds. He associated literature with the parental attachments that enable infants to survive. As he recalled, when Philip would read to him, the young Sendak felt subsumed by his father's body, becoming connected to his chest and arm. Accordingly, he would compare children to puppies and other animals who crave to be licked, groomed, and touched by their parents, on whom they depend to survive. Children who remember being held and read to by their parents, he felt, may develop a sensual, lifelong connection to literature, solidified through the memories of a beloved parents' physical proximity during story time—their smell and touch.[137] With this notion in mind one might best understand Sendak's later claim that one of the highest compliments he ever experienced was from a young child who, upon receiving an autographed drawing of a Wild Thing from the artist, expressed excitement over the gift by literally devouring it.[138]

For a child raised to fear kidnapping and to mourn the traumatic losses of relatives, nothing could be more comforting than the fantasy of fusing with loved ones. As Max exclaims to his mother in a moment of psychologically disorganizing rage, "I'll eat you up!" As the Wild Things proclaim to Max when faced with the possibility of losing him, "Oh, please don't go—we'll eat you up—we love you so!" Endangered bonds and imagined fusions occupy much of the content of Sendak's work. Using metaphors of eating and devouring, his creations dramatize the emotional and physical mergers that small children feel with their intimate caretakers, as well as the sometimes comical anxiety that accompanies the idea that this merger might lead to one party consuming the other, or the terror that an act of overstepping might terminate the precious relationship, leaving the other endangered. The grotesque, horned monsters of his *Where the Wild Things Are* would creatively conflate the explosiveness of early childhood emotion with the unkempt wildness of the greenhorn stereotype, imbuing the parent-child bond—both its rewards and its dangers—with markedly ethnic notes. The book grapples with the line between familiar and foreign. It also represented the emotional confusion of a child who both loves and fears his parents, sensitive to their fragilities and aware of the possibility that some external stimulus might elicit parents' emotional undoing, transforming them from gentle caretakers into threatening monsters. Like his immigrant parents and relatives, the Wild Things were both dangerous and familiar members of his tribe. Moreover, Max's fantastical mobility owed itself, in part, to his relationship with his mother. It is the rage he feels toward her that spawns a jungle in his room, where he is free to re-create and process his real-life family drama within the personal abandon of a wild rumpus.

Haunted by the strong feelings of his immigrant parents, Sendak would imagine American children who step into the shoes of their own overwhelmed and demanding caretakers to reach creative resolutions. In *Kenny's Window*, for example, Kenny travels to the Old World and asserts too much control over a goat, a sort of surrogate child: "I have come all the way from America to make you my only goat," he proclaims to the animal he wishes to possess. Kenny initially prohibits this goat from playing outside but then becomes more understanding of her loneliness. Max would act similarly, imagining the possibility of ruling over the Wild Things. Max ultimately returns home to his punishing mother, because he longs to be somewhere safe where he feels loved, despite the emotional chasm that may exist in his relationship with her. Sendak offers a complex message about the inevitable loneliness of both children and caretakers—of those "in charge" and of those cared for by distressed authority figures. Max, as King of the Wild Things, like his own mother back at home, has the challenging task of maintaining both social order and loving bonds in a chaotic context.

As a child of beloved immigrant parents castigated by the wider society as "wild" or socially corrosive, Sendak created from a place of ambivalence about the child's genuine need for love and for "home," even when parents were rough or emotionally incoherent by public standards. Wild rumpuses and threats of "I'll eat you up!" assert one's power to develop even beyond parental constraints. Moreover, acculturating caretakers and American children alike might long to "eat each other up," or to love in ways denied by a wider culture of restraint and individualism. They may also punish each other for behavioral missteps and sublimate their longings, each ultimately eating their own hot supper alone—an American prerogative even in the most loving of families. Confronting the limits of what feels safe, Sendak's children end their journeys with a degree of internalized comfort but also with a greater acceptance of their serious, burdensome positions as mediators between conflicting social and personal realities.

Drawing on a culturally hybrid childhood experienced in the currents of parent-child separations that characterized the 1930s, especially for immigrant families, Sendak's work would dramatize how parents become unavailable, distracted, or even dysfunctional. The emotionally overwhelmed or absent parent would be a staple of Sendak's creative work in the latter twentieth century, as would be the solitary, flying child whose freedom comes with its own dangers. His illustrations for Randall Jarrell's *The Animal Family* (1965) and *Fly by Night* (1976) would interpret Jarrell's words as expressing "a great hunger pain . . . a looking-for-mama pain . . . my pain." The latter book features a nude, blonde American boy soaring past his lost mother, drawn as a carefully rendered portrait of Sadie holding the infant Maurice on her lap. In another image, a younger Sadie tends a flock of sheep in what may be an imagined Old World pasture.[139] Similarly, Sendak's illustrations for the book jacket of *In Grandpa's House* (1985) would depict a boy flying on the back of a bird, uprooted and solitary in the night sky, disconnected from the adult couple who clasp hands below. *In the Night Kitchen* would situate the child protagonist as both a bourgeois child who cries,

"Mama! Papa!" and a hungry, urban hero who follows his own dreams, sculpts an airplane, and flies naked through the nocturnal cityscape on a sensual journey while his parents sleep.

Channeling the zeitgeist of 1930s popular culture, the artist actively employed the visual language of comic books as a shorthand for the emotional qualities of his childhood years, using a fast-paced, musical approach to catch readers' attention through a jazzy flow that would animate a text and hurry it to a beat.[140] While working on *Night Kitchen*, he would write himself notes in his journal to remind him to keep the page spreads varied and fast, exciting like a comic book.[141] Mickey's name is, in part, a nod to the surname of the cartoonist Winsor McCay, creator of *Little Nemo in Slumberland* (1905–11, reprinted in the 1920s). Like *Little Nemo*, *Night Kitchen* features elongated panels to dramatize a surreal, urban dreamland. Like the comic book form, *Night Kitchen* uses a language of simplified planes and shapes, a collapsing of time and space, a fast-paced rhythm, separated panels, speech bubbles, popular cultural references, and a kind of dream logic in order to articulate a serious, self-reflexive message. By visualizing a book like *Night Kitchen*, about a child's newfound agency, as a sort of comic book, Sendak playfully expressed that some modern human needs are only met beyond the purview of parents and inherited traditions. However, by framing Mickey's nocturnal tryst in a domestic household scene, dedicating the book to his parents, and using their names on brand labels for the oversized kitchen products of his tactile fantasy, he also offered children a world in which individual drives might somehow manage to relate directly to a particular familial belonging. The cream container, for example, lists two addresses from Sendak's Brooklyn childhood.[142]

As a project immediately following Sadie's death and finished as Philip was dying, *Night Kitchen* would also help Sendak ward off anxieties about his mortality. Mickey would begin like the endangered Lindbergh infant—a child displaced from his bed at night and nearly baked in an oven by three bakers sporting Hitler moustaches.[143] But this oven is a "Mickey Oven," and Mickey takes charge of the narrative, ultimately towering above these men and distributing the precious milk they require. Mickey is a unique and seemingly audacious child for taking control over the adult prescriptions imposed on his body and experience. The determined young protagonist emerges defiantly and flies an airplane that he fashions from dough, aligning himself symbolically with the Lindbergh baby's parents, Charles and Anne, the celebrated aviators, authors, and inventors. The bakers howl, "Milk! Milk! Milk for the morning cake!" Mickey responds, "What's all the fuss? I'm Mickey the pilot! I get milk the Mickey way!" He proceeds to fly over the Milky Way, into a milk bottle that is also a skyscraper, and asserts power by pouring milk down from the sky like a self-appointed god of dairy. Pointing to the emotional seriousness of very young people as well as to the external social forces that children perceive, *Night Kitchen* explodes traditional assumptions and expectations of modern American childhood. It also invites readers to take note of the processes by which society misjudges and acts upon the uninitiated and the powerless, as well as the creative vitality with which the latter might resist unwelcome social advances and proclaim their truths.

Decades after *Night Kitchen*, Sendak's *We Are All in the Dumps with Jack and Guy* (1993) would lovingly celebrate both of his parents. For the text, he recovered a forgotten nursery rhyme: "We are all in the dumps / For diamonds are trumps / The kittens are gone to St. Paul's! / The baby is bit / The moon's in a fit / And the houses are built without walls." In a critique of capitalist greed that would have delighted Philip, Sendak depicts Sadie as the savior of the narrative, merging the good intentions of a harried caretaker with a universal vision of the excluded social outsider. Fiercely caring but also removed, the unsung hero of *Dumps* is a boundary-crossing, micromanaging moon, a maternal stereotype that also captured elements of how Sendak experienced Sadie while playing on his Brooklyn block. He described this sort of anxious, hovering mother as one who breaks the cosmic law, as Sadie did, crossing established boundaries in order to come to Earth and save her children. She "watches and watches . . . and says, 'You *shmegegies*, come with me.'" Sendak recalled his worried mother watching him play on the street from the window of their second-floor apartment building: "If I turned the corner, she'd run to the window on the other side of the building. Her head darted out of three windows, like a cartoon. I remember wherever

I looked, her head *was*. . . . I knew it was a worried, Jewish moon . . . a *nudgy* moon."[144] Ultimately, the moon transforms into a giant cat who destroys the greedy rats and carries Jack and Guy to St. Paul's Bakery and Orphanage, where they are able to save a bruised, dark-skinned child and offer him a braided loaf of challah.

Philip's presence lurks here too. Applying his father's Yiddish-inflected social consciousness to late twentieth-century capitalist exploitation and its human casualties, Sendak sidesteps the idealized bourgeois family to empathize with the boundary-breaking closeness and caring of unconventional families. In the vein of Lauren Berlant's "cruel optimism," the artist problematizes cultural focuses on upward mobility, material gain, and social conformity to instead prioritize empathy and social justice vis-à-vis contemporary crises.[145] And he does so, in part, by the graces of his alienated, socially critical immigrant parents and what they represented for him within a society set on denigrating foreigners and shaping compliant American children in contrast to their parents. Amidst the mayhem of corruption, disaster, and filth, Jack and Guy are a sort of same-sex couple or sibling pair fighting socioeconomic injustice in their community under the cosmic sanction of a Jewish maternal moon, adopting a lost orphan boy of color and declaring, "Let's buy him some bread / You buy one load / And I'll buy two / And we'll bring him up / As other folk do." Though the abject Jack and Guy physically cling to each other and, visually, almost lose their individual boundaries, they also demand admiration as resilient and generous life-givers. They contrast the giant rats, whose imposing robes and mammoth deck of cards suggest reckless competition and, perhaps, blame for the crises headlined in the newspaper fragments worn by the destitute children: "AIDS," "War," "Shootin[g]," "Homeless," "Meaner Times, "Chaos in Shelters," "Famine," "Babies Starv[e]," "Layoff!" A landscape of robust skyscrapers pronounces a dispassionate establishment culture ruled by capital and indifferent to its most vulnerable subjects. If the project of modernizing childhood had in the twentieth century helped standardize middle-class culture and separate immigrants' children from their parents, who were imagined as inherently "outside" of domestic social norms, Sendak's work insisted that all children, by virtue of being human animals, begin "outside" too, like Jack and Guy and their peers. If some parents were "rough" and broke cosmic laws, they usually did so to fight falsity or injustice and to help their children survive. Sometimes their roughness offered valuable exposure to emotional honesty—a rare resource within the emergent culture of middle-class childhood innocence.

CHAPTER 2

LOVE IN A DANGEROUS LANDSCAPE

Queer Kinship and Survival

AT THE HEIGHT OF SENDAK'S CAREER in the 1970s, an essay in the underground *Gay Alternative* pointed to him, along with James Marshall and Edward Gorey, as characteristic proponents of a "gay sensibility" in children's literature that prioritized a "lushness and peculiarity of imagination" generally "disinclined to present the happy, radiant nuclear-family situation so characteristic of conventional children's literature."[1] Indeed, a great part of Sendak's appeal to those modern children bound to domestic norms has been his emotional bravery to search beyond them. In his own life, he perceived the rhythms of the traditional nuclear family as directly at odds with his needs and capacities as an artist. He would contrast himself with the late Herman Melville, who was "ill equipped" to be a husband or father but became so anyway, causing suffering to himself and his family. Sendak, instead, consciously avoided social expectations, reserving himself to focus fully on his art and accepting any associated limitations this imposed on his life.[2] Perhaps as a reminder to himself of this conviction, Sendak painted a portrait of Melville to hang above his own drawing table, depicting the writer as a wistful and handsome dandy in a red necktie, his eyes soft and blue.[3] The artist's atypical stances on kinship, like his interest in the dark and complex sides of childhood, were inseparable from his queerness and his proximity to Jewish historical trauma. Though the Sendaks lived in

Brooklyn during World War II, the Holocaust destroyed Philip's and Sadie's communities of origin and took the lives of most of their relatives.
Reactions to these events thwarted some of the formative moments in
the artist's adolescence, complicating his initiation into adult society, but
they also intensified his internalization of family mythology and his creative meaning-making around parent-child and sibling bonds.

Sendak once stated that his relatives "showed us love in ways that
were very heavy—when I learned their history, it broke my heart."[4] His
parents and maternal grandmother, for example, conveyed historically
based anxieties to him: Jews are targeted with violence, children lose
their parents, and children also die. Philip had, as a boy, lost his own
little sister.[5] But families like Sendak's also imbued their children with
values of resilience and survivalism. They stressed the importance of
political consciousness and in-group loyalty, even as they pushed their
children to achieve American success. As Tony Kushner writes, Yiddish Brooklyn children of the 1930s "were loved while at the same
time inculcated with ghetto-bred tribal fearfulness and insecurity,"
and Sendak's home, as no exception, was "an atmosphere of pressur-
ized familial closeness."[6] Throughout Sendak's upbringing, their home
remained infused with a tone of ongoing mourning and exasperation.
The Sendaks' wartime losses psychologically depleted an already
strained household, pervading the emotional climate of their tight-
knit family.[7] Philip assured Sendak that "the Holocaust could happen
here" and told him to "keep a suitcase packed in the closet" just in
case. Sendak despised these reminders of his own vulnerability as a
Jew, even in America.[8] He internalized the fragility of his existence,
troubled by what he perceived as a lack of safety and social foundation. Philip's whim to chase a girl all the way to the United States was,
he felt, all that separated his American childhood of "lollipops and
bar mitzvahs" from his other potential childhood of concentration
camps and gas chambers in Poland. He recalled, "[W]henever a kid
died, when I was a kid, it was a very big thing; it reflected back on
the fact that my being here was arbitrary."[9] The Sendaks' proximity to
migration and collective trauma colored the tone of their household
and separated it from other American homes, a difference reflected

in wider studies of posttraumatic immigrant families. Scholarship on
the European Jewish family during World War II, for example, is rife
with accounts that emphasize the need to be flexible about suspend-
ing personal boundaries and social roles in endangered circumstances,
in order to pool resources together, care for each other, and attend to
stressors as a group.[10] American individualist ideals, however, starkly
contrasted this tightknit relational style. Put simply and profoundly
by Eva Hoffman, who immigrated from Poland to America after her
parents survived the Holocaust in hiding, "[F]amilial bonds seem so
dangerously loose here."[11]

Sadie and Philip continuously received news of Jewish deaths in
Europe by way of American Jewish agencies and Philip's social club.[12]
In Philip's home *shtetl* of Zambrow, where all of his close relatives
remained, antisemitic violence and economic boycotts had become
routine by 1936, and half of the town was destroyed in air raids at
the start of World War II.[13] According to Zambrow's *yizkor* book, the
Germans conquered the city on the first day of the outbreak of war
between Germany and Russia: June 22, 1941, during the month of Sendak's bar mitzvah in Brooklyn.[14] The Nazis plundered and confiscated
Jewish property and businesses, sending the town's Jews to complete
forced labor in a ghetto from which transports to death camps began
that September. These transports, along with typhus outbreaks and the
shooting of those Jews who sought to escape imprisonment, entirely
eliminated the remaining Jewish population of Zambrow.[15] As for Sadie's *shtetl*, Zakrocym, located in the Warsaw district of Poland, about
70 percent of it was destroyed at the onset of the war, forcing most
of its Jews to flee. In July 1941, remaining Jews without resident per-
mits were expelled to Pomiechowek, the rest sent to the Nowy Dwor
ghetto that November.[16] Sendak's parents had brought Sadie's mother,
Minnie, Sadie's three sisters, and one brother to the United States before the war, but Sadie would lose another brother, Aaron, as well as
aunts, uncles, nieces, nephews, and cousins. On Philip's side, only two
second-cousins made it to America.[17] Philip and Sadie displayed photographs of nieces and nephews sent to concentration camps, including
newlyweds and babies. These images were all that Sendak knew of

most of his extended family. "It was suffocating, unhappy," the artist would later recall, "almost like my father was blaming me for being alive. Dead Jews hung all over the place."[18]

Still, Sendak invested intensely in the memory of those dead relatives, perhaps as one means through which to solve the problem of his own perpetual feelings of depression. Agnieszka Bedingfield's concept of "trans-memory" informs an analysis of this investment in family memory.[19] Trans-memory resembles the more familiar notion of "postmemory," coined by Marianne Hirsch. Postmemory refers to what it means to grow up in the shadow of a parent's overwhelmingly meaningful, but also inaccessible experiences of endangerment and loss. The parent's unresolved and all-pervasive psychology, as it manifests in the parent's behavior and relational style, leads postmemorial children to feel haunted or threatened by a past that they did not directly experience, as well as compelled to piece that past together and relate to it through creative investment in the parent's traumatic history.[20] Trans-memory, which is also a kind of secondhand memory, focuses not necessarily on trauma but on the emotional or psychological difficulty of cultural and linguistic adjustment from the language and memory of parents' origins to the language and culture of a new, adopted home country. According to Bedingfield, the subject's stability may be threatened by the inability to narrate the past in a language that is meaningful to the present.[21] This surely characterized Sendak's experience in a Yiddish-speaking household in a context that pressured assimilation, and decades before the emergence of mainstream Holocaust memory in Anglophone culture. As Bedingfield writes, subjects of "trans-memory" have an impulse to "return" to the imagined origins of an uneasy heritage that overshadows them and defines them in order to find closure with unresolved internal conflicts in the present.[22] Sendak's work gives shape to such past-oriented familial longings, and to the frustrations and impotence such longings sometimes induced by virtue of their second-hand nature. These feelings, however, interacted dynamically with the concerns of a queer artist who positioned himself as a subject in tension with bourgeois nuclear family models.

The Family That Tells Scary Stories Together . . .

Play, danger, and improvisation were the bread and butter of story time in the Sendak household. As a sickly, highly sensitive child, Sendak spent much of his early years indoors, both alone in his bedroom and absorbing traditions and stories from his parents and maternal grandmother, Minnie.[23] Sendak was specifically intrigued by the dybbuk trope, in which Sadie fervently believed. In Yiddish folklore, a dybbuk—named from the Hebrew root "davok," which means to cling or adhere—is a spirit that attaches to a living being through "ibbur," the "impregnation of another living soul." Dybbuks were sometimes queerly invoked in traditional Yiddish culture as excuses for betrothed brides who did not wish to marry the men of their parents' choosing. To be possessed by a dybbuk was to be carrying too much of another person to be fit to offer oneself fully for marriage, to be pregnant with or dispossessed by another person who had somehow penetrated the victim's depths. In this way, possession—including the emotional possession of secondhand memory—carries receptive, traditionally feminine connotations and offers a creative possibility for queer sidestepping. Possession aligns with the power to resist constraining social expectations, perhaps especially for unusual members of traditional Ashkenazi communities.[24] A queer or rebellious subject, for example, might claim possession by an external being in order to resist the unwelcome advances of a tradition that negated their internal experience, as a heterosexual union would have been for most individuals who might today identify as gay or lesbian.[25] Less intentionally, Sendak, from his earliest years, also invited associations of possession. Sadie recounted finding him during a fever at age two standing up in his crib, speaking fluent Yiddish, and reaching toward a photographic portrait of his maternal grandfather, Moishe Schindler, hanging over him. A neighbor in the apartment building warned Sadie that her father's dybbuk was trying to lure his grandson into the *yene velt*, the afterlife, through his photograph, which led Sadie to tear the picture to shreds. In his adulthood, Sendak would later find the torn picture, hire a specialist from the Metropolitan Museum to reconfigure it, and hang the reassembled portrait above his bed.[26]

In the Sendak home, frightening stories were not limited to the dyb-buk trope. Minnie and Sadie, for example, recounted more concrete horrors, including memories of pogroms in Zakroczym, during which "Jew-haters" would come into their little grocery store, Minnie pushing Sadie and her siblings into the cellar, where they hid as Cossacks ran-sacked the store above them.[27] Perhaps related to this story, Sendak had a recurring nightmare around age four about seeking protection in a cellar. A complex nightmare, it conveys the child's absorption of terror, but also his fear of his own caretakers. As he narrated it, it was about "being chased by a very frightening something and . . . I'm desperate to get the cellar door open, but this thing is right behind me. And I finally turn. And it's my father. And his face is hot on my face and his hands are out: murder. That's all it is: he will kill me." But, like the reviled relatives who became the models for his beloved Wild Things, dream-Philip was ultimately redeemed through a plot twist. Experiencing the dream again, seventy years later, Sendak would discover, "The same thing hap-pened and . . . I did something I never did before. I turned around and there he was, but I stood my ground and his face was so close to mine and his nose was pressing my nose and then I saw that he was laugh-ing—that it was a joke. He wasn't trying to kill me, he was playing with me."[28] The blend of aggression and play evinced in this unconscious image of Philip reflects the violent, fantastical bedtime stories he shared with his children. Likely drawing from the *mayses* (stories), midrashic tales, and folklore of his childhood *kheyder* and community in Zambrow, Philip embellished otherwise truthful renderings of his youth with el-ements of fantasy, biblical narratives, and ghost stories. Sendak most recalled one story about a game Philip played as a small boy with his friends—they would dig sticks into the ground of a graveyard at night. One night, while doing this, they heard a scream. The next morning one of the boys was found dead by a coronary, because, having pierced the stick through his own garment on its way down, lodging himself to the earth, he thought the dead were seizing him.[29]

Philip's stories would blend in Sendak's imagination with earlier versions of the Brothers Grimm tales, which had also used metaphor, repetition, and hyperbole to offer wild, poignant truths to children and

adults alike. During Philip's childhood, as he recalled, his own grandfather had been transparent with him about mortality and made the
explicit connection between death, storytelling, and family memory; he
had spoken frankly with Philip about the transience of human life and
the importance of telling grandchildren meaningful stories to maintain a
positive legacy.[30] Bedtime stories in many Yiddish-speaking, immigrant
families, like Sendak's, reflected the need to nourish the child's capacity
to locate and heed dangerous situations. Philip's cliff-hanger *mayselekh*
(little stories), which often extended over multiple nights, included the
terror of Cossacks and Polish peasants who wielded clubs studded with
nails.[31] They also featured children who get lost, fall asleep in the snow,
or struggle to get their parents to recognize them after a period of separation.[32] In one story, for example, a child loses his way in the winter,
sobbing under a tree. After he dies from the cold, the souls of the biblical
Abraham and Sarah usher him to heaven. In another, a boy named David
finds his lost parents among a hunter's horde of kidnapped slaves and,
despite his eagerness to reunite with them—pretends not to recognize
them so that the hunter will not suspect him of intending to free them.[33]
Later, in Philip's book *In Grandpa's House* (1985), which Sendak would illustrate, the child protagonist would similarly struggle to get his captured
parents to recognize him after he frees them from their captor.

The Sendaks were not alone in narrating dark or upsetting situations to their children. Reflecting generations of oral storytelling in
Poland, it was not uncommon to address gruesome and frightening
content as a family through narrative improvisation. Moreover, Yiddish children's literature published in interwar Europe and the United
States handled difficult themes of war, violence, mortality, racism, and
lynching. Tapping into American racial issues, for example, a Yiddish
children's story published in the May 1933 issue of the *Kinder Zhurnal*
depicts and condemns the public lynching of an African American man
in Georgia.[34] As Daniela Mantovan shows, Yiddish children's literature
of the 1930s, like Philip's bedtime stories, reflected the harsh realities
Jews experienced in Eastern Europe, as well as other terrors to which
minorities were subjected at home and abroad.[35] Broadly speaking, Yiddish literature for children did not shy away from the horrors that could

be inflicted by fellow human beings and oppressive regimes alike. For example, Der Nister's 1934 *Dray mayselekh* (three little tales) and his 1939 *Zeks mayselekh* (six little tales), published in Kharkov and Kiev, respectively, handled themes of cannibalism and murder, with human beings killed without hearing or trial. As Sendak would later do, Der Nister's stories used animals to symbolize those human elements that were socially othered, regulated, or forbidden: small, benign animals attempt and fail to participate productively in human society, and larger predatory animals are killed as enemies. Not unlike Sendak's position as a queer child of immigrants in an assimilationist era, Krutikov imagines Der Nister's identification with the "wild animal" figure as reflecting his incompatibility with the new disciplinarian Soviet society.[36]

During Word War II, Yiddish children's periodicals such as the *Kinder Zhurnal* also detailed accounts of ghettos, gassing, and other atrocities committed against Jews in Poland. An April 1942 issue reported the Nazi murder of over eighty-four thousand civilians in Poland, including women, children, and the elderly—most of them Jews. It described the Nazis' treatment of the city of Barysaw, where they killed fifteen thousand Jews, imprisoned the rest in a barbed-wire ghetto, and—fearful that the Jews were helping the Red Army—plundered the ghetto, leading the remaining Jews, including small children, to hide in the open graves they had dug for their dead.[37] Yiddish writers even made emotional appeals to Jewish children; an August-September 1942 issue, for example, features a front-page story about the hundreds of homeless Jewish refugee children in America, rescued from the war by the Jewish Joint Distribution Committee and the United Palestine Appeal. It includes photographs and asks what will become of them. The article describes the invasion of Jews' homes by storm troopers at night and masses of Jews forced into starvation, panic, and death in concentration camps. One photograph depicts a group of refugee children in America, explaining that they cannot muster a smile, because their hearts are weighted with grief.[38] Yiddish schools, writes Naomi Prawer Kadar, discussed events of the Holocaust almost immediately, beginning with Kristallnacht on November 9, 1938.[39] Accordingly, in 1947, Yiddish linguist and educator Yudl Mark pondered whether it was a sin against child psychology that children of Yiddish schools were taught about gruesome tortures, crematoria, and gas chambers. However, he also understood "the urge to take our children in as partners in our harsh fate, and to arm them with firmness and to brighten their spirits with the luster of the recent martyrdom of fellow Jews."[40]

From infancy, Sendak claimed, he internalized the fragility of his existence. He once stated, "I only have one subject. The question I am obsessed with is, how do children survive?"[41] His art would repeatedly ask the questions, "How do you prevent dying? How do you prevent being eaten or mauled by a monster?"[42] Though later in life he would own at least one volume of Yiddish poetry and enjoy works of Yiddish theater on VHS, there is no evidence that he read Yiddish literature as a child. He claimed to prefer American books like *Tom Sawyer* but also to have read his father's books.[43] Philip was an avid reader of the Yiddish stories serialized in the *Jewish Daily Forward*, especially those by I. J. Singer, Sholem Aleichem, and Sholem Asch, and it's possible that he or others read them to the Sendak children. These writers' sensibilities may have also had an impact on Philip's Yiddish oral tales, which mystified the artist as a child.[44] The books Sendak co-created and illustrated with his brother and sister as a boy extended the makeshift plays they improvised to soothe and entertain their world-weary parents, whose morale they needed to maintain for their own safety. Following the model of Philip's stories, Sendak's work in later decades would explore themes of parent-child role reversals, of children protecting parents from external dangers or "parenting" themselves and other children, tasked with mature responsibilities in the absence of adult protection. Max of *Where the Wild Things Are* (1963) would become a sort of disciplinarian to the Wild Things, serving as their king; Mickey of *In the Night Kitchen* (1970) would seize control of the symbolically maternal milk that gets dispensed in the Night Kitchen and, thereby, of the adult buffoons who try to bake him into a cake; Ida of *Outside Over There* (1981) would save her kidnapped baby sister while her parents were away or too despondent to notice; and the children of *Brundibar* (2003) would set out to ward off a villain and to find milk for their mother, bedridden in the ghetto.

Children as Ghostly Redemption

Sendak described an adolescence characterized by self-erasure and private fantasy. A painful dynamic arose within his household as Jewish relatives were murdered overseas. Sadie and Philip constantly contrasted the young Sendak's irreverent childhood energies with idealized cousins whom they mourned:

> If I was staying out late and dinner was on the table and I'd been called three times, I was playing stoop ball or something outside in the street, my mother's voice would tell me that I'd better go up now. And I'd go up. And she'd say, "Your cousin[s], they're in a concentration camp. You have the privilege of being here. And you don't come up and eat. They have no food." . . . I was made to feel guilty all the time. Because I had the great, good luck and it was only luck that my father came here. I mean really just dumb luck. . . . It was so cruel of my parents. It constantly made me feel that I was shamelessly enjoying myself when they were being cooked in an oven.[45]

This dynamic created a morose and emotionally oppressive atmosphere:

> I'd hear about Leo and Benjamin and the other children who were my age who . . . were good to their mothers but now they were dead, and I was lucky. . . . I hated [them] for dying because all they brought was violent scenes in the house between my mother and father and her pulling hair out of her head, my father diving onto the bed . . . vivid memories.[46]

As a teenager during the war, Sendak became close with a girl named Pearl Karchawer while their families vacationed at Charlie's, a kosher hotel in the Catskills, in the summer of 1944. Sendak and Pearl bonded over the shared hardship of having an older brother drafted and missing in action. Pearl died suddenly the following year from a surgery-related infection, at age twelve. This direct experience of a young friend's death left a lasting mark on Sendak and would lead him to dedicate his *Sign on Rosie's Door* (1960) to Pearl.[47] In his eighties, he would state, "She was my personal Anne Frank. She died during the war, she was Anne's age. . . . I still have every letter she wrote me. . . . It affects me now as much as it did back then."[48] The artist would insist that he carried Anne Frank, and her dream of becoming a writer, with him in his own artistic career—achieving his professional accomplishments for the both of them.[49] Perhaps this conviction also helped preserve an emotional tie to Pearl and to his own adolescence, which he experienced as threatened by the emotional absence and secondhand trauma that surrounded him during the war years.

The systematic murder of Jewish relatives in Europe during World War II added complicated dimensions to American Jewish parents' expectations of their own children. Literary scholar David Roskies argues that the parent-child relationship became a "universal trope" in Jewish folk songs and literature during World War II, children signifying the endangerment all felt, regardless of age, as well as the possibility of future regeneration.[50] In the Sendaks' Bensonhurst neighborhood, the Orthodox Congregation Sons of Israel emphasized the role of the Jewish child for the rebirth and destiny of postwar American Jewry. Rabbi Benjamin Morgenstern's letter in a 1947 yearbook asserted, "When we behold children of seven and eight studying Chumesh, then indeed we hear the youth saying to us, 'Do not despair, a brighter dawn awaits us on the morrow.'"[51] The synagogue's president, Dr. Meyer Cohen, further emphasized the role of the child in the community's symbolic future: "We are told further that the faces of the Cherubim bore the features of youth, of children; meaning that the only guardians of the Ark . . . were the children, the ones who would see to it that the Ark and all it stood for were handed down to future generations."[52] Hitler would thus be doubly defeated by a shining new generation of Jewish children on safe American ground. Often, however, new children also reminded parents of those relatives and friends who did not live to know them, or who could never be sufficiently replaced, even by these new births.

Comparisons and associations made between Jewish children and lost relatives were understandably burdensome for those children. Some parents paradoxically demanded that their postwar offspring both preserve the family's painful history while also becoming exceptionally successful and happy, to compensate for losses and to spite Hitler. Speaking for himself and for his siblings, Sendak would later lament, "We didn't know who we were, and whatever we chose to be was seemingly in opposition to what our parents wanted us to be. . . . They wanted us to be wealthy Americans," he mused, "A doctor, a professor. My sister could be a rich wife."[53] These culturally fraught pressures also speak to a wider reality about childhood in general. Children are regularly asked to surrender themselves to powerful others' emotional needs in order to secure the care required for survival. They may at times disappear emotionally while remaining present in the performances expected of them. As writer Clifton Fadiman articulates, this tendency in children cultivates a natural talent for acting and for fantasy. Children are experts at emptying their consciousness to become whatever role they are enacting; a child playacting as "Snoopy," writes Fadiman, knows he is not actually Snoopy but "can empty his consciousness of all except Snoopy feelings."[54]

Sendak, inhibited in his own personhood and sensitive to his parents' emotional suffering, was primed to serve as witness to his family's difficult feelings by creatively disappearing, so to speak. Accordingly, he would later claim, "I skipped my adolescence. Total amnesia."[55] Ambiguous nursery rhymes, fairy-tale motifs, and metaphors of supernatural possession offered him pathways into conveying this sort of experience. Claiming artistic control over the process by which his subjectivity was "undone" by external forces, he would later describe a favorite activity in the mid-1950s of "sitting in front of the record player as though possessed by a dybbuk, and allowing the music to provoke an automatic, stream-of-consciousness kind of drawing."[56] Sendak's Rosie in *The Sign on Rosie's Door* would model the experience of "possession" as a means of self-preservation and child's play, as she sits beneath a blanket and insists on having lost her identity, waiting for the supernatural intervention of "Magic Man" to rescue her. Like Rosie, the child Sendak awaited the inspiration of "magic"—in his case, that of a personally recalled emotion, of the movie palace, of the comic book, and of the dime novel—to conjure outrageous narratives of flight and suspense, as well as to provide the dramatic plots he narrated to other neighborhood children as a means of connecting, if only momentarily, with otherwise indifferent or hostile peers. In 1997, he would illustrate the cover of Tony Kushner's adaptation of S. Ansky's *A Dybbuk: and Other Tales of the Supernatural* with a distraught bride in white and a solemn groom with sidelocks beside a Hebrew-lettered gravestone at night. Justin Almquist would also interpret the "ladies dressed in white" and the "ghostly lady" used in Sendak and Kushner's stage production of *Brundibar* as possible dybbuks.[57]

Similar to Fadiman's notion of children's playacting, Sendak saw the creative act as the throwing of one's self into a "void" or into one's own "private ocean without an oxygen mask."[58] This vision suits Roland Barthes's understanding of literature as a void that diffuses the self, a space that merges an author's voice with various elements of invention, cultural tradition, psychology, and philosophy, "that obliquity into which our subject flees, the black-and-white where all identity is lost, beginning with the very identity of the body that writes." Barthes believed that the writing of literature begins with a disjunction in which "the voice loses its origin" and "the author enters into his own death," becoming an active vessel of symbol and creativity.[59] By this logic, children—as beings for whom "reality" is new and subject to takeovers by the feelings and demands of powerful others—are *designed* for literature and primed for navigating jolts and unknowns through play and fantasy. It is specifically the plasticity of young children's conceptions of reality and their ambiguous levels of agency and self-control, especially within the family context, to which Sendak's creative work speaks, reflecting his own emotionally challenging youth and his creative survival through fantasy.

Having sometimes felt like a receptacle of his immigrant parents' memories and losses, Sendak was practiced at contemplating the personal significance of once-removed realities of other worlds and eras—of coming into one's own identity between the cracks of other people's overwhelming stories, so to speak. He would come to view illustration as a means for illuminating hidden interpretations or expressing his own emotional truth between the lines of a personally evocative text. He identified with children for the burdens traditionally placed on them by parents and adult society to carry the timeless torches of the collective past, including those discarded cultural elements that adults no longer actively used. The original meanings of most Old Mother Goose rhymes, for example, are usually no longer comprehensible to the adults who relegate them to children in order to preserve those early lyrics, but they offer contemporary children a creative opportunity to make personally satisfying meaning of them beyond the perimeters of "sensible" society. In his *Hector Protector* (1965), for example, Sendak would enliven an old, ambiguous rhyme: "Hector Protector was dressed all in green; Hector Protector was sent to the Queen. The Queen did not like him, No more did the King; So Hector Protector was sent back again." Drawn from his own defiant emotional life, his interpretive illustrations for this picture book would pit a wild boy riding on the back of a lion against a scandalized, rotund Victorian queen reading Mother Goose. Like nursery rhymes, fairy tales also offered folk relics for children to claim and interpret. As Sendak enjoyed recalling, fairy tales, which were first collected by scholars to preserve threatened cultures, were linked with childhood only after children themselves took interest in grappling with their meanings, attracted to how these stories handled pressing concerns around mortality, parental abandonment, and sexuality.[60] Like illustrators activating a text with new complementary meanings, children, Sendak felt, accomplished the task of remembering by reinterpreting and revamping the old, nonsensical material. They had the opportunity to either regurgitate the interpretations that adults wanted or to reimagine the available material in context and on the basis of immediate, embodied feelings.

Quests for self-preservation and emotional survival featured in Sendak's books are likely related to the heavy emotional expectations against which Sendak struggled during his own upbringing. He felt selfish for being a child with energies and needs of his own in the face of such collective tragedy. Even in his old age he would continue to recall feeling guilty for wanting to enjoy his adolescence while his family suffered the news of World War II. He described a memory from age twelve in 1940: "Everybody was very unhappy. And I was ashamed of being so happy, because I wanted to see *Pinocchio*. . . . I was ashamed also, because my mother and father were crying because Jews were dying . . . and I had gotten everything I wanted, and I was ashamed."[61]

The following June, on the morning of Sendak's bar mitzvah, a tele-gram alerted Philip to the news of his father's death.[62] Philip was in the process of trying to bring his relatives to the United States. All those remaining in Poland would also perish.[63] Sendak's outrage at a father who collapsed on the most important day of his young life battled his concern for Philip's well-being. As he remembered Philip that morning,

> He lay down in bed. I remember this so vividly. My mother said to me, "Papa can't come." I was going to have the big party at the colonial club, the old mansion in Brooklyn. And I said, "How can Papa not come to my bar mitzvah?" And I screamed at him, "You gotta get up, you gotta get up!" And of course he did. The only thing I remember is looking at him when they broke into "For He's a Jolly Good Fellow." . . . And my father's face was vivid, livid, and I knew I had done something very bad; that I had made him suffer more than he had to. What did I know? This thirteen-year-old ersatz man.[64]

Philip and Sadie's tendency to induce shame in their children, in-tentionally or not, contrasted with popular contemporary American approaches to parenting, which saw parents' imposition of guilt on chil-dren as a psychologically damaging behavior.[65] Perhaps in the service of overcoming his distraught parents' feelings and proving to himself that he was *not*, contrary to their claims, a selfish ingrate who took others' deaths too lightly, Sendak would later create a boy protagonist onto whom he projected those same accusations. He would illustrate his Pierre of the *Nutshell Library* (1962) in a spirit of ungrateful irrev-erence, dismissive of his distraught parents and a dangerous world. Indifferent toward his mother and father, Pierre yawns and repeats his mantra, "I don't care," even while reclining against a hungry lion. Once devoured by the lion, Pierre is rescued by his distraught parents whom he ultimately comes to value. Sendak would later write, "I was never Pierre at any point in my life. Perhaps I harbored his thoughts, but I would not have dared speak to my parents in such a way. That's why I wrote the book."[66] Speaking on the Holocaust's influence on his work, he offered, "It forced me to take children to a level that I thought was more honest than most people did. . . . If Anne Frank could die, if my friend could die, children were as vulnerable as adults, and that gave me a secret purpose to my work, to make them live. Because I wanted to live. I wanted to grow up."[67] His way of helping children "live" was to portray their inner lives, fears, and unspeakable fantasies with more honesty, without the purification imposed on childhood by adult constructions of it, perhaps especially by postwar ideals. Pierre was a far cry from such ideals, as would be Max, the protagonist of *Where the Wild Things Are*, who runs about the house in a wolf costume, shouts at his mother, and threatens to eat her.

Sendak thus created more room for his child self by retroactively claiming his right to *be* a child, with the prerogative to be selfish and rebellious at times, despite the constraints of parents' perpetual mourning and their constant fixations on external dangers. His *Hector Protector* and *Higglety Pigglety Pop!* (1967) would, like *Pierre*, similarly pit self-indulged, reckless child protagonists against the threat of a hungry lion's jaws. *In The Night Kitchen* (1970) would in addition feature a cranky child who dreams about escaping his bed and flying to colossal heights after breaking out of an oven into which he has been ushered by three giant bakers. In *Outside Over There*, Ida's physically and emotionally absent caretakers would be consumed by an "Over There," the same phrase commonly used by traumatized and reticent survivors to describe Europe during the Holocaust, and whose ambiguity left their offspring paralyzed by its worst possible connotations.[68] Ida's father is present only in words, a sailor shouting from across the ocean and sending the occasional letter; her mother is despondent and unresponsive, staring into the distance as Ida cares for her crying sibling. The loss of Ida's parents to "Over There" would enable the kidnapping of her infant sister, but it would also embolden Ida to plunge *herself* into "Over There," where she would dissolve an emotional haze with her art, literally melting the goblin kidnappers through a musical performance that restores order to her weary family—as Sendak and his siblings had tended to do for their own parents with makeshift plays and stories.

Sendak too ventured into the "Over There" of his parents' lost worlds, at least in the realm of his art-making. Illustrating *Zlateh the Goat* (1966) by I. B. Singer, a Yiddish writer and contemporary, was especially therapeutic for him, connecting him to his parents' cherished *shtetl* stories. In Singer's foreword to the book, he connects the writing of literature with a transcendence of time and space, a means of reviving and immortalizing the "many moods" and subjects of the past.[69] The opening story, "Fool's Paradise," follows Atzel, a boy who, lured by his old nurse's stories about the delights of paradise, tries to will himself dead by the powers of his imagination in order to convince his parents to bury him. The artist based Atzel's appearance on photographs of Sadie's mother, Minnie. He drew the baby in another story, "The First Schlemiel," from a photograph of himself as an infant.[70] Other illustrations included faces drawn from the photographs of relatives murdered in the Holocaust who had haunted his adolescence. Sendak cried with his parents as they identified images of Philip's handsome younger brothers and women relatives with long hair and flowers. He chose to draw these murdered loved ones, from both sides of his family, in a realistic style, to revive them for his parents.[71] The careful, intricate cross-hatching of those drawings is tenderly executed—the fine pen work gives a fuzzy softness to light and space, which, lacking strong contours, hums like a dreamscape that dissolves at its seams. *Zlateh* delivered Yiddish folklore to mainstream American readers; Sendak described it as a collection of Jewish stories that everyone could appreciate.[72] In this project, his creativity functioned not only as a personal exorcism, but also as a living memorial to loved ones and their lost worlds.

Reviving the Dead

As Eugene Glynn would later write, the fantasy of narcissistic fusion, the "merging or fusing or blending of the self with the other," helps the artist feel a sense of mastery over the world and its objects. It offers a way of creating or reviving any given person or object by radically empathizing with and figuratively *becoming* them.[73] The fluid boundaries of the young Sendak's subjectivity led him to overempathize with endangered others and troubled or underappreciated historical figures, sometimes to the point of confusing his identity with theirs. He felt compelled to imagine himself into the shoes of deceased heroes from bygone eras whose social tensions spoke to his own internal struggles.

Sendak wrote of Lindbergh's murdered infant son, whom he depicted in *Outside Over There*, "I was that child—and my sister rescued me."[74] Such overempathizing with other people, however disorienting, allowed him to enter into and convincingly convey the emotions of a child whose boundaries are continuously in flux and potentially threatened.

In *Higglety Pigglety Pop!*, baby Maurice, rendered female, would fuse with Mother Goose and with the moon, his own cosmic mother. Sendak wrote and illustrated the book during Sadie's later battle with cancer. It stars his dog Jennie, who was also dying at the time of the book's creation.[75] Jennie arrives at the home of an infant whose parents have "been away ever so long," and no one else remembers her real name. As it turns out, however, the infant, drawn from baby photographs of Sendak himself, reveals herself to be the ultimate mother: she is in fact "Mother Goose," drawn as a matronly and stout woman, resembling photographs of Sadie. She then ascends into the sky as an everlasting moon. "To babies, mothers are cosmic," wrote Sendak, "You expect them to protect you from everything, become trees, become houses, become beds, become fountains of milk, become all the things that babies have every natural right to expect."[76] In his *Fantasy Sketches* (1970), a series of free-association drawings done to classical music, the artist would also depict infants, parents, and animals devouring and regurgitating each other. In the 1980s he would be drawn to the Brothers Grimm tale *Dear Mili* (1988), a wartime story of a mother arbitrarily separated from her daughter in the midst of feeling safe and blissful in their forest cottage. As Donald Haase notes, fairy tales offer an ideal literary context for articulating feelings about things that are both beloved and frightening, like traumatized parents or socially forbidden desires. "The settings of fairy tales," he writes, "are polarized and valorized according to whether they offer characters familiarity and security, or threaten them with exile and danger . . . including imprisonment and death. Even familiar locations—including home—can become defamiliarized and threatening."[77] For *Dear Mili*, Sendak illustrated the girl's return home to her aged mother with a fiery autumn sunset in a landscape that sprawls across a full, wordless page spread. The mother, wrinkled with eyes closed and hands reaching out to her child—who may be just a flicker of her dying imagination—sits before a cottage whose door and window swing open to a jet-black interior— death awaits them both inside. A turn of the page confirms this fate in the words of Wilhelm Grimm: "All evening they sat happily together. Then they went to bed calmly and cheerfully, and next morning the neighbors found them dead. They had fallen happily asleep, and between them lay Saint Joseph's rose in full bloom." Sendak would leave this last page without illustration, as though to grant full impact to the devastating words themselves.

Perhaps most striking among his imagined fusions, the artist often described himself as "pregnant" or "birthing" when discussing his creative process.[78] For Sendak, the inspiration for a new book felt like "getting pregnant when you've just gone crazy and you've found out your house has burned down."[79] Despite his ultimate disinterest in creating a traditional nuclear family, the artist "acted out" the emotional tribulations of his Jewish immigrant family's parent-child relationships in his personal conceptions of the bookmaking process. With the "kvelling" of the stereotypical Jewish mother, Sendak described Max, the protagonist of *Wild Things*, thusly: "How many people have a child who goes out and does so well by them? Max is the kind of son I should have been for my parents."[80] As Jodi Eichler-Levine argues, Sendak not only conveyed the emotional rhythms of a Jewish mother, he metaphorically *became* a sort of Jewish mother himself.[81] Gregory Maguire has also made this connection, characterizing Sendak as possessing "the hectoring, scowling affection of a Jewish mother—one who wields a cudgel-like rolling pin against her enemies as adroitly as she might lean over a table with a sable-haired paintbrush, to draw her loved ones again, and again, and again."[82] In his later life, the childless Sendak would own and treasure John Keats's original death mask, occasionally stroking its forehead, and feeling "maternal."[83] While working on *Outside Over There*, Sendak expressed,

[W]e men are all so jealous of birthing—and making a book becomes having a baby. I talk about it endlessly, and my friends have taken up the habit. They ask, "How's the baby coming? What month are you in?" Well, I am now deep into pregnancy. I'm definitely going to have a full-term child, but whether it'll be alive or dead, I don't know yet. And that's the state I am in with the book.[84]

Something complex is at work in Sendak's tendency to understand his artistic work as a process of pregnancy and birthing. Perhaps imagining himself pregnant helped him to process the powerlessness he experienced as a child bombarded with the news of lost relatives, possessed by the mourning of others, but also cosmically bound to those inaccessible others, as pregnant mothers are to their emergent offspring. Phantom pregnancy may have also helped Sendak find some control over the process of emotional impregnation involved in postmemory or trans-memory, of growing up affectively arrested by preceding traumas, narratives, or cultures to which one cannot gain sufficient access but nevertheless remains bound. Creating more personal meanings around his own emotional experience of indirect traumas, Sendak described his finished books as his offspring, which he could birth and mourn on his own terms, as though granting himself access to his own obstructed genealogical roots and reenacting their loss:

> And then finally it is a book. And you become extremely depressed, because you realize that what was so superb and different is really just another book! How strange. . . . And then it goes out into the world, and your child, who was so private and who was living with you for two years, now is everybody's child. Some people knock him on his head, some kick him in the rump, and others like him very much. It's a totally different experience. It takes me a long time to shift gears.[85]

From a queer perspective, Sendak's male "pregnancy" also speaks to the unusual interiority of his work as a deeply personal harvesting of buried emotional content for public consumption—a traditionally unconventional venture for the American man. If the queer or allegedly threatening child is forbidden from existing as such during childhood, that child might be retroactively recovered, rebirthed. This queer birthing touches feelings usually forgotten or suppressed by the socialized adult. In this way, according to Eve Kosofsky Sedgwick, it follows a tendency of the British realist writer Henry James (1843–1916), one of Sendak's favorite authors. Sedgwick writes that James repeatedly "invokes Frankenstein and all the potential uncanniness of the violently disavowed male birth . . . in order to undo it . . . by offering the spectacle of—not his refusal—but his eroticized eagerness to recognize his progeny even in its oddness."[86]

On some level, Sendak, like James, may have used the motif of male birthing to affirm the worth of what Sedgwick calls the "maimed or slighted, the disfigured or defeated, the unlucky or unlikely child."[87] The specter of a man birthing might symbolically deem his offspring "queer" in their odd, exceptional nature, and it might position Sendak as a parental protector of those who do not belong in conventional, bourgeois families that restrict certain possibilities. Sendak's pop-up picture book *Mommy?* (2006) would depict a small boy seeking his mother among a cast of male creatures. One of them, resembling popular depictions of Frankenstein's monster, stands beside his own framed baby picture; another monster shares Sendak's physical build and wears red high heels like Dorothy in Oz. The dominant visual conception of Frankenstein's monster, as originally performed by Boris Karloff, derives, of course, from the 1931 film *Frankenstein* from Sendak's childhood. Sendak sympathized with this and other misunderstood monsters of Old Hollywood, calling them early Wild Things. Hollywood monsters, depicted as lumbering, helpless creatures who invoke fear in others and struggle to communicate in coherent English, were like immigrants, traumatized subjects, or children who struggle to bridge inner feelings with concrete social language. The real monsters, Sendak felt, were not these unfortunate beings but the people with torches who assaulted them in the films—the dangerous masses who scapegoated and demonized outsiders.[88]

The artist would struggle to bridge his immigrant parents' emotional lives with realities of his own in Manhattan's Greenwich Village of the culturally tumultuous late 1960s. Even at the height of his fame, he would remain sensitively attuned to his parents' feelings and health, also keeping a framed photograph of Philip's parents, his "rabbinical grandfather" and grandmother, in his studio.[89] During Philip's unexpected back surgery in 1965, Sendak would desert his Fire Island vacation to join the family, writing to a friend about the reemerged childhood feelings and closeness reinforced during this reunion.[90] Three years later he would acquire for his father an inscribed copy of I. B. Singer's *The Séance*, bringing Philip to tears.[91] So intertwined was Sendak with his own parents' emotional worlds and their preservation that their inevitably impending deaths, he felt, threatened something essential inside himself. While Sadie lay dying of cancer in May 1968, Sendak's own heart would also give way. At age thirty-nine, a near-fatal heart attack would interrupt an interview in England, from which he would excuse himself upon losing the ability to speak.[92] For the *Saturday Evening Post* that same month, he would illustrate I. B. Singer's story "Yash the Chimney-Sweep" with a drawing of his father and mother, Sadie's eyes hidden under a draped headdress. Later that year, following Sadie's death, he would write to Singer about how proud she had been that her youngest son had worked with such a great Yiddish writer.[93] But Sendak would lose Singer's friendship over his refusal to sell him the original drawing for "Yash," being so attached to this image of his declining parents.[94] After his mother's death, he would complain of an inner chaos, a feeling of not existing, of having died along with Sadie, and of lacking the drive to work.[95] He would yearn to express such feelings in a book.[96] While Sendak worked on this book the following year, Philip too would grow ill and move into his son's studio.

Pangs of queer activism would erupt in his West Village neighborhood as Sendak continued his book project and cared for his ailing father. By the end of June, within steps of his West Ninth Street apartment, the dramatic Stonewall Riots would catalyze the gay liberation movement at the Stonewall Inn, which stood a mere 0.3 miles from Sendak's residence. Though it is not clear where the artist would have been during the actual riots or their immediate aftermath, he would have been finishing the story of *Night Kitchen* and beginning the pictures, as well as arranging to have Sadie's grave unveiled quickly to ensure that Philip would still be alive for it.[97] As Philip lay dying in the hospital, Sendak would persuade him to put down one of his stories and to tell him more about his life in Poland. Philip would do so in Yiddish, Sendak transcribing his words in a notebook.[98] Unfinished and untitled when Philip died in June 1970, the text took over a decade to reach publication, as Sendak fretted over doing justice to his father's memory.[99] His editor would later write to the artist of her recollections of him in the hospital as he tended to Philip and transcribed his Yiddish dictations: "I saw a part of you I'd never seen before," she offered, "the manly tenderness and love with which you treated him in the hospital. . . . [Y]ou did so much for him in the final years, gave him so much love and understanding and support."[100] Three months after Philip's death, Harper would publish *In the Night Kitchen*. The book showcases Sadie and Philip's everlasting presence through their absence—Mickey's parents are not visible, but the names "Sadie" and "Philip" appear in both the author's dedication and in product labels of the kitchen cityscape.

Night Kitchen fused Sendak's relationship to his parents with feelings connected to his own suppressed sexuality and the liberating energies surrounding his neighborhood in the aftermath of the Stonewall riots.[101] On one page, a skyscraper named "Eugene" towers over one named "Philip." At the end of the story, a giant milk carton labeled "Glynn" is accompanied by the words "open" and "pure," as though to celebrate his union with Glynn as itself a triumph worthy of reverence. *Night Kitchen* was, Sendak wrote, a "good-by[e] to a large part of childhood . . . to New York, a good-by[e] to my parents." It was also "a victory over death."[102] He made sure to include the name "Q.E. Gateshead" on a building at the end of the story—a nod to the Queen Elizabeth Hospital in Gateshead, where he had survived his heart attack.[103] On a symbolic level, *Night Kitchen* was a triumph over the social and emotional forces that had for decades suppressed and deadened the artist's inner life, evacuating him from himself. Despite popular neo-Freudian anxieties that spending too much time in the sentimental sphere of the home, with one's mother, might cause a boy to "become" gay, *Night Kitchen* connected the stereotypically feminine, kitchen symbols of milk, dough, and oven with a boy's sensual awakening in a fantasy of men baking together at night while parents slept in ignorance; Sendak described the book as expressing "a profound love of . . . the lusciousness of cooking, . . . of undressing and floating in the sentuosity [*sic*] of milk."[104] Mixing Romantic, psychoanalytic, and modernist sensibilities, Sendak breathed new life into what might have been vacuous depictions of childhood play and domesticity by infusing those scenes with emotional qualities generally misinterpreted, ignored, or forgotten by adults. Home was a site of warmth and comfort but also the battleground of childhood's inner emotional wars, of helplessness, awkwardness, pain, and revelation.

Sibling Refuge

In the context of Sendak's creative vision, the symbolic role of the sibling operated as a flexible survival bond, as well as a connective tie between various realms. A sibling, as both a "double" and an "other," could become a mirror, a foil, or a rare companion in one's struggle to exist authentically inside and between one's marginal heritage and surrounding society. Accordingly, Sendak's artistic vision emerged in cooperation with his siblings, in whom he invested an almost romantic level of desire and identification. If he associated literature with the feeling of merging with his father's body, he also associated it with the secret worlds he shared with Natalie and Jack. Natalie had first introduced him to reading by bringing him books—a discovery he would describe with semi-erotic undertones. As he would later assert, "I think I spent more time sniffing and touching them than reading. I just remember the joy of the book; the beauty of the binding. The smelling of the interior. . . . A book is really like a lover. It arranges itself in your life in a way that is beautiful."[105] Jack, on the other hand, was his "best friend," artistic collaborator, and gentle and wonderful "savior."[106] Jack drew pictures and wrote stories with his younger brother. By age nine, Sendak was pasting together comic strips, newspaper photographs, sketches of his family, and hand-lettering on paper and shirt cardboard that he decorated to illustrate Jack's stories.[107] Natalie, whom he recalled as a shrewd businessperson, hired neighbors to make bindings for her brothers' books and sold bound copies on the street to collect profits.[108] Sendak "wanted to do everything that [Jack] did," so it became "an utter necessity" that his "whole life be devoted to being an artist."[109]

Against the social pressures on immigrants' children to individuate away from parents, close sibling bonds and other relationships rooted in mutual experiences of difference offered lateral opportunities for preserving cultural particularity and resisting normalization. Together the Sendak children also cared for Philip and Sadie. The siblings were extraordinarily close—Sendak sometimes referred to Jack and Natalie as his "real parents," the people who spent the most time and emotional energy on him during early childhood: "I felt more parent affection coming from my brother and sister [than from my own parents]," he once said, "I was very lucky to have two siblings of opposite sexes, so I could have another mother and another father and ones I really adored."[110] In a room with two beds, Jack and Maurice shared one bed, Natalie sleeping in the other. Some nights all three siblings chose to huddle into one of the beds together. Sendak shared, "My parents would come in—sometimes with my uncle and aunt—and they'd say: 'Look, see how much they like each other.'"[111] Sendak also recounted memories of holding onto his own brother in bed at night: "There was no privacy. And we had bed bugs. And to protect me, my brother said, 'Lie on top of me.' And I said, 'I'll fall.' And he said, 'No, you won't, not if you clamp your teeth on my nose.' I didn't fall. . . . The bed bugs didn't get me. They got him."[112] Decades later, after coming out as gay to the mainstream press and speculating also about his late brother's sexuality, Sendak would reminisce in one interview about the nights he shared a bed with Jack, "He used to hold me close; we never did anything, but it was the happiest time I remember." Speaking for Jack years after his passing, Sendak would muse, "We intended our lives to be entwined like those of the Grimm brothers."[113]

Already in childhood, Jack and Maurice had sublimated their feelings of intense closeness. As young adolescents, the brothers wrote and illustrated "We Are Inseparable," a story about a brother and sister who fall in love, much to their parents' dismay, and ultimately commit suicide together by jumping from the seventeenth floor of the Brooklyn Jewish hospital. As Sendak jested, "Sigmund Freud passed over our house in Brooklyn. In any case, as the wedding day approached, my brother—instinctively smelling trouble, I suppose—contrived to have the young hero mortally injured in an accident."[114] The brothers dedicated the book to their beautiful, sixteen-year-old sister, whom they both admired.[115] As a teenager, Sendak offered substantial emotional companionship to Natalie. When her fiancé was killed as an American soldier in the invasion of Anzio, she became inconsolable for months, and Sendak instinctively took on a "full-time" role as her caretaker.[116] Soon it would be Sendak's turn for grief when Jack was drafted to serve in the Pacific invasion of Okinawa. The artist recalled watching his mother sit by a small table radio in the kitchen in those years, listening and not hearing anything from Jack, who was missing in action for months at a time. When Jack finally returned, he was, Sendak claimed, "a totally unrecognizable man," and the "intense communication" the brothers had shared was gone.[117]

From the start of Sendak's career, however, he would depict the close-knit sibling relationships he recalled from his own youth. In *Happy Hannukah Everybody* (1954) a brother and sister share a room, talking at night across their beds.[118] *Good Shabbos, Everybody* (1951) also featured a drawing of a brother and sister clinging to each other in a dramatic, tight embrace.[119] About a decade after Jack's return from military service, the artist depicted a boy cared for by soldiers in tender, almost romantic poses for Dutch-American writer Meindert DeJong's *The House of Sixty Fathers* (1956).[120] In this story, Tien Pao, the boy protagonist, is separated from his family and tended by a group of sixty American soldiers during the second Sino-Japanese War. In one of Sendak's pencil studies, a soldier with a gentle expression carries the barely clothed Tien Pao in his arms, the boy shy and gleeful as the soldier gazes at him, their faces almost touching, Tien Pao's hand curled around the soldier's neck. Perhaps this story spoke to Sendak's memory of his affectionate relationship with Jack, his own "savior." In the published illustration, however, Sendak would draw a shirt on the boy and change his gentle smile to an anxious frown, minimizing the intimacy between these figures.[121]

Close sibling relationships took on a mystical quality in Sendak's work by the late 1960s. For George MacDonald's *The Golden Key* (1967), Sendak carefully rendered a brother and sister holding hands as together they struggle through the fog of crosshatched ink. In *Dear Mili*, the girl protagonist meets a sister spirit in the woods in her symbolic journey to the afterlife, as a child lost in wartime. As the text declares, this "guardian angel" looks "just like the poor little girl, except her eyes were larger and brighter and she may have been even more beautiful." The illustrations, rife with oversized blossoms, tangled tree trunks, and intricately detailed expanses of vegetation, emulate Van Gogh's pantheistic style, which, Sendak felt, infused nature with a lively spiritual element. Sendak had devoured Van Gogh's letters in the 1960s and frequented the Van Gogh Museum in Amsterdam in the 1980s. He may have also related to Van Gogh's biographical closeness with his own brother, Theo. Studying the Dutch artist's letters, Glynn wrote that Theo became a "mother-father-wife-husband-other self" to Van Gogh in the latter's adult years.[122] Sendak, having suffered his parents' grieving and their comparing of him to his cousins murdered in Nazi Europe, likely also related to the emotional ambivalence Van Gogh felt toward his unborn older brother—a year before Van Gogh's birth, his mother had birthed a stillborn also named Vincent. The Dutch painter, by Glynn's estimation, also struggled with homosexual shame and parents who, Van Gogh felt, disapproved of his animal nature and emotionally neglected him, always mourning their stillborn child and suffering guilt for having tried to replace him. Thus, Glynn wrote, Van Gogh "felt unloved, unwanted, *outside* . . . a big, rough dog with wet paws everyone feared to have in the house . . . an intruder, hopelessly inferior to the idealized lost child, forever inadequate, himself fixated on the dead as rival and model [and with] unmanageable conflicts over homosexual and passive urges" (my emphasis).[123]

Like Van Gogh's need for Theo and Sendak's for Jack, close sibling bonds could help a child alienated by parents to remain "inside" the spaces of family and domestic safety. In *We Are All in the Dumps with Jack and Guy* (1993), Sendak imagined himself and his own brother as the eponymous abandoned children, who form a sort of makeshift family in a wasteland of corporate greed and poverty, rescuing a wounded child to adopt as their own. On one page, their heads press against each other, without contour to distinguish one head from the other. Together, they restore a sense of family and social accountability in the midst of homelessness and abjection. Even in Spike Jonze's 2009 film

Where the Wild Things Are (based on the 1963 picture book), on which
Sendak worked as a close consultant, two of the Wild Things, Carol and
KW, would be presented, in Eichler-Levine's words, as an ambiguously
"estranged, perhaps romantic (or sibling) couple."[124]

Sendak's depiction of intense solidarity between siblings, as well
as his own closeness with Jack and Natalie, speaks to the survivalist
importance of clinging to "one's own" to endure the demands of traumatized parents and a traumatizing world. Jonathan Cott understands
the literary tradition of intensely close sibling bonds as symbolic com-
pensation for parental neglect in emotionally strained families, perhaps
most epitomized in the Grimm Brothers' tale of Hansel and Gretel.[125]
Boundary-crossing closeness between siblings is a prevalent theme in
narratives of posttraumatic families and of families in which children
band together to compensate for parents who are absent, abusive, or
unwell. A common trend in Holocaust survivors' narratives is the perception that creating a tight-knit kinship unit of mutual devotion offers
redemption from the wartime deaths of one's previous, destroyed family, as well as reliable support in potential future crises. Such survivors
emphasize the importance of protecting sibling bonds at all costs. De-
scendants of some survivors also rely on sibling bonds to share the
responsibility of caring for wounded parents, as well as to support and
protect each other *against* those parents, who may have invaded psychological boundaries, acted out their traumas in frightening ways, or
were altogether emotionally unavailable.[126]

As Sendak aged, he longed most for Jack, who had passed away in
1995. The year of Jack's passing, Sendak would dedicate his erotic illustrations for the Kraken edition of Melville's *Pierre* "in remembrance
of Jack Sendak my Melville-loving brother."[127] Throughout his old age,
the artist mourned this loss, crying, "I want to be free like when I was
a kid, working with my brother and making toy airplanes and a whole
model of the World's Fair in 1939 out of wax."[128] He claimed that Jack's
death dealt him a humbling blow, leading him to feel more rational and
less "chosen by God."[129] Five years after Jack's death, Sendak began the
text for *My Brother's Book*, which would be published posthumously
in 2013.[130] Stephen Greenblatt introduces the book as Sendak's "final

expression to be reunited with his dead brother."[131] Sendak again depicts himself here as "Guy" journeying to the afterlife to find his brother Jack and bite his nose once more. The frontispiece of *My Brother's Book* includes an illustration of "Jack and Guy, two brothers dreaming the same dream," their sleeping bodies almost fused together in a surreal abstracted landscape. The stumpy, cartoonish children of *Dumps* have become muscled, sexually mature, and balletic, writhing in William Blake–inspired poses. Sendak admired Blake's ferocity, his bold depictions of sexuality, and his ability to simultaneously convey "two worlds": a surface world of "what we approve of ourselves to be like when we're with other people" and a world of "what we're really like, what we dare and reveal to other people."[132]

Perhaps recalling Jack's long departure as a soldier in World War II, the book begins with the trauma of two brothers' separation from each other, the earth split in two as "Jack" is catapulted to "continents of ice." Illustrations show a bewildered younger brother strewn on the ground and then nude and small in a winter landscape, his despairing head in his hands, with Jack embedded in a block of ice in the foreground. The book reveals Sendak's longing for the early childhood feeling of playing with and creating stories with his brother, who became somewhat estranged from him after military service and even more so as the artist rose to great fame in adulthood. Creative play with Jack in childhood was perhaps Sendak's deepest experience of integrating uninhibited fantasy with a sense of shared social meaning—of merging his notions of "inside" and "outside" to achieve a sublime sense of harmony and connectedness beyond himself. *My Brother's Book* glorifies and ambiguously eroticizes this relationship with Jack, the brothers longing for each other when separated, even to the point of following each other into the afterlife. The book concludes with Jack "enfolded in his brother's arms," Guy whispering, "[Y]ou will dream of me." When *My Brother's Book* was published, critics interpreted a fusion of feelings Sendak held for Jack with emotions reserved for Glynn.[133] Tony Kushner called the book "Maurice's elegy for his brother Jack, for his partner of fifty years, Eugene Glynn, and for himself. . . ."[134] Sendak himself suggested the similarity between these two men, admitting that

Eugene was "so much like my brother. He was a psychoanalyst. I was very proud of him. He was a man who loved music and reading. And when I worked in the studio, he would be reading."[135]

Such blurring of romantic and familial love might have helped Sendak express his experience of widely misunderstood queer affect and desire. Sendak was doubly "buried" as a child expected to restrain joy and excitement for the sake of his grieving family, and as an emerging gay subject in a world that would not see or validate him as such. For a queer youth to express "incorrect" or unacceptable feelings was, it may have seemed, to become like the Wild Things or Sendak's elderly Yiddish-speaking relatives, whose loving advances were mistaken for aggression—the Sendak children were petrified of those relatives, not understanding "that [their] gestures [were] meant to be affectionate."[136] In their inability to express love without eliciting terror, the Wild Things, whom Sendak called "foreigners, lost in America, without a language," are also like queer people, experiencing love and attraction in "wrong" ways, according to a prejudiced society. Entranced by boundary-crossing, ambiguous emotions that—at least on the surface—ring of incestuous eroticism, Sendak staged apocalyptic, alternate worlds to embody forbidden longings from the safe distance of the picture book, which both channels and diffuses overwhelming meanings.

Fusion with siblings or other loved ones might also promote survival strategies—the pooling of resources, the flexible sharing of roles, and an intuitively empathic solidarity that helps one anticipate and respond to dangers as a family. However, in psychological literature, the condition of being unable to distinguish boundaries between self and other subjects "is to be psychotic."[137] As Glynn would write, "The danger of the artist is . . . to remain fused with objects."[138] For Sendak, the risk of being an artist who conveyed childhood emotion was the necessity of repeatedly flirting with psychosis. As he would explain to Art Spiegelman in the comic strip interview the two would co-create for *The New Yorker* in 1993, "Childhood is cannibals and psychotics vomiting in your mouth!"[139] Accordingly, Sendak struggled to differentiate between himself and the objects of his affection, including the people he loved. After inciting his novelist friend Coleman Dowell's annoyance, for example,

Sendak pleaded for his forgiveness in February 1969, comparing himself to an infant and apologizing for his inability to understand boundaries between himself and those with whom he formed close relationships.[140] Within the interiority of his creative process, he would fuse temporarily with the objects of his obsessions and desires. In this sort of vacuum, the artist could blur or reimagine painful divisions: between the living and the dead, family and sexuality, heritage and lived experience. Or, more broadly, artistic work enabled him to explore how endangered subjects join an endangering society without losing who they are. Sendak addressed this question perhaps most dramatically in the late 1940s and 1950s, as he entered adulthood, grappled with his sexuality, and moved to Manhattan.

CHAPTER 3

SURVIVING THE AMERICAN DREAM

Early Childhood as Queer Lens at Midcentury

SENDAK BECAME AN ADULT in the aftermath of World War II, as the American nation sought to rebuild itself. On average, Americans married more often and at younger ages in the 1940s and 1950s. Supporting the cause of social regeneration after the war, a dominant middle-class morality restricted sexual intercourse to the context of marriage. Postwar American youth embraced the goal of rebuilding the nation, producing over four million babies per year from 1946 through 1964, during its "baby boom."[1] In this context, the artist stood outside of the optimistic, reproductive culture of his peers. In addition to the weight of managing a covert sexuality at midcentury, he had also internalized his family's suffering in response to the genocide that annihilated their relatives in Europe—a catastrophe that placed even more pressure on him to marry and reproduce. Sendak would attempt sexual relationships with women in his twenties, despite his being gay, even becoming engaged to and impregnating a certain young woman. This arrangement was dissolved, however, after an argument that became physical. "I blame myself," he later lamented. "We had a fight. I pushed her after she pushed me and she fell. I assumed it killed the baby."[2] An unlikely children's book artist, indeed. Or was he? A single, unmarriageable young man pressured from multiple directions to become someone he was not, the young artist, like countless other artists, was at odds with the social ideals of his time. But this very stance of social incoherence positioned him to speak directly to others alienated by the dominant culture—including children and others who had lost something precious in the process of "growing up."

In the first decades of his life, Sendak was remarkably lonely. He was most alone in his queerness. To be queer in midcentury America was to be in danger in almost all contexts—often within one's own family, as well. Queer youth, as Eve Kosofsky Sedgwick notes, often internalize anti-queer prejudice from within their would-be support systems. They learn to accept and protect themselves through indirect, retroactive pathways, sometimes through "chosen family" found later in life.[3] For much of the twentieth century, when American youth recognized themselves as queer, they could expect problems not only of emotional isolation but also of social and physical endangerment. Politicians and social commentators painted queer people as obscene outsiders and predators in relation to the exclusively heterosexual bourgeois family, linking them with pedophiles and vampires.[4] In the years of Sendak's Brooklyn childhood, New York police forces repeatedly harassed and jailed queer people when they failed to conform to the norms of heterosexuality and its related binary gender expectations. Simply being present at a gay establishment meant risking arrest in those years. Historian George Chauncey notes that in the 1930s New York State's highest court upheld regulations that explicitly forbade gay men and women from congregating in licensed public establishments; other measures also threatened to destroy any bar or restaurant owner serving gay men or lesbians, to ruin any theater that permitted the inclusion of gay characters, and to impede the distribution of any film handling gay subject matter. These rules explicitly turned the act of a man hitting on another man into a criminal offense.[5] As one New York journalist for *Commentary Magazine* recalled, "The police . . . were a presence, if only as a theoretical possibility, in the life of virtually every homosexual. As were other embodiments of authority whom we heterosexuals never thought about except to suppose that they were working for us."[6]

It is not surprising that Sendak struggled to accept his sexual orientation, given the risks and consequences that threatened him in his youth. The artist later shared on National Public Radio that discovering that he was gay was "a shock and a disappointment. . . . I did not want to be gay."[7] Being gay set him apart from basic social meanings and thus from participating openly with others around him. He recalled that it felt dangerous and alienating, calling it "another sign of isolation." Into his old age, Sendak never "stopped beating myself up about it. . . . I missed a lot of fun . . . to me it's a dilemma, it's like how do you cross the Alps? How do you have fun?"[8] The artist struggled to understand his intimate urges, which were widely considered symptoms of a perverse disease at odds with American, middle-class family values, especially during a time that imagined those same values as the very foundation of the country's postwar recovery. "All I wanted was to be straight so my parents could be happy," he would tell the *New York Times* in 2008.[9] Jewish children like Sendak internalized the message that marriage was a cultural and religious duty, both for American belonging and for Jewish continuity.[10] As Jacob Kohn wrote in *Modern Problems of Jewish Parents* (1932), "For clean young people marriage should mean a keying up of all of life's promises, social and individual, spiritual and physical."[11] Traditional Yiddish-speaking culture did not openly acknowledge homosexual unions and generally frowned upon those who remained unmarried, discouraging childlessness and self-imposed isolation from the community.[12] Moreover, for immigrant and ethnic minority families, like Sendak's, the prospect of violating middle-class norms was perhaps especially threatening to the acculturation process, as such families struggled to gain American acceptance and belonging. Like most other Americans of their time, many English-speaking Jews derided and rejected homosexuality and queer gender expression; popular Jewish American performers like Milton Berle and Jack Benny, for example, made fun of gay people, effeminate men, and cross-dressers. Caricaturing such "others" helped acculturating performers and audiences to feel passably American by contrast.[13]

Amidst these challenges, the young Sendak did find at least one male role model that spoke to his queer sensibilities in the Jewish milieu of his Brooklyn surroundings. In preparation for his bar mitzvah, Maurice developed a crush on his Hebrew school teacher, Mr. Berdichevsky, whom he affectionately called Mr. Berd. Hebrew school, which he attended from around 1938 through 1941, was on the corner of the Sendaks' street at the time (West Sixth Street in Brooklyn, off of Kings Highway). Mr. Berd, a sort of hero to the young Sendak, took a special interest in the boy. Sendak described him as a kind and gentle Polish immigrant with beautiful, fragile features and a fedora hat. Mr. Berd had immigrated with his mother, who wore a *shaytl* and lived in a back room in the tiny apartment where her son taught.[14] It is unclear whether the young Sendak would have recognized the queer irony of Berdichevsky's nickname: the bird was a sometimes-queer symbol in Yiddish culture, the word *feygele* ("little bird") being popular slang used to describe a gay man. Moreover, when the Motion Picture Production Code ("Hays Code") forbade all references to homosexuality in film from 1930 through 1968, directors sometimes used depictions of birds, or even the word "bird," to suggest the gayness of a given character.[15] In Joseph Green's popular Yiddish film *A Brivele der mamen* (1938), for example, the Jewish immigrant "Arele" Berdyczewski, who coincidentally shares Mr. Berd's surname, becomes a fanciful singer named "Irving Bird," rides in limousines, and snubs his immigrant mother. Sendak was about ten years old at the film's release, already studying with his own Mr. Berd. The young artist began to cultivate his own liberation by connecting with sensitive mentors like Mr. Berd and diving inward to harness the endangered feelings that he harbored.

Starting around age fifteen, in the summer of 1943, Sendak tapped into his queer feelings by illustrating stories in private for his own pleasure. Twenty years before Max would don his famous wolf suit, Sendak made his first serious illustration attempt for the story of *Peter and the Wolf*. He followed this effort with pictures for the late Oscar Wilde's "The Happy Prince," a story he then found "extraordinary," about impossible love between a statue and a sparrow—again, the symbolic fusion of bird and man to signify a forbidden union. Next was Bret Harte's *The Luck of Roaring Camp*, which was his favorite story—about an illegitimate infant adopted by a group of rough lumberjacks after the mother's death.[16] Already then he began to identify interests in how young individuals survive insufficient emotional guidance, physical and social danger, and forbidden desires. As a student at Lafayette High

School, "mild-mannered Maurice," as his classmates recalled him, contributed work to the yearbook and literary magazine.[17] One classmate remembered him as "sensitive," "very different," and "driven," always immersed in art-making while other students prioritized sports and fun.[18] For the school newspaper Sendak created a comic strip featuring a sort of queer outsider named Pinky who gets enlisted to sweep the floor at the senior prom while his peers pair off and dance.

Teenage Sendak became familiar with the comics industry by working after school at All-American Comics on adapting popular strips such as *Mutt and Jeff, Tipsy,* and *Captain Stubbs* from their newspaper strip format into comic books. Sendak's role was to fill in background scenery and add visual cues, like puffs of dust to indicate speed.[19] This job entranced the young artist, who had idolized the richness of detail in the background visuals of Disney films like *Fantasia* (1940).[20] Sometimes skipping school, which he was failing, he would take home his assigned pages, shut his door, make his parents believe he was doing homework, and pour himself into those comics. But his opportunities at All-American were limited, as his drawing tendencies clashed with the heterosexual male aesthetic of highly sexualized women and heroic male saviors.[21] In general, commercial artists of the time needed to emulate the sexually and ethnically conservative zeitgeist if they wanted to find work. As the United States moved from a largely manufacture-oriented economy to a service-sector one after the war, increasing social importance was placed on restoring prewar gender norms and on ensuring self-esteem among young Americans expected to socialize cheerfully and reproduce the nation.[22] Seeing himself as "a serious person in an unserious society," Sendak chose to remain a misfit focused on creatively excavating endangered personal truths.[23]

"Mark" in Manhattan

When World War II finally ended, a seventeen-year-old Sendak bolted from Brooklyn to make it to Manhattan before the soldiers did, to witness the moment of celebration. Doors were opening, he felt: "Young people were welcomed. New things were happening, a surge of energy: a surge of hope. A surge of happiness."[24] The summer after graduating high school in 1946, he made his big move to Manhattan and found a first full-time position at Timely Service, a warehouse for which he fashioned props for store window displays. Deeming "Maurice" too fanciful for his surroundings, Sendak generally went by "Mark" in those years, a choice that suggested also his desire for a new beginning and, perhaps, a means of separating his professional and private lives.[25] He claimed to have become fully conscious of his sexual orientation by age nineteen, his first year on the island.[26] He lived for a while in a first-floor studio at Tenth Avenue and Forty-Ninth Street, in the center of what George Chauncey described as a poor gay enclave that developed in the Forties west of Eighth Avenue, as large groups of gay youth crowded into Hell's Kitchen's tenements.[27] Hell's Kitchen may have served as Sendak's very own "Night Kitchen," decades before he created his story of sensual awakening, *In the Night Kitchen* (1970), during the throes of the Stonewall riots and the emerging gay liberation movement. Almost twenty years before Max donned his wolf suit, the artist traversed an urban landscape of "wolves" and "trade," old terms for men who, unlike "fairies," maintained masculine social personas while engaging discreetly in same-sex encounters.[28] Sendak described this period as "one of the best times in my life." He had made it to Manhattan and "was meeting all kinds of people I'd never met in Brooklyn. . . . They were really artists."[29] The artist's full, wild embrace of the Manhattan he had once idealized as a child would inspire drafts by the late 1950s of what would later become *Where the Wild Things Are* (1963) and *In The Night Kitchen*, celebrations of a triumphant child's secret knowledge and of urban, nocturnal delights.

But Sendak first struggled to find creative success as a painfully shy figurative artist in the age of abstract expressionism, sometimes attempting in vain to work in the more "sensible" field of advertising, which in those days hired fewer Jews. In 1947, his Lafayette High School physics teacher, Hyman Ruchlis, had reached out to commission the young artist's illustrations for his forthcoming textbook.[30] These first published Sendak illustrations earned the artist $100 and a 1 percent royalty of McGraw-Hill's profits. Like his high school comic strip, the pictures reflected his awkward position on the fringes of mainstream, heterosexual youth culture. An illustration titled "The Chemical Dance Floor," for instance, shows three chlorine atoms represented by chloride boys pairing up with sodium girls, a sort of testament to the "natural" science of heterosexuality in which the artist lacked a place of his own.[31] On the other hand, of course, the result of this heterosexual sodium-chloride pairing was less than glamorous: salt. In any case, the illustrations are emotionally vapid and mechanical, if sometimes slapstick. They convey concepts such as the "chain reaction" with faceless figures connected by repetitive motions. The stiffness of these drawings reflects the teenage artist's reserve within a culture that did not welcome queer expressions or unusual desires.

Despite the excitement of meeting other queer youths and artists in Manhattan, Sendak went to war with himself. As he recalled, "There was something wrong, always. . . . Whatever was wrong . . . manifested itself when I was becoming a teenager and then going to live on my own in New York. I was permanently frightened."[32] After a promotion at Timely Service, he grew markedly unhappy and quit his work altogether, moving back into his parents' Brooklyn apartment in 1948. There he sketched children from his parents' window—mostly a Sicilian American child named Rosie who entertained her peers with exhibitionist antics. He also created handmade toys with his brother, Jack, which they tried to sell to FAO Schwarz. Not suited to mass production at a reasonable cost, however, the toys were rejected. But Sendak accepted the company's unexpected offer to work as a window-display assistant at their store on Fifty-Ninth Street and Fifth Avenue. Commuting from his parents' home in Brooklyn, he sometimes lingered in the city after work, taking evening classes at the Art Students League in oil painting, life drawing, and composition. This would be the only formal art training he ever pursued. A self-portrait from this period captures an emotionally blank stare from under a towel draped on the teenager's head like a lion's mane or a feminine hairstyle.[33]

Coming into his fraught sexual orientation, the artist experienced his first physical encounter with a man while at FAO Schwarz. Strangely enough, as Sendak would recount to a journalist in his old age, it happened "in a giant doll's house on the second floor" of the toy store.[34]

Continuously battling difficult feelings, the artist soon began long-term psychotherapy. As he put it, he "keeled over. I just really ran out of steam and I was too frightened. I just lost it. And a very good friend of mine then paid for my first session [of therapy]. He said, 'You have to help yourself.' And I went and I stayed for 10 years."[35] Speaking of his therapist, Bertram Slaff, who was also gay and Jewish, Sendak would later admit, "I wanted him to hammer me straight, but of course that failed."[36] But the artist would later praise Slaff, telling *Rolling Stone*, "a large part of my 20s was spent on the analyst's couch. And it enriched and deepened me and gave me confidence to express much that I might not have without it."[37] Slaff and Sendak had much common ground from which to draw during their years of dialogue. Like Sendak, Slaff loved the arts and had even made several earlier attempts at playwriting. In the summer of 1954, while attempting to write a play in a rented house on Nantucket, Slaff would meet a flamboyant writer who lied about his age and invented his family's past. This writer, Coleman Dowell, would become Slaff's domestic partner, as well as a close friend of Sendak's for decades.[38] While Slaff's playwriting fell by the wayside, Dowell's daring novels would earn him the friendship of authors like Gilbert Sorrentino, John Hawkes, George Whitmore, and Edmund White.[39] Like Sendak, Dowell was an alienated queer artist concerned with complexities of "the self" and accompanying questions of the physical body, and he too partnered romantically with a psychiatrist interested in the arts.[40]

Slaff might have offered Sendak valuable insight related to his own experience as partner to Dowell. His clinical research surely also spoke to Sendak, focusing in part on the emotional plight of gifted youth, whose creative interiority isolated them from the wider society. Slaff's publications on adolescent psychiatry would advocate against pathologizing those whose distress reflected merely the suffering of a misunderstood, "creative personality," rather than a character disorder. Interestingly, in an era that still used coded language for homosexuality, terms like "creative" and "artistic" also referred to gay people.[41] This understanding may have colored Philip Sendak's uneasiness about the fact that his two sons were working as artists.[42] "Growing up differently from most people," Slaff wrote of the "gifted individual," this person "is likely not to have developed successfully the kinds of support systems more generally available, such as stable and predictable family and career anchorages. He is likely to be unique and alone, sometimes gloriously so, sometimes devastatingly so."[43]

Slaff's conception of the "gifted individual" could have described Rosie, the child who caught Sendak's attention from his parents' window in 1948 and who became the greatest muse of his career. Sendak would recall her as "a fierce child who impressed me with her ability to imagine herself into being anything she wanted to be, anywhere in or out of the world. She literally forced her fantasies onto her more stolid, less driven friends."[44] Rosie epitomized Sendak's belief about the nature of early childhood as a time concerned with the workings of reality itself—a time in which fantasy could be more freely employed to process overwhelming emotions and create new possibilities of meaning. Rosie had saluted Sendak, spontaneously calling him "Johnson" and including him in her game of make-believe.[45] The artist was impressed by her inclination to invent his identity "on the spot" and at a time when he was perhaps least sure of who he himself was.[46] As he would remember, "I was out of a job, out of sorts and money, and (worse) had to live at home with my parents, without a clue as to what to do next. Rosie occupied both hand and head during that long, languishing time and filled my notebooks with ideas that later found their way into every one of my children's books."[47] Rosie struck something important in Sendak. Though often withdrawn and stammering as a boy, Sendak had also been a "Rosie" at heart. He had enthralled other neighborhood children with highly exaggerated retellings of Saturday-morning movie classics like *The Mystery of the Wax Museum* and *Phantom of the Opera*. Also like Rosie, he had feared social abandonment once the captive attention of his peers was lost.[48] For about nine months after encountering Rosie, he had filled a sketchbook with her antics, labeling it "Brooklyn Kids, August 1948" and later calling this period his "Rosie fever." As he described her:

> She must have been aware of the pasty-faced youth (me) watching from a second-floor window. It seems, on the evidence of that sketchbook and the ones that came quickly after, that the better part of my day was spent

at that window, Rosie-watching. The [sketch]books are jammed with drawings of Rosie, her family and friends, and—along the sides of the pages—frantically jotted bits of precious Rosie monologue.... Her games were based mostly on the movies. She managed both the Charles Laughton and the Maureen O'Hara roles in *The Hunchback of Notre Dame*.[49]

Sendak remembered her as suffering and pained—qualities he identified with "real" children, beyond the "Dick and Jane" ideals.[50] At a time in which he explored his own childhood with Slaff, Rosie became the model of most of the children he would depict, and he would later remark on the "essential Rosieness" of all his child protagonists. Some of her peers would later also find belated glory as the children of Sendak's *Nutshell Library* (1962). But their first appearances were in Sendak's early sketchbooks. Looking back on these drawings, the artist would admit, "These early, unprecise, wavery sketches are filled with a happy vitality and a joy that was nowhere else in my life at the time."[51]

Children appealed to Sendak's creativity as socially uninitiated, sensitive human beings who resided "before," "outside," and sometimes even *despite* dominant social meanings. Children exhibited the powers of comic-book heroes who traverse time and space—children, he felt, "live in fantasy *and* reality; they move back and forth very easily in a way that we no longer remember how to do.... [T]hey can move with you very easily from one sphere to another without any problems."[52] Children, in other words, spoke the language of those adults like Sendak who lived between worlds. The artist sought to bridge his multiple worlds by exploring how to comprehend and survive the generic socialization that discounts one's passions and most urgent feelings. In his picture books, children would do the same, moving "from the inside out," despite what the wider society demanded of them. They would experience the world through more direct emotion and sensation, learning how to remain *themselves*, within and despite the dominant conventions that confine and police them.

By 1952, Sendak's financial success as a Harper illustrator would enable him to leave his job at FAO Schwarz and move to an East Fifty-Fourth Street apartment between Madison and Park Avenue. The young

artist savored New York's nocturnal rhythms and claimed to love walk-
ing the city around midnight, despite getting mugged three times.[53]
His new apartment stood just a few short blocks from what was then
called the "bird circuit," a popular district for gay nightlife between
East Forty-Fifth Street and Fifty-Second Street on Third Avenue. The
bird circuit was a favorite evening destination of Slaff, who was only
seven years older than Sendak, and Dowell, three years Sendak's senior.
It included bars with names like the Golden Cockerel, the Swan, the
Yellow Cockatoo, and the Blue Parrot.[54] Slaff and Dowell resided near
the circuit and had connections in an upscale milieu of gay and bisexual Jewish artists and cultural figures in New York, such as composer
Leonard Bernstein.[55] Some wealthy and covertly queer artists, art collectors, and their lovers held private soirees, including Lincoln Kirstein,
who co-founded the New York City ballet. These circles involved other
Harper children's illustrators such as Clement Hurd, who did the pictures for *The Runaway Bunny* (1942) and *Goodnight Moon* (1947), and
who posed nude for the homoerotic photographs of George Platt Lynes,
another figure in the New York gay arts scene.[56]

Surely Sendak had some exposure to Manhattan's various gay cultural realms, as well as their associated dangers, though he was still
quite timid in his early years of success. Discussing gay New York in
the 1950s, Sendak would admit that it was an exciting subculture, but
also that "gay bars were tiresome."[57] The young artist was generally
reclusive, more interested in books than in late-night parties, which
made him anxious and compromised his work the next morning. As a
twenty-four-year-old, he later admitted, the center of his universe was
an Eighth Street bookshop in Greenwich Village.[58] Through his brother's recommendation, he became specifically engrossed in those years
in the works of Herman Melville, whom Sendak would later perceive as
a potentially repressed gay or bisexual man. The artist started by reading *Moby-Dick* (1851), a work known for themes of male-male eroticism
and an eponymous sperm whale who represents a lurking psychological
danger.[59] So drawn was Sendak to the culture of the Village that he became a resident by the end of 1952, befriending local artists and *Village
Voice* contributors and staying put for almost two decades. Evenings

there in the 1960s and early 1970s would be memorable, to say the least. At one party, for example, a middle-aged Sendak would find himself utterly speechless when making the acquaintance of a woman who turned out to be none other than Margaret Hamilton, known for her role as the Wicked Witch of the West in MGM's *The Wizard of Oz*. Decades earlier, the boy Sendak had fixated fearfully on the scenes in which Hamilton holds Judy Garland's character hostage and then "melts" under Dorothy's pail of water; facing this star of childhood terrors in the flesh, now, over cocktails in New York's Bohemia, the artist trembled and nearly spilled his drink on her![60]

Following the Generic Child

Children's literature, previously marginal in American publishing, exploded in the postwar decades as a profitable beacon of middle-class American idealism. The postwar baby boom and its accompanied rise in funding for public schools and libraries created a thriving market that prompted publishers to expand their lists, as well as inspired new companies, such as Golden Books, to create innovations. Children's editors, librarians, and critics rose to influence, empowered by their authority to designate the prestigious Newbery and Caldecott Medals.[61] However, despite these advances, children's publishing in the 1950s was still relatively obscure and marginalized in the publishing world, a fact that attracted socially insecure artists like Sendak. These artists could create their most genuine, heartfelt work "off the map," relatively unseen within the broader culture. As Sendak would recall decades later, using a favorite metaphor of "diving" as truth-seeking, "Back in the '50s and '60s, the decades I define as the golden age of children's book publishing, we—the then new generation—were actually encouraged to dive—an unimaginable situation today. There were no temptations except to astonish, there was not much money, and 'kiddie books,' as they were called, were firmly nailed to the bottom of the 'literary-career-totem-pole.'"[62]

Sendak's career in children's books took off at an auspicious historical moment as a new class of "child experts" championed emotion-centered approaches and critiqued social conformity for its

effects on children. These ideas held special resonance as postwar antagonism toward communism and fascism loomed large. Social fixations
on a limited postwar child symbol, along with a gradual renaissance in
children's book publishing, paved the way in the early 1950s for critical
interventions. By the end of World War II, Neo-Freudian, child-centered approaches had largely replaced established behaviorist notions
of "child-training" within the field of child psychology. Commentators
warned that the child exposed too early to the harsh will of adult problems or ideologies might become a feeling-suppressed automaton like
the fascist youth overseas. Questioning the authoritarian undertones of
Superman comics, for example, Dr. Dallas Pratt of the National Mental
Health Foundation warned in 1950 against the use of "preachy materials" in children's literature, suggesting that children would respond
most to work that met them at eye level.[63] Neo-Freudian, "permissive"
approaches, however, were themselves also a product of the socially
conformist era that they critiqued. Even as they turned attention to the
child's emotions and individuality, they privileged and sought to elicit
the emotional experiences of a *specific sort* of child—namely a child
who would replicate the existing middle-class social order—a largely
White, Anglo-Saxon, gender polarized, and exclusively heterosexual
order.[64] Sendak knew firsthand how it felt to be a different sort of child
prodded with generic expectations, noticing "the cheated, missed-luck
look" in his father's eyes as Philip "turned from the radiant image of
Shirley Temple back to the three un-golden children he'd begotten."
Generic children were, Sendak felt, "yodeling, tap-dancing, brimming-
with-glittering-life miniature monsters."[65] Real children, by contrast,
were "as different and as varied as adults. Some have more taste, some
have less. Some are interesting, some are dull." Accordingly, the artist
considered it a "terrible mistake" to view children as a single, unified
entity of "Child," a mistake also directly connected with imposed pressures of assimilatory socialization.[66]

The symbol of the generic child—as a largely White, middle-class
fantasy—operated as a cultural site of debate for social scientists, ed-
ucators, politicians, and popular media determining who would be
included in the nation's desired future, and under which conditions.[67]

Postwar American social welfare initiatives incorporated child images in their efforts to expand acceptance of minority groups within the nation's idealized future vision.[68] The Manhattan-based National Social Welfare Assembly, for example, created a Comics Project from 1949 through 1967 that sought to both reinforce the social order and promote multiculturalism, combatting young Americans' inherited ethnic, religious, and racial prejudices. Its educational inserts in popular DC comic books reached an average of forty million Americans each month.[69] The generic child operated as an object of empathy that traversed social divisions. The emotionally dependent, vulnerable nature attributed to modern, middle-class children supported the idea that all children were blank slates of shapeable human matter and thus, on some level, constituted a unifying element across ethnicities, religions, and other divides—so long as such children and their caretakers followed the ideal of the generic child.

Populations seeking entry into middle-class American belonging were often eager to obey the prescriptions of the generic child. Children's books about ethnic minorities in the immediate postwar years helped integrate the image of White "ethnic" families, including most Jewish, Irish, and Italian Americans, as "normal," light-hearted, decorous, and thoroughly American. Jewish children's periodicals, for example, reflect American Jews' emotional shift from feelings of endangerment to suburban optimism and belonging at midcentury. One such publication, the *Kinder Zhurnal*, revamped its cover art by the late 1940s with a more childish aesthetic. In April 1946, the periodical shifted from its previous cover art, which had featured ornamental patterns, majestic lions, deer, birds, and decorative plants, to introduce wide-eyed, cartoonish children—one of them dressed in a sailor outfit—accompanied by dolls, baseball bats, and small, playful cartoon animals.[70] In the 1946–47 *Jewish Book Annual*, a librarian at the Boston Public Library noted that the twentieth century had turned out to be what she called "The Children's Century" because, with the help of public education and higher living standards, "everywhere people are striving to create for their children a more ideal environment and a more secure future." In the same breath, she pointed to the role of children's books as key affective tools in such endeavors, because they helped normalize children's emotions and behaviors, guiding them on how to integrate into the wider society.[71] Sydney Taylor's children's book, *All-of-a-Kind Family* (1951), offered optimism about such integration, even becoming the first children's book series about Jews to attract a large *gentile* readership.[72]

If Yiddish accents, religious rituals, or the recent events of genocide in Europe painted Jews as outsiders, the visibility of iconic Jewish child victims such as Anne Frank helped coalesce mainstream American values of the time with difficult facts of Jewish history and social difference.[73] The symbol of the child Holocaust victim, as an object of emotional investment, spoke to wider American feelings regarding the next generation. In figures like Frank and the child narrator of Elie Wiesel's *Night* (1956, translated to English in 1960), Americans could relate their investment in protecting all children, as material of the symbolic national future, from psychological harm and physical danger. While child Holocaust symbols, like Taylor's characters, explicitly identified as Jewish, their emotional styles and behaviors were virtually indistinguishable from the ideals of the gentile middle class, unlike Sendak's Brooklyn children. The innocence and mutability of generic Jewish child symbols allowed them to serve as a stand-in both for European Jewry and for universal human vulnerability and courage as America recovered from war.[74]

Sendak's representations of children in the early 1950s—as troubled, awkward, flamboyant, and wildly expressive—sat uneasily within this cultural moment. His pictures for *Good Shabbos, Everybody*, written by Robert Garvey, were published by the United Synagogue Commission on Jewish Education in 1951, the same year as Taylor's bestseller. He also illustrated *Happy Hanukah, Everybody* by Hyman and Alice Chanover, for the same commission, in 1954. His images for these books emphasize closeness between siblings and family in an ethnically Jewish atmosphere, a slouching grandfather in *Good Shabbos* appearing bald with a large nose and arched eyebrows—his countenance almost child-like. These books portray the Jewish family and home as emanating tightknit warmth, mysterious interiority, and weighty, ritualized meaning. In 1955, Sendak also contributed to the ongoing fight against antisemitism and other social prejudice by illustrating *Seven Little Stories on Big Subjects* by Gladys Baker Bond, published by the Anti-Defamation League Of B'nai B'rith. One of the included stories described the experience of Johnny, a child, drawn with dark hair. Johnny is tricked by a group of boys, whose staring "blue eyes and gray eyes and green eyes" make him "uncomfortable" and warn him of the danger that awaits him.[75] At the story's end, however, Sendak depicts Johnny in a tender moment of connection with another boy, placing his hands on this boy's shoulders. Johnny's new friend has lighter hair and stands taller with more confidence, gazing warmly at the bullied protagonist. In this work, Sendak began to express his creative vision more directly. The endangered ethnic outsider here survives most authentically not through assimilation but through inner resolve paired with transcendently queer recognition of humanity across social boundaries.

The same year as *Seven Little Stories*, Sendak turned to a vision generated in therapy—a vision of "something, or someone, or some little animal, getting out of some enclosure." Thus began his conception of *Wild Things*, which originated for him as "Where the Wild Horses Are," a wordless "sequence of drawings . . . of a little boy who stumbles almost haphazardly into a strange place where wild horses are running tempestuously about. And he tries his best to stop the stampede."[76] The evocative image of a child running after wild horses awakens countless associations, not least among them the artist's memory of racing a parade of American soldiers at the end of wartime, a queer youth's escape to new spaces of freedom in Hell's Kitchen, or, more abstractly, a troubled subject tackling his inner demons. In Sendak's evaluation of this initial idea, "There was something orgiastic and strange, and I knew there was some seed in it."[77] In November 1955, he created a tiny dummy of the book in which a moping protagonist decides to put on his winter gear and steal glances at wild horses from behind a tree, like a child spying on adult behavior or a lonely soul cruising Central Park. Posted signs warn him, "go slow," "don't let them see you," and "hide your eyes." The boy cannot help himself and grabs one horse by the tail, which leads the latter to whip the boy out of his clothes. "Beware!" reads a following sign, as a series of hostile creatures appear—a furry mustached being, a bat, and a wolf—like plainclothesmen busting up an illicit gathering, or adults denying a child's need. These creatures chase the boy, who dives naked into the ocean and climbs into a boat, where he dresses himself in yellow sailors' garb. The boy survives a stormy sea and arrives at "Happy Island," where a comically idealized ending awaits him—a house labeled "your house"; a woman dressed as a bride who brings him cake and screams, "surprise"; and an infant, a dog, and a cat for good measure. Thus, in this early iteration, the boy returns from his wild departure not to *himself* or to his punishing mother, as Max would later do in *Wild Things*, but to a future, heterosexual vision Sendak still wished he might accomplish.[78] Sendak would keep this project on the backburner for years. He would harvest the ripest fruits of his prime only in retrospect, after reworking his story and facing the parts of himself that did not fit his surroundings.

Queering the Generic Child

As Maria Popova writes, "Modern childhood's most benevolent patron saint turned out to be a childless gay woman."[79] This woman was Ursula Nordstrom, and she was among the most important factors in the making of Sendak. Frances Chrystie, a children's book buyer for FAO Schwarz, first introduced her to the twenty-two-year-old window decorator during one of her visits to the store.[80] A witty, impassioned, and self-educated daughter of divorced vaudevillians, Nordstrom had become director of Harper & Brothers' children's book department in 1940.[81] Far from a bourgeois moralist, she viewed family life as "an impediment to creativity," lived with a same-sex partner, Mary Griffith, for decades, and cared a great deal about children and their plight.[82] She claimed that her authority in the field derived from being "a former child" who had forgotten nothing. Nordstrom was, Leonard Marcus writes, "the field's most audacious editor and inspired mentor," striving to free children's books from sentimental propriety and unleash their modern literary potential.[83] At the heart of her agenda was a desire to take the unruly child's side in its struggle against what she perceived as a desensitized adult world designed to reproduce itself by breaking the child's instinctual energies. She hoped to put an end to "bad books for good children"—the moralizing, vapid *Dick and Jane* stories—and begin a culture of what she called "good books for bad children," of work that acknowledged and supported young people, not as angelic symbols but as human beings who experience frustration and emotional struggle. In addition to rethinking gender and sexuality expectations, she believed American youth should become more familiar "with 'non-Wasp' backgrounds" to expand conceptions of acceptable social norms. This impulse would lead her, for example, to publish Isaac Bashevis Singer's *Zlateh the Goat* (1966) collection of Yiddish folktales, which Sendak would illustrate.[84] Nordstrom cared most about offering unusual beauty and interesting realities to children, regardless of whether a departure from social convention might embarrass adult librarians or critics.

Nordstrom also saw in children something she felt was missing among adults in midcentury society, who stigmatized and conformed all too easily—children had an unalloyed emotional perceptiveness and openness. As she wrote to Singer, "[M]ost adults are dead and beyond hope by the age of thirty."[85] In children's books, by contrast, the reader's identity was expected to exist in a state of flux and "becoming," of passionate truth-seeking. Sendak too adopted this perspective, later declaring,

> Grown-ups desperately need to feel safe, and then they project onto the kids. But what none of us seem to realize is how smart kids are. They don't like what we write for them, what we dish up for them, because it's vapid, so they'll go for the hard words, they'll go for the hard concepts, they'll go for the stuff where they can learn something, not didactic things, but passionate things.[86]

Thus Nordstrom helped Sendak evolve from a meek, self-doubting person into a direct and forceful visionary with confidence about the seriousness of his work.[87] She had a penchant for nurturing the suppressed emotional world of artists—both in her book creators and in her readers. Nordstrom's first encounter with Sendak, however, was far from dynamic. She found him so withdrawn that she felt compelled to ask his age.[88] Still, the following day, after studying his sketchbook, she hired him to illustrate Marcel Aymé's *The Wonderful Farm* (1951).[89] The artist described their immediate connection and his "knowing instantly my life was with her. . . .

I would do anything she said."[90] The powerful editor surely saw the fragility and raw, creative potential of Sendak's interiority—the inner world that his reserved, child-like manner sought to preserve and to protect. She challenged and educated the young artist by assigning him two books in 1952, four books in 1953, three in 1954, and three more in 1955. In 1958, she assigned him nine. As Leonard Marcus notes, by the time of his first major press profile, in the *Village Voice* on September 26, 1956, Sendak had already published twenty-four books.[91]

As mentor, Nordstrom also built Sendak's confidence in private, addressing insecurities and introducing him to influential critics and career connections. In her letters to him in the 1950s and 1960s, she assuaged his anxieties about his identity as an artist, calling him "Marlon" after Brando the film star.[92] Nordstrom would write to him in August 1961, "You love and admire the work of some other contemporary artists and writers today but really, think how few of them have any vigorous emotional vitality? What you have is RARE."[93] Challenging convention, her letters used a tone that was at once maternal, goofy, and jokingly flirtatious. She sometimes lightened the artist's serious moods with self-effacing humor about her own failures to perform gender expectations—recounting, for example, how, for a Newbery-Caldecott awards dinner, she wore an unflattering lavender lace dress and, ditching her glasses, fumbled to see anyone who spoke to her. "I've just seen the photographs," she wrote to Sendak, "Oh God . . . who is *that*? Or rather, *what* is that? Surely it isn't a woman, or even a human being. No, it is more a sort of *expanse* of something, and so why would it be in the picture?. . . . Oh, I know what it is, it is Jones Beach—a picture of Jones Beach. Jones Beach Nordstrom."[94] Nordstrom both modeled and participated in freewheeling, unabashed banter with the young Sendak, who found in her an adopted, wild caretaker as well as a friend similarly alienated by conventional gender and sexuality norms of the time.

Nordstrom also introduced Sendak to children's book writer Ruth Krauss, who, along with her husband, Crockett Johnson, became makeshift parental figures to the young artist. A childless couple, Sendak claimed them as his "weekend parents," visiting them for as many as two weekends a month in Rowayton, Connecticut. He sought their guidance when his own parents doubted his ability to make a living or refused to acknowledge his sexuality.[95] Krauss had already changed the face of children's literature with *The Carrot Seed* (1945, Harper & Row), illustrated by Johnson, offering young readers an unconventional message about prioritizing dreams and desires above accepted logic and social expectation—a message Sendak would deepen through serious artistic treatments of childhood's most painful, dark, and fantastical moments. But it was Johnson who suggested the word "rumpus" to Sendak, a word that would, through Max and the Wild Things, come to signify a sort of reckless abandon and transcendence the artist had craved amidst social restriction. While visiting Krauss and Johnson in Connecticut, Sendak also befriended Doris Orgel, whose young son might have inspired Max's outfit; according to Leonard Marcus, this boy wore "fanciful leopard pajamas, complete with big-cat ears and tail."[96]

Krauss collaborated with Sendak on several works and likely helped him to overcome his erotic shame in his early twenties, freeing his creativity. Sendak contrasted Krauss, who "boasted of her sexuality," with his own mother, who characterized men as "plunderers and pigs" whom married women had to "endure" without enjoyment.[97] In his eulogy for Krauss, Sendak would later call her a "fiercely liberated woman" who met him at a time when he was a "hopelessly middle-class kid."[98] She had a sizable circle of gay friends, including Frank O'Hara and Remy Charlip, who illustrated some of her books, and she lived beside a partnered couple named Harry Marinsky and Paul Bernard.[99] A previous anthropology student of Margaret Mead's, Krauss spoke unabashedly with Sendak about anatomy and human sexuality. As he later remembered,

> Ruth—to me, [a] timid Brooklyn boy—her ability to talk about the body and its orifi[ces] was an amazing adventure. I was both shocked and so elated that my thoughts were not sick and putrid, as I thought they were, as I suspect most young people of that generation thought that what they were thinking was sick. Because how could you know? No one else talked about it. No one would confirm your fantasies or answer your questions.[100]

Krauss's shocking sensibilities had an impact on the young artist's tastes and painfully highlighted for him the disservice done to youth raised without a positive education about the body and the naturalness of human sexuality. He once stated, "I think my entire training was Ruth Krauss, working with her."[101] Sendak internalized her daringly blunt disposition and aversion to prudish, "middle-class" sensibilities. This form of education proved crucial to accessing the wildness and primal vitality of early childhood feelings, which were yet to grace American picture books.[102] He would credit her and Nordstrom as the fundamental shapers of his bold, irascible voice: "I've taken on so many of her traits and Ursula's traits. These were my models. And I will not tolerate oblique language. [Ruth] taught me how to say 'fuck you.' I never said things like that until Ruth said them."[103]

Sendak's chemistry with Krauss translated to a successful creative output. The first Krauss-Sendak collaboration, A Hole Is to Dig (1952), sold over eighty thousand copies by its fifth year in publication and first established Sendak as a powerful new creator in the field.[104] The artist called it his "baptism into picture books."[105] The book is a series of childlike definitions, many supplied by actual children. Krauss studied young children at the progressive Bank Street School, collecting definitions offered to her by the toddlers and preschoolers on 3x5-inch index cards.[106] She assembled and typed lists of these definitions. The book was an "anomaly" for lacking a plot. It was also the first modern children's book to come largely from the mouths of living children.[107] A Hole Is to Dig also defied normative gender expectations. Following Krauss's direction, Sendak changed some of his girls to boys and vice versa. Thus, the final drawings present girls wearing false mustaches, building with plywood, and leading a processional march, as well as boys with limp wrists and frilly aprons washing dishes and pushing strollers of kittens. Sendak would note, with delight, that some of the children drawn in this book appeared as not obviously male or female.[108]

A Hole Is to Dig also broke with children's book convention by featuring ethnically marginal subjects who defy the normative Anglo ideals of childhood innocence and obedience. Leonard Marcus aptly characterized the awkward proportions, firmly resilient stances, unruliness, and heavy line quality of Sendak's children and the page designs in *A Hole Is to Dig*, contrasting the sunny idealism of existent picture-book norms.[109] Commenting on his drawings of Brooklyn children, Sendak shared, "[T]hey're all a kind of caricature of me. They look as if they've been hit on the head and hit so hard they weren't ever going to grow up any more."[110] These Brooklyn kids were "old before their time. . . . Most of them were Jewish, and they may well look like little greenhorns just off the boat. They had—some of them, anyway—a kind of bowed look, as if the burdens of the world were on their shoulders."[111] Sendak had not meant for the children of these early books to look like nervous, elderly people, as commentators viewed them. He simply drew kids the way his Brooklyn peers had looked to him—much unlike the depictions of previously existing picture books featuring uncomplicated children from "other neighborhoods and planets."[112] Perhaps his characters' awkward stances drew also, on some level, from the hours spent rehashing his own childhood while seated across from his therapist, Bert Slaff, who had clubbed feet.[113] In the course of the artist's treatment and his subsequent friendship with Slaff, the latter may have in addition shared anecdotes from his work with gifted children whom others called "prematurely aged."

Beyond *A Hole Is to Dig*, Sendak and Krauss's artistic visions continued to share an appreciation for the oddities of children's creativity, serious feelings, and play. Their collaborations spoke to young people in their own language, however queer or inscrutable to adults. In *I'll Be You and You Be Me* (1954), for example, a boy describes another younger boy: "He can't talk yet / But I can understand him. . . . He answers when I call. / I call 'Honey, come here, Honey,' / And he comes."[114] In this way, Sendak began the work of reviving his own child self, a queer child who was not allowed to grow up without becoming someone else. This child's emotional predicament continued to speak to the queer adult's position as insider-outsider. Sendak would constantly reference the afterlife of his suppressed inner child when discussing his interventions in children's literature, once stating,

> Too many parents and too many writers of children's books don't respect the fact that kids know and suffer a great deal. My children show a

lot of pleasure, but often they look defenseless, too. Being defenseless is
a primary element of childhood. And often, I am trying to draw the way
children feel—or, rather, the way I imagine they feel. It's the way I know
I felt as a child. And all I have to go on is what I know—not only about
my childhood then, but about the child I was as he exists now.[115]

Like the children he depicted and admired, Sendak worked "from the
inside out," struggling to understand and hold himself together in a social context that preferred either to maintain his incoherence on the
margins or forcibly to assimilate him. For Ruth Krauss's *I Want to Paint
My Bathroom Blue* (1956), he painted a boy who leaps flamboyantly upward toward an image of a horse, the text declaring, "upstairs a horse in
the bedroom."[116] Like the boy in Sendak's emerging story of wild horses,
this boy too dreams of a house on an island. This house, however, contains not a wife and child, but all of the boy's friends living together,
their skin tones comprising different colors of the rainbow. The individuals are partnered in couples that seem to include at least one
same-sex pair holding hands, whether lovers or confidantes. As Max
and the Wild Things would later do, these friends dance in the woods
together. A 1955 book dummy presents this scene with more creative
pairings—boys with boys, girls with girls, boys with girls, and lone children hugging tree trunks, their eyes closed with longing.[117]

In addition to learning from mentors like Krauss and Nordstrom,
Sendak was an autodidact and avid reader of classic literature that challenged conventional restrictions on the emotional life of children and
others. He delighted, for example, in Henry James's writing, with its
child protagonists who are permitted to stay up late and observe and
judge their elders' behavior in strange and uninhibited states. This tendency in James complemented the artist's outrage against those who
held children back from learning about the world and "becoming who
they are." A fantasy come true, James's novels would influence later
Sendak creations such as *In the Night Kitchen*, in which Mickey defies
his bedtime in order to find out what happens in the world after dark.
Night Kitchen would address children made to feel unduly naïve, igno-
rant, and manipulated by adults—put to bed before the important events

of any given evening and denied access to knowledge about their own bodies and physical drives.

The experimental energy that Sendak championed in the mid-1950s drew also from European influences, as books from overseas began to circulate for American children in those years, including works by Hans Fischer and Carigiet. Consequentially, the look of American books became more European.[118] In 1956, Nordstrom introduced Sendak to Tomi Ungerer, a rebellious twenty-two-year-old French artist at Harper. Nordstrom hoped that Sendak would teach him how to do the color separations used in publishing of the time. In the 1950s and 1960s, Selma Lanes writes, Ungerer was Sendak's closest colleague and friend; both lived in the Village, and they would often meet for coffee and late-night strolls to talk about life, illustration, and their goals.[119] Ungerer's work reflected World War II's disruption of his own boyhood home in Alsace under German occupation, as well as his resulting emotional alienation. In a later documentary about his life, Ungerer would offer the mantra, "If you are faced with nothing, you can fill it up—with your mind."[120]

Similar to Ungerer in this respect, but heavier in the tone of his artwork, Sendak created child heroes who, situated in a gulf between competing forces of urgent feeling and imposed, social expectation, face a void of meaning and address that void through fantasy. Sendak too conveyed the potential marginalization and creative meaning-making of children from within the spaces of generic childhood, collective traditions, and their own middle-class homes. *Circus Girl* (1957), for example, written by Jack Sendak and illustrated by Maurice, depicts Flora, the protagonist, in what resembles a fascist nightmare in which all of the village's men, women, and children huddle silently around her and appear to have vacant eyes and the same exact face, as though manufactured by the same rubber stamp.[121] Published the same year, Sendak's drawings for Else Minarik's *Little Bear* rebel against the Victorian, bourgeois self-restraint imposed on the child. Steeped in the mores of a buttoned-up culture, the young protagonist sheds his clothes and pursues adventures, connecting with his animal needs and personal curiosities.[122] His illustrations for Minarik's *No Fighting, No Biting!* (1958) also critique the well-mannered, emotionally suppressed child ideal. These Victorian-era children cannot sit still, so their caretaker tells them stories of a wild alligator and her two rambunctious children. Formally dressed and slouching on a drawing-room sofa, they appear purposefully out of place.[123] Sendak heightened the emotional boldness of the children in these works through visual contrast, drawing them in the restrained, crosshatching style of Victorian illustrator George Cruikshank.

Kenny's Window (1956), the first book Sendak both authored and illustrated, reflects touchstones of his personal and creative journey in dialogue with broader American norms. It is dedicated to Sadie and Philip, to Slaff, and to Nordstrom, and it takes place on Rosie's street. Sendak worked on the book at Yelping Hill, a summer literary community established on the property of Henry Seidel Canby, founder of the *Saturday Review* and the Book-of-the-Month Club. *Kenny's Window* focuses on the solitary indoor play of a withdrawn boy in his urban home, drawing on the artist's early childhood memories of recovering from sicknesses in Brooklyn. Kenny appears blonde and thin, like the idealized American child. However, this child evinces queer longings, experiences moments of spite and greed, and has dreams that seem to draw from Old Testament narratives and cultural motifs of Old-World Europe. The book borrows symbols from Genesis's creation story: the division of light and dark, a wondrous tree blossoming in a garden, and a supernatural call to seek hidden knowledge. In place of the biblical serpent, a winding train carries a rooster who poses seven questions that Kenny must answer. The rooster's symbolic presence suggests both virile independence and the mythological *shtetl* landscape, but his unusual body—he has four feet—also marks him as a queer outlier, not unlike the bed-ridden Kenny. This rooster seems to prefigure the phallic energy of Sendak's future protagonists, especially Mickey, the naked hero of *In the Night Kitchen*, who would later crow "COCK a DOODLE DOO!" during his triumph of self-mastery in a dreamscape composed of items from the family's kosher pantry. Starting with *Kenny's Window*, Sendak wedded his suppressed queer feelings with the very sources of their denial: the constraining, but cherished traditions of his heritage, as well as the confinement imposed by generic childhood and midcentury ideals.

As a realm associated with asexual innocence, children's literature has been, counterintuitively, a context in which queer affections could emerge without implying social taboo. What words could not condone might still suggest itself in the emotional texts of images. Some of Sendak's early published illustrations feature same-sex affection, regardless of its absence from the accompanying text. His cover art for Ruth Krauss's *A Hole Is to Dig*, for example, depicts one small boy offering flowers to another. In a painting for Meindert DeJong's *Wheel on the School* (1954), the artist drew a tender moment between two boys in an open field—one lays on his back, smiling, while the other rests on him.[124] In *I'll Be You and You Be Me*, Sendak chose to depict "Skippy" and "Hoppy" as boys holding hands. He also drew two boys sitting on each others' feet to illustrate Krauss's words: "You sit on my cold feet and I'll sit on your cold feet." For the line "You take my name and I'll take yours," Sendak again imagined two boys, now leaning head-to-head.[125] These moments are the first visual representations of same-sex affection in any of Krauss's published work and perhaps in any American children's books. Even more boldly, Sendak would later depict two boys cuddling and smiling in a narrow bed together for Janice May Udry's *Let's Be Enemies* (1961).[126] In another pencil study for that book, a picture of the boys reconciling, Sendak writes himself a note to move the boys closer together. Perhaps he was thinking purely of spatial layout, or striving to emphasize a platonic sort of friendliness. Or maybe these minor decisions reflect a longing to see himself better reflected in print, for his sake and for the sake of other young people with unpopular feelings. Nordstrom would have supported such a stance. As she later declared, "I had for years also said that I wished somebody would write a book that would just give a hint that there could be a romantic feeling between two persons of the same sex." Nordstrom even published her own picture book, *The Secret Language* (1959), about a special, intimate friendship between two boarding-school girls who use the code word "leebossa" to indicate when something is "lovely" or "just right."[127]

In a culture saturated with heteronormative representations that pair sweet, submissive girls with brave, confident boys, Sendak's early work challenged children to face the constructed nature of those representations when they did not feel included in them. In a drawing for Krauss's *I'll Be You and You Be Me*, a clueless boy scratches his head beside a frustrated girl, with hand-lettered text proclaiming, "If you kissed me, I'd kiss you back, I guess." A child's play at conventional gender roles meets anticlimactic indifference in *Kenny's Window*: when hosting a make-believe party, Kenny's teddy bear asks about inviting "lady guests," so Kenny summons Baby, his female dog. Baby, Sendak writes, "promptly curled up and went back to sleep." The protagonist he drew for *I Want to Paint My Bathroom Blue* sprinkles colorful seeds across the world, leaps through the air flamboyantly, and dreams of a "house like a rainbow" where all his friends can live with him. In *A Kiss for Little Bear* (1968), Little Bear would anger a male skunk by lifting his skunk bride off her feet to kiss her on the lips in the midst of their wedding. The groom holds a drawing by Little Bear of the skunk couple kissing and holding hands— the two skunks look identical, lacking any distinct gender signifiers.[128] As an adult, Sendak might have seen himself, like Little Bear and countless actual children studying their parents' relationships, as something of a playfully welcomed intruder and anomaly. Similar to how children stave off the marginality they feel in the context of their parents' marital relations, he carved out a relational position for himself in heteronormative culture through subversion and make-believe, with Krauss and Johnson as his "weekend parents" and all. At his last visit with an elderly Krauss before her passing, he would lift her face for a kiss, as Little Bear had done at the skunks' wedding. In his eulogy for the bold author, Sendak would write, "I took her face in my hands and kissed her on the mouth. And I was rewarded once more with her growing belly laugh. . . . This was the same seductive Ruthie, the high-flying Ruthie who gave all of herself to her art. What a lucky kid I was."[129]

Undergoing his own therapeutic process and thawing his emotional defenses in the service of his work, the reserved artist pondered and expressed his sexuality in more open ways by the 1950s, at least privately, with his friends and in the margins of his drafts. Doodles in his pencil studies for *A Hole Is to Dig* show two nude youths drawn with a loose line, one approaching the other, genitalia in view.[130] In a draft of his illustrations for Krauss's *I'll Be You and You Be Me*, in which a boy and girl speak to each other on the telephone in a series of playful poses, the artist doodled the lower half of a leaping male nude.[131] Sendak was about twenty-five at the time. A year or so later, at the top of a page draft for *Kenny's Window*, he sketched two nude figures at the focal point of Kenny's upward gaze: a man crawls in a position of desperation or despair beside a crouching headless female. The text below reads, "What looks inside and what looks outside?" These figures occupy the space above the protagonist's window, out of which he gazes upward at the falling snow.[132] Like Kenny, who was learning to engage with the world beyond his bedroom window, Sendak also stood before a window in those years, peering into his buried desires in private. In a draft for *Let's Be Enemies*, beneath one of the pencil studies in which the boys share an umbrella and blow bubble gum into each other's faces, Sendak would again doodle, with a shaggier line, the form of a reclining male nude, muscles rippling.

Perhaps these hints of sexuality in the margins of his drafts merely reflect the wandering imagination of the adult artist. But they might also reveal what Sendak could not so explicitly include in his stories—the child's lonely curiosity about the physical and social implications of a gendered, sexually emergent body and the queer desires that may emanate from that body—as well as confusion about adults' notions of sexual shame. In later adulthood, he would write, "To deny children's sexuality is a crime which we in this country are very guilty of."[133] His nude sketches in the upper-page regions of his drafts, the "sky" regions, foreshadow his artwork for *In the Night Kitchen*, *Fly by Night*, and *The Light Princess*, in which nude children float through the sky while parents are missing, distracted, or asleep. Sendakian flight connotes the uninhibited, unconscious rhythms of the mind when dreaming, as well as the movement of birds, another important symbol invoking histories of Jewish and queer associations.

Like Sendak's sexual marginalia, free-associated fantasies and Freudian projections help the protagonist of *Kenny's Window* to gain control over his anxieties about growing into himself. But Sendak's voice as a covertly gay and highly sensitive artist was not always welcome, as a study of the book's omissions suggests. *Kenny's Window* presents a wordier, less polished Sendak who sought to expose his emotional struggles in detail through extended metaphor. It took direct inspiration from psychoanalyst Dorothy Baruch's 1952 study of a developmentally challenged boy named Kenneth.[134] Baruch describes validating Kenneth's jealousy of his younger brother, addressing his mother's dislike of maleness and his Oedipal struggles with his emotionally distant father, and dispelling his fear that touching his penis was a "bad" behavior that would cause it to "burn off." Sendak was overwhelmed by Kenneth, "by his inability to communicate," because Kenny's struggles reminded the artist of his own, of how lonely and lost he had felt.[135] Ongoing conversations with Baruch while playing with finger paint and clay help Kenneth tackle his difficult feelings and free him to better express himself and connect with others. Sendak pursued a similar process for his own Kenny protagonist as he developed this first book. In early typescripts, Kenny envisions a snow-covered landscape of waterfalls and rainbows, where he discovers a secret—that he is special and different from others. Sexually suggestive metaphors in this unpublished episode feature a milky white torrent of water and a rainbow arching its back.[136] In this fantasy, a moonlit Kenny, dusted in the white of snow, his eyes colored rainbow, realizes that the secret he seeks is inside of him, rather than outside of his window.[137] In the spirit of Baruch's Kenneth and of Sendak's relationships with Krauss or Slaff, Kenny seems to find validation of his own nature here, despite social and emotional obstacles.

Earlier drafts of *Kenny's Window* also present intimate, tender moments between male characters. During a sort of lovers' quarrel between Kenny and his sulking teddy bear, Bucky, the two parties threaten to never speak to or sleep with each other again.[138] Reacting to Kenny's announcement about his plan to draw a special, secret picture, the two toy soldiers appear pleased, and Kenny whispers kind remarks to them. An anonymous reader's handwritten reaction, however, condemns these instances as fussy and confusing, recommending their erasure.[139] It is not clear whether these notes—a challenge to Sendak to clarify a foggy or coded vision—came from Nordstrom or some other colleague at Harper. Penciled throughout the typescripts, they beseech the artist to be more direct, cheerful, and outward, rejecting the inwardness

and perceived strangeness of Kenny's perspective.[140] The young Sendak
ultimately obliged, also eliminating the motif of Kenny's secret, rain-
bow-infused difference. An early draft in addition has Kenny ask the
rooster if another boy, "David," may reside with him in the garden and
ride with him in the caboose of the train. The rooster affirms this request, including David in the dreamlike vision he paints for Kenny.[141]
Though David is omitted from this scene in the published book, he does
appear on Kenny's block toward the end of the story. In an almost romantic pose, Kenny gazes downward at David from his window like
Juliet answering Romeo's call. Sendak's interest in lonely soldiers,
secret difference, and private pleasantries exchanged between male
companions might reveal an eagerness to handle the frustration of a
queer boyhood. But it did not suit the social climate of the 1950s. He
consequentially neutralized Kenny's voice from its initial sensuality
and secretiveness to a more universal, generic tone. However, he creatively infused Kenny's fantasies with queer undertones and honored
the alienated child's frustrated, forceful emotions and dreams of agency
and belonging. At one moment in the published story, for example, a toy
soldier asks his comrade to run away with him. Kenny stops them, telling them he loves them, whispering sentimentally to them and rubbing
his finger over the chipped parts of their bodies.

Kenny's Window reflects the midcentury tension between idealizing
a generic child that would rebuild the nation with the existing American ideals and the desire for children to have their own individual
voices. Reflecting this ambivalence, Kenny's dog, Baby, worries about
being herself without losing others' love. Baby dreams of becoming an
elephant but fears that Kenny would stop loving her if she no longer
looked and behaved like a dog, admitting, "I was afraid you'd stop loving me. I thought, 'Kenny has lots of love for a little dog, but does he
have enough for an elephant?'" Baby's fear is, of course, the same fear
harbored by Kenny and by any young person who feels or loves differently: Am I undesirable or excessive to others? Will I remain so once
I've grown? Do others know the expansiveness that is the "real" me (the
elephant), or do they know only the surface of me? Overtly queer or
not, *Kenny's Window* transcended generic childhood representations to

offer advice to alienated children about how to manage psychological imprisonment, pursue unique dreams, and anticipate authentic growth. The seven questions posed to Kenny by the four-legged rooster may reflect insights from their twenty-six-year-old creator's own life at the time as he underwent therapy, pursued dating, and negotiated levels of closeness with his parents and new role models. Through imagined interactions with his teddy bear, for example, Kenny learns how to apologize with sincerity and how to use playfulness to mend relationships. Projecting onto his dog, Baby, he learns to see others through their own self-conceptions, or at least to respect those conceptions. When Kenny attempts to catch a goat in his fantasized trip to Switzerland, he learns that relationships can be lonely when they are based on force instead of on understanding. Kenny also learns not to rely exclusively on parents or to expect them to understand his dreams—"I won't tell mama or papa [about the horse on the roof]. They'd say it was a dream. They don't know how to listen in the night." Last, he learns to be flexible about adjusting his assumptions as he grows and develops new capacities—"I thought I wanted to live in the garden [but] I wish I had a horse, and a ship with an extra room for a friend."

Following *Kenny's Window*, children in Sendak's books would depart the domestic spaces of their homes in more drastic ways, sometimes in disguise, as does Martin in *Very Far Away* (1957), also set on Rosie's street.[142] Fleeing a mother distracted by the new baby, Martin seeks a place where others do not ignore him. In Sendak's illustrations for *Circus Girl* the same year, Flora ventures away from the circus in which she was born in order to spy on people in a residential community and learn about "how the outside people live." Child readers stretched precariously between competing realities, perhaps especially in families with stark divisions between notions of "inside" and "outside," might relate to Flora when she tightropes across the neighborhood street on this journey. With Flora, the reader stands physically outside of "normal" or socially privileged homes where children play with obedient house pets and sit down for dinners served by their culturally refined caretakers.

In his own life, Sendak too ventured further "outside" in the mid-1950s. The artist pursued friendship and the delights of live music in a social group whose gatherings rotated between the apartments of its participants. Sendak became romantically involved with a particular piano player in the group, Eugene Glynn, who worked as a psychiatrist in public medicine and specialized in treating adolescents and supervising social workers.[143] Two years his senior, Glynn reminded Sendak of his brother, Jack. Like the artist, Glynn had also faced a troubled childhood. His mother had died of pneumonia shortly after Glynn's birth, and his father was fatally shot during a hold-up at the family's grocery store when Glynn was nine.[144] Sendak found in Glynn a fellow appreciator of the arts and a fellow intellectual averse to fads and trends. Glynn was named after Socialist icon Eugene Debs. His parents, members of the Workmen's Circle, were secular Jewish immigrants whose surname had been shortened from Glynbuski after migrating from present-day Belarus by way of Liverpool, England. Like Sendak, Glynn navigated cultural homophobia and antisemitism in his youth. He had graduated high school at sixteen or seventeen and could not yet be drafted, so he began college coursework early. With persisting anti-Jewish sentiments and quotas in universities, Glynn knew in the 1940s to withdraw his other medical school applications after being offered a spot at NYU, so as not to obstruct other Jewish applicants elsewhere.[145] Beyond his primary profession, Glynn was a brilliant and opinionated critic of art and culture who also played the piano and cooked wonderfully. Though in social settings he often played a supporting role to the more effusive Sendak, wearing his genius lightly and shying away from spotlights, Glynn's presence was a commanding one, and his ideas were original and surprising. Sendak, for his part, walked a tightrope in this relationship, knowing others' desire not to acknowledge it. Thus, although Sendak and Glynn remained supportive and protective of each other, they kept their professional lives markedly separate and avoided displays of affection, even at some of their own dinner parties.[146] While the artist's parents met and respected Glynn, they did not want to know about his relationship to their son: "They never knew I was officially gay," Sendak would recount, "Of course, they knew. . . . Nothing was said, but if something had been said I would have been thrown out of the house. Don't ask, don't tell."[147] Therefore, Sendak "lied to them constantly.

They couldn't have dealt with it."[148] Once he found his sister weeping over his fate: "my little brother, sitting there drawing pictures . . . what's going to happen when I die? You're going to have no one." "Wait a minute," Sendak recalled answering, "I have Eugene." "No, no," insisted Natalie, "you've got to have a woman to take care of you."[149]

Though open about his sexuality with most friends and collaborators in his adult life, Sendak sensed what the public wanted to keep in shadow, and he would remain discreet with the press until his eighties.[150] A committed, cohabitating couple, Glynn and Sendak lived for half a century in varying degrees of circumspection with those beyond their inner circle. Years after the former's passing, however, Sendak would publicly admit, "I dream of him constantly. I'm always feeling guilty that I didn't do enough for him. . . . I wish I had been more demonstrative. . . . Being gay in the old days was hard."[151] But if Sendak had fallen at all short of his expectations for himself as a companion, he might have found solace in what he had done for the world—he'd harnessed his own hardships in ways that helped children and others at odds with constraining social norms to know that they mattered and that they were not alone. Through a focus on early childhood and his own coming of age, Sendak's creative vision increasingly blared and demanded dignity for queer truths that he could not always speak directly.

CHAPTER 4

"MILK IN THE BATTER" AND CONTROVERSY IN THE MAKING

*"Camp," Stigma, and Public Spotlight
in the Era of Social Liberation*

SENDAK TREADED INTO FAME AND SUCCESS in the 1960s with greater confidence, humor, and grit. Passing age thirty with multiple successes under his belt, he carried valuable insights from Rosie, Nordstrom, and Krauss. His work interacted energetically with a zeitgeist of emergent liberation and cultural surges riding on the wings of the civil rights movement. Though by no means free of stereotyping or exploitation, the mainstream "ethnic revival" of the 1960s and 1970s began to present protagonists who wore their Irishness, Italianness, Jewishness, or Blackness with dignity and pride. These decades celebrated the likes of Ed Sullivan, Sidney Poitier, Lenny Bruce, Barbra Streisand, Diahann Carroll, Eddie Murphy, Bette Midler, Al Pacino, Mel Brooks, and countless others who performed variations of minority culture with confidence and humor. As Americans increasingly welcomed a vision of their nation as an ethnic conglomeration and yearned to engage with roots beyond those of White Anglo-Saxon Protestants, more Jewish writers and artists turned to distinctly Jewish content: pre-immigration narratives, the young state of Israel, and the tragedies of the Holocaust. Sendak's honesty and interest in difficult emotional truths refreshed postwar parents who had grown up spiritually alienated and disengaged from their own ethnic and religious roots in the conformist 1950s, and who sought to cultivate richer existential foundations for their children.

Like the fiction of Philip Roth, Sendak's work spoke specifically to intergenerational conflicts between postwar youth and acculturated parents who had focused on earning or protecting their American belonging and on building institutions. The artist enlivened representations of the domestic sphere by subverting the sentimentality that colored mainstream images of childhood. He did so by painting children and the home with startling emotional honesty, unruliness, and snark—children airborne and endangered, not protected at the hearth; mothers absent or threatening, rather than "angels of the home"; rage and ecstasy instead of empty displays of tamed feeling; the affective storms of the unfiltered individual over the affected sweetness of the curated family image. He described his approach of reaching others by speaking to their "brutal, happy, rough roots," which he envisioned as "little quiet jets that go off in us and that make us respond to people." Fighting for the freedom to express such "roots," the artist condemned a cultural establishment focused on propriety that was unwilling "to confirm in children's minds and hearts . . . that we understand" the frightening, erratic, and even unseemly elements of a developing person's inner world.[1] He explicitly employed Krauss's frankness, Nordstrom's subversive wit, and his parents' animated mannerisms and political consciousness. In doing so, he addressed what most children, even comfortably middle-class children, feared and pondered about the world, including taboo feelings of fury and sensual desire, as well as the harsh realities of social inequality, abuse, and mortality, to which the artist had been exposed during his Brooklyn youth. A career focused on recovering and communing with his earliest emotions was, for Sendak, the natural progression of a long-internalized battle to preserve social and creative difference against pressures of assimilation.

On "Camp" and "Growing Up"

From May 9 to September 8, 2019, the Metropolitan Museum of Art presented an exhibit called "Camp: Notes on Fashion." The exhibition catalog featured Philip Core's 1984 declaration, "Camp is the heroism of people not called upon to be heroes."[2] One route to understanding Sendak's evolving tone by the 1960s is to examine his interaction with the sensibility of "Camp," which Susan Sontag made most famous in a 1964 essay. Though Sendak's work is generally more grim and Romantic than "campy," it drew on Camp strategies, which Sontag characterized as a "love for human nature" that "relishes, rather than judges, the little triumphs and awkward absurdities of 'character,'" including discarded artifacts of popular culture and of sentimental collective memory.[3] Camp "sees everything in quotation marks. It's not a lamp, but a 'lamp'; not a woman, but a 'woman.'"[4] Camp allows one to espouse larger-than-life emotions, characters, and states of extremity but without the usual social repercussions. As Sontag writes, it is a "sensibility of failed seriousness, of the theatricalization of experience," and it "refuses both the harmonies of traditional seriousness, and the risks of fully identifying with extreme states of feeling."[5] Camp also celebrates artifice, exaggeration, and the unnatural for the edification of a knowing group of insiders, whether ironically or nostalgically. It takes the cool, cutting wit of the nineteenth-century dandy and adjusts it to the "low culture" of mass production and consumption—in Sendak's case, to ethnically marginal and otherwise queer children playacting Hollywood films and comic-book heroes on the street. Thus Camp is a theatrical "modern dandyism," building on the cynically witty and highly stylized culture of Oscar Wilde, whose "Happy Prince" Sendak once loved and privately illustrated as a teenager, and who famously characterized art as "a lie that tells the truth." Camp transforms the old dandy's classist snobbery and moral superiority into values of self-indulgence, aesthetic illusion, and pleasure.

In 1960 Sendak published a picture book about a neighborhood queen of Camp, the muse who'd first inspired his drawings of children in the 1940s. Initially titled *Alinda the Lost Girl*, it was published as *The Sign on Rosie's Door* (1960).[6] The book stars Rosie, a dramatic child with a proclivity for borrowing different selves as a means of fighting off feelings of insignificance, loneliness, and boredom.[7] The archetypal theater artist, Rosie both coerced and delighted her peers by imagining characters and scenarios for them to enact—outlets for demoralized or lost children to spiritually unleash themselves. Sendak aimed to show how children suffered emotional voids in a normalizing, commercialized society of escapism, whose meanings are largely determined by preoccupied, inconsistently available adults. "Camp" and self-made fantasy serve these children as defenses and as generative survival strategies. Rosie's mother, for example, is usually depicted from behind as a faceless figure doing the dishes, like Martin's mother in *Very Far Away*, who is "busy washing the baby" and does not hear Martin's pressing questions, leading him to disguise himself in cowboy clothes and a false mustache and to run away in search of a place where he is not ignored. While Kenny of *Kenny's Window* (1956) had struggled with confusion and Martin with frustration, Rosie combatted "boredom and a sense of personal inadequacy." Evaluating these child creations, the artist would conclude, "On the whole they are a serious lot." But Rosie's theatrical, flamboyant techniques for warding off loneliness and obscurity inaugurated a new sort of child protagonist for Sendak. These children, he explained, "all have the same need to master the uncontrollable and frightening aspects of their lives, and they all turn to fantasy to accomplish this."[8] These child heroes of the latter twentieth century exhibit Romantic flamboyance, monstrosity, and stardom with passion and heightened investment in their feelings, even as they flounder. They do so as children of the social liberation eras immersed in aesthetic and cultural tones that Sendak recycled from his own interwar childhood, with its fast-paced, spectacle-driven ethos of consumerism, early Hollywood, comic books, and advertising.

In *The Sign on Rosie's Door*, Rosie exudes the stylized, awkward triumph of Camp. Lonely and constrained, she fashions her mother's discarded dress, an oversized hat, and a black feather boa into a showy sort of "drag" to entice others with an inventive, farcically exaggerated performance. After announcing with pomp that she is "Alinda, the lovely lady singer," she is promptly overshadowed and abandoned by the other children. Eliciting pity and humor simultaneously, the colorful Rosie improvises by transforming instantly into a "lost girl," waiting with a blanket over her head for her best friend, "Magic Man," who will tell her who she is and what she should do. Rosie may be lost, but it is this very quality—her undefined, boundlessly experimental agency, even in moments of degradation—that positions her as a creative icon and leader among her peers. Her alignment with what Sontag lists as the "exaggerated, the fantastic, the passionate, and the naïve" values of Camp, allows her to "dethrone the serious," to diffuse tragedy with style, theatricality, and frivolity.[9] Rosie is self-absorbed, as physically suggested by the way she refuses to let others steal the spotlight, and the way she sits outside with a red blanket wrapped over her head, announcing that she is waiting to find herself. But she is also motivated, creatively driven by her own need to matter. The neighborhood children turn to Rosie to save them from their boredom and lack of direction. When they are not allowed to play with dangerous firecrackers on the fourth of July, for example, Rosie ignites their imagination by proclaiming that Magic Man has given her the power to *become* a "big red firecracker" and that the other children may become "little silver firecrackers!" Fusing into the forbidden object of their desire, the children satisfy their emotional needs through creative improvisation. The book closes with Rosie switching places with her cat Buttermilk at bedtime. Not ready to leave fantasy behind, she curls up to sleep on the floor, her cat tucked under the covers of Rosie's bed.

Two years later, Sendak also channeled Camp in *The Nutshell Library* (1962), introducing a family of alligators who engage in exaggerated behaviors following each letter of the alphabet. A group of children in this collection romp through New York's brownstones and outdoor delights across the months of the year, watering flowers with chicken soup in June, *becoming* a pot of chicken soup in steamy August, and transforming into Christmas trees adorned with soup bowls in December. *In the Night Kitchen* (1970) would also recycle family imagery and "low culture" icons, like Mickey Mouse and the comic strips of Winsor McCay, and discarded cultural references, such as Oliver Hardy, whose countenance manifests as three bakers who sing and dance amidst a skyline of oversized, branded kitchen products. Creating his own repository of sentimental, antique treasures, Sendak amassed a major collection of early Mickey Mouse paraphernalia for his studio to help him remember the emotional tone of interwar-era cartoons.[10]

In *Really Rosie*, the 1975 CBS-network animated special based on both *The Sign on Rosie's Door* and *The Nutshell Library* books, with lyrics and music by popular musician Carole King, Rosie appears even campier than in her first iteration, her voice now audibly commanding the other children, "Believe me!"[11] Though the other children mock Rosie's unusual antics, she pays them no apparent heed. Instead, she shakes her hips, closes her eyes, and unflinchingly declares, "Yes! My name is *Rosie. I am a star*! I'm *famous*, and *wonderful*, and everybody loves me and wants to be *me*. Who can blame them?" Capturing her peers' interest for a time, Rosie plays at directing and starring in a "movie" she declares will be all about her life. As a "director," she must respond to the actors' desires, and she must learn to accept that they will abandon her fantasy by the time their mothers call for dinner. The nostalgic mingles with the ridiculous here, with Rosie introducing her little brother as "Chicken Soup," and Moby Dick appearing, as in the *Nutshell Library,* his blowhole "spouting chicken soup with rice."[12] Singing joyously about the endless virtues of this particular soup in a raucous musical number that traverses a colorful cityscape, Rosie and her friends helped Sendak to jab affectionately at his mother's tendency to offer chicken soup as a universal medicine for all ailments. "Chicken Soup with Rice," together with accompanying numbers like "Such Sufferin'," "One Was Johnny," and "Alligators All Around," produced a playful spectacle of nearly forgotten childhoods in which insiders and outsiders alike could revel. So appealing were Rosie's human plight and exaggerated antics that *Really Rosie* would find success as an off-Broadway stage musical in 1980 and again in 2017.

Beyond its celebrations of repurposed nostalgia, ironic artifice, and the excess of the unsung hero, Camp is also a strategy associated explicitly with queerness. As Sontag painted it, modern forms of Camp emerged as a sensibility of pre-Stonewall queer people forced to approach their lives as an elaborate, extended game of role-play within a culture hostile to the truths of atypical gender identities and sexualities. In Scott Long's understanding, Camp offered some protection against homophobia, using performative means to turn a spectator's potentially hateful or violent reaction into an amused one.[13] Sendak too engaged in Camp through colorful, role-playing correspondences with friends, including the novelist Coleman Dowell, whose partner, Bertram Slaff, was Sendak's therapist decades earlier. He shocked, disarmed, and tickled such friends with his bawdy, creative sense of humor. He could shift seamlessly from playing the self-indulged diva to becoming the "dirty old man" or imitating a harried, Yiddish-inflected immigrant in a tone both affectionate and sardonic. The artist would also use "boytshik" or "dahlink" as pet names for younger friends and collaborators.[14] Despite the public's desire not to see Sendak's queerness, he eschewed the stereotypical emotional resolve and restraint of American masculinity ideals for most of his career, flamboyantly emulating children, women, and foreigners who inspired him—including his own Polish Jewish immigrant mother and relatives who migrated as interwar refugees—his "Wild Things."[15] Campy interactions helped Sendak refine and express the contours of his own complex subjectivity by playing exaggerated roles, as children and young people do to help them determine their identities amidst confusing social constraints. These imaginative friends participated with Sendak in trying on such stereotypical parts as the Slavic Romantic and the sexually liberated gay man free of shame or discretion.

Dowell, an ideal playmate for Sendak, was known to live for fantasy, youth, and the exploration of human sexuality. The novelist often lied about his humble, rural family background to project a cosmopolitan pedigree that matched his extravagant dinner parties, and he did everything "flamboyantly," turning a picnic supper into a "Calvary," a tea-party into "a martyrdom." He performed an exaggerated machismo, despite his feminine mannerisms and sexually submissive preferences. Eugene Hayworth writes that Dowell "sought out a series of uneducated, impoverished lovers, men he often paid for sexual favors" to counterbalance "the otherwise placid home life he shared with Bert."[16] Through flamboyant, imaginative banter with friends like Dowell, Sendak could play with the line between fantasy and reality, which seemed all the blurrier as the nation underwent sexual and cultural revolutions. He enjoyed what he called "cackling gossip" with fellow gay picturebook creator and dear friend James Marshall at "a table set brightly, exquisitely."[17] He also playacted in letters exchanged with Dowell, relieving himself of the limitations and pressures of his public image.[18] Sendak peppered his letters to Dowell with charming Yiddishisms and invitations for Dowell to describe his exploits with other men. While working on the text for *Night Kitchen*, the artist asked Dowell for ideas for words related to baking that he might use in the book, as well as details about Dowell's exploits on Shelter Island, where he vacationed and wrote.[19] Sendak ended another letter to Dowell with a sexually explicit compliment penned as though from *Night Kitchen*'s protagonist, Mickey, a stand-in for the seed of Sendak's own sensual self and its relegation, in a prejudiced world, to dream spaces.[20] The artist also sometimes played a Slavic Natasha character to Dowell's Aryan Max in a game of dramatic make-believe, drawing on the cultural differences of their backgrounds and jokingly submitting Natasha to the character performed by the Anglo-Saxon Dowell.[21]

Though Sendak was openly gay among his own friends and colleagues, his choice not to explicitly announce it to the popular media until 2008, after Glynn's death, related, in part, to his concern as a children's book artist about prejudicial public associations made between gay men and pedophilia—associations that prevented the public's desire to question the beloved artist's sexuality in the first place. In the privacy of his intimate correspondence with Dowell, however, the artist bit back against the unsubstantiated modern demonization of gay men as pedophiles. Together they playfully mocked the roles of ancient pederast and pupil on which Western civilization itself had ironically rested since the Greco-Roman era and which it had only in most recent decades projected onto the specific population of "homosexuals."[22] In February and March of 1971, Sendak jested in his letters to Dowell about seducing young people at his university talks and in other imagined spaces.[23] Switching into the complementary perspective of the receptive student, he expressed yearnings for a wise man who might arouse his mind from aimlessness into action.[24] As in other forms of fantasy play, Sendak found in role-play and sexually ironic conversation among confidantes a means of bridging the gaps in his subjectivity, finding company in his queer feelings, and easing the emotional dissonance of misrecognition by a homophobic public that sought to paint queer people as predators. All in all, however, Camp served serious and sensitive aims. Between and through the colorful banter, Sendak consoled and encouraged Dowell during his bouts of serious depression, as well as confessed his own spiritual restlessness and his challenges with boundaries in relationships, including his difficulty internalizing others' love.[25]

The Island of Fire and Wild Things

Sendak performed heterosexual bachelorhood for his family members, as well as for a twentieth-century public that, he felt, would cringe or anger at the idea of a gay children's book artist. One *New York Times* article, for example, painted him in terms of a stereotypical unmarried straight man who "copes with the intricacies of an elaborate kitchen as best he can. The bachelor has bought a beginner's cookbook that doesn't take for granted you know what a skillet is."[26] The fact that Sendak could neither drive nor cook did not hurt his public image as an eccentric, urban "bachelor" and "uncle." In a later article in *Parents Magazine*, he accounted for his own childlessness, explaining that his last name was Hebrew for "godfather," and describing himself as "the ultimate uncle . . . and a consummate watcher of children." Indeed, "Sendak" likely derives from "sandak" or "sandek," the medieval Ashkenazi term for a child's godfather, traditionally tasked with holding a male infant during his circumcision ceremony.[27] Sendak's *One Was Johnny* (1962) of his *Nutshell Library* collection, about a boy who "lived by himself / And liked it like that," also seems like the story of a young bachelor-in-the-making, but in actuality the artist had based Johnny on his partner, Glynn, who was a bookworm, even dedicating the book to him. Glynn had much to read in the 1960s, pursuing graduate studies in intellectual and art history at Columbia.[28] Sendak too may have felt like the reclusive Johnny who reads alone in his empty room. He had written to Nordstrom in 1961 that he had "the sense of having lived one's life so narrowly—with eyes and senses turned inward. An actual sense of the breadth of life does not exist in me. I am narrowly concerned with me. . . . All I will ever express will be the little I have gleaned of life for my own purposes. . . . My world is furniture-less. It is all feeling." Nordstrom's reply sought to reassure him: "Yes, you did live 'with eyes and senses turned inward' but you had to. Socrates said 'Know thyself.' And now you do know yourself better than you did, and your work is getting richer and deeper, and it has such an exciting, emotional quality."[29]

The artist continued to cultivate his idea for a story about a boy who chases wild horses, becomes the target of a wolf and other wild creatures, and eventually finds shelter on "Happy Island," where a bride and child await him. By the early 1960s, this sequence had evolved into a prose piece of approximately eight chapters. But Sendak was not satisfied with the piece, because it was too "sentimental." He rewrote the story as a concise poem, "very abrupt and quick. . . . Very tight and very immediate, and very breathless, like . . . a child chanting . . . or fantasizing to himself."[30] He first considered naming the protagonist Johnny, then Kenny.[31] The project really took off after Sendak discovered Fire Island. His friend Amos Vogel, who had fled Nazi Austria as a child and would co-found the New York Film Festival, invited Sendak to rent an island home in the Seaview neighborhood on Beachwold Avenue ("B Street") near his own.[32] Vogel bonded with the artist over their European heritage and their interests in literature, art, and music. They laughed about life and enjoyed the free-flowing culture of the beach. Amos and Maurice, as well as their partners, Marcia and Eugene, were part of a Greenwich Village social circle that included *Village Voice* columnist Nat Hentoff and his wife, Margot. Intimate friends with a taste for counterculture, the three couples referred to their group as "the Nintimates," celebrating the freedom and creativity afforded to them on the island, where one wore less clothing and could spend uninterrupted hours sketching, writing, resting, and talking in the open air, with less inhibition.[33] Photographs of the Nintimates on the island show the group piled together in the sand, Eugene reclining on Marcia, his head thrown back in wide-mouthed laughter; Sendak, smiling with a cigarette, lounges behind him in a swimsuit.[34] As the latter came further into himself as an artist and as a gay man, Fire Island became the "Happy Island" he had first imagined as a heterosexual family realm in his wild horses story several years prior. Eric Pederson, who later befriended Sendak and worked as his assistant at Harper, believes that the artist suffered persistent fears and insecurities in the wider public sphere, especially beyond New York, and that he felt particularly safe on Fire Island, not only as a gay man but also as a Jew.[35] Sendak began a habit of staying on the island in the warmer months for weeks at a time, beginning in the early 1960s. Rather than staying in Cherry Grove or the Pines—which have been famous as gay spaces of liberation since at least the 1950s—Sendak chose to stay further west where he could more easily rest and write. Sometimes he resided in the Seaview neighborhood, known as the Jewish family area, where acclaimed writer Herman Wouk had co-founded an Orthodox synagogue in 1952 in his home with a Rabbi Adrian Skydell, importing a Torah scroll from the Conservative congregation of Long Island's Bay Shore community.[36] While writing in that neighborhood one summer, Sendak's wild horses poem transformed into what would become one of the most beloved works of children's literature: *Where the Wild Things Are*, whose text Sendak claimed to write in a single hour.

The project went on hold again as Sendak illustrated several other books, including Vogel's *How Little Lori Visited Times Square*, a humorous story that similarly follows a boy, named after Vogel's son Loring ("Lori"), who gets lost on a solitary outside quest. Among Lori's toy collection, Sendak featured the soldiers and model train from *Kenny's Window*. On the cover of the published version of *Little Lori*, Lori appears with a pigeon on his head, the frontispiece featuring him in a helicopter on which three additional pigeons perch. The artist once again expressed an urban child's need for flight and coincidentally honored Vogel's surname, German for "bird." Wild horses continued, however, to leap through the artist's mind as he worked on this project in early 1963. In the upper margins of one penciled draft page for *Little Lori*, Sendak rendered them galloping in blue ink. It might have been at this very moment that the horses became "things," Sendak deciding that he was no good at drawing horses. On May 25, 1963, he finished a dummy in which Max wears a wolf suit, and the "Wild Things" look like lions, horned bears, goats, and griffins. These creatures teach Max "many new wild ways" but ultimately do not love him "best of all," failing to "show him how to call long distance," thus preventing him from reaching his abandoned parents. In this version, the child estranged by his emotional storm becomes the lone wolf who had chased him in the original dummy.[37] Max's wolf suit recalls both the pajamas of the "lost boys" in Disney's film *Peter Pan* (1953) and the hooded donkey costumes used in the woodcuts of Sebastian Brant's fifteenth-century *Das Narren-schiff* (Ship of Fools).[38]

Writing on an island famous for its sexually liberated enclaves, Sendak conceived of a rumpus of Wild Things whose depictions would draw from his disheveled immigrant relatives. He would illustrate the rumpus as an energetic gathering that begins at night among the trees, ending in the morning light, Max and the Wild Things swinging satisfied from branches suspended over leaves that look like puckered lips in profile, or fleshy crevices. If sexual associations were not clear at the time of publication, they became distinct in the book's afterlife, in which the artist repeatedly referred to Max's rumpus as an "orgy." Sendak would end his 1996 commencement address to Vassar College's graduating class by exclaiming, "And when the hard work is done, have safe sex and let the wild rumpus begin!"[39] Stephen Colbert would flatly ask the artist in January 2012, "is 'rumpus' sex?," to which Sendak would playfully reply, "Sure. Yes. The whole bed going up and down . . . and being happy."[40] Similarly, Sendak would later describe the rebellious, party-throwing protagonist of his *Bumble-Ardy* (2011) as engaging in an "orgy," like Max's rumpus, in order to test his limits and measure his own safety beyond the protection of his caretakers: "The orgy he has is a way of testing himself. How much can he resist? How much can he understand? How much can he live through?"[41] Like the drag balls of Fire Island, Bumble-Ardy's ninth birthday party would be a secret masquerade of pigs who don extravagant costumes that range from the beaked masks of medieval Italy to the cowboy regalia of country western films and the fur-trimmed dresses of the 1930s and 1940s.

Sendak would disappear to Fire Island for weeks or months at a time during summers and sometimes autumns in the 1960s to write and dream and decompress from obligations of a fast-paced public sphere in which he managed his famous persona.[42] This tendency reflected a trend among queer people of his social orbit of retreating to gay-friendly islands and beach towns. Dowell and Slaff, for example, bought a home in 1968 in Shelter Island's Harbor View neighborhood, which was known as the summer residence of several prominent gay and lesbian couples. For eight years, Dowell spent most of his time on that island, Slaff joining him on weekends. He wrote to Sendak in the late 1960s about his emotional isolation and sexual exploits there, also basing his novel *Island People* (1976) on these experiences.[43] Though relatively shy beyond his close circles and not one for heavy drinking, it's likely that Sendak too explored both literary and queer spaces during his island retreats. His snarkier correspondences cast a critical eye on both the partygoers and the less glamorous bathers. In a letter from July 1967, for example, he told cartoonist Jules Feiffer and his wife, Judith, that Seaview was overrun by *yentes*. The letter included a drawing of Sendak as one of the Wild Things with a bewildered expression, sitting in the sand beside the bones of a dead fish, an older woman in a bikini passing in the distance. Sendak became more focused on his own fitness and physical appearance in those years, writing to Selma Lanes in March 1968, for example, that he was smoking less and dieting.[44] Two months later, he wrote to his friend Mary Jarrell that he was growing out his sideburns and that he had started to run at the YMCA, noting a decrease in his waistline and a flatter stomach.[45] To his friend and former lover, Leroy Richmond, the artist painted a picturesque vision of his lifestyle on the island, writing in August 1966 about reading Kafka on the beach and tanning his body in the sun.[46]

Though Sendak often resided in the Seaview and Ocean Beach neighborhoods while on the island, he must have also visited Cherry Grove and the Pines, neighborhoods known for their LGBTQ communities. Shel Silverstein recalled speaking with him in Cherry Grove in 1965 while the former collected notes for a cartoon travelogue for *Playboy* Magazine. The travelogue appeared with the title, "Silverstein on Fire Island: foot-loose Shel visits the gay side of Gotham's offshore bohemia— where the fruits are unforbidden."[47] The vignettes playfully explore the island neighborhoods' gay flirtations, social life, and drag culture. Silverstein, who later asked Sendak to illustrate his *Where the Sidewalk Ends* to no avail, conveyed the liberating dimension of Cherry Grove in the early years of the gay liberation movement:

> In the last few years homosexuality as a social phenomenon has emerged from the shadows, to the extent that today there are clearly

recognized gay enclaves in most big cities. . . . Here, sans stares, homosexuals of every stripe gayly enjoy the amenities of a thriving vacation community. And here, through this summer fairyland, strolled our
straight John, bewhiskered, bare-pated and bewildered, recording for
posterity his walk on the Wilde side.[48]

Drawing attention both to the heavy Jewish presence on the island and
to the controversy of that fact for the twentieth-century Jewish family, Silverstein sketched two women in bed, one answering her mother's
phone call: "No . . . I didn't take my pink chiffon gown, because I don't
have any use for it here. . . . Well, sure, Mom . . . sure there are lots of
nice Jewish boys around, but. . . . " Another cartoon, narrated by a male
drag artist, conveys a culture of fluid gender expression:

> I'm relaxing in my cottage yesterday afternoon, when the doorbell
> rings—and me—thinking it's Philip, I run and put on my best cologne,
> I put on my garter belt, I put on my nylons and spike heels, I put on my
> black negligee, I put on my wig and make-up, and I run to the window
> and peek out—and it's my *parents*!! So I run back into the other room, I
> wipe off my make-up, . . . put on a pair of blue jeans, a flannel shirt and a
> pair of loafers, and run back to the door.[49]

Not a far cry from the theatrics of Sendak's Rosie, inhabitants of the
island's gay enclaves enjoyed a rare context in which certain social stig-
mas were normalized and even celebrated as avant-garde creativity or
as a subversive social statement.

In the wider culture of the 1960s, however, journalists and politicians painted queer people as tragically lost in fantasies of youth and
glamour, refusing to "grow up." Popular conceptions of homosexuality
at the time critically emphasize child's play and disguise. Midge Decter, a heterosexual writer who frequented Fire Island's mostly gay Pines
neighborhood in the 1960s, recalled gay men "taken up with various
forms of play," which included "great elaborate celebrations, costume
balls" colored by "a fierce social competitiveness" and contempt for
the entrapments of and mundane burdens of heterosexual family life.
Noting their hairless bodies on the beach and their playful, competitive

creativity, she concluded that "the reigning homosexual fashion" was based on "the worship of youth—youth understood not even as young manhood but rather boyhood."[50] Even Sontag explicitly connected the queerness of Camp with the value gay men placed on youth, writing, "The Camp insistence on not being 'serious,' on playing, also connects with the homosexual's desire to remain youthful."[51]

While these writers identified certain superficial aspects of gay male culture, they failed to grasp the underlying meaning of youthful appearances for the queer subjects they scrutinized. Idealizing "boyhood" or youth, more generally, was not a predatory or delusional stance but a means to find vitality and beauty in a life at odds with the socially available options for "growing up" in a conservative society, which had required adherence to traditional notions of gender, heterosexuality, and bourgeois family structures. In a context that imposed conformity to those models and forbade alternative ways of loving or being, to "grow up" might have actually meant, for a queer person, either to lie and conform or to disappear.[52] Is it a surprise, then, that queer people preferred styles associated with a stage of life situated *before* sexual maturation and mandatory heterosexual development? At a time preceding gay rights or positive cultural recognition, "growing up" for a gay person meant forcing oneself to deny one's physical drives and emotional orientations. Thus queer rejections of the expected adult roles that required one to remain closeted were not "immaturity" but rather creative acts of self-defense, self-preservation, and communal searching in response to the lack of understanding one received in the wider culture. As Decter herself was aware, before the 1970s, gay men "lived in a rather different relation to, say, the police than we [heterosexuals] did. Any one of them, caught in the wrong attitude in the wrong bar in the wrong neighborhood on the wrong night, might be subjected to humiliations that no record of good citizenship and no amount of high position in society would protect him from." Cherry Grove and the Pines, then, were a valued respite from a daily existence in which queer people were barred from desirable housing and certain professions, socially shamed, and forced into lives of secrecy in order to survive.[53]

Social commentary about queer performance and disguise in the 1960s and 1970s also reflects the homophobic, misogynist, and antisemitic claims of the early twentieth century. Havelock Ellis had written in 1900, for example, that the "dramatic and artistic aptitudes of inverts are . . . partly due to the circumstances of the invert's life, which render him necessarily an actor—and in some few cases lead him into a love of deception comparable with that of a hysterical woman—and partly, it is probable, to a congenital nervous predisposition allied to the predisposition to inversion."[54] Alisa Solomon also notes that "anti-Semitic and homophobic rhetoric warned of the Jew's and homosexual's predatory ability to pass unnoticed, to masquerade as 'normal,' and characterized dissembling itself—a propensity for *acting*—as an inborn attribute of Jews and of queers."[55] Creative artists, stigmatized individuals, and children alike all regularly employ strategies of disguise and play used by outsiders who learn to "pass" for their survival. To varying degrees, children all begin, like these stereotypes of women, Jews, and queers, as developmentally vulnerable, "congenitally nervous" beings in a world in which power resides beyond their grasp. This is perhaps especially true of those children born within oppressed or culturally marginal families. Those youth forbidden from adult society without first changing or hiding who they are, are thus known to become "actors"—a feat that garners both fascination and pathologization. This predicament is what Eve Kosofsky Sedgwick has dubbed the "double bind" of the subject endangered both by exposure and by hiding—a predicament familiar to Jewish and queer histories alike.[56] Sendak, in using the form of the children's book to write "not for children" but for himself, conveyed the synergy that exists between children, artists, and other cultural outsiders. All learn to cultivate the modernist ability to be of (at least) two minds, to transcend any singular perspective of reality that may isolate or entrap.

Psychoanalysis, of course, insists that any given subjectivity is inherently always divided, an interplay that includes submerged unconscious feelings and desires. In the neo-Freudian era of childrearing that also popularized talk therapy, Kenneth Kidd demonstrates, Sendak's achievement came not only from his own genius but also from his sophisticated use of psychological concepts. The artist rewrote Freudian analysis while making it "more palatably American."[57] Sendak's exposure to psychoanalytic ideas came from his own years in therapy, from Glynn, and from Nordstrom, who, as Kidd writes, mentored Harper's illustrators in conveying their deep feelings and frequently joked with them about picture books' "psychotherapeutic power."[58] Accordingly, Sendak's language is often strikingly psychoanalytic in his discussions of art and process. Merging uncomfortably separate facets of his identity, his work contains ingredients that mix to produce a flavor at once American, queer, and Old World. These facets of identity waver between the space of a "normal" home and the wild emotion of a subjugated realm that is, like the psychoanalytic "id," always also connected. Readers of all ages appreciate the artistic depth, specificity, and serious psychological discipline evident in a Sendak book, which works through tangles of real social and emotional predicaments in layered ways. Sendak's articulation of his own multiplicity has forever raised the stakes of the picture book and of children's literature as a whole.

Stigma and Buried Meanings

It would be inaccurate to paint midcentury America as a context completely devoid of queer vitality or to suggest that no LGBTQ individuals of the time led fulfilling lives.[59] Despite pervasive prejudice, George Chauncey argues, queer people maintained dual realities, resisting the shame imposed on them. Their diaries from those years reveal detailed, exuberant accounts of their erotic experiences. Some of Sendak's friends participated in what Chauncey describes as "a vast underground of cruising areas and public sex venues in urban streets, parks, subway cars, and tearooms, not to mention the standing-room section of New York's Metropolitan Opera and well-known men's rooms in department stores and university buildings across the country."[60] In a book published in 1963, the same year as *Wild Things*, sociologist Erving Goffman wrote of stigmatized individuals who suffer a "secret differentness." Having learned that the "normal point of view" disqualifies them, they learn to pass in secrecy, navigating three types of spatial contexts: "forbidden" places in which "exposure means expulsion," "civil" places in which public manners obstruct others' underlying prejudice, and "back" places—like Cherry Grove or the theater—in which concealment

is unnecessary and secret differentness might even be indulged or celebrated. A contemporary of Sendak's who stemmed also from an Eastern
European Jewish family, Goffman included homosexuals, mentally
disabled people, sex workers, and addicts among his examples.[61] He asserted that these stigmatized individuals anxiously managed lives that
could be "collapsed at any moment."[62] Perceiving and articulating feelings within multiple simultaneous registers, stigmatized subjects find
themselves at odds with the demands of the social status quo, which
prefers that human beings fit within straightforward categories, bina-
ries, and hierarchies. A subject who resists such assimilation, even if
only partially, grows along creative pathways. By refusing to conform
and holding fast to "outside" or "submerged" meanings, this subject may
consequentially expose hidden truths that both clarify and propel social
structures within the blind spots of dominant "reason." In this regard
we can understand literary critic George Steiner's observation in 1983
that "[t]here is simply no counterpart in mathematics, or physics or as-
tronomy or engineering to set beside the high catalogue of homosexual
poets, novelists, plastic artists, composers, aesthetes and thinkers," or
the proverbial adage that "Jews are like other people, only more so."[63]

Historically speaking, children might have also belonged in Goffman's list of social groups stigmatized in public life, at least prior to
the solidification of modern childhood, which sanctioned a shielded,
diminutive place for minors within the wider society. Sendak sensed a
synergy between his own stigmatized identity and that of children, to
whom he could speak more relevantly and passionately than to adults.
He once stated, "[C]hildren read the internal meanings of everything.
It's only adults who read the top layer most of the time. . . . Children
know that there are mothers who abandon their children, emotionally
if not literally. . . . They don't lie to themselves. They wouldn't survive
if they did. My object is never to lie to them."[64] The artist saw more
freedom in creating the sort of work that children consumed, because
"when you write for children you don't limit yourself; there's no need
to. They know everything. Or they sense so many things that, as adults,
we presume they don't know or don't sense."[65] Traversing the liminal
spaces between private and public, particular and universal, sensory

and civil, children, like stigmatized subjects and artists, often lack the luxury of an empowered social position yet sustain a faculty of human insight unimaginable to those who easily and publicly belong.

Goffman's analysis of stigma speaks to understandings of what illustrators and theater artists do and why they are often socially marginal. He described situations in which human beings grow under pressure to *maintain* a flexible, in some ways child-like plasticity, an ability to shift between realities and to intuit social cues that are not important to other adults.[66] He paints socially stigmatized adults as masking their difference and studying realities that most people mindlessly accept and take for granted. Such subjects scan for and predict various possible outcomes in any given situation, and they analyze social dynamics for multiple meanings and contextual clues of how they might be allowed to behave, and what they may be allowed to reveal about themselves. Likewise, Tony Kushner links the lack of social respectability given to illustrators and theater artists with the focus in those professions on reading between the lines of concrete realities and conjuring buried elements and associations. Both professions aim to disrupt "the silent literary dyad of writer and reader" to excavate and animate meanings buried within the language of a text.[67]

Sendak identified with the marginality of illustration and the theatrical arts, seeking to express himself so fully and profoundly within those fields as to elevate the fields themselves. The disruptive nature of the illustrator's and theater artist's role coalesced with his sense of existing socially "apart" and "in between." He felt that a good illustrator, like a psychoanalyst, reads the emotional meanings hidden beneath the surface of the text, rather than merely depicting the text literally. Thus, when illustrating others' work, Sendak saw himself as one who interrupted and expanded the words on the page, like a director or actor bringing a script to life. Theatricality was a central feature of his process, and sensibilities of the theater pervade his picture books. The artist described, for example, approaching the picture book form as a "tabletop theater," a fantastical space that drew on children's impulse to improvise and reinvent themselves, as he and his siblings did in performances for their relatives.[68] For example, his *Higglety Pigglety Pop!*

or There Must Be More To Life (1967) follows a protagonist to stardom on the stage of the "World Mother Goose Theatre," where she performs a range of experiences from playing dead to affronting a lion. "The pictures," Sendak said of his books, "are like the operatic stage, and the words are the orchestral accompaniment."[69] The act of fantasizing and playing farcically dramatic roles offered Sendak a cathartic wholeness and connectedness to his surroundings; it prompted him to step *beyond* his conceptions of himself, committing to the performance of other selves. Recognizing the relativity and flexibility of the self as an ongoing and ever-changing performance offered comfort to a subject made to feel consistently incoherent and unduly ashamed within prevailing social structures. Disguises and carnivalesque scenes in Sendak's work express an ironic knowledge of the unreliability of appearances and of the questionable, constructed nature of any dictated reality. Sendak's protagonists use costumes to convey the transformative potential of creative play as a universal value most clearly expressed in childhood dress-up. Martin, Rosie, Max, Mickey, Ida, and Bumble-Ardy all captivate through uses of clothing, props, and make-believe.

More personally, Sendak's work in the latter twentieth century conveys a struggle to preserve and express his own embodied relationship, both generally and as a gay man, with a specific Jewish cultural past. This was a past laden with collective and personal traumas, characteristic types and personas, and traditions carried into an American social reality that threatened to neutralize those elements through assimilation. Three years after *Fiddler On the Roof* opened on Broadway, Sendak's *Higglety Pigglety Pop!* placed the label "Ketzle & Company" on a milk wagon modeled after a favorite toy given to him by his Aunt Esther and also reminiscent of popular Old World depictions. *Ketzele*, meaning "kitten" in Yiddish, was a pet name that Philip used for Sendak as a boy. Consciously or not, presenting this private Yiddish name on a milk wagon offers a decidedly queer gloss. In Yiddish, to call a man *milkhik* (dairy based), signifies that he is the opposite of *fleyshik* (meaty), which can imply that he is emasculated, as in the case of the text that inspired *Fiddler*—Sholem Aleichem's "Tevye der Milkhiker" (Tevye the dairyman).[70] Tevye, whose masculinity is already playfully critiqued by his position as a dairyman, directly queers himself in the text by comparing himself to an abandoned mother hen, and one who hatches *ducklings* who swim away, rather than chicks who remain—a metaphor to cope with the loss of his beloved daughters as they mature and leave him to claim their own lives and embrace the attractions of modernity.[71] In Sendak's story of his own dog Jennie, who flees her human parent, the "Ketzle" [*sic*] milk wagon stands against a building labeled "Glynn," thus connecting a Yiddish-infused heritage with the artist's own same-sex relationship.[72] Here the artist blended his family's Yiddishkeit with subtle queer confessionalism in a story about parent-child separation and the finding of one's self on the theatrical stage of the World Mother Goose Theatre, an imaginary stage that, he claimed, took inspiration from Kafka's "Nature Theater of Oklahoma" in the latter's story *Amerika*.[73]

Theatrical devices thus helped Sendak resist uncomfortable internal clashes related to his ethnic and social positions. It offered Sendak a means of honoring his emotional truth-seeking and Old World identifications. Sometimes a shift in chronological era, for example, allowed characters to more seamlessly perform moods associated with another place or time. Shifting away from mainstream, twentieth-century American cultural norms, Sendak exalted children who play the parts of royalty, nobility, monstrosity, and celebrity with passion and emotional seriousness. Peter Dobrin described Sendak as an unusual artist for being engaged simultaneously in contemporary social concerns and nineteenth-century aesthetic and literary forms.[74] Since the late 1950s, his intricate cross-hatching and somewhat sentimental depictions of early modern and Victorian settings, as in his drawings for Else Minarik's *Little Bear* series (1957–68), departed from the splashes of color and futuristic abstraction that were in vogue at the time.

Beyond his picture books, Sendak's "second career" in the performing arts, beginning in the 1970s, allowed the artist to devise larger-scale sets and costumes for opera, theater, and dance productions. As Tony Kushner writes, this work drew from Sendak's own memories of "stoopside theatrics, the intense drama of a childhood lived in an urban neighborhood, in public, on the concrete stages that are New York City sidewalks, the grandiosity and the opulent imagination that arise in counterpoint to the poverty and deprivations of working-class life."[75] Children of Jewish immigrant households like Sendak had experience playing two roles as Jews and Americans, as well as navigating urban landscapes studded with the illusions and deceptions of advertising and department store windows, drawing on linguistic phrases and emotional styles that their parents may not have understood or accepted.[76] To varying extents, the world of theater, dance, and opera—like the field of children's literature—has historically functioned as a "back" space, to use Goffman's term, in which queer and ethnically marginal identities flourished since before the turn of the century, at least behind the scenes. With the broader American cultural establishment theatricalizing "ethnic revival" by the 1960 and 1970s, the mainstream welcomed explorations of new aesthetic and social possibilities beyond Anglo Saxon Protestant ideals, presenting minority cultures for public consumption. Nordstrom wrote to Sendak in 1971, "I think I am just about as Jewish as you are."[77] Four years later, Sendak's televised musical *Really Rosie* showcased Jewishness far more explicitly than the 1960 picture book on which it was based. As Leslie Tannenbaum notes, this animated Rosie, voiced by the Jewish Carole King, peppers her performance with an ironic, brash, subversive tone characteristic of Jewish female stars like Fanny Brice, Barbra Streisand, and Bette Midler. Tannenbaum even describes "The Ballad of Chicken Soup" as a *bobe mayse* and notes the exclamations of *oy vey* in Yiddish.[78] The 2017 off-Broadway production of *Really Rosie*, directed by Leigh Silverman, would further champion the spirit of Sendak's immigrant roots and his belief in the dreams of the disadvantaged. This performance would feature a cast reflective of New York's dynamic cultural landscape; a Black Rosie, Taylor Caldwell, would command a chorus of youth reflecting various ethnic backgrounds and a range of neurodiversity, including a young actor with Down syndrome.

Sendak would continue to channel forgotten Jewish personalities and archetypes throughout his career, describing the child protagonists of his *Some Swell Pup* (1976), for example, as "an aggressive and hysterical yenta" girl and a passive, "real *vaserdiker gornisht* type" boy.[79] Illustrating a group of tiny people described in his father's book, *In Grandpa's House*, he drew what Kushner believed were "memories of relatives and neighbors of Philip Sendak's generation, . . . malnourished homunculi."[80] Sendak's 1985 poster for the Jewish Book Council's Jewish Book Month would feature a dark-haired boy and girl with squinted eyes and prominent noses sitting on "Bernard" the Wild Thing, who holds an open book. Sometimes Sendak's draft work revealed even more explicit references to Jewish culture, such as the giant Gefilte Fish jar originally conceived in one of his *Night Kitchen* dummies, and the inclusion of "Sipurei Shalom Aleichem" (The stories of Sholem Aleichem) written in Hebrew along the book spine for a draft of the Jewish Book Month poster.[81] A far leap from the artist's earlier sentimental depictions of Jewish children for the ADL and United Synagogue Commission on Jewish Education in the 1950s, these images were unapologetically and subversively "ethnic," and audiences of the latter twentieth century relished in the vicarious opportunity to embrace the liberated, playful energy they conveyed. Against deep-seated pressures to disconnect from a heritage of Old World Jewish traditions, as well as from his own queer feelings as a sensitive, gay American, his theatricalizations preserve and integrate disparate, embodied investments, while also diffusing the weighty meanings connected to them in the spirit of social liberation.

Like other Jewish creatives before him, Sendak also followed a perennial impulse to comment playfully on mainstream Christian culture from an outsider's perspective. On the cover of *Rolling Stone*'s December 30, 1976, issue, two dark-haired Sendakian children with smug expressions would put their own stamp on the Christmas tradition, decorating "Moishe," one of the Wild Things, instead of a tree. A queer take on Christmas appears also in I. B. Singer's *Zlateh the Goat* collection (1966), which Sendak illustrated. In "Grandmother's Story" of that collection, a jolly, big-bellied devil arrives by sleigh during Hanukah with a bottomless purse, joined by a gang of "goblins in red caps and green boots." Sendak drew these goblins as tiny elves with the pointed hats of those so often depicted in Christmas folklore.[82] Years later, he was invited to enliven set and costume designs for the beloved Christmas ballet *The Nutcracker*, premiering in Seattle in 1983. These became the basis for his 1984 picture book based on E.T.A. Hoffman's original text, and they were used in a motion picture of the ballet directed by Carroll Ballard (1986). In this production, queerness and Jewishness offer visual signals of deeper thematic challenges intended by Sendak, who sought to dissolve the ballet's saccharine surfaces in order to reveal Hoffman's original brilliance. As Rachel Federman argues, Sendak and his collaborator, Kent Stowell, who directed the Pacific Northwest Ballet, revised the character of Clara, the protagonist, who is originally depicted as a young child, to present her instead as a prepubescent girl of twelve who becomes a grown woman after defiantly throwing her shoe at the mouse king. This revision reveals what Sendak viewed as the "throbbing, sexually alert" meanings embedded in Hoffman's original text. The artist also perceived *The Nutcracker* as a story about the suffering of the creative child, of the "artist in the family who puzzles the parents" and grows up feeling alone.[83] Likewise, other important characters in Sendak's rendition appear "strange," queer, or "other," but also as more impassioned and alive. The Nutcracker himself is reconceived as a squat figure with a pronounced hook nose and dark features, including giant bulging eyes. Drosselmeier, the story's genius inventor, dons drag, including Mother Ginger's mammoth dress, the black fur trim on his sleeves recalling Rosie's campy feather boa in *Really Rosie*. Like Sendak, whose own countenance appears caricatured in large scale on the show curtain as the face of a wooden nutcracker, Drosselmeier dominates the stage as a giant grandfather clock whose head crowns the proscenium arch, queering time and its age-based meanings.[84]

By dignifying children's emotions, even those that contemporary society associated with ethnic minorities or deemed queer, Sendak's work articulated a wider cultural shift. The patriarchal, institutional ethos of earlier decades increasingly faced emotionally attuned approaches that sought to empower those at the bottom and on the margins. This shift is clearly reflected in the history of American Judaism, as large institutional congregations and federations gave way to spiritual renewal, Havura, and do-it-yourself movements by the 1960s and 1970s. Titles like *Very Far Away* (1957), *The Sign on Rosie's Door* (1960), *Where the Wild Things Are* (1963), *In the Night Kitchen* (1970), and *Outside Over*

There (1981) all evoke the emotional journeying of alienated, devalued, or misunderstood children who, left in the figurative dark, depart into unknown territory on their own in order to solve the problem of emotionally existing and preserving self-worth in a fast-changing culture when adults do not see, understand, or care. They helped fill a need in the culture of the postwar decades, which hungered for a literature that would harness the materials of contemporary life into meaningful, positive values amidst the cynicism that followed generations of American acculturation and a magnitude of wartime destruction and loss.[85]

From Spotlight to Torchlight

Sendak's work in the latter twentieth century increasingly fought those social elements that alienated him from his own embodied feelings as a young child. As he'd long complained, "In most children's books in this country . . . you would never even know that children had normal bodily functions, because it's an unmentionable kind of thing. And children must think it very peculiar."[86] Against critics who saw *Wild Things* as inappropriate for children, he created *Hector Protector* (1965) as a "vendetta book." The artist admitted to consciously playing with the book's serpent images in suggestive ways. Tangled around Hector's sword in the shape of two coiled spheres, the snake's head lunges forward to emphasize the protagonist's phallic defiance. One young male reader sent a letter to the artist, asking, when I grow up will mine be as big as Hector's?[87]

Several years later, *Night Kitchen* became a similarly subversive account of children's awareness of the physical pleasures of which they are expected to pretend innocence, such as sexuality and the nocturnal amusements of urban life.[88] For his own gratification, Sendak infused the book with coded references to his own narrative battle of overcoming obstacles impeding his maturation. On one of the buildings of his kitchen cityscape, Sendak divided the word "trademark" into "Trade Mark," potentially referencing the name he sometimes used as a discreetly gay young man in Manhattan, qualified by the term "trade," which in gay slang refers to a straight-identified man who also engages sexually with other men. While working on the text for *Night Kitchen*,

Sendak wrote to Dowell, requesting in the same breath suggestions for words to use in the picture book, as well as details about Dowell's sexual exploits on Shelter Island.[89] Sendak finished the book in an apartment just a few short blocks from the Stonewall Inn as the gay liberation movement erupted. About a week after the Stonewall Riots, he created a dummy in which a naked Mickey displays what appears to be a full erection and cries "Cock-a-doodle-doo!" as he slides down the side of a giant bottle labeled "The Milky Way."[90] Never published, these rather explicit elements would be neutralized in later drawings, Mickey's penis shrunken and flaccid, the "Milky Way" label removed, and Mickey's arms now imitating rooster wings, rather than raised above his head. Speaking about the process of creating the book, which he described as a farewell to his own childhood, the artist declared, "I was now old enough to stay up at night and know what was happening in the Night Kitchen."[91]

In the wake of *Night Kitchen*, American attitudes moved to favor increased censorship in popular culture, as the nation negotiated definitions of decency following the liberal social revolutions of the 1960s. Without noting the personal references from Sendak's own life, critics deemed *Night Kitchen* an "inappropriate" urban fantasy of a naked boy mixing batter and spilling milk in the moonlight among men while his parents slept at home in ignorance. As one book review stated, "Something very sexy is going on in 'In the Night Kitchen.' . . . It celebrates eating and staying up late, and the child's voracious desire to participate in those grown-up activities."[92] Another review in *Elementary English* saw *Night Kitchen* as striking "a literary blow for the Kid Lib movement" in its invitation to "vicariously wallow nude in cake dough and skinny dip in milk."[93] Sendak's assistant Eric Pederson recalled a flood of letters from the Northwest disapproving of Mickey's nudity, as well as related hate mail throughout the artist's later years.[94] But Nordstrom stood by Sendak's decision to draw the protagonist, Mickey, in full-frontal nudity, because "the hero of a story about forbidden pleasures and the awakening sense of self needed to be naked."[95] She distributed a press release on June 9, 1972, comprising 425 signatures of professors, librarians, artists, authors, and publishers condemning librarians' censoring of Mickey's genitalia as artistic "mutilation," as it unfairly altered public engagement with the artist's original work. To one mutilating party, she would personally write in Sendak's defense, "Should not those of us who stand between the creative artist and the child be *very careful* not to sift our reactions to such books through our own adult prejudices and neuroses? . . . I think young children . . . will react *creatively* and *wholesomely*. It is only adults who ever feel threatened by Sendak's work" (Nordstrom's emphases).[96]

In 1973 the Supreme Court case of *Miller v. California* set the parameters for defining obscenity, and thus determining censorship guidelines. An obscene work, according to the Miller or "SLAPS" test, was one with an "indecent" main theme, a lack of serious artistic or societal value, and a perceived offensiveness by community standards.[97] Though never deemed legally obscene, *Night Kitchen* would be repeatedly challenged and banned in various American libraries. Sendak suffered those who deemed his work too frightening or sexual. "I have this idiot name tag," he would complain, "which says 'controversial.' . . . It's like Pavlov's dogs: Every time I do a book, they all carry on. It may be good for business, but it's tiresome for me."[98] Somewhat ironically, Sendak's choice to convey his creative vision through the emotional qualities of early childhood—its uninhibited rage, unabashed sensuality, and boundless self-indulgence—was exactly what led the adult artist to be named "inappropriate for children."

Fellow picture book artist Tomi Ungerer, an old friend of Sendak's known for children's books like *The Three Robbers* (1961), became a tragic warning to the artist about playing with the boundaries of "indecency" as the nation pushed back against the liberal movements of the 1960s. Once a beloved figure in the United States, Ungerer self-published works for mature audiences that destroyed his reputation in America as a children's artist and made him the object of scandal. These works included radical posters against the Vietnam War, controversial erotic drawings, and a satirical book called *The Underground Sketchbook*. Ungerer's children's books were then "virtually banished in the United States" in the early 1970s, banned from libraries and pushed out of print.[99] Unable to find work, he left the U.S. in 1971, later concluding,

"At that time, my European sensibilities weren't appreciated or un-derstood by the Americans."[100] In his old age, Sendak would sit with Ungerer on a bench outside the former's Connecticut home, and they would cry together over what had transpired.[101] Sendak would continue to fight for the cause of subversive artistic freedom in his own way. In the mid-1970s, anticipating negative criticism for choosing to depict the protagonist of Randell Jarrell's *Fly by Night* (1976) in the nude, Sendak would complain to a writer from *Rolling Stone*, "I had a picture show-ing a girl with her vagina in full view in *The Light Princess*, and nobody made a fuss about that, which makes me think that the whole world is male chauvinist—vaginas don't count."[102] Sendak would indeed receive the criticism he expected for depicting David nude in *Fly by Night*. John Updike would write, "The nudity is unspecified in the text but looms specific in Sendak's illustrations, one of which shows a prepubescent penis and another a rather inviting derriere."[103]

Even after achieving great fame, Sendak suffered social anxiety as he fought for his wild, but highly sensitive inner child against what he perceived to be an encroaching cultural wasteland of puritanism and capitalist greed, which placed profit and defensive patriarchal values above emotional truth-seeking. He would admit to Dowell that social grace did not come naturally to him, and that he struggled to speak can-didly with people about his real feelings.[104] According to Eric Pederson, who assisted Sendak in the late 1980s and early 1990s, the artist suf-fered an inferiority complex related to his background, never felt safe, and worried before each public-speaking engagement that the audience might perceive him as "just another Jew from New York City getting in their way."[105] As a sort of social enigma, he often conceived of him-self through metaphor. For example, reflecting the internalized stigma ascribed to his Jewish background and to his sexual orientation, he imagined himself as an ominous "bird of prey," a dangerous loner who collects and "steals" from different places to synthesize a new work of art, rather than inventing from scratch.[106] Birds have also long symbol-ized Jews in antisemitic rhetoric about the Jewish body, as "beaked" and flat-footed, and about the alleged Jewish temperament, as flighty and neurotic. Bernard Malamud's short story "The Jewbird" (1963), for example, relied on this motif the same year as *Wild Things*, depicting a Jewish crow named Schwartz who flees persecution and endlessly nags the human protagonist.[107] In *Fly by Night*, Sendak drew his nude child beneath the face of a giant owl who encompasses the entire sky—perhaps a stand-in for the artist himself. Years later he would make this visual association even more directly, painting his head on an eagle's body, for the frontispiece of *I Saw Esau* (1992), along with the book's authors and publisher.[108]

Being bird-like also suggested the generative, sometimes Camp tendency of finding nourishment in "waste," or making meaning of tragic pasts and of hostile associations made by others. Discussing his integration of painful family memories in his work, Sendak once declared, "I am like a vulture. . . . I will feed off these memories because that's the only way I can handle them."[109] The bird, as a symbol, connected the artist directly to his own family's obscured past. As he told *Rolling Stone*, "[B]irds were my father's favorite fairy tale symbol. He used to tell stories of birds taking children away. And I think that they enter into a lot of my things because it's an image of his that has always appealed to my heart."[110] Philip's stories might have drawn from the Abrahamic tradition in which birds symbolize divine redemption from bondage, as in God's address to Moses in the Book of Exodus, "You have seen what I did to the Egyptians, how I bore you on eagles' wings and brought you to Me."[111] Sendak from his earliest work merges children with birds in stories of fantasy and survival. *Night Kitchen* and *Fly by Night* both depicted naked children in flight. His *Fantasy Sketches* (1970), which he composed in a free-association manner while listening to music, also include children devouring and being devoured by birds, fish, and their parents.[112] Later, in his drawings for *Brundibar* (2003), children would fly on the backs of blackbirds; these birds are as threatening as they are liberating—they carry children away from the hunger and suffering of a wartime ghetto, but also, presumably, deliver these children to their deaths, as suggested by the text's dark lullaby and by the kerchiefed mothers weeping beneath them.[113] The drawings for *Fly by Night* had used a similar composition, with Sadie depicted in a pasture below the nude boy who floats into the owl-marked sky above her, suggesting a parent-child separation rooted specifically in the boy's emergent sexuality. Queer connotations of birds and flight are evident in the term *feygele* and in other references to birds that have signified homosexuality in both secular and Jewish contexts, especially when overt references to gay people were forbidden, as in film during the Hays Code.

Like J. M. Barrie's archetypal Peter Pan, Kathryn Bond Stockton argues, children play at merging with the animal world in order to grow "sideways," or even backward, rather than "upward" in the direction of social maturity, when the process of social maturation feels threatening, foreign, or overwhelming.[114] In Barrie's *The Little White Bird* (1902), the story that would inspire his *Peter Pan*, all children begin as birds before they are born. Thus Peter becomes birdlike and flies away in direct protest to the prospect of growing up.[115] Likewise, Sendak's children merge with animals when they feel lost or disconnected from their caretakers or the wider adult world. In *Brundibar*, a brother and sister physically transform into grizzly bears in their animal desperation to fight the bully who stands between them and the money needed to help their dying mother. In *Wild Things*, Max dresses in wolf pajamas and imagines a wilderness in his bedroom. Beyond childhood, the threat that a coercive socialization may imply for a sensitive or unusual subject may remain constant in adulthood within conformist cultures, a fact that reinforces the harmful idea that queer people, foreigners, and other stigmatized "outsiders" are somehow "immature" or "won't grow up."

Akin to Stockton's idea of "growing sideways," J. Jack Halberstam's notion of "queer time" responds to the impending threat of "no future," of potentially lacking the option to belong or to survive. Crystalized in the late twentieth century among gay men facing impending mortality during the AIDS crisis, "queer time" emphasizes a present-minded "urgency of being" that "squeezes new possibilities out of the time at hand."[116] Harnessing the strange boundlessness of child's play, Sendak resisted oppressive, socially imposed timelines to instead explore emotional realities of shamed and endangered subjects. Max sails "through night and day and in and out of weeks and almost over a year" on his imaginary journey to the Wild Things. In *Night Kitchen*, Mickey's story *begins* during bedtime. Children's fantasies rupture normative

temporality, but Sendak viewed them as "the normal and healthy outlet for corrosive emotions such as impotent frustration and rage; the
positive and appropriate channeling of overwhelming and, to the child,
inappropriate feelings."[117] Child's play bends time and space to suit the
demands of a given subjectivity as it grows and seeks coherence across
constricting or contradictory realities. Fantasy involves temporarily
shifting one's conscious social orientation and emotional position in the
service of exploring other roles and perspectives. Play may carry the
liberating capacity to diffuse feelings of being overwhelmed or incoherence within the confines of one's experience. When time and space
become plastic or fluid, they create "wiggle room" for expressing and
exploring tangled and suppressed elements of self. Creative personalities engage in play for these reasons, reaching possibilities beyond
normative ideas about time and space.

As Slaff would write, the creative personality has the unusual capacity "to bounce within the various time levels of his experience, actual,
imagined, past, present, or future. He is likely to be open intellectu-
ally and affectively."[118] Accordingly, Derick Dreher described Sendak
as "a nineteenth-century man who happened to live in the twentieth
and twenty-first centuries."[119] Sendak's prominent antiquarian side,
which prompted his collections of eighteenth- and early nineteenth-
century literature, gave him the appearance of one possessed by spirits
of another time.[120] Like a Victorian parlor, his duplex displayed various treasures, books, and old curiosities, with rows of first-edition
illustrated books from different eras, a hand-painted tin tray, seashells,
antiques, and blue-plate tiles.[121] Noting the contrast between the bustling Manhattan streets of the early 1970s and the dark stillness of
Sendak's Greenwich Village apartment, Muriel Harris described his
home as "a time tunnel" and "a fortress against any of today's distrac-
tions, a fortress for contemplation and immersion in one's work" with
books "lining walls, books lining staircases, books comfortably lying on
almost every step."[122] Indeed, the artist treated his home as a hideaway
from time and other strictures in which to grapple with his complex
inner life by traversing worlds, an occupation punctuated by outings to
Harper, book signings at the Strand, and work parties.

Much later, *Bumble-Ardy* (2011), the first picture book the artist would create after a seven-year break from the form, exemplifies the use of queer time to cope with feelings of misrecognition and endangerment. His return to the form reflected his desperation to use child's play as a means for healing the pain, guilt, and fear he experienced as Glynn lay dying of lung cancer. The artist would admit, "[T]hat amalgamation of emotions led me back to doing a book for children. . . . I had this little story in my head for a long time. I couldn't figure it out, I couldn't solve it. Then, during this horrendous time, I solved it. And it was like heaven sent to preoccupy me during a terrible, terrible, terrible time."[123] The protagonist of *Bumble-Ardy* exemplifies the notion of queer time when he promises his caretaker, Aunt Adeline, that he "won't ever turn ten"—this follows his breaking Adeline's rules, throwing himself a wild costume party for his ninth birthday. Guests arrive in a frenzy of fashion statements that blend history and collapse geography, drawn by Sendak in a mix of paints and crayon. Interspersed with skeleton imagery, the word "nine" appears graphically on banners and signs in Yiddish, Greek, Dutch, and Russian, like comic-book interjections reflecting the diversity of Ardy's guest list. Ultimately, Ardy realizes that his emotional development and reward must be suspended or channeled elsewhere if he is to sustain the love and protection of his caretaker, Adeline, who, with crazed, gaping eyes and an aggressively contorted face, wields a cleaver and threatens to slice his fantastical friends into ham. Ardy's parents, the reader learns, had met a similarly drastic end: they "gained weight. And got ate." Ardy's own safety requires maintaining his relationship with a dangerous caretaker with whom, he senses, he must "never turn ten." Ardy's predicament exemplifies Stockton's notion of queer childhood, with its "fascinating asynchronicities, its required self-ghosting measures, its appearance only after its death, and its frequent fallback onto metaphor (as a way to grasp itself)." Ardy, like Stockton's queer child, is made to identify his own dreams and desires as inherently forbidden and dangerous, experiencing childhood as "a frightening, heightened sense of growing toward a question mark. Or growing up in haze. Or hanging in suspense—even wishing time would stop, or just twist sideways, so that one wouldn't have to advance to new or further scenes of trouble."[124]

Like Martin in *Very Far Away*, Ardy dresses up as an American cowboy. But unlike Martin, who finds only a horse, a bird, and a cat for company and ultimately tires of them, Ardy hosts "orgiastic, crazy, fantastical creatures," as Sendak called them. They are a crowd of pigs, like Ardy, dressed as humans—including a wide-eyed infant with facial stubble, a feminine sheriff in a fur-trimmed purple dress with a sheriff's gold star, a Napoleon-like figure, and others in long-nosed Italian carnival masks. Ardy's promise to "never turn ten" explicitly protests the confined obedience his aunt expects of him, as well as slyly preserves the potential for queer pleasure: his promise implies that he will never grow up, not that he will never indulge his desires. Discussing *Bumble-Ardy*, Sendak stated that inspiration came from feeling unsafe as a child in a dangerous world with foreign parents who "knew nothing" about how to properly protect or guide him: "You had to form a kind of fake life, to protect yourself," he claimed.[125] During the creation of *Bumble-Ardy*, Sendak similarly sought emotional protection as Glynn faded away from him. Ardy drew also from the bravery of real children Sendak encountered in his own life. For example, a child cancer patient whom he met in a London hospital exemplified for the artist how disempowered people dramatize, pretend, and occupy multiple roles simultaneously to placate the emotions of powerful others, negotiating between authenticity and safety. Introduced to Sendak by her mother, the child patient had offered the artist a "chilly" welcome and answered his questions with shrugs. She then insulted the sketch that Sendak made for her alongside his autograph. As he recalled,

[She] murmured her astonishment that I drew so badly and couldn't possibly be the real illustrator. There was just a faint hint of comedy in her voice, and I snatched it up and said it was a portrait of her. She yielded finally and giggled and, as though by accident, leaned up against me. . . . I glanced at [her] mother and what I read in her face made me look quickly away. In her great dark, wet eyes, I read astonishment and wonder at her seemingly healthy, happy, clever girl so completely twisting me, the renowned artist, around her littlest finger. I read, too, the anguish of her knowing that this fine creature would soon die. Meanwhile, the girl laughed loudly, one arm encircling my neck. . . . She never looked at her mother. Her face was, so to speak, in mine, her eyes shining with pleasure, her touch affectionate and trusting. Her other arm . . . crept stealthily along the bed until it reached her mother's arm —it drifted down that mother's arm and gently, firmly clasped her hand. I watched. The clasp was tight, reassuring—it rocked the mother's hand gently, knowingly. "Knowingly" because she knew. The doctor confirmed this fact.[126]

Limits of Fantasy

Sendak believed that, despite children's proclivity for fantasy, "every child's dream" was ultimately "to survive and to become a grownup." Though he often jested that he was himself a child who had stopped growing, he usually did so in lamentation. "To be an adult and live in childhood," he once proclaimed, "is to inhabit a limbo land. Not a Peter Pan land, not a Disneyland. It is an eerie, truth-demanding land."[127] Working through fantasy was a serious means of survival, not an end in and of itself.[128] People like Sendak identified and desired in ways that made growing up particularly counterintuitive, isolating, and painful. Some of these individuals creatively pioneered new pathways into actualization and belonging. They also struggled to resist the temptation of "too much" fantasy, which might keep them victim to their own emotional storm, like Neverland's "lost boys" or the passengers on the metaphorical ship of fools—a position Sendak sought to escape in his own life, even as he recognized the importance of staying connected to that storm in the service of creating his truest work.

The artist would similarly comment on Rosie's insistence on remaining in fantasy, contrasting her with her fictional friend Kathy in *The Sign on Rosie's Door*, a well-adjusted child able to shift between fantasy and reality. Unlike Kathy, the price Rosie paid for remaining stuck in fantasy was perpetual loneliness, a problem she addressed by further escaping her social reality, becoming different characters, and even different animals.[129] Sendak perceived this problem even in the "real" Rosie, the child on whom Rosie was based. This child struggled madly to maintain the star role and to guard her creative control as other children offered competing ideas about what to do and how to play. Though she enchanted Sendak, she also ultimately disturbed him with what he perceived as her immense suffering—she seemed stuck in fantasy play, almost *losing* her humanity in her endless refusal of social reality, covering unhappiness and desperation with one-way departures into imagination.[130] He associated Rosie with a certain dramatic "type" of person he knew in his own life, including his own mother and her sisters. He described this "type" as narcissistic, unhappy, absorbed in sad things, crying, and prone to making dramatic scenes.[131] As chance would have it, he had crossed paths with the "real" Rosie while visiting Brooklyn in the late 1950s, years after he had sketched her as a child from his window. Noting the teenage Rosie's high heels and heavy makeup, and the lethargic manner with which she hung onto an unseemly man's arm, Sendak was overtaken with grief at what he perceived as evidence that his early muse had remained a victim of her fantasy play.[132] Rosie was a cautionary tale—a child lost on her own island. "Fantasy," Sendak would insist, "makes sense only if it's rooted ten feet deep in reality."[133] Fantasy disconnected from any real experience was vacuous, even dangerous.[134]

Dowell, for all his imaginative generosity, would also serve as a cautionary tale about how an alienated dreamer might disappear from "reality" without means of return. Succumbing to his emotional storm, Dowell isolated himself from others, including Sendak, and drowned himself in alcohol and compulsive sexual encounters. In the late 1970s, as the American mainstream began to wax conservative and retreat from social liberation movements, the novelist dove into written correspondences with incarcerated men whom he exoticized, conjuring fantasies of violent sexual union with them.[135] In 1985, overcome by his own loneliness and pain, he jumped from the window of the fifteenth-floor apartment he shared with Slaff.[136]

About a year after Dowell's suicide, Sendak reflected on his own relationship to fantasy: "Primarily, my work was an act of exorcism, an act of finding solutions so that I could have peace of mind and be an artist and function in the world as a human being and a man."[137] He described the act of making a picture book as "the only true happiness I ever, ever enjoyed in my life. . . . It's sublime. Where all your weaknesses of character and blemishes of personality and whatever else torments you fades away."[138] But creativity did not always succeed in exorcising unwanted elements of the artist's subjectivity. In a 1977 article, Glynn wrote that because art does not actually transform the self or restore the dead, an artist's internal conflicts generally resume after the completion of a work of art, when the artist "wakes up" from the partial fantasy that the creative process of "discharging aggression" or "externalizing hated parts of the self" has only temporarily enabled.[139] In other words, Glynn observed that weaknesses of character and unwanted elements of self return when fantasies end. Sendak accordingly described the process of finishing a project as one that involved catharsis followed by depression.[140] Sometimes he bemoaned the inevitable experience of loss, of banishment from another completed world.[141] He knew the importance of existing meaningfully with others beyond fantasy play, but he struggled to do so. In close correspondences he reflected on his experience of emotional emptiness, of not being able to internalize or accept his worth to those who maintained relationships with him.[142] Ultimately, however useful fantasy may have been for survival and psychic evolution, it was also as ethereal as the waves of emotion that inspired it. Even Max grows tired of the Wild Things once his rage has subsided, opting instead for concrete nurture somewhere in which a real someone "loved him best of all."

Conveying the emotional experience of early childhood and the queer positions of stigmatized subjectivities, Sendak's works demonstrate his scanning for social possibilities, hidden meanings, and new associations. Like the artist himself, his protagonists are overextended and emotive about their plights, unsure if growing up is even a possibility for them, given their social exclusion and internalized anxieties. They solve the problems of violated boundaries, neglect, loneliness, and the overwhelming feelings of powerful others through their own emotional play and embodied instincts. Throughout his career, an intuitive and improvisational "grappling in the dark" helped Sendak reclaim emotional agency against internalized queer shame, ongoing social misrecognition, and self-policing. Camp and theatricality offered some strategies for celebrating the drama of human nature—its awkwardness, suffering, and gratifying pleasures. These aesthetic approaches also resonated with the bold, boundary-breaking arts scene and gay subculture that emerged around Sendak in Manhattan and Fire Island as he came into his thirties and forties, offering opportunities to foster further personal cohesion as a gay man across what Goffman called "civil" and "back" spaces. In an era that predated socially respectable roles for queer adults, what social commentators might have viewed as a "gay obsession with youth" might have actually reflected an interest in children's talent for creative, playful resistance against threatening forces of normalization—a goal shared by many adult artists and social outsiders. Sendak's obsession with childhood, in particular, conveys not the mere desire to remain physically youthful or to speak specifically to children, but rather the need to preserve and cultivate the sensitive flexibility of young subjects for his own psychological survival and self-determination.

At a time when the wider culture turned to social liberation, "ethnic revival," and the reevaluation of societal divisions, Sendak helped universalize the emotional experience and significance of insider-outsider performativity by demonstrating to the wider culture how most young children related to it, even across social divides of class, religion, and ethnicity. Children's ability and need to playfully suspend and temporarily replace their subjectivity was for Sendak an optimal, if imperfect, position from which to communicate creatively, and one that humanized stigmatized adults through the prism of universal child's play. Thus he used the feelings and flexible conceptions of self and time recalled from childhood to work through and exorcise difficult emotions connected to his marginality, stigma, and spiritual longings. He spoke to young children's psychological plasticity, testing various reactions to embodied drives in an ongoing process of performative trial-and-error in the construction of early selfhood. He also spoke to those stigmatized or alienated adults who, maintaining strategies of child's play and fantasy, fought to keep a grip on reality in contexts that might have alienated, shamed, or eradicated them. Professionally channeling the creative play, psychological flexibility, and fantasy of early childhood was a double-edged sword for Sendak: it allowed him to give voice to a subjectivity that felt chaotic, overextended, and strange, but building his name and identity through this work also perpetuated that internal chaos, confining him within the emotional limbo required to continue to produce "Sendakian" art.

CHAPTER 5

INSIDE OUT

*Processing the AIDS Crisis and Holocaust
Memory Through the Romantic Child*

"IT'S HARD TO BE HAPPY," Sendak would conclude in 2012, the year of his death. "Some people have the gift of pulling themselves up and out and saying there is more to life than just tragedy. And then there are those who can't. I'm one of them."[1] If Sendak nourished his own unhappiness, he used it to fuel an ongoing artistic response that conveyed the endangered individual's grappling with a void of meaning in the aftermath of collective tragedies. Heightened differentiations between "inside" and "outside" color his work, from the first book he authored, *Kenny's Window* (1956), in which the protagonist is stuck inside, through the artist's posthumously published *My Brother's Book* (2013), which conveys deeply personal feelings harbored for his older brother, Jack, amidst a dangerous and hostile landscape. Katie Roiphe understands the latter project as driven by a question that underlies much of Sendak's work: can a person "be close to another person without being consumed"?[2] Sendak's investment in the boundary between inside and outside reflects what Robert Rosenblum calls "a familiar Romantic polarity between near and far, enclosure and freedom."[3] This trope conveys Sendak's position as a queer and self-identified "Old World" Jewish man in a heteronormative, Christian-secular majority culture, as well as a truth-seeking artist within a field that increasingly shifted its focus, he felt, from unearthing buried meanings to chasing exorbitant profits. During the later years of his career, the artist's queerness and Yiddishkeit continued to speak through the sensitive, disenfranchised children of his creative vision. Having matured his voice and established his cultural significance by the late twentieth century, Sendak more directly tackled the problems of sexual alienation, as well as more boldly responded to the century's collective traumas, including the Holocaust and the AIDS epidemic. He did so in original picture books, in illustrations of texts by canonical writers, and in his second career as a designer for the performing arts, where muscled, sexually potent adult figures could expose their desires, wrestle with death, and wage bloody wars onstage.

Sendak's picture books in the last several decades of his life garnered notably mixed reviews. Critics such as Ellen Handler Spitz appreciated his tendency to capture children's "often well-hidden but inescapable feelings of being misperceived, overlooked, and estranged . . . alone—an outsider, a victim," as well as the resulting need "to retreat into some sort of a private space, some refuge far away from others."[4] However, they also worried about the message his work sent about indulging personal feelings at the expense of social participation. Spitz argued, for example, that "Sendak's children inhabit a vacuum that, as we go from Max to Mickey to Ida, becomes increasingly obtuse, freakish, and unintelligible," that these child protagonists are "profoundly alone" and "remain mentally isolated and apart," retreating into "private worlds" of "transitory pleasure" and "delusions of grandeur" without ever returning to a real relationship or sense of belonging.[5] Jean Perrot similarly concludes that Sendak's *Dear Mili* (1988) "shows the same allegiance as *Outside Over There* . . . to the principle of writing based on the hermeticism of quotations and personal humour."[6] The artist, on his part, generally detested criticism and found reviewers lacking in their analyses of his work. He bemoaned the tendency to focus on concerns of child development, rather than on the artistic merit of his particular point of view. Longing to be read as a self-reflective artist who spoke to greater truths, rather than as a guardian of bourgeois childhood mores, he complained, "Everything I've done is so personal. God, if people could read what I've written about myself . . . it reveals everything. But they don't."[7]

This final chapter focuses on the intensification of the always-present notions of "inside" and "outside" in Sendak's life and work, especially in the latter decades of his life. Interior-exterior metaphors are historically salient tropes of Jewish and queer lives, which have endured different forms of ghettoization, hiding, passing, eventful exposure, and hybridity. Interrogations of "inside" and "outside" reflect Jewish concerns about endogamy, distinctiveness, and collective continuity, as well as symbols of the closet and of "coming out" in queer narratives. Though Sendak remained an atheist generally nonobservant of Jewish holidays, he identified wholeheartedly with "Old World" Jewish sensibilities, even as much of the Jewish American world embraced modernity. Though he remained hesitant about publicizing his own sexual orientation until his final years, he infused his work with erotic introspection and political statements supporting queer people. Sendak struggled throughout his career and personal life to remain both distinct and connected to others—a struggle shared by most minority groups in a progressive American cultural context. His creative universe is paradigmatic of queer subjects and of diaspora experiences, broadly conceived. Within a powerful majority culture, the heightened fear of losing an endangered self or subculture complicates relationships and social participation, and it encourages a protectively inward focus. Thus the following pages explore Sendak's antimodernist, Romantic emphasis on introspection, as well as his determination to protect his urgency of feeling, a quality on which he depended both for self-preservation and as a means of public outcry in the latter half of the artist's life.

Pulling Up the Drawbridge

In 1970, a journalist visiting Sendak's Manhattan duplex noted that the artist "limits his friendships" and "lives an ascetic life."[8] Suffering health problems and puritanical criticisms of his *In the Night Kitchen* (1970), he considered a move. The following year, he and Glynn purchased a home in Ridgefield, Connecticut, that reminded Sendak of the grand estates of the 1930s movies he cherished. Relocating there by 1972, the artist began to reserve months at a time to work on his projects, refusing to leave home or accept speaking engagements.[9] His correspondences from those years are filled with apology after apology, as he declined invitations from various individuals and institutions. Selectively welcomed visitors described his studio, situated in an extended wing of the house, as a kind of darkened cave, lit by a single desk lamp as he painted to classical music into the late hours of the night. The image symbolically evokes Sendak's lifelong quest to illuminate how the emotionally abandoned or marginal individual survives by grappling in the dark. The artist used his answering machine as a buffer to filter the outside world. His dear friend James Bohlman recalled needing to announce who he was before Sendak would answer: "Each time he did that I felt wealthy beyond any tabulation, rich and privileged that I was allowed into his private life."[10] Sendak counted the reclusive, never-married Emily Dickinson (1830–86) among his most favorite poets, claiming that she taught him, "Don't open the door, don't let them in!" and that she "kept the world OUT."[11] In his later years, Sendak described the book-making process as "an isolationist form of life."[12] As he worked on locating and reshaping his own boundaries, the "outside" world became increasingly intolerable to him in the twenty-first century, representing elements from which he urgently wished to differentiate himself.

Chief among Sendak's complaints at the time was what he perceived as the "spontaneous combustion" of the children's book industry by the 1980s. He watched with disgust as the industry "sold out," abandoning craft for money and self-promotion. From 1978 to 1988, the profits of Harper & Row's children's division jumped from fourteen million to forty million. *Dear Mili* would run an unprecedented number of copies for a children's book at its first printing in 1988—250,000, compared to a previous record of 140,000 copies for a children's book's first printing.[13] Bemoaning how commercially oriented publishing had become, he reminisced about "the great days in the 1950s and after the war, when publishing children's books was youthful and fun."[14] Children's books were now, he felt, "churned out in the hopes they will make money, rather than make children happy. . . . They're directed at parents, grandparents and the possibility of movies."[15] The artist also specifically bemoaned the machismo that entered the field and the shifting of emphasis from boundary-breaking art to bourgeois-sanctioned profit. As he recalled, "[W]hen we succeeded, that's when they dumped the women. Because once there's money, the guys can come down and screw the whole thing up which is what they did. They ruined the whole business."[16] Spotlighting the hypocrisy of such men, he recalled "embarrassing parties" of the earlier years, in which "only the women talked to me because I was the man who wrote the book that put little Jane to sleep. The macho daddies didn't know what to make of a man who did that for a livelihood."[17] In his eulogy for Ruth Krauss, Sendak would similarly condemn the men in children's book publishing who "wouldn't be caught dead in a 'kiddie book' department" until a "whiff of Big Bucks reassured their masculinity."[18] Reflecting this dissatisfaction with the field, he rerouted much of his energy toward a second career in the performing arts by the late 1970s, creating song lyrics and animated pieces for television; set and costume designs for opera, ballet, and dance; and his own children's theater company with Arthur Yorinks.[19]

A Queer Mentor

Sendak's later years also reflect a tendency to mentor and care for the queer, the unlucky, the forgotten. In 2010 he would inaugurate the Sendak Fellowship for early-career illustrators, offering month-long residencies in a house neighboring his own in Connecticut and providing his own direct feedback on these artists' work.[20] Preceding this formalized program, he continuously helped kindred spirits to launch their careers, including such illustrators and writers as Richard Egelski, Peter Sís, Chris Raschka, Brian Selznick, and James Marshall—a best friend and colleague of Sendak's most known for his "George and Martha" picture books published in the 1970s and 1980s. While studying early editions of L. Frank Baum's *The Wonderful Wizard of Oz* (1900), Sendak also befriended antiquarian bookseller Peter Glassman, a gay twenty-year-old Brown University dropout. The artist helped Glassman to establish his Books of Wonder, an independent children's book store, which opened in 1980 on Hudson Street in Greenwich Village.[21] Sendak would later illustrate the cover of Glassman's edited volume for HarperCollins, *Oz: The Hundredth Anniversary Celebration* (2000). In the early 2000s, while reading Walt

Whitman for the first time, Sendak would meet illustrator Brian Selznick, also gay and Jewish, who was between jobs and struggling to find his creative voice. The two enjoyed long conversations, Sendak urging Selznick to unlock his greater potential by diving deeper, encouraging the younger artist to create the book that he *wanted* to create, regardless of what he thought would sell. Selznick would credit this motivation as a driving force behind his *The Invention of Hugo Cabret* (2007), which topped the *New York Times* bestseller list, achieved a Caldecott Medal, and earned a finalist spot for the National Book Award.[22] With Selznick, Sendak also discussed Whitman's "Live Oak, with Moss," a series of poems constituting a love story between two men who ultimately part; Whitman had cut the poems into fragments, hiding them within his 1860 edition of *Leaves of Grass*. Selznick would revive and illustrate "Live Oak, with Moss" in 2019, dedicating his beautifully imagined edition to the memory of his own wild mentor, with love.[23]

Sendak, in his old age, reflected on the connection between his social queerness and his proclivity to mentor others:

> I can make friends with young people much more easily than with the people who are older, who normally would be friends of my age, but I'm an unmarried man, I'm a gay man, my choices are limited. I don't want to belong to anything. I don't want to be anybody. I wish I could be disembodied. But it's only my body that's going to die and decay. That's all there is. . . . I don't know why friendships are so hard to be made. I feel useful to the younger people. I can help them.[24]

Such sentiments make clear the degree of pain and loneliness with which the artist contended, even in his later years, and despite his successes and his lively, intimate friendships. Decades of engaging primarily with internal meanings may have perpetuated the feeling of disembodiment and of not truly existing beyond his interior world. Sendak complained that "just being alive is troublesome. . . . I've been ready to die since childhood. . . . It's time to go. . . . I'm old enough to die. . . . I will be nothing and nowhere, and that will be such a relief. To be something and somewhere is very tiring."[25] This perspective also relates to stark contrasts felt in emotionally strained subjectivities between the "inside" world of feeling and the threatening "outside" world in which the public's wider mentalities callously erode and neutralize individual truths. To exist authentically for Sendak was a constant physical battle.

Against discomforts in the public sphere, Sendak and Glynn created their own unusual variation of home and "chosen family" in Ridgefield, developing a household that blurred boundaries and relational styles. Lynn Caponera, who first came to Sendak's home as an eleven-year-old neighbor to help care for the dogs, dropped out of high school to live and work at Sendak's home at age sixteen and began running the household two years later.[26] The artist came to depend on Caponera to remarkable extents, claiming that he felt sick if she came home late and insisting that only Lynn prepare his sandwiches. As Roiphe writes, "The dependence was absolute, draining, flattering, consuming; the quasi-maternal care demanded of her was magnificent in scope. The particular quality and seductiveness of the need will be recognizable to mothers of very small children, most of whom won't rise to it."[27] In his old age, Sendak called Caponera "my best friend, the person who has sacrificed herself for me, the person who thinks I'm worth the trouble of being cared for. She's everybody. She's everything. She's the most devoted friend I have, and I'd like to think I'm her most devoted friend."[28] Roiphe writes that Caponera was "a servant and not a servant. . . . She was a part of the household in a way that could not be defined or pinned down with pedestrian words like 'daughter' or 'mother' or 'friend' or 'lover' or 'assistant' or 'housekeeper.'"[29] Roiphe describes Caponera's job as "the constant caretaking of larger-than-life, kvetching theatrical characters," but a job that she enjoyed. As an ultimate last gift to her, Sendak would later designate Caponera as the legal executor of his estate and president of his foundation.

Particularism and Self-Preservation

In some respects, Sendak's emotional conundrum—his need to remain "apart" despite his cultural renown, as well as his internalized pressure to turn inward and preserve a threatened queer and Yiddish-inflected identity—reflects wider tensions in Jewish and queer American conditions of recent decades, as both groups reach record levels of integration in powerful sectors of American society. Belonging too well may breed complacency, dull one's connection to specific cultural rhythms, and blind one to potential dangers. Sometimes when minorities gain public platforms in America, they also become visible targets or undergo cooption by the majority culture, which can ultimately induce their assimilation or disappearance. By the time Sendak reached middle age, for example, Jews had intermarried and integrated into American society in record numbers, with synagogues and Jewish federations increasingly fretting over the preservation of Jewish distinctiveness. Also by the late twentieth century, for many American Jews, Jewishness had been fragmented from the all-encompassing communal identity of immigrant forebears into a set of sanitized symbols in public, and personal or familial emotions and rituals in private.[30] Largely acculturated and viewed as "White" Americans, writes historian Eric L. Goldstein, most American Jews no longer expressed their particular, deep attachments through the language of "race" but relied instead on the "echoes of Jewish racial identity, a discourse of 'tribalism,' which gives voice to the feelings of loss Jews experienc[e] in a world resistant to seeing them as a group apart."[31] The more removed Jews became from a minority status, Goldstein argues, the more Jews felt the need to insist on their distinctiveness from the majority culture. One means of doing so has been to align with other minority groups and to fight for their civil rights. Another route has been the ongoing study and discussion of antisemitism and the Holocaust as a means for actively remembering the contingencies of social privilege even within "universalist" societies when they are built on racism and ethnic nationalism.[32]

As a public figure by the late twentieth century, Sendak would have experienced firsthand the tensions of belonging "too well" in some respects to take his Jewishness or queerness for granted. His history, as an artist grappling with concerns of nonacculturated identities, offers a useful springboard for thinking about how incoherent or socially intangible subjectivities operate and survive. It also raises difficult social questions about the nature of integrating or acculturating identities that rely on a minority status, a need to remain distinctive and apart in order to exist with authenticity. The spaces of literature and art, as connected to but also distinct from public life and society at large, offer a means for contemplating and shaping meaning, especially regarding facets of experience obscured or neutralized in socialization or assimilation. They are also spaces of play and problem-solving that, through fantasy, interweaving, and improvisation, help endangered subjects to determine how they might survive subtle and systematic forms of oppression while simultaneously cultivating social worth and connectedness.

Young children continued to inspire Sendak's creativity as beings inherently positioned between "inside" and "outside," belonging and isolation. Children were masters at juggling multiple registers of reality. As Sendak would repeatedly assert, most children protect their parents by keeping parts of themselves inside—paralleling histories of subjugated peoples, more broadly, as evidenced in minority literary traditions. Kushner, for example, reads Sendak through Harold Bloom's notion of Jewish interiority, of "Being a self, alone, committed to oneness, whether through predilection or through a conviction of the necessity of the condition of aloneness," a conviction to pursue the divine most decisively in one's own heart, mind, and *neshome*, one's soul.[33] The Sendak universe is concerned with matters of distinctiveness, belonging, self-preservation, memory, and survival; it is also ambivalently wedded to a majority culture that does not always accept or understand outsiders without the caveat of their disappearance into the mainstream. Sendak's life offered him multiple early perspectives into what it meant to survive on the fringes of twentieth-century society and its emotional norms.

In the last decades of the twentieth century, Sendak's interiority shaped work that more explicitly referenced the Holocaust. Such references might have also met greater appreciation as America officially sanctioned its commitment to Holocaust memory, President Jimmy Carter establishing the President's Commission on the Holocaust in 1978. Sendak was deeply impacted by his frequent visits to the Anne Frank House in the 1980s while working on an opera in Amsterdam. Frank had decorated part of her family's secret annex with magazine cut-outs of American celebrities, aspiring to stardom, like Sendak's beloved Rosie. The preserved rooms of the annex demonstrated the profound claustrophobia of a family forced to remain inside, and Anne's diary further demonstrated the feelings children keep inside of themselves. Upon reading her diary after the war, her father, Otto Frank, would express surprise at the depth and seriousness of his daughter's thoughts and feelings—revealing a different Anne than the one he had known. A strange synergy existed for Sendak between his perception of those Jewish children, like Frank, whose lives had been forcibly cut short and those queer, excluded, or terrified children, like himself, who had struggled to "grow up" but found it difficult in a society that ignored, misunderstood, or targeted them. He believed that Jewish artists "piggyback" or carry those fellow Jews of the past who did not survive, helping them fulfill what they could not live to do.[34] Thus he claimed to carry Frank, metaphorically speaking, and he repeatedly featured her in his drawings and later costume designs for live performances.

In Sendak's designs for *The Nutcracker* ballet in the 1980s, he would present Clara as a lonely, creative child whose dreams of the future are weighted with references to grim realities. The artist reinterpreted the ballet's original text as a story about the pain of growing up misunderstood. Among the darker elements that punctuate Clara's fantasies are visual references to Auschwitz—lurking above the ship on which a suddenly matured Clara sets sail, boys sit in structures that resemble guard towers and wear shirts striped vertically in white and faded blue, like camp prisoners.[35] Even more explicitly, in *Dear Mili*, the artist would feature a scene in which a group of children are marched to Auschwitz.[36] He drew them crossing a shaky bridge with a guard tower looming behind them. If the Holocaust association is at all ambiguous in the published image, one has only to look to a 1985 pencil study completed for this painting, which includes yellow Stars of David sewn onto the children's overcoats. Sendak also depicted Anne Frank herself in this book, together with a group of children from the French town of Izieu who had been murdered under Klaus Barbie at the end of World War II. Together they form a choir led by Mozart in Heaven, at the far reaches of St. Joseph's garden. Like French writer and Auschwitz survivor Charlotte Delbo's postwar account of living "a double existence," a split consciousness that enables a living self to ward off traumatic brushes with death, *Dear Mili* follows a child who hides alone in the forest, followed by a doppelgänger, a guardian angel who eventually claims her for heaven.[37] In the original 1984 storyboard for the book, the girl has cropped dark hair, like Frank, but becomes blonde when she dies in the woods, upon meeting her ghostly golden-haired double. The cover image of the storyboard presents the girl and her guardian angel, both already blonde and leaning head-to-head on their way to the afterlife. For the final paintings, however, Sendak would lengthen their hair and keep the darker color of the protagonist's locks intact, preserving her distinctiveness, perhaps, within the implied grip of Aryanization and impending death. The year following the book's publication, a sixty-one-year-old Sendak noted that Frank would have been sixty at the time, and that she had dreamed of being a writer. He insisted that he achieved his own literary successes, in part, to share them vicariously with her.[38]

Years later Sendak collaborated with Tony Kushner on a staging of *Brundibar*, based on the 1939 opera of the same name by Hans Krása and Adolf Homeiste and performed over fifty times by child prisoners in Theresienstadt, most of whom were subsequently murdered by the Nazis. The artist also worked with Kushner on a picture book version of the opera in 2003. For visual research, Sendak borrowed František Zelenka's original 1943 watercolor of the stage design used in the camp, in which the word *škola* ("school" in Czech) hangs from the sky in a red-and-white circle, like a futile traffic sign or an angry sun.[39] In Sendak's crayon and watercolor rendition, childhood in a Nazi-occupied town appears vital and resilient against the visual subtexts of poverty, cruel competition, and tragic loss. A mother's lullaby about babies who grow up and fly away like blackbirds accompanies Sendak's darkened images of weeping women situated beneath giant crows that carry their children into the night sky.

While working on *Brundibar*, Sendak also joined Glenn Dickson's Shirim Klezmer Orchestra on a project called *Pincus and the Pig*, a klezmer version of Sergei Prokofiev's *Peter and the Wolf*, which happened to have been one of the first stories Sendak illustrated at home as a teenager. While writing the script, Sendak made "Peter" into "Pincus"

after his father's Yiddish name; the wolf became "Chozzer" (pig), an
epithet Sendak's aunt had used to refer to antisemites in Poland. Sendak
offered his own voice for the recorded narration, infusing the language
and tone with the sounds of his late relatives. His script for this piece,
which he created with help from Arthur Yorinks, delighted in Yiddish-
inflected banter between a bird and a duck, the former drawn by Sendak
in the cover art with a yarmulke, the latter with a black hat and sidelocks. Bickering with each other, the bird calls down to the duck in
his pond, "You should only sink to the bottom like a stone!" and then
quickly squawks "Gevalt!" as a cat attempts to eat him. The script for
Pincus ends with a glossary of over twelve Yiddish terms, their definitions humorously composed.[40] Having been emotionally drained by
Brundibar, the artist appreciated the opportunity to work on a more
playful project about his roots that ended in a child's tangible triumph:
collaborating with his animal friends, Pincus sees Chozzer captured and
sent to the unkosher butcher. In addition to this collaboration, Sendak
offered his service several years later to New York's Jewish Museum
for a 2011–12 exhibit titled "An Artist Remembers: Hanukkah Lamps
Selected by Maurice Sendak." The artist chose thirty-three menorahs
from various historical eras to be displayed alongside original drawings
from his *Zlateh the Goat* and *In Grandpa's House,* both of which feature
images of traditional *shtetl* scenes and likenesses of Sendak's deceased
relatives. The process of selecting menorahs was, however, a painful
one for the artist, returning him to his feelings of first learning of his
relatives' deaths in Nazi Europe around the time of his own Bar Mitzvah in Brooklyn.[41]

Germany as Forbidden Love Object

Complicating his mourning of Holocaust victims and his conceptions of
spaces that were "inside" or "outside" for him, the artist's paradoxical
love of German culture helped him express his particular feelings as a
queer, "Old World" Jew in America. He considered German music and
literature "unquestionably [his] favorite," the German language induc-
ing dizziness, in a positive way.[42] As young men, Sendak and his brother,
Jack, had emulated German craftsmanship, creating six animated toys

in the eighteenth-century German lever-controlled style in the summer of 1948, despite having been "force-fed on anti-German feeling" by their parents.[43] Sendak believed that one of the most graphically beautiful books ever produced was *Der Struwwelpeter* (1845), a German children's book depicting fatal choking, cutting off of fingers, and the burning of people alive.[44] Many of his own early books were strongly influenced by German artists. For example, in a study for *Kenny's Window*, during a scene in which Kenny travels to Europe to find his "only goat," Sendak depicts the boy, his back to the viewer, in a contemplative stance over a misty, mountainous landscape, the pose highly reminiscent of "Der Wanderer über dem Nebelmeer" (Wanderer above the sea fog), painted in 1818 by Caspar David Friedrich.[45]

To Philip's fury and disappointment, Sendak had also visited Germany in his twenties for the Salzberg music festival, as well as for an opera festival in Munich and Bayreuth featuring Wagner.[46] In May 1971, the month of Philip's gravestone unveiling, the artist returned to Germany. Referring to this trip as his "Grimm *Reise*," he went in order to look at German illustrations of Grimm Brothers stories at the Grimm Museum in Kassel, West Germany—including those by Otto Ubbelohde—as visual research for illustrating a collection of Grimms' tales.[47] So determined was Sendak to immerse himself in German cultural sensibilities that he fashioned his Connecticut property like a German landscape, circling his home with ash, sugar maple, dogwood, and locust trees, as well as roses, lilies, irises, and phlox. He connected his domestic retreat to that of Mahler and Mozart, who worked in isolation and knew that "[t]he only way to find something is to lose oneself." Mahler had written symphonies from within his "Waldhütte," his forest hut, and Mozart had worked on his opera *The Magic Flute* alone in Vienna and within a tiny cottage beyond the theater grounds.[48] Sendak wrote that Mozart's letters were to him what the Bible is to many. It moved him how everything Mozart wrote exuded his individuality and brutal honesty.[49] The artist also acquired what he called his "goyishe dogs," German shepherds whom he depicted in his *Outside Over There* and *Some Swell Pup*. Naming one of them Herman after Herman Melville, he would cynically amuse himself by telling some visitors that the dog's namesake was Hermann Göring, the infamous Nazi leader, because in another life this dog might have been trained to kill Jews.[50] A later shepherd was named Runge, after the German Romanticist painter Philipp Otto Runge (1777–1810).[51]

Needless to say, Germany is a strange love object for a Jew who came of age during World War II, as well as for a child of a Yiddish-speaking family. German culture would have carried negative associations for families like the Sendaks even before the war. Since the Haskalah, Berlin and its secularizing influence on the Jewish world had posed a threat to the traditional way of life that characterized Sadie's and Philip's families for generations.[52] German culture thus likely signified the doubly upsetting associations, for Sadie and Philip, of Nazism and of Jews' abandonment of Jewish tradition. In some respects, the perceptions of childhood held by those German Romantic painters whom Sendak idolized would also bolster the racialized supremacism of the Nazis. Even Hitler himself owned an original child portrait by Runge.[53] Runge's and Friedrich's Romantic notions of "children as tough, animal beings, deeply rooted in nature" fed into "the growingly nationalist view of Germany's cultural past" by the 1920s with its *Wandervogelbewegung*, the German "wandering bird" youth movement stressing Teutonic roots and self-reliance in nature—a movement subsequently replaced by the Hitler Youth.[54]

But the child paintings of Runge and Friedrich also offered something of a "primal scene" of queer and Jewish endangerment for Sendak, who, like his Ida flying "backwards in the rain" in *Outside Over There* (1981), looked rebelliously to the source of his mournful family's losses and his own internalized terrors to free himself of them and create new meanings. His identification with German music and culture as a Jew descended from families destroyed by the Holocaust may have also reflected his conception of himself as a stigmatized queer person, invested in mastering overwhelming feelings about his precarious place in the world. There is thus a queer sort of logic to his love of the German Romantics. The Teutonic, "über alles" mentality espoused by antisemitic figures like Wagner repelled Sendak as a queer Jew but enchanted him aesthetically as an artist obsessed with early childhood feelings, including grandiosity and yearnings for an emergent self-worth. Immersing himself in prewar German culture, he explored the artistic ferment of the nation that would produce his family's own collective traumas. In doing so, he separated himself, symbolically, from his parents' conception of him as a living reminder of relatives murdered by Nazis but also exacerbated his own feelings of inevitable displacement. He channeled Romantic narcissism and hubris, but in the service of his own aims as a queer Jewish artist. As Glynn wrote, "The artist, repeating a long-forgotten pattern of linking up, serves his originality and history together, belonging, yet working himself free."[55]

The Romantic "Inner Child"

Sendak's reconfiguration of the Romantic child positioned this symbolic figure to stand in for the valuable power of the marginal individual, rather than for the reification of hegemony. Romantic notions of childhood had emerged in the late eighteenth and early nineteenth centuries in a rapidly industrializing world that bred nostalgia for a simpler past imagined as organic and divine. With the onset of modern democracies in Europe and America, the social primacy of class-based hierarchy shifted to favor power structures based more on race, as constructed by European and American colonialist powers. These powers had enforced their dominance, in part, through symbols of their own children as somehow anointed by God, designed for greatness. In racialized societies, Romantic depictions separated "White" children, varyingly defined, from the transactional realms of labor, connecting them instead with the awe-inspiring qualities of nature, the soul, and the unconscious.[56] The Romantics positioned their children, according to Robert Rosenblum, as "mysterious vessels of primitive energy through which nature's most awesome secrets could be intuited."[57] This conception offered Sendak early models for his own understandings of childhood, but the artist complicated those models to suit his vision of a dangerous and unjust society that targets difference. Sendak's "Romantic child" is not an Anglo-Saxon angel of the natural order, but an ethnically estranged hybrid figure who wrestles with hurricanes and beasts. Sendak's Romantic child is not a justification for a particular people's social power but a reverence for presocial nonconformity and inward truth-seeking.

All children, for Sendak, live at the mercy of social circumstances beyond their comprehension, and any child may experience unrealized social identities or turbulent emotions. The artist worked through confusing boundaries internalized as a child in a tightknit Jewish immigrant family in which his close sibling relationships and fantasies held overwhelming significance against an impersonal, sometimes hostile public culture. Private feelings of same-sex desires, public condescension toward his Yiddish-speaking parents, and the mourning of Jewish relatives in Nazi Europe made it harder to "grow up" and actualize in his environment. Accordingly, Sendak's children are often either left outside or constrained inside, almost always liminal and in need of creating their own meaning, separate from a wider society that would exclude, misperceive, or threaten them.

Working in the latter twentieth century's "confessional culture" of autobiographical comic books and talk shows, as notions of the "inner child" and the "subconscious" invited deep self-exploration, the artist romanticized his connection to his own childhood emotions. As an aesthetic paradigm, Romanticism—like folk superstition, psychoanalysis, or "the sentimental"—prioritizes passionate feelings over "reason," subverting modern scientific, systematized knowledge and power in order to privilege deep longings and unmet emotional needs. Romanticist works are characterized by an eruption of feeling that cannot be sufficiently contained within the language or practices of the social order. As a mode of creating, Romanticism thus also poses a means by which a subjugated person might survive the danger of their own obscurity *without* a facility of language, a wealth of social capital, or a mastery of political tools. Kushner accordingly described the children of Sendak's picture books as culturally ambiguous Romantics:

> eyes often closed, stiff-gaited, top-heavy, and heavy-footed, smilingly sensual, obviously bright, theatrically temperamental, self-satisfied tiny egoists vulnerable in bare feet or in their parents' shoes, prone to stomping, dressed and groomed in a style neither American nor European, neither familiar nor unfamiliar. They are immigrants' kids, Brooklyn kids, the most kid-like of any kids ever to march through a children's

book, exasperating and delightful as children are and know themselves
to be, preposterous and lovely in equal measure . . . holding themselves
and their world together.[58]

Sendak expressed early childhood in all its awkward vulnerability as
a state of ego-formation, self-determination, and negotiations of one's
own abilities and self-worth. His books came to him as feelings and fantasies that "well up," like dreams at night, leading the artist to "rush to
put them down" in physical form. He described each story as a "house"
built around a fantasy, the bookmaking process as "the painting of the
house."[59] As he further explained, "An idea to me is an emotion, a need,
that gets louder and louder and more demanding that I must express
myself in a certain way."[60] Discussing *Where the Wild Things Are* (1963),
for example, he claimed that children's potential reactions were not on
his mind when he created the book, but rather, it "was written to exorcise certain things in myself." Like all creative work, he believed, "it's
simply done for yourself. I mean, you have a need to express some particular feeling. . . . *Wild Things* is not an idea, it's a *feeling*. And you have
to catch the feeling in both words and pictures."[61] To focus on a feeling
as *itself* the basis of a serious aesthetic or literary project is, like Heather
Love's conception of "gay shame," not only to acknowledge an internal
experience but also to sharpen awareness of those "Xs marking the spot
where the social is at work on us."[62] For Sendak, to be led by feelings
also meant challenging himself to investigate and discover connections
across disparate realms, even in cultures marked as dangerous. His creative process for *Outside Over There*, for example, relied heavily on the
intuitive integration of separate components of public and private life
that he yearned to see together: the Lindbergh kidnapping of 1932, the
girl depicted in a rainstorm on the Morton Salt shaker, and the artist's
feelings about his own childhood. As he expressed, "[S]omehow as an
artist you have a funny kind of faith that they *will* come together. The
unconscious has such a need to make an artistic whole out of these disparate elements that it's going to happen."[63]

The artist's intuitive, open-ended approach of uniting disconnected
elements could be personally maddening. Kushner once noted "how

deeply Maurice *suffers* a picture book."[64] Sendak's description of the mania that accompanied his creative periods suggested the phenomenon of working through disorganizing feelings that were difficult to master: "It becomes some monstrous thing that's got its fangs in your neck. . . . But while you're miserable . . . you are very happy because you know your misery and suffering is special and you're very proud of it and you're very vain glorious [sic] about it. But it's hard. It's damned hard!"[65] During this all-consuming creative state, Sendak would work morning until night, seven days a week; isolate himself from other people; and read only works of history, biography, or other general interest topics so as not to be distracted from the emotional wave of inspiration. He described his workday as being "like a zombie's," working about ten hours a day, on and off until midnight or one o'clock a.m.[66] In the midst of working on his *In the Night Kitchen*, for example, he virtually eliminated his social contact with the outside world, feeling like he was "under some magic spell."[67] But this state of "seizure" also offered "great pleasure" and "a tremendous chorus of celebration." As he explained, "I was caught up in something so intoxicating, I didn't know where it came from. I just believed totally in its reality."[68]

For Sendak, self-absorption was necessary to do the hard work of emotionally surviving and understanding himself in a context that offered few positive mirrors for sensitive queer people marked by an enduring ethnic particularity and Holocaust losses. Overcoming the traumas of queer shame and emotional obscurity happened in secret, in the cracks of respectable society, and it sometimes involved the self-protecting defense mechanisms of inflated narcissism, of seeing oneself as special, even magical, to cast away feelings of defectiveness. The artist thus described his creative bursts in narcissistic terms, as moments of possessing a secret, almost supernatural energy that sets one apart from others—a position he associated with both ecstasy and torture.[69] Accordingly, he would reflect at age forty-three that he needed help thinking beyond his own inflated ego.[70] Ideally, art could help one find a satisfactory balance between feelings of insignificance and grandiosity, rather than perpetuating the maddening experience of alternating between the two. Kushner writes that one of art's powers is its capacity to help individuals recognize, understand, and name themselves, as well as to see themselves relative to others in wider contexts.[71] Glynn believed that creativity emanated from artists' earliest relationships, to others and to one's self, and that an artist, like a neurotic patient, returns compulsively to the originating trauma in generally unsuccessful attempts to master it. Art-making, however, keeps an artist "tied to reality, a defense against psychotic breakdown."[72]

Sendak's relationship to notions of a Romantic child cannot be understood without considering his relationship to his own adopted "children"—his dogs. As mediating figures between himself and a broader social world, canine companions served an important role for the artist and feature prominently in his work. Raising and caring for his dogs helped Sendak develop a greater capacity to transcend his own personal concerns, to recognize others more clearly as separate individuals and to understand his impact on others. He disclosed a tendency to see all of his dogs first as extensions of his own infant self, a problem he finally overcame with his last dog, Runge. Sendak later recounted, "Runge is the first dog I've had who has been fully transformed. . . . He's not me anymore; . . . he's finally a beautiful German shepherd and no longer a cranky kid . . . finally my vision is focused and I see a dog."[73] The artist's relationships with his dogs were unusually emotional and meaningful. As he stated, "With our dogs, we wear no masks. A dog is so ruthlessly and unashamedly honest in the demands it makes of you; it is entirely dependent. . . . [T]he way you relate to your dog is a subtext to the way you relate to everything and everybody. Since dogs are so transparent, they mirror you back to yourself, and the challenge for us is to take that seriously."[74] Because a dog, like an infant, is nonverbal, the relationship can be "incredibly intense and basic," allowing for the creative, primal intimacy connected to early human emotions and also inviting a "self-training." Sendak demonstrated this insight in a picture book called *Some Swell Pup* (1976), in which children modeled on Jewish immigrant prototypes learn the responsibilities and challenges of raising a dog in an extended metaphor for human development. The book playfully modeled how socially liminal children might socialize themselves through relationships with others, as Sendak had done, first with his siblings and later with his friends and dogs. His dogs' transparent, basic physical dependence on him allowed him to experience "very primitive feelings" in *himself*, forcing him to recognize and control those feelings, or to sublimate them through art-making, which ultimately led him to feel "emotionally calmer, more conscious."[75] His preliminary studies for *Outside Over There*, the project he deemed most painful to create, began in 1977 with pencil sketches on tracing paper of his German shepherd Aggie, cracked eggshells, and hooded shrouds engulfing faceless figures.

Drawing "Outside" In

Sendak called the process of making *Outside Over There* (1981) a difficult "religious experience" that changed his life.[76] He would admit, "Something went amiss in me, a kind of panic, a kind of fear. I had touched on a subject, which is *not* in the book, but which had to be touched on to do the book. . . . I went back into therapy. . . . "[77] Sendak likened his process to that of a miner's work: "At that point in my still-young life, I felt I *had* to solve this book, I *had* to plummet as far down deep into myself as I could: excavation work." But unlike in the creation of *Wild Things*, in which he felt "like a miner getting out just before the blast," *Outside Over There* overtook Sendak in a full-blown psychological crisis.[78] In addition to undergoing psychotherapy, he studied the work of eighteenth- and nineteenth-century masters, such as William Blake's watercolors for Milton's "L'Allegro" and "Il Penseroso," displayed at the Morgan Library, which gave him the courage to make paintings out of the initial drawings he had done for the book.[79] Blake's art reaffirmed Sendak's belief that societies misunderstand, mistreat, and hurt children by socializing them into zombies, like the "ice baby" of the latter's story.[80] The artist created his paintings for *Outside Over There* with a four-hair brush that enabled incredible precision with watercolor.[81] Their content blends references to the popular culture of his youth with traditional German Romantic elements. The paintings of Ida and her sister beside a dwarfed white picket fence and sunflowers draw directly from Runge's portraits of Hülsenbeck children, depicted in an almost identical composition in a garden near Hamburg in 1805.[82] James

Marshall would poke fun upon the book's publication, playfully inscrib-
ing a copy of one of his own books for Sendak with a caricatured child
in a Romantic gown among sunflowers, accompanied by the words "For
~~Wolfgang, Carl, Gustav~~ Maurice."[83]

Outside Over There follows Ida's journey to rescue her infant sister,
kidnapped by goblins that have left an icy changeling in the infant's
place. The story's setting, in a luscious, rolling landscape populated by
oversized German shepherds, is at once dangerous and intoxicating.
Sunflowers grow furiously through a window into the sisters' room as a
storm rages outside, where their mother sits in a trance. On a "hornpipe"
whose coiled shape connotes a fallopian tube, Ida plays "a frenzied jig"
that "makes sailors wild beneath the ocean moon" to churn the babies
into "a dancing stream"—all but Ida's sister, who remains "cozy in an
eggshell" just "as a baby should." This dancing stream, which dissolves
the goblins in their cave of cracked eggshells, might read as a sort of
birth reversal, whether interpreted as a miscarriage, an abortion, or a
backward leap from baby to seminal fluid. Ida's backward journey also
returns the goblins, like the *melting* Wicked Witch of the West, to the
stream from which they came, revealing her sister—the last remaining
baby—in an eggshell in the cave: a natural, young creature, saved from
the goblins' fate. With all its symbolism of backwards motion, marriage,
honeymoons, sailors, babies, churning, and eggs, *Outside Over There*
spins a wild denaturalization of childbirth within a cave-like womb in
the moonlight. Ida's backward motion may signify the "widdershins,"
counter-clockwise motion deemed unlucky in Christian folk superstition, as a movement against the prescribed order that defies "patriarchal
centuries of time keeping" and unleashes powers "beyond reason," including demons from the underworld.[84] More important, *Outside Over
There* moves backward to an eighteenth-century German landscape to
investigate the meaning of the artist's own birth and identity in relation
to it. Once fearful of his own queer feelings and frustrated by his mother's blindness to his sensitivities, Sendak had felt like the changeling
ice baby the goblins exchange for their kidnapped victim, a traumatized shell that his own caretakers could not understand. One of his
diary entries states, "I was the ice baby—and my mother didn't notice

that I'd been replaced. She could have done the magic trick to get her real baby back but she was too distracted and I stayed an ice baby."[85]

Sendak's fearful association between his sexuality and social endangerment resound beneath the surface of his stormy, oceanic picture book. Like Melville's *Moby-Dick*, *Outside Over There* uses the word "honeymoon" with ominous undertones. Much speculation surrounds Melville's sexuality, his *Moby-Dick* sometimes read as a man's fight to suppress the homosexuality lurking in his unconscious and embodied by a sperm whale in the ocean's depths whom he strives to kill. Sendak believed Melville was a misunderstood gay or bisexual man drawn to the secluded, homosocial dynamics of men at sea. He would later joke with Pederson, his Harper assistant, about the sexual attractions of the sailor's life, Pederson teasingly reminding the artist, who struggled with his health and didn't drive, that he would not have lasted a minute on a boat.[86] While Melville's novel describes two men intertwined in bed, "in our hearts' honeymoon," Sendak's Ida ventures to interrupt the "honeymoon" that the goblins will have with her infant sister.[87] And if the hooded, dancing goblins have any connection to a demonized sexual orientation or stigmatized subculture, they are also humanized as misunderstood, "just babies like her sister!" The goblins turn out to look like naked human babies, all crying and wailing in a dark, womb-like cave filled with cracked eggshells, and "in the middle of a wedding." What first seemed a monstrous celebration of indiscriminate intimacy and aborted life is revealed to be profoundly human, powerless, and misunderstood—like outsiders condemned as predators or trapped in the unchecked emotions of a creative fantasy, cast away from the wider society. "Outside Over There" was the territory of the Wild Things, *Pinocchio*'s Pleasure Island, and the final destination of Dowell and Rosie, a place where dreams consume and destroy those who give up on the pursuit of a life beyond the realm of fantasy. It is also the realm of the condemned outsider who cannot belong, the shadowy grip of an enduring disgrace or stigma, beyond the ever-shifting line societies draw to separate "us" from "them." The book became, as Sendak described it, "the pursuit of the theme I had been tracking since *Kenny's Window*, but now I had it trapped in a corner. I was really like Sherlock Holmes, sniffing it out in myself."[88]Sendak repeatedly claimed that, in *Outside Over There*, Ida and the infant symbolize two separate stories. The infant was a fusion of the murdered Lindbergh baby and the child Sendak himself, feeling emotionally cheated by his immigrant parents and physically endangered by external interferences against which they seemed unprepared to defend him.[89] Sometimes his parents even were themselves threatening. Philip, for example, told Sendak during his early childhood that he and Sadie had unsuccessfully attempted to abort him in utero.[90] In *Outside Over There*, the infant's kidnapping and near-death experience—which takes place while Papa is away at sea, Mama despondent and neglectful—may, in some regard, relate to the artist's understanding that his own parents rejected and even sought to eradicate him before he was born. Ida, on the other hand, was another sort of conglomeration. She was, in part, the artist's older sister, Natalie, who was forced to babysit him from a young age. She was also partly Pamina of Mozart's *Magic Flute*, who is forcibly separated from her beloved mother, unaware that her mother is not sane, and in love with a prince who loves her back but can never reveal it, due to a vow of silence.[91] And she was also Ida Perles, a beloved Brooklyn Jewish woman and friend of the family—a cheerful, humorous, and resilient role model who, in addition to being the only pet-owning Jewish person that the child Sendak knew, was emotionally available to him in ways his mother could not be.[92]

Ida, in addition, symbolized "the favorite child he never had," a child who, Sendak imagined, might have rescued him emotionally.[93] As he fantasized, "A daughter would be drawn to me. A daughter would want to help me."[94] This fantasized daughter may have been the miscarried child that Sendak nearly fathered in his youth while engaged to a woman—a time close to his first emotional breakdown and psychoanalysis. He sometimes imagined that this unborn child had in fact survived, that the miscarriage had never happened. He once claimed, "I have lived my whole life with a dream daughter."[95] As he reflected in the last year of his life, Sendak "never saw the fetus" of that miscarried child. The would-be mother had kept in touch with him until her death, enduring "a very sad marriage," perhaps in the vein of Ida's mother, presented as endlessly despondent while her husband is off at sea.[96] Sendak had a recurring dream about their lost child, imagined as a teenager. In the dream, the artist was on a train arriving to Saint-Izaire, France, and "My eyes are looking for my daughter. I know she is waiting for me. I get off the train, I see her, she is pretty, I don't talk to her. The dream fizzles out."[97] If Ida is, on some level, the unborn offspring of Sendak's would-be heterosexual life, her lost seafaring father is partially the artist himself, having left Ida and her mother despondent—the bride and child waiting on "Happy Island" in Sendak's original dummy for "Where the Wild Horses Are," but this time without the concluding arrival of the boy sailor. In this iteration, the boy—their father and husband—changes his mind, pursues his truths, and abandons the island in the form of a seafaring father. Ida restores his kidnapped infant, for whom she offers care, allowing him to remain far away at sea. Fitting Sendak's belief that "[a] daughter would want to help [him]," Ida, like Natalie, Lynn Caponera, or his own "dream daughter," is a rescuer with special access to the artist's emotional world.[98] Ultimately, she is a fantasy, never born in life, but immortally present in the book—a redeemer from pain, guilt, and isolation beyond the queer displacement of his physical reality.

As a final interpretive possibility, Ida might symbolize Sendak's own capacity to redeem himself through art, succeeding in his struggle to conquer his fears and achieve his own agency. As he would declare about Ida and the effect that her journey held on his life, "[W]hat she did is what I did and what I know for the first time in my life I have done. The book is a release of something that has long pressured my internal self . . . when Ida goes home, I go home."[99] The instructions offered by Ida's father are a call internalized by Sendak to use art to save himself from the grip of his own demons: "If Ida backwards in the rain would only turn around again and catch those goblins with a tune she'd spoil their kidnap honeymoon!" All Ida needs to do to reconnect with the lost infant, as Sendak strove to do with his own early childhood feelings, is to change her direction from backwards to forwards and utilize her musical horn—an instrument of embodied, creative truth-seeking.

While the narrative climaxes in differentiating and reclaiming a "natural" baby—the discovery and rescue of Ida's sister—Sendak also identified with those goblins and changeling "ice babies" who were products of ambiguous marriages in secret, womb-like darkness. Those hooded and ice-cold creatures were mistaken for aggressors against children; they looked like kidnappers, or even sexual predators, Ida fearing that her sister was to become a "nasty goblin bride." They were like wild sailors beneath an ocean moon, in fluid homosocial waters outside of conventional society, exuding queerness, subjugation, and death. Considering the unkind associations made across the twentieth century between gay men, the worship of youth, and social corruption, it seems far from a coincidence that Fire Island crossed Sendak's mind as he visualized the setting for this narrative; in an August 1977 study for the opening scene in which Ida and her mother face Papa's ship fading into the horizon, Sendak specifically wrote himself a note to paint a Fire Island sunset for that composition.[100] Fire Island, a space of freedom and creative community for the artist, also offered a stand-in for imagined social dangers and the liminality of the ocean and those called to it. Sendak may have even recalled tabloids from his childhood in the 1930s that had conflated gay men and sailors, satirizing both, along with prostitutes, as members of an erotic subculture of urban ports. Cartoons that caricatured the competition between gay men and female sex workers to win the interest of docked sailors may have been some of the first artifacts of popular culture to which the young Sendak was exposed. In the art world, painters such as Paul Cadmus had also displayed homoerotic paintings of seamen in those years. His piece The Fleet's In! (1934), for example, depicts solicitations between sailors, gay men, and prostitutes on New York's boardwalks. Cadmus wrote, "I always enjoyed watching them when I was young. I somewhat envied them the freedom of their lives and their lack of inhibitions."[101] Sailors would continue to stand in for uninhibited eros in the collective imagination of the latter twentieth century, not least of all in the homoerotic drawings of artists like "Tom of Finland" (Touko Valio Laaksonen). Creating his own sensual drawings of men, including pictures of voluptuous sailors he imagined from Melville's maritime novella Billy Budd, Sendak too would continue to explore erotic truths within a climate increasingly anxious about gay male sexuality.

Accompanying the release of *Outside Over There*, the year 1981 would see Americans introduced to a mysterious virus that appeared most evidently among gay men and that would unleash a polarizing epidemic. Amidst the AIDS crisis and the Reagan administration, Sendak's emotional turmoil and conflicted relationship with the dominant culture found expression in the fairy-tale genre. Reviewing the mechanisms of this genre, Donald Haase has noted how the "fundamental themes of separation and exile" signal inner journeys, as isolated characters endure the travails of the outside world.[102] Sendak's attraction to fairy tales is evident in his depiction of endangered children faced with supernatural forces in Romantic German landscapes, as in *Outside Over There*. The artist was intimately familiar with fairy-tale conventions from having earlier illustrated a number of traditional tales, including a collection of the Brothers Grimm titled *The Juniper Tree* (1973). His friendship with Justin Schiller and Raymond Wapner, collectors who ran a Manhattan antiquarian rare books shop, led to his discovery of a four-page autographed letter Wilhelm Grimm wrote in 1816 to a child named Amalie ("Mili") von Zuydwyck as she grieved her lost mother. Mili's parents were part of a Westphalian aristocratic circle that supported the Grimms' efforts to collect fairy tales.[103] Sendak illustrated Ralph Manheim's 1983 translation of this letter, published as *Dear Mili* (1988) and dedicated to Sendak's sister, Natalie.[104] He used a German Romanticist aesthetic with inspiration from Runge and Friedrich, hiding the name "P.O. Runge" in the bottom right of the cover's floral design. The story presents a blissful mother-daughter relationship interrupted by warfare. Darkened clouds of smoke circled by lurid flames suggest the sunflowers of *Outside Over There*, whose kidnapped infant, Sendak claimed, had grown to become the unnamed child protagonist he conceived for *Dear Mili*. Faced with encroaching danger, this child is sent alone by her mother into the forest to hide. "You can imagine how the child felt at being left all alone," reads the text, beside an illustration that recalls Snow White's escape from her evil stepmother in Walt Disney's 1937 animated film, which had made its lasting impact on Sendak as a child viewer. The jagged, gnarled branches of trees frame the girl's small figure from both sides and from above, like a menacing trap against a darkening sky: "[S]he was terrified, for she thought that wild beasts had seized her in their jaws and would tear her to pieces. . . . [T]he farther she went, the heavier her heart grew." The following wordless page spread is an overwhelming tangle of roots, tree trunks, branches, and shadows, the recesses and hollows in the lumpy trunks resembling orifices or hooded figures, like the goblins of *Outside Over There* or *Snow White*'s Evil Queen in her cloaked disguise. In the distant background, a group of children march solemnly across a bridge supported by crooked tree trunks before a concentration-camp guard tower. The girl makes her way to Saint Joseph's hut, deeper in the woods.

Despite loving German art and the Grimms, Sendak struggled at first to relate to the Christian elements of this story. He sought advice from a friend at the New Skete monastery in Cambridge, New York, who reminded Sendak that Saint Joseph was just a good-natured Jew. Following this notion, the artist decided to base Joseph's likeness on Sam Perles, a Brooklyn friend of the family from Sendak's childhood. He would also model the gravestones in the story on the Czech cemetery where Rabbi Loew of the Golem of Prague legend is buried, including a lion of Judah on one of them.[105] He thus embellished the Grimm story with his own history as an American Jew for whom Old World Europe presented familiar and dangerous associations. Joseph's hut appears without doors, the overgrown lilies, sunflowers, and vines making their way inside, as sunflowers do in *Outside Over There*, even reaching the space under the bed. Joseph's home, in which nature creeps indoors, also recalls Max's room in *Where the Wild Things Are*, in which the harsh feedback of the external world could be safely worked through via imagined scenes and conflicts—bedposts turned to tree trunks, private rage into monsters. This visual transgression of natural law reflected an emotional message in the letter accompanying the original text of *Dear Mili*. Wilhelm Grimm had written Mili that the outside world of "meadows, cities and villages . . . cannot be moved, and humans cannot fly. But one human heart goes out to another, undeterred by what lies between."[106] Sendak's depiction of the afterlife thus blended notions of inside and outside to illustrate the transcendent capacity of human beings to enter each other's inner worlds through leaps of empathy—even across boundaries of time, space, nation, religion, or gender.

Gay Sex and Death

As the AIDS crisis ravaged the United States and took many of the artist's contemporaries, Sendak made even bolder steps outside of himself to memorialize losses and condemn the indifference and exploitation of the conservative capitalist establishment. The American public reacted anxiously to AIDS and to the social liberation movements of the previous two decades in ways that recalled the conservative zeitgeist of Sendak's childhood years. AIDS took many of Sendak's loved ones and ushered in a new kind of homophobia from a society that often framed it as a "gay disease," a punishment for sexual "sin," or as a problem not worthy of governmental resources. Countless infected youth were abandoned by their bigoted or fearful families. Sedgwick and others have written of the terror and grief that gay men and their friends and families experienced in the late 1980s, as continuous loss, mourning, and fear led many to feel utterly abandoned and dislodged from social protection.[107] In 1986, for example, the Supreme Court's *Bowers v. Hardwick* decision upheld the constitutionality of criminalizing gay sexuality, responding in part to the AIDS public health crisis and its concentration in the gay male community.[108] On Halloween of 1989, the AIDS advocacy group Act Up, founded by Larry Kramer, led a public demonstration by Trump Tower on Fifth Avenue, protesting the fact that Donald Trump and other billionaires were enjoying multimillion-dollar tax breaks at a time when thousands lay homeless. Activist Ronny Viggiani dressed in drag as Dorothy from *The Wizard of Oz*, raising a sign that demanded in cursive, "Surrender Donald," mirroring the "Surrender Dorothy" message traced in smoke by the Wicked Witch on broomstick in the MGM film. Thousands had lost their apartments due to skyrocketing medical bills related to HIV/AIDS, as well as to the common legal inability of same-sex companions to remain in their sick or deceased partners' residences in a time preceding civil unions and gay marriage. The presence of a Dorothy at this demonstration, evoking the lament of "There's no place like home," called attention to the reconfigured state of "home" and "family" for tens of thousands of infected people displaced and abandoned in this era. The use of the Wicked Witch's words acknowledged and challenged the demonization queer people experienced. Many infected individuals in those years were banished and derided like witches or lepers, losing their jobs and the support of their nuclear families. Some found "chosen family" in political assemblies, community centers, cultural hubs, volunteers, nurses, and physicians.[109] Home became, for many of those affected, "inside out."

During these years, Glynn worked tirelessly at the Gay Men's Health Crisis (GMHC) to help those fighting the disease, and Sendak visited close friends and colleagues who were dying, donated to the GMHC, and later painted a mural of his Wild Things in the "Child Life Program" room of their Manhattan building, for children with HIV and children of GMHC clients.[110] The artist once remarked, "It's amazing, just dumb luck, that I didn't die of Aids [sic]. Some of my very dearest friends died."[111] In 1998, Where the Wild Things Are merchandise raised $25,000 to support pediatric AIDS care at Boston's Latino Health Institute.[112] In 2010, three years after Glynn's passing, Sendak would donate a million dollars in Glynn's name to the Jewish Board of Family and Children's Services to support mental health and social services in the New York metropolitan area. A notice about the donation published that year in the Chronicle of Philanthropy would recognize Glynn as someone who treated young people at the Jewish Board for about thirty years, as well as "helped people affected by the AIDS epidemic throughout the '80s and '90s."[113]

If Sendak was limited by the wider culture's impulse to paint homosexuality as perverse or deadly, he also followed in a tradition of artists and thinkers who reimagined it on their own terms. His portrayals of homoerotic sexuality and death became more explicit in the late 1980s and the 1990s, reflecting his sensitivity to mortality and his internalization of sexual danger. As Kushner notes, only after the first years of the AIDS epidemic did Sendak create older boy protagonists who confront social perils without the safety net of a loving family or home.[114] Death occupied much of Sendak's contemplation in those years, AIDS losses fusing with early internalizations about the fragility of human life and the pain of losing loved ones. Moreover, Sendak's own health declined as he aged. In 1980, he suffered nearly fatal blood poisoning, writing to Selma Lanes about his inability to walk.[115] In 1988 he wrote to Bohlman about the tendinitis he suffered in both hands and the drug he took for it that was destroying his gut, as well as fears about his dogs dying. Wondering whether he loved with too much intensity, he concluded that the price of love was terror.[116] James Marshall died of AIDS-related causes in October 1992. At the time Sendak felt that Marshall had been his last genuine connection to book publishing. Processing this painful loss, he felt himself emerging from his emotional fog with a new forceful energy fueled both by rage and by acquired wisdom.[117]

We Are All in the Dumps with Jack and Guy (1993), a merger of two little-known Mother Goose rhymes, fused the artist's amazement at his own survival with feelings of social abandonment experienced by gay men condemned during a media-sensationalized health epidemic, despite the social gains of the gay liberation movement. It depicts a city run by capitalist rats who play cards while a horde of children are made homeless, like the thousands of Americans evicted due to HIV/AIDS. These children clothe themselves in scraps of newspaper that advertise products and that report on AIDS and other tragedies, one of them even memorializing Marshall's burial: "Oct. 17, 1992. Jim Goes Home." The book integrated memories of dirty, naked, homeless children whose feet stuck out of cardboard boxes at night near the posh Rodeo Drive in Los Angeles, as well as memories of brave, bald-headed children fighting cancer in the London hospital Sendak once visited. It channeled the artist's "misery over the loss of gifted students and colleagues to AIDS."[118] As he stated in 1999, "[M]y later books will be haunted by AIDS . . . it's because of the need to . . . keep it up front and to stop it."[119] The epidemic encouraged Sendak to step beyond his private world, if only temporarily. Speaking about *Dumps*, the artist called it the first book of his that was "not preoccupied with my private concerns and dilemmas. By being absorbed in politics for the first time in a long time, by watching friends die of AIDS . . . I've become a more social, political animal. *Dumps* reflects this . . . getting out of myself into a place where real things happen, not psychological, magical things anymore." The artist lamented, "[C]hildren get shot on the way to school, children contract AIDS, children are in the most vulnerable position imaginable. If we aren't honest with them, they'll die. . . . If we don't look, and if we don't listen, and if we don't do something, kids will be lost."[120] While preparing to publish *Dumps,* it seems Sendak was almost on the verge of coming out to the world. Art Spiegelman met with Sendak that year and told the *New Yorker,* "Maurice was about to have a book come out . . . that he felt had to do with AIDS. And he was wondering whether he was going to come out of the closet at that moment publicly."[121]

Following *Dumps,* Sendak's illustrations dealt more explicitly with sexuality and its connection to death and doom: he completed violent, sexually graphic paintings for the 1995 Kraken edition of Herman Melville's *Pierre; or, The Ambiguities* (1852) and for Heinrich von Kleist's *Penthesilea* (1998), which follows the attack of warrior Amazon women on Achilles and his men, whom the Amazons take as prisoners and sexual servants. Sendak's drawings for *Penthesilea* delight in the physicality of gore and sex; he paints the captured Achilles embracing his clothed Amazon captor, his own nude form rippling and ruddy, his uncircumcised penis engorged.[122] He painted a row of raging blonde Amazon women with flaming torches behind a shadowed foreground of crouched, androgynous Greek men with smooth bodies, long blonde hair, and strained, forlorn faces reminiscent of Leonardo da Vinci's drawings of the Virgin Mary. In his illustrations for the Melville, Sendak dressed Pierre in a skin-tight bodysuit, emphasizing his muscular body and pronounced genitalia. Pierre moves from poses of confidence and bliss to ambiguous romantic entanglements with male and female figures alike.[123] Photographer John Dugdale sold Sendak images of male nudes posed according to the stances Sendak needed for his drawings. The artist read between the lines of *Pierre,* understanding its coded motifs of secrecy and brotherhood used to propel the narrative drama; the protagonist hears a spirit call, "Come into solitude with me, twin-brother; come away: a secret have I; let me whisper it to thee aside; in this closet. . . . " This leads him to a secret, "gay-hearted" portrait of his deceased father from his youth, hidden in "a locked, round windowed closet" connected to Pierre's room.[124] Though still not officially "out" to the mainstream media, Sendak read selections from *Pierre* in one of Manhattan's gay bookstores to mark the book's publication in 1995. In his final illustration for *Pierre*, the protagonist crouches fully nude, holding up a falling, dark sky that threatens to consume him, his eyes wild and pained. As one reviewer wrote of these illustrations, "The AIDS epidemic and America's panicked retreat from liberalism . . . pushed the artist into a stronger commitment to sexuality in his work. Until now, Sendak's orientation has not been hidden so much as warily positioned vis-à-vis homophobic America."[125]

Considering the underlying notes of incestuous desire and homosexuality involved in *Pierre*, it's interesting that Sendak was first introduced to Melville's writing by his brother, Jack, a Melville aficionado whose relationship with Sendak was an intimate and influential one. Jack encouraged Sendak to read Melville when the latter was in his twenties, a time in Sendak's life in which he began to accept his own gay sexuality. Kushner, who first befriended Sendak through a shared love of Melville, wrote that "Melville idolatry" functioned as a sort of "calling card, a point of introduction, particularly among gay men," describing Melville's character Pierre as a fatherless, beautiful man "engulfed in a moral, sexual, political and artistic fog."[126] Sendak surely knew this association, stating that he believed his brother was also "probably gay but he married, and his wife hated me because I was more famous than him" (after writing a few books for children, two of which Sendak illustrated, Jack worked at the Emerson radio company and at a post office).[127] The ambiguous conflations of sibling bonds, sexuality, and morbid danger in some of Sendak's later work reveals how he allowed elements of his "inside" world—home, family, sex, and death—to mix in unrestrained, intuitive ways.

The artist explicitly connected his feelings of outrage and endangerment as a gay man during the AIDS crisis with his memories of growing up Jewish during World War II, stating, "having my parents' families wiped out in the Holocaust, and then another holocaust later in my life—it's a hideous century."[128] In 1998 he brought these feelings to a collaboration with Pilobolus Dance Theater, lending his efforts to a piece called "A Selection." The Pilobolus dancers' "playful, almost shameful use of the body" reminded Sendak of babies and young children.[129] *Last Dance* (2002), Mirra Bank's documentary about the production process, shows the artist improvising and interjecting with dark, sexual, and Yiddish-inflected humor as he expresses sensibilities connected to queer Jewish endangerment and desire.[130] When disagreement erupts between the Pilobolus artistic directors and Sendak, who refuses to budge on his desire to include a scene of a family waiting for a train to Auschwitz, one of the directors tells the camera, "[H]e's a sensitive guy . . . we should take that into account and deal with him differently than we would one of us." Watching the dancers improvise, one reaching into the folds of another dancer's torso to pull out an imaginary object, Sendak cries, "Dr. Mengele!" When another dancer puts on a hat and makeshift sidelocks, the artist declares, "Yeshiva bocher!" Later, playing a folksy tune, Sendak has the dancers chant, "Jews, Jews, Jews, I've got news for yous!" His costume designs for the piece include a sketch of Anne Frank at age thirteen, as well as a glamorous, swastika-patterned dress in a style reminiscent of Eva Braun and Marlene Dietrich.

Last Dance conveys Sendak's intent on making visual connections between Holocaust elements and queer sexuality, highlighting and fusing these as unjustified dangers of the twentieth century. As a wartime family is torn apart in "A Selection," a dancer named Otis, personifying Death, wrestles the father out of his clothes, gripping the exposed, naked male dancer from behind. The costume for Otis is a white, skintight bodysuit worn under a striped concentration camp uniform. Behind the scenes, Sendak hand-paints the elastic bodysuit as it sits directly on Otis's muscular body. Bending over as the artist paints the dancer's rear-end, Otis jokingly compares himself to an "Assyrian boy" among "the Greeks," proclaiming, "canvas is too expensive; the boys are cheaper." The figure of a shrieking child dangles from the groin area of the painted bodysuit, simultaneously devoured and birthed by Death's loins. The costume explicitly, and perhaps ironically, links a stigmatized, allegedly "unnatural" sexuality with child endangerment, but also with a child's origins. Sendak despised criticism of his work as "too sexual for children," because of both the implication that children were essentially asexual and the misconception that Sendak's work existed only for children or for the sake of promoting a specific sort of child development. As an artist marketed to children, however, he felt pressured to stay publicly discreet about his gayness until his old age due to homophobic associations made between homosexuality and pedophilia. In "A Selection," the costume of Death, however, queerly conflates the powerful male artist, who, Zeus-like, births his own creations, with the menacing, demonized forces of unrestrained passion, which also threaten politically vulnerable subjects by fusing with or devouring them.

As Katie Roiphe notes, Sendak's obsession with death may also be explained by the message from his immigrant family that "he should be grateful to be alive, that his continued existence involved some aspect of luck that should not, if he was smart, be pushed." Roiphe notes Sendak's stereotypical Jewish diasporic instincts of reserving personal information from the public, expecting the worst, and not "jinxing" good luck—instincts internalized through a history of expulsions, the Depression, and the Holocaust.[131] Cultural theorists also point to the symbolic imposition of morbidity upon gay men. Popular representations position gay men as negators of reproduction, self-obliterating pleasure-seekers, and gravediggers of society. According to Lee Edelman, for example, the symbolic childlessness of queer people creates a lasting cultural association with sterile, narcissistic pleasures perceived as destructive to collective, future-oriented values, like the costume for Death in "A Selection" as a sexualized man whose loins birth and eat a shrieking child.[132] Did Sendak fear that others might view him this way, as a gay man who made his name by amplifying marginalized feelings in children's picture books?

Sensitive literary treatments like Larry Kramer's play *The Normal Heart* (1985), Sendak's *We Are All in the Dumps* (1993) and Kushner's play *Angels in America* (1991–93) worked to humanize gay men and others suffering AIDS and social neglect in the last decades of the twentieth century. When *Angels in America* aired as an HBO miniseries in 2003, Sendak appeared in the very first episode. In a cemetery on a cold autumn day, he sits beside Kushner himself and actor Meryl Streep, costumed in drag as an elderly male rabbi. All wear long beards, black hats, spectacles, and forlorn expressions. Following a funeral, this scene takes place in the deathly space of a graveyard as Louis, a gay Jewish protagonist, discovers that his partner has AIDS. The funeral is not for an AIDS victim, however, but for Louis's grandmother. In a preceding eulogy, recited in a heavy Slavic accent by Streep's character, the viewer learns that Louis's grandmother was an immigrant who "carried the old world on her back across the ocean. . . . " to raise a family "in this strange place," perceived optimistically as "the melting pot where nothing melted," a land where social differences were imagined to coexist in peace.[133] The specter of this Jewish grandmother's sacrifice frames the piece's exploration of Louis's guilt-ridden abandonment of his lover, a gentile who battles AIDS against a backdrop of domestic, political, and theological chaos. More than addressing the AIDS crisis, however, the play addresses the fear of "melting"—of dying physically of AIDS, or dying spiritually in a "melting pot" that burns away difference in the service of conformity. Kushner presents an open, pressing question—is America a place where minorities survive and maintain their innermost dreams, or a place where they must choose between assimilation and dissolution?

Five years after his television appearance, Sendak spoke with a *New York Times* writer who wondered whether the eighty-year-old artist wanted to share anything new with the public. "Well, that I'm gay," he answered, explaining his previous reticence through the logic of a fierce child of immigrants: children protect their parents.[134] The *Times* ran the article on a September morning on which Sendak found himself recovering from surgery and attending to his other "parents," Ruth Krauss and Crockett Johnson, whom he'd once affectionately called his "weekend parents" during his early years at Harper. Philip Nel was then writing their biography, and the artist had agreed to review portions of Nel's draft. He spoke with Nel by telephone on the day of the *Times* article's printing. The latter recalls a distracted Sendak interrupting himself during their conversation, changing the subject to fret over his remarks in the paper that day—that they might have sounded odd or jarringly frank.[135] Uncommon concerns for the wild truth-teller, for whom oddness and frankness were celebrated virtues, Sendak's fretting reflected his understanding of the delicate but treacherous relationships between exposure and endangerment, liberation and retaliation. As the villainous dictator of *Brundibar* hauntingly reminds the reader after his defeat, bullies don't disappear; they recede temporarily.

Tensions of Jewish, queer, and other minority groups pervade Sendak's drive to remain distinct from a generic public and from a potentially dangerous "outside" world that continuously fluctuates in its valuation of distinction. His creative attempts at resolving those tensions hermetically from the "inside" reflect nothing less than a fight for survival. He fought to survive a society whose subsuming acceptance, on the one hand, threatened to neutralize his unusual "inner child" and his creative talents; he fought to survive coercive social expectations, on the other hand, that appeared bent on reshaping or "melting" him like a soluble ingredient—the Wicked Witch of the West, the ice baby in *Outside Over There*, or Mickey in the bakers' cake. Thus he reflexively built walls and empowered his "own kind" against a potentially insensitive or hostile world in which he experienced his personhood as an endangered rarity. The artist's cultivation of a creative interiority, differentiating in stark ways between "inside" and "outside," helped him to clarify his own understandings of love, family, and mortality. Exploring the meaning and boundaries of his relationships and desires, Sendak sought to define and preserve the contours of his elusive and historically tenuous identity. He fought to express the survivalist impulses and unusual vitality of a life predicated on multiple forms of marginal distinctiveness, interiority, and emotional catharsis against limited public acceptance and understanding.

A GARDEN ON THE EDGE OF THE WORLD

THERE IS A TRUISM that the worst thing a teacher can do for a child is to paint a picture of the world in which that child cannot imagine existing. That kind of painting erases potential mirrors for growth and belonging. In some cases, however, unseen or rejected hearts energize underground to challenge convention, to emerge from social incoherence into the light of vital, clarified vision, to decry the limitations of a society that would bury them. "They tried to bury us," begins an adage of the Greek poet Dinos Christianopoulos, "they didn't know we were seeds." Sendak's history, like the archetypal Sendakian narratives that survive him, tells of a buried subject who becomes the seed of a creative revolution.

From the artist's perspective, a modern culture of "childhood innocence" buried human beings in at least two ways: it infused a protected realm of development with emotional coercion, and it endangered those left outside of it. Such an approach punishes those, like Sendak, who question or puzzle social authorities. In the most disastrous of cases, it sanctions exclusion and physical violence against those denied access to favored social roles. Children's literature scholar Robin Bernstein has shown this to be true in the case of Black American children denied access to the cultural category of "childhood innocence."[1] From the age of American slavery to cases like that of Trayvon Martin (1995–2012),

whose killer claimed to have mistakenly perceived the unarmed seventeen-year-old youth as a dangerous adult man, the denial of Black
children's "innocence" has been a testament in America to the lies society tells itself about which social categories of people are truly at risk
and truly deserving of protection.[2] Sendak, as a visionary who dreamed
against the grain of his time, saw children as liminal and misunderstood
figures, like himself. "I refuse to lie to children," he insisted. "I refuse to
cater to the bullshit of innocence."[3]

The present study has examined Sendak as an American-born but
ethnically and sexually queer artist committed to an emotional stance
both within and apart from mainstream American culture. Taken together, his life and work compose a feelings-led story of a passionate
insider-outsider who pushed through the soils of callousness, conservatism, and conformity to offer the world his heart—a queer, "Old
World" Jewish American, achingly human heart. The contested space
of childhood and the shifting field of postwar children's literature offered Sendak contexts in which to articulate new cultural sensibilities
and survival strategies for endangered subjects in hostile environments.
Though the picture-book form had grown as a modernist innovation,
Sendak's contributions to it were unusual in their intermixing of modernist influences, such as psychoanalysis and comic-book conventions,
and antimodernist influences, including the traditional "high art" of
German Romanticism and Victorian illustration, Yiddish folk rhythms,
and family memory. He offered children's literature and the wider culture an unprecedented creative model for taking seriously the emotions
of early childhood, a domain aligned in his work with his own historical
and social position, one he experienced as a permanent state of question
and endangerment, an endless problem to solve by diving inward.

His life and the trajectory of his creative output are intertwined
with broader social histories of marginal Americans, as well as with an
unfolding history of modern children's literature. The artist grew up
endangered in ways that were often imperceptible, and that came from
multiple directions. His need to learn the "laws of the land" as a child of
immigrants and to gain social acceptance while enduring the effects of
family trauma and his own atypical feelings as a queer person evokes the

central concern of his art: the process by which a vulnerable subject determines how to survive and face dangers beyond comprehension. The circumstances of his life indirectly offered him insights into modern children's complicated social positions. "Old World" ethnic roots and the feelings of a queer youth were both targets belittled by twentieth-century American socialization processes aimed at creating a specific national future—a goal for which most children were also symbolically flattened, or "melted," under the banner of the "generic child." Twentieth-century immigrant families had struggled to acculturate amidst nativism and prejudice, frequently perceiving mainstream America as hostile. They were the objects of diligent reform initiatives that sometimes approached new Americans condescendingly as children in need of instruction, or as raw matter to be trained and sculpted. Surpassing their parents in American social capital, first-generation children of immigrants like Sendak painfully learned how their older relatives appeared to others through the eyes of the American establishment: as "Wild Things." Children of immigrant families like Sendak's navigated both the plight of childhood in a modernizing culture foreign to their parents and the plight of surviving overwhelming emotional pressures at home connected to losses of World War II. Midcentury Jewish Americans endured the second-hand effects of genocide in Europe, where many of their relatives and communities were destroyed. Across these decades, American Jews' experiences led them to place additional value on their children as compensatory symbols of redemption, as links in a threatened lineage, and, sometimes, as the only relatives left alive. Thus any childish indiscretion could make Sendak, too, a "Wild Thing" in the eyes of grieving parents who lacked energy to handle misbehaving children and who needed those children to stand in for their own murdered families abroad. The Sendakian child is one wary of caretakers' feelings, feelings that may grow so large as to displace everything else, feelings which are to be feared but also lovingly addressed.

Moreover, the position of embodying a gay or queer subjectivity, especially in a context that did not offer socially valid options for queer desires or self-concepts, also contributed to Sendak's experience of emotional obscurity or invisibility, of an isolating difference even among one's closest kin. This frustrating experience faces most of the children in his stories. Queer children navigate the personal travails of accepting and surviving physiologies that mark them as socially "deviant," often without the help or understanding of even their own caretakers. Sendak expressed a vision in which isolated and disenfranchised subjects become profound creative artists, deserving of representation and redemption without acculturating to the behavioral ideals of the society that would erase them. He changed modern conceptions of childhood with his compelling artistic depictions of misunderstood children forced into dangerous situations for which they were not yet prepared. His protagonists are punished for unleashing their difficult emotions, yet also victorious by harnessing inner resources, fantasy, and play.

Throughout the twentieth century, Sendak believed that the adult public would not have accepted the idea of a gay man writing books for children due to problematic and unfounded associations made between homosexuality and pedophilia.[4] This problem perpetuated his fluctuation between feelings of hiddenness and self-exposure, as well as his enduring sense of not being fully known or understood by others. A personality both porous and guarded, he fluctuated in his own life and work between the internalized weight of others' emotional worlds and the drive to clarify and protect his own. The worlds he came to straddle—including New York's stigmatized and wildly creative gay subculture, the rapidly expanding but conservatively critiqued field of children's literature, and the tight-knit atmosphere of his suffering immigrant family—were, in some respects, impossibly far apart. His experience of emotional overextension and social incoherence demanded unrestrained bouts of fantasy, release, and invention. Playing in this way, he made work that appealed to young children, who learn to function socially by trusting their urgent, if unclear emotions, and, like Rosie, by using strategies like Camp to test different performances, roles, and disguises while orienting toward external powers and new possibilities. Guided by these strong internal currents, Sendak applied his perspectives to the space of childhood, seeing children as kindred spirits: children were, like himself, human beings on the edge of the world.

In some respects, the artist used the space of childhood to recon-
ceive concrete, specific dangers of puritanism, posttraumatic family
life, and social coercion. He linked the anxieties of his own embodied
position with universal reservations about socializing vital, sensitive
children into superficial, deadened adults. America and the wider
Western world could more easily share these concerns especially after
World War II warned of the dangers of social conformity and fascism,
prompting an inward search for renewed human values. As American culture looked to children and childhood to champion a symbolic
collective rebirth, Sendak fought to dignify the queerness, emotional
seriousness, and sensitivity of children. With enormous humor and
vitality, he helped poke holes in the culturally biased optimism of
midcentury, championed the zeitgeist of emergent social liberation in
the 1960s and 1970s, and alternated in the following decades between
political confrontation and hermetic meaning-making as the public
retracted anxiously toward more conservative ideals during the AIDS
crisis. The artist's life and work offer a fascinating history of critically
resisting pressures to sacrifice particularity for the safety of belonging,
as well as a model of untangling "reality" from fantasy, social expectation from emotional truth.

Sendak's legacy is vast. As *New York Times* art critic Brian O'Doherty
described him, the artist was "one of the most powerful men in the US"
due to his ability to "give shape to the fantasies of millions of children."[5]
About three hundred people were present at his memorial service at the
Metropolitan Museum of Art in New York, according to James Bohlman,
who attended.[6] As one obituary declared, *Where the Wild Things Are* had
changed the history of children's books.[7] At the time of Sendak's passing in 2012, his books had sold almost thirty million copies in the United
States alone, *Wild Things* having sold over nineteen million copies
worldwide. As John Cech notes, even the term "Wild Thing" has gained
near-universal currency as "a general descriptor for a wide spectrum of
mischievous, outside-the-box behaviors—from the innocently playful to
the knowingly erotic."[8] The phrase even made its mark on social movements, such as radical feminism, with a grassroots collective of queer
Jewish women choosing in 1982 to be called Di Vilde Chayes (Yiddish

for "the wild beasts") under the leadership of such influential figures as Evelyn Torton Beck, Irena Klepfisz, Melanie Kaye/Kantrowitz, and Adrienne Rich.[9] *Wild Things* has inspired several literary and dramatic adaptations, it has been used successfully as a tool in art therapy for children, and it was even read by President Barack Obama at the White House's 2015 annual Easter Egg Roll.[10] In January 2020, the largest public library system in the United States, the New York Public Library, reported that *Wild Things* was the fourth most circulated book in the library system's entire one-hundred-and-twenty-five-year history.[11]

Beyond his own creations, Sendak helped establish *Sesame Street*, which changed television and children's engagement with learning. He influenced Jim Henson's conception of the Muppets and inspired new directions in embracing allegedly "monstrous" elements of self, humanizing "othered" figures in media for both children and adults.[12] Sendak's legacy also opened the door for an outpouring of representations of wild, dark, and unapologetic children who reject socially imposed expectations, follow their inner compasses, and sensitively attune to menacing forces beyond their grasp. Such figures have included "Jonas" of Lois Lowry's *The Giver* (1993), "Harry Potter" of J. K. Rowling's fantasy series (1997–2007), and the Baudelaire siblings of *A Series of Unfortunate Events* (1999–2006) by Lemony Snicket (the pen name of Daniel Handler), not to mention the countless examples found in contemporary television and film. Such representations are virtually unimaginable, in children's literature and beyond, without the example of queer Jewish Sendak. They remain vital in a century that has continued to threaten the basic rights of those most vulnerable and that has even enforced prolonged separations of parents from children at national borders. Sendak's *We Are All in the Dumps with Jack and Guy* (1993) presciently informed political dangers of the early twenty-first century, including the "zero tolerance" immigration policy, which separated thousands of migrant children from their parents at the U.S.-Mexico border in 2018. In *We Are All in the Dumps* Sendak placed "Trumped Tower" above a dystopian landscape of homeless children, who must form a makeshift family in order to survive. Reflecting on these images, Eric Pederson muses, "If he was alive today, he'd be busy working on multiple books about Trump and the border, and the wall would probably look like a [concentration] camp wall."[13]

Sendak channeled the internalized peculiarities of a queer, Yiddish-infused, Brooklyn "ghetto" childhood to irreversibly expand children's literature and the wider culture. During his own youth, the artificial boundaries placed around bourgeois childhood had stood in tension with the familial norms of working-class homes, acculturating immigrants, and those marked by war traumas. As Art Spiegelman argues, Sendak saw that "the distinction between children and adults is probably one of hypocrisy more than anything else."[14] Adults project onto children aspects of character and personality that they seek to banish from their own identities, whether angelic or wild. Throughout his work, Sendak answered hypocrisy with creative force and with snark, enjoying an enormous sense of humor, sometimes dark and ironic. His persistently skeptical and cantankerous disposition drew from his life-long identification with emotional states of a "rough" childhood and from his guiding principle that his own early years were not sweet or innocent, but rather sensual, terrifying, thrilling, and lonely. Growing into a man out of sync with mainstream adult society, the artist found solidarity in child readers, whom he viewed as more honest, raw, and perceptive than adults. In his own words, "nothing but the truth will suffice for children."[15] He believed that children were the most sophisticated and daring readers, that they "dive right into symbols and metaphor. They just go, and they get it. They know how to get right to the heart of the matter [because] fantasy is all-pervasive in a child's life."[16] If Sendak was guilty of essentializing children in his own way—children as always perceptive and emotionally resilient—it's likely that he did so to defend important childhood possibilities precluded in the wider culture.

Working through terrors and untangling social fictions, Sendak's artistic obsession with childhood has built existential foundations for buried and endangered souls of all ages, offering outrageous fantasy, brave emotional release, and generative play as paths more effective for "becoming one's self" than those of blind submission to power. He reminds us that we all begin as children and that children are profoundly

human animals—corporeal, discerning, and in need of love and recognition, without the bullshit of innocence. In the world of Sendak, children
want to grow up, but not to lose their childhood selves. The artist's creative vision and identity cannot be essentialized to any single facet of his
personhood, even as each lends rich territory for analysis. "Old World"
Yiddishkeit, queerness, and positionality vis-à-vis war, memory, kinship, and trauma, for example, are all mutually influential prisms that
contribute to the larger pursuit of positioning and appreciating the artist's life and work. Metaphorically speaking, they are fused ingredients
within the archetypal Sendakian cake that Mickey offers the world each
morning. They are mixed and scattered seeds of the Sendakian garden
that blooms perennially, reaching like sunflowers through windows for
receptive readers on the edges of all conformist and unfeeling worlds.

Appendix

Timeline of Selected Life Events, Works, and Influences

1928   Maurice (Moishe) Bernard Sendak is born as the third and youngest child of Sadie (Sarah) (1895–1968) and Philip (Pinchas) (1896–1970) on June 10 in Bensonhurst, Brooklyn, New York

1932   Charles and Anne Lindbergh's infant son is kidnapped and found dead; a four-year-old Sendak is struck by a photograph of the infant's corpse on a front-page issue at a newspaper stand

1934   Birth of the identical Dionne quintuplets

1937   *Snow White and the Seven Dwarfs* (animated film, Walt Disney Productions)

1939   *The Wizard of Oz* (live-action film, Metro-Goldwyn-Mayer)

1939–1940   World's Fair held in Queens, New York, April 30–October 27; an eleven-year-old Sendak attends with his sister, Natalie, who loses track of him there; Sendak returns home to Brooklyn in a police car

1940   *Pinocchio* and *Fantasia* (animated films, Walt Disney Productions)

1941   The Nazis conquer Zambrow, Poland, Philip's town of origin, where most of his relatives remain (June 22)

1941   Sendak's bar mitzvah (June)

1945   World War II ends, and Sendak witnesses victory
          celebrations in Manhattan

1946   Sendak graduates Lafayette High School and relocates to
          Hell's Kitchen in Manhattan to work at Timely Service's
          warehouse

1947   Hyman Ruchlis, a physics teacher from Sendak's high school,
          commissions his illustrations for a McGraw-Hill science
          textbook

1948   Sendak moves back to his parents' apartment in Brooklyn,
          where he makes handmade toys with his brother, Jack, and
          sketches "Rosie" and other neighborhood children from his
          window

1949   Sendak accepts a job at FAO Schwarz in window-display
          construction

1950   Sendak meets Harper editor Ursula Nordstrom through
          introduction by an FAO Schwarz book buyer

1951   *The Wonderful Farm*, pictures by Sendak, written by Marcel
          Aymé (Harper & Brothers)

1951   *Good Shabbos, Everybody*, pictures by Sendak, written by
          Robert Garvey (United Synagogue Commission on Jewish
          Education)

1952   *A Hole Is to Dig*, pictures by Sendak, written by Ruth Krauss
          (Harper & Brothers)

1952   Sendak relocates, first to Midtown East and then to
          Greenwich Village, where he remains for about two decades

1954   *Happy Hanukah, Everybody*, pictures by Sendak, written by
          Hyman and Alice Chanover (United Synagogue Commission
          on Jewish Education)

1954   *I'll Be You and You Be Me*, pictures by Sendak, written by
          Ruth Krauss (HarperCollins)

1955   *Seven Little Stories on Big Subjects*, pictures by Sendak,
          written by Gladys Baker Bond (Anti-Defamation League of
          B'nai B'rith)

1955   "Where the Wild Horses Are" book dummy by Sendak, dated
          November 17

1956   *The House of Sixty Fathers*, pictures by Sendak, written by
          Meindert DeJong (Harper & Brothers)

1956	*I Want to Paint My Bathroom Blue*, pictures by Sendak, written by Ruth Krauss (Harper & Brothers)
1956	*Kenny's Window* (Harper & Row)
1957	*Circus Girl*, pictures by Sendak, written by Jack Sendak (Harper & Brothers)
1957	*Little Bear*, pictures by Sendak, written by Else Minarik (Harper & Brothers)
1957	*Very Far Away* (Harper & Brothers)
1960	*The Sign on Rosie's Door* (Harper & Brothers)
1961	*Let's Be Enemies*, pictures by Sendak, written by Janice May Udry (Harper & Row)
1962	*The Nutshell Library* (Harper & Row)
1962	Sendak composes the text to what would become *Where the Wild Things Are* during a stay in Fire Island's Seaview neighborhood
1963	*How Little Lori Visited Times Square*, pictures by Sendak, written by Amos Vogel (Harper & Row)
1963	*Where the Wild Things Are* (Harper & Row)
1964	Caldecott Medal for *Where the Wild Things Are*
1965	*Hector Protector and As I Went Over the Water* (Harper & Row)
1966	*Zlateh the Goat*, pictures by Sendak, written by Isaac Bashevis Singer (Harper & Row)
1967	*Higglety Pigglety Pop! or There Must Be More to Life* (Harper & Row)
1968	*A Kiss for Little Bear*, pictures by Sendak, written by Else Minarik (Harper & Row)
1968	Sendak suffers a heart attack in England (May)
1968	Sadie passes away (August)
1969	Philip moves in with Sendak (Greenwich Village apartment)
1969	Stonewall Riots catalyze the gay liberation movement (June–July)
1970	Philip passes away (June)
1970	*In the Night Kitchen* (Harper & Row)
1970	*Fantasy Sketches* (Philip H. & A.S.W. Rosenbach Foundation)
1970	Hans Christian Andersen Award

1971   Sendak's "Grimm *Reise*," his trip to Kassel, West Germany, to
            complete visual research for *The Juniper Tree*

1972   Sendak relocates to Ridgefield, Connecticut

1973   *The Juniper Tree*, pictures by Sendak, written by Jacob
            and Wilhelm Grimm, translated by Lore Segal and Randall
            Jarrell (Farrar, Straus & Giroux)

1975   *Really Rosie*, a CBS animated film based on *The Sign on
            Rosie's Door* and *The Nutshell Library* books, music by Carole
            King (book and lyrics by Sendak)

1976   *Some Swell Pup or Are You Sure You Want a Dog?* (Farrar,
            Straus & Giroux)

1976   *Fly by Night*, pictures by Sendak, written by Randall Jarrell
            (Farrar, Straus & Giroux)

1980   *The Art of Maurice Sendak* by Selma Lanes (Abrams)

1980   *Really Rosie*, Off-Broadway musical production directed and
            choreographed by Patricia Birch (sets, costumes, and lyrics
            by Sendak)

1980   *The Magic Flute*, opera composed by Wolfgang Amadeus
            Mozart, directed by Frank Corsaro (sets and costumes by
            Sendak)

1980–1984   *Where the Wild Things Are*, opera composed by Oliver
            Knussen (sets, costumes, and libretto by Sendak)

1981   *Outside Over There* (Harper & Row)

1982–1984   *The Nutcracker*, ballet score by Pyotr Ilyich Tchaikovsky,
            directed by Kent Stowell and Francia Russell (sets and
            costumes by Sendak)

1983   Laura Ingalls Wilder Award

1984   *Nutcracker*, pictures by Sendak, written by E.T.A. Hoffman,
            translated by Ralph Manheim (Crown)

1985   *In Grandpa's House*, pictures by Sendak, original Yiddish text
            written by Philip Sendak (Harper & Row)

1988   *Dear Mili*, pictures by Sendak, written by Wilhelm Grimm,
            translated by Ralph Manheim (Michael di Capua Books/
            Farrar, Straus & Giroux)

1988   *Caldecott & Co.* (Michael di Capua Books/Farrar, Straus &
            Giroux)

1992   James Marshall dies of AIDS-related causes

1993 *We're All in the Dumps with Jack and Guy* (Michael di Capua Books/HarperCollins)

1995 *Pierre; or, The Ambiguities*, pictures by Sendak, written by Herman Melville (HarperCollins)

1995 Jack passes away (February)

1996 *Hänsel und Gretel*, opera composed by Engelbert Humperdinck, directed by Frank Corsaro (sets and costumes by Sendak)

1998 *Penthesilea*, pictures by Sendak, written by Heinrich von Kleist (Michael di Capua Books/HarperCollins)

2001 *A Selection*, dance performed by Pilobolus (sets, costumes, and creative input by Sendak)

2003 *Brundibar*, opera composed by Hans Krása, libretto by Tony Kushner (sets and costumes by Sendak)

2003 *Brundibar*, pictures by Sendak, written by Tony Kushner (Michael di Capua Books/Hyperion Books for Children)

2003 Tony Kushner, *The Art of Maurice Sendak: 1980 to the Present* (Abrams)

2004 *Pincus and the Pig* (audio recording) Shirim Klezmer Orchestra, Tzadik Records (script, voice narration, and cover art by Sendak)

2006 *Mommy?*, pictures by Sendak, written by Arthur Yorinks (Michael di Capua Books/Scholastic)

2007 Eugene Glynn—psychiatrist, art critic, and Sendak's partner of over fifty years—passes away

2008 Sendak shares his sexual orientation with the popular press

2009 *Where the Wild Things Are* (film), directed by Spike Jonze

2010 Sendak donates a million dollars in Glynn's name to the Jewish Board of Family and Children's Services, for whom Glynn was a consulting psychiatrist

2010 Inauguration of the Sendak Fellowship, a residency and workshop for developing artists

2011 *Bumble-Ardy* (Michael di Capua Books/HarperCollins)

2012 Sendak passes away (May 8)

2013 *My Brother's Book* (Michael di Capua Books/HarperCollins, posthumous publication)

2013 P.S. 118 in Brooklyn renamed "The Maurice Sendak Community School"

2018   *Presto and Zesto in Limboland*, pictures by Sendak, cowritten
          with Arthur Yorinks (Michael di Capua Books, posthumous
          publication)

NOTES

Introduction

1. Robert Haddock, "Sendak Doesn't Kid 'Kids,'" *News-Times*, January 26, 1975, box 3, folder 28, Truman A. Warner Papers, MS 026, Western Connecticut State University Archives, Danbury, CT.

2. Hazel Rochman, "The Booklist Interview: Maurice Sendak," *Booklist* (June 15, 1992), 1848, box 1, folder 21, Blaine Pennington Papers, University of Missouri-Kansas City Archives.

3. Maurice Sendak, "Enamored of the Mystery," in *Innocence and Experience: Essays & Conversations on Children's Literature*, eds. Barbara Harrison and Gregory Maguire (New York: Lothrop, Lee & Shepard, 1987), 371.

4. Muriel Harris, "Impressions of Sendak," *Elementary English* 48, no. 7 (November 1970): 825–832, rpt. in *Conversations with Maurice Sendak*, ed. Peter C. Kunze (Jackson: University Press of Mississippi, 2016), 39.

5. "Questions to an Artist Who Is Also an Author: A Conversation Between Maurice Sendak and Virginia Haviland," *Quarterly Journal of the Library of Congress* 28, no. 4 (October 1971): 262–280, rpt. in *Conversations with Maurice Sendak*, ed. Peter C. Kunze (Jackson: University Press of Mississippi, 2016), 273.

6. Maurice Sendak, September 14, 1993, Public Education Program sound recordings, Manuscripts and Archives Division, The New York Public Library.

7. Harper & Row publicity material, box 1, folder 15, Joanna Foster Dougherty Papers, Special Collections & University Archives, University of Oregon, Eugene.

8. Edna Edwards interviews Maurice Sendak, sound recording, 1973, box 2, folders 8–9, Edna Edwards Interviews with Children's Authors and Illustrators, Loyola Marymount University Archives & Special Collections, Los Angeles.

9. Leonard S. Marcus, ed., *Dear Genius: The Letters of Ursula Nordstrom* (New York: HarperCollins, 1998), 156.

10. Maurice Sendak, foreword to *R.O. Blechman: Between the Lines*, ed. Bea Feitler (New York: Hudson Hills Press, 1980), 9.

11. Jean Mercier, "Sendak on Sendak," *Publishers Weekly*, April 10, 1981, 45–46.

12. Harriet Stix, "Sendak Draws on Childhood Truths," *Los Angeles Times*, December 7, 1984, box 1, folder 103, Arne Nixon Papers, Arne Nixon Center for the Study of Children's Literature, Fresno, CA.

13. Gerry Brigada and Warren Taylor, "Sendak's Childrens Books Come from Personal Life," *The Connecticut Daily Campus*, April 29, 1981, Francelia Butler Papers 1997.0056, series 2, box 9, University of Connecticut Archives & Special Collections, Thomas J. Dodd Research Center, Storrs, CT.

14. Edna Edwards interviews Maurice Sendak, 1973.

15. Selma G. Lanes, *The Art of Maurice Sendak* (New York: Harry N. Abrams, 1980), 27.

16. *The ABC of It*, New York Public Library exhibit, curated by Leonard S. Marcus, June 21, 2013–March 23, 2014, Stephen A. Schwarzman Building, New York.

17. Dagmar Langlois, "The Influence of Maurice Sendak, Leo and Diane Dillon, and Chris Van Allsburgh on Contemporary American Children's Book Illustration," (master's thesis, Syracuse University, 1991), 200.

18. Leonard S. Marcus, "Chapter I: The Artist and His Work: Fearful Symmetries: Maurice Sendak's Picture Book Trilogy and the Making of an Artist," in *Maurice Sendak: A Celebration of the Artist and His Work*, ed. Leonard S. Marcus, cur. Justin G. Schiller and Dennis M. V. David (New York: Abrams, 2013)," 15; Seth Lerer, *Children's Literature: A Reader's History, from Aesop to Harry Potter* (Chicago: University of Chicago Press, 2009), 276; Marcus, *Dear Genius*, xxii.

19. Barbara Bader, *American Picture Books from Noah's Ark to the Beast Within* (New York: Macmillan), 32, cited in Langlois, "The Influence of Maurice Sendak," 199.

20. John Cech, *Angels and Wild Things: The Archetypal Poetics of Maurice Sendak* (University Park: Pennsylvania State University Press, 1995), 49.

21. Philip Nel, "Wild Things, Children and Art: The Life and Work of Maurice Sendak," *The Comics Journal* 302 (2013): 14.

22. *The ABC of It*.

23. Fanny Goldstein, "The Jewish Child in Bookland," *Jewish Book Annual* 5 (1946-1947): 89. The Jewish Book Council, founded in 1944 as an affiliate of the National Jewish Welfare Board, published lists and reviews, promoting higher-quality literature for youth. Sophie N. Cederbaum, "American Jewish Juvenile

Literature During the Last Twenty-Five Years," *Jewish Book Annual* (1967–1968): 193. *K'tonton*, published by the Women's League of the United Synagogue, was based on S. Y. Agnon's tale of Rabbi Gadiel Hatinok, a tiny hero who rescues the Jews from a blood libel. Jonathan Sarna, *JPS: The Americanization of Jewish Culture, 1888–1988* (Philadelphia: Jewish Publication Society, 1989), 86, 171–172. For more on the book's history and context, see Jonathan B. Krasner, "A Recipe for American Jewish Integration: *The Adventures of K'tonton* and *Hillel's Happy Holidays*," *The Lion and the Unicorn* 27, no. 3 (September 2003): 344–361; and Jonathan Sarna, "From K'tonton to the Torah," *Moment Magazine* (October 1990): 44–47.

24. David Michaelis, *Schulz and Peanuts* (New York: Harper, 2007), cited in Maria Popova, "Peanuts and the Quiet Pain of Childhood: How Charles Schulz Made an Art of Difficult Emotions," *Brain Pickings*, January 20, 2015.

25. Joseph E. Illick, *American Childhoods* (Philadelphia: University of Pennsylvania Press, 2002), 122.

26. Cederbaum, "American Jewish Juvenile Literature," 196.

27. Michaelis, *Schulz and Peanuts*.

28. Sara Evans, "The Wild World of Maurice Sendak: A Visit with the Most Celebrated Children's Author of Our Time," *Parents*, November 1992, 583, box 6, folder 67, Phillip Applebaum Collection, American Jewish Historical Society, Center for Jewish History, New York.

29. Roger Sutton, "An Interview with Maurice Sendak," *The Horn Book Magazine* (November-December 2003): 687–699, rpt. in *Conversations with Maurice Sendak*, ed. Peter C. Kunze (Jackson: University Press of Mississippi, 2016), 150.

30. Riv-Ellen Prell, "Family Economy/Family Relations: The Development of American Jewish Ethnicity in the Early Twentieth Century," in *National Variations in Jewish Identity*, ed. Steven M. Cohen and Gabriel Horenczyk (Albany: State University of New York Press, 1999), 178.

31. Gennady Estraikh, introduction to *Children and Yiddish Literature: From Early Modernity to Post-Modernity*, ed. Gennady Estraikh, Kristin Hoge, and Mikhail Krutikov (Cambridge, UK, and New York: Legenda, 2016), 1–2.

32. Ibid., 2.

33. See David Biale, "Eros and Enlightenment," in *Eros and the Jews* (Berkeley: University of California Press, 1997), 149–175.

34. Ibid., 150.

35. Magnus Hirschfeld, preface to N. O. Body, *Memoirs of a Man's Maiden Years* (Philadelphia: University of Pennsylvania Press, 2006), 109.

36. Jonathan Cott, "Maurice Sendak, King of All Wild Things," *Rolling Stone*, December 30, 1976.

37. Ellen Handler Spitz, "Maurice Sendak's Sexuality," *New Republic*, February 21, 2013.

38. For example, Jerry Griswold, "Outside Over There and Gay Pride," *The Horn Book Magazine*, June 28, 2017.

39. See Golan Moskowitz, "Before *Wild Things*: Maurice Sendak and the Postwar Jewish American Child as Queer Insider-Outsider," *Images: A Journal of Jewish Art and Visual Culture* (2019): 1–10; Nick Salvato, "Queer Structure, Animated Form, and Really Rosie," *Camera Obscura* 33, no. 2 (2018): 139–159; Caitlin L. Ryan and Jill M. Hermann-Wilmarth, "Already on the Shelf: Queer Readings of Award-Winning Children's Literature," *Journal of Literacy Research* 45, no. 2 (2013): 142–172; Kenneth Kidd, *Freud in Oz: At the Intersections of Psychoanalysis and Children's Literature* (Minneapolis: University of Minnesota Press, 2011), 125; Philip Nel, "In or Out? Crockett Johnson, Ruth Krauss, Sexuality, Biography," *Nine Kinds of Pie* (blog), February 17, 2011.

40. John Mitzel, "An Approach to the Gay Sensibility in Literature," *The Gay Alternative* 11 (Spring 1976).

41. Nel, "In or Out?"

42. Jesse Green, "The Gay History of America's Classic Children's Books," *The New York Times*, February 7, 2019. See also Barbara Bader, "Five Gay Picture-Book Prodigies and the Difference They've Made," *The Horn Book Magazine*, March 5, 2015, and Kelly Blewett, "Ursula Nordstrom and the Queer History of the Children's Book," *Los Angeles Review of Books*, August 28, 2016.

43. Bader, *American Picture Books*, 252.

44. Susannah Cahalan, "'Goodnight Moon' Author Was a Bisexual Rebel Who Didn't Like Kids," *New York Post*, January 7, 2017.

45. Aaron Rosen, "Bernard Perlin: Europe's American," in *In Focus: Orthodox Boys 1948 by Bernard Perlin*, ed. Aaron Rosen, Tate Research Publication, 2016; David Leddick, *Intimate Companions: A Triography of George Platt Lynes, Paul Cadmus, Lincoln Kirstein, and Their Circle* (New York: St. Martin's Press, 2000), 93.

46. Colin Stokes, "'Frog and Toad': An Amphibious Celebration of Same-Sex Love," *New Yorker Magazine*, May 31, 2016.

47. Nel, "In or Out?" In a 1972 letter to Nordstrom, Sendak deemed Gorey a "mensche." Marcus, *Dear Genius*, 338.

48. Tim Teeman, "Maurice Sendak: I'm Ready to Die," *The Times*, September 24, 2011.

49. Emma Brockes, "I Refuse to Cater to the Bullshit of Innocence," *The Believer* (November-December 2012); Jodi Eichler-Levine, "Maurice Sendak's Jewish Mother(s)," in *Mothers in the Jewish Cultural Imagination*, ed. Marjorie Lehman, Jane Kanarek, and Simon J. Bronner (Oxford, UK, and Portland, OR: The Littman Library of Jewish Civilization, 2017).

50. Cott, "Maurice Sendak, King of All Wild Things."

51. David Drake, "Born to Be Wild: Interview by David Drake," *Poz* (September 1999): 89, ONE Archives Foundation, Los Angeles.

52. Cech, *Angels and Wild Things*, 79.

53. Patricia Cohen, "Concerns Beyond Just Where the Wild Things Are," *New York Times*, September 9, 2008. Though Cohen's interview for the *New York Times* was Sendak's first direct announcement of his sexuality to a popular press, his sexuality had also been noted in a *New Yorker* profile of him published two years prior, as well as in Tony Kushner's study in 2003. Cynthia Zarin, "Not Nice: Maurice Sendak and the Perils of Childhood," *The New Yorker*, April 17, 2006; Tony Kushner, *The Art of Maurice Sendak: 1980 to the Present* (New York: Abrams, 2003).

54. Amy Sonheim, *Maurice Sendak* (New York: Twayne, 1991), 12; Stix, "Sendak Draws on Childhood Truths."

55. Bill Moyers, "Maurice Sendak: 'Where the Wild Things Are,'" *PBS NOW*, March 12, 2004.

56. John Klapper, *Nonconformist Writing in Nazi Germany: The Literature of Inner Emigration* (Rochester, NY: Camden House, 2015), 70–71.

57. Mikhail Krutikov, "An End to Fairy Tales: The 1930s in the *Mayselekh* of Der Nister and Leyb Kvitko," in *Children and Yiddish Literature: From Early Modernity to Post-Modernity*, ed. Gennady Estraikh, Kristin Hoge, and Mikhail Krutikov (Cambridge, UK, and New York: Legenda, 2016), 113.

58. Jennifer Young, "'A Language Is Like a Garden,': Shloyme Davidman and the Yiddish Communist School Movement in the United States," in *Children and Yiddish Literature: From Early Modernity to Post-Modernity*, ed. Gennady Estraikh, Kristin Hoge, and Mikhail Krutikov (Cambridge, UK, and New York: Legenda, 2016), 154.

59. Daniela Mantovan, "Reading Soviet-Yiddish Poetry for Children: Der Nister's *Mayselekh in Ferzn* 1917–39," in *Children and Yiddish Literature: From Early Modernity to Post-Modernity*, ed. Gennady Estraikh, Kristin Hoge, and Mikhail Krutikov (Cambridge, UK, and New York: Legenda, 2016), 108.

60. Estraikh, introduction to *Children and Yiddish Literature*, 3–4.

61. See Klapper, *Nonconformist Writing*, especially Chapter 2. Thank you, Eugene Sheppard, for introducing me to the concept of "inner emigration" and to Klapper's work.

62. Moyers, "Maurice Sendak."

63. Brockes, "I Refuse to Cater to the Bullshit of Innocence."

64. Maurice Sendak to Gene Friese, September 15, 1966, box 1, folder 4, Morton E. Wise Collection of Maurice Sendak—Manuscript MS-1038, Dartmouth Rauner Library, Hanover, NH.

65. Maurice Sendak to Selma Lanes, March 25, 1968, MS 292, Smith College Library Special Collections, Northampton, MA; Maurice Sendak to Selma Lanes, February 19, 1969, MS 292, Smith College Library Special Collections.

66. Kathryn Bond Stockton, *The Queer Child* (Durham, NC: Duke University Press, 2009).

67. Steven Bruhm and Natasha Hurley, eds., *Curiouser: On The Queerness Of Children* (Minneapolis: University of Minnesota Press, 2004); Stockton, *The Queer Child*; Michelle Ann Abate and Kenneth B. Kidd, eds., *Over the Rainbow: Queer Children's and Young Adult Literature* (Ann Arbor: University of Michigan Press, 2011).

68. Evans, "Wild World of Maurice Sendak."

69. Edna Edwards interviews Maurice Sendak, 1973.

70. Miranda Fricker, *Epistemic Injustice: Power and the Ethics of Knowing* (Oxford, UK: Oxford University Press, 2007), 5. Thank you, ChaeRan Freeze, for introducing me to this source.

71. For further analysis of Sendak's artistic styles and influences on his artwork for *Dear Mili*, see Leonard S. Marcus, *The Art of Maurice Sendak: A Conversation with Maurice Sendak Conducted by Leonard S. Marcus*, November 22, 2002–January 12, 2003, The Eric Carle Museum of Picture Book Art, Amherst, MA; Gregory Maguire, *Making Mischief: A Maurice Sendak Appreciation* (New York: Harper-Collins, 2009); Paul G. Arakelian, "Text and Illustration: A Stylistic Analysis of Books by Sendak and Mayer," *Children's Literature Association Quarterly* 10, no. 3 (1985): 122–127; *Sendak at the Rosenbach*, exhibition catalog, curated by Vincent Giroud and Maurice Sendak, April 28–October 30, 1995, The Rosenbach Museum & Library, Philadelphia; Brian Anderson, Catalogue for an Exhibition of Pictures by Maurice Sendak, December 16–February 29, 1975–76, Ashmolean Museum, Oxford, UK (London: Bodley Head, 1975); and Hamida Bosmajian, "Memory and Desire in the Landscapes of Sendak's *Dear Mili*," *The Lion and the Unicorn* 19, no. 2 (1995): 194.

72. Eugene Glynn, "Desperate Necessity: Art and Creativity in Recent Psychoanalytic Theory," *The Print Collector's Newsletter* 8, no. 2 (May-June 1977): 29–36, reprinted in *Desperate Necessity: Writings on Art and Psychoanalysis*, by Eugene Glynn, ed. Jonathan Weinberg (Pittsburgh: Periscope, 2008), 139–140.

73. Jonathan Weinberg, introduction to *Desperate Necessity: Writings on Art and Psychoanalysis*, by Eugene Glynn, ed. Jonathan Weinberg (Pittsburgh: Periscope, 2008), 11.

74. Peter N. Stearns and Carol Z. Stearns, "Emotionology: Clarifying the History of Emotions and Emotional Standards," *American Historical Review* 90, no. 4 (1985): 813; Nicole Eustace, "AHR Conversation: The Historical Study of Emotions," *American Historical Review* 117, no. 5 (2012): 1490. The participants included Nicole Eustace, Eugenia Lean, Julie Linvingston, Jan Plamper, William M. Reddy, and Barbara H. Rosenwein.

75. Maurice Sendak, "Sources of Inspiration," Inaugural Zena Sutherland Lecture, May 20, 1983, Zena Bailey Sutherland Papers, box 7, folder 4, Special Collections Research Center, University of Chicago Library, Chicago.

76. Patrick Rodgers, "Chapter X: Where the Wild Things Are: Mad Max: On Three Preliminary Drawings for Where the Wild Things Are," in *Maurice Sendak: A Celebration of the Artist and His Work*, ed. Leonard S. Marcus, curated by Justin G. Schiller and Dennis M. V. David (New York: Abrams, 2013), 195.

77. Marcus, *Dear Genius*, 184.

78. Ann Cvetkovich, *Depression: A Public Feeling* (Durham, NC: Duke University Press, 2012); Lauren Berlant, *Cruel Optimism* (Durham, NC: Duke University Press, 2011); Sara Ahmed, *The Promise of Happiness* (Durham, NC: Duke University Press, 2010).

79. The present study takes explicit interest in the cultural and historical intersections of a queer Jewish experience as informed by the dynamic coalescence and dissonance involved in occupying queerness and Jewishness simultaneously. It does not, however, use the term *intersectionality*, a term conceived in order to identify those structural intersections of systemic racism and sexism that produce blind spots in policy and negatively affect, or even endanger, individuals who occupy multiple minority positions, specifically Black women in America. Intersections of queerness and Jewishness influenced Sendak's inner life and sometimes carried social implications for him, but they did not erase his access to all privileges associated with Whiteness or maleness. For more about the intentions of intersectionality as a critical tool and its afterlife in academic discourse, see Kimberlé Crenshaw, "Intersectionality and Identity Politics: Learning from Violence Against Women of Color," in *Reconstructing Political Theory: Feminist Perspectives*, ed. Mary Lyndon Shanley and Uma Narayan, 178–193 (University Park: Pennsylvania State University Press, 1997); and Sirma Bilge, "Intersectionality Undone: Saving Intersectionality from Feminist Intersectionality Studies," *Du Bois Review: Social Science Research on Race* 10, no. 2 (2013): 405–424. Thank you, Sara Shostak, for discussing this matter with me.

80. William M. Reddy, *The Navigation of Feeling* (Cambridge, UK: Cambridge University Press, 2001), 129.

81. Cech, *Angels and Wild Things*, 65.

82. Quoted in Cech, *Angels and Wild Things*, 49.

83. Kidd, "Wild Things and Wolf Dreams: Maurice Sendak, Picture-Book Psychologist," in *The Oxford Handbook of Children's Literature*, ed. Lynne Vallone and Julia Mickenberg (New York: Oxford University Press, 2011), 216.

84. Quoted in Cech, *Angels and Wild Things*, 51.

85. Cech, *Angels and Wild Things*, 256.

86. Bruno Bettelheim, *The Uses of Enchantment: The Meaning and Importance of Fairy Tales* (New York: Knopf, Distributed by Random House, 1976). It should be noted that Bettelheim criticized *Wild Things* in his column in the *Ladies' Home*

Journal, asserting that it would frighten children to see a mother cruelly with-
holding supper from her child. Marcus, *Dear Genius*, 265.

87. Kenneth Kidd, "'A' is for Auschwitz: Psychoanalysis, Trauma Theory, and
the Children's Literature of Atrocity," *Children's Literature* 33 (2005): 131. See also
Kenneth Kidd, *Making American Boys: Boyology and the Feral Tale* (Minneapolis:
University of Minnesota Press, 2004).

88. Justin Wintle interviews Maurice Sendak, in Wintle, *The Pied Pipers: Interviews with the Influential Creators of Children's Literature* (New York: Paddington Press, 1975), 28.

89. For an extensive list of Sendak's works through 2001, as well as descrip-
tions of first-edition markers, see Joyce Y. Hanrahan, *Works of Maurice Sendak:
Revised and Expanded to 2001* (Saco, Maine: Custom Communications, 2001).

Chapter 1

1. Cott, "Maurice Sendak, King of All Wild Things."

2. Jill P. May, "Envisioning the Jewish Community in Children's Literature:
Maurice Sendak and Isaac Singer," *The Journal of the Midwest Modern Language
Association* 33, no. 3 / 34, no. 1 (Autumn 2000–Winter 2001): 148.

3. Tony Kushner, *Art of Maurice Sendak*, 190.

4. Lanes, *Art of Maurice Sendak*, 25–26.

5. See Jonathan B. Krasner, *The Benderly Boys and American Jewish Education*
(Waltham, MA: Brandeis University Press, 2011); Eliyana R. Adler, *In Her Hands:
The Education of Jewish Girls in Tsarist Russia* (Detroit: Wayne State University
Press, 2011); Naomi Prawer Kadar, *Raising Secular Jews: Yiddish Schools and Their
Periodicals for American Children, 1917–1950* (Waltham, MA: Brandeis University
Press, 2017); Avraham Greenbaum, "The Girls' Heder and the Girls in the Boys'
Heder in Eastern Europe Before World War I," *East/West Education* 18, no. 1 (1997):
55–62; Shaul Stampfer, *Families, Rabbis, and Education: Traditional Jewish Society
in Nineteenth-Century Eastern Europe* (Oxford, UK: Littman Library of Jewish Civ-
ilization, 2010); Steven J. Zipperstein, "Transforming the Heder: Maskilic Politics
in Imperial Russia," in *Jewish History: Essays in Honor of Chimen Abramsky*, ed.
Ada Rapoport-Albert and Steven J. Zipperstein, 87–109 (London: Halban, 1988).

6. See Chapter 2 of Naomi Seidman, *The Marriage Plot: Or, How Jews Fell
in Love with Love, and with Literature* (Stanford, CA: Stanford University Press,
2016); and Biale, *Eros and the Jews*.

7. See Sarah E. Chinn, *Inventing Modern Adolescence: The Children of Immigrants in Turn-of-the-Century America* (New Brunswick, NJ: Rutgers University
Press, 2009).

8. Nicholas Sammond, *Babes in Tomorrowland: Walt Disney and the Making
of the American Child, 1930–1960* (Durham, NC: Duke University Press, 2005), 19;

Peter N. Stearns, *Anxious Parents* (New York and London: New York University Press, 2003).

9. Chinn, *Inventing Modern Adolescence*, 39.

10. Sholem Aleichem was the penname of Solomon Naumovich Rabinovich (1859–1916). Selma G. Lanes, interview transcript, June 22, 1989, box 76, no. 3, American Jewish Committee Oral History Collection, New York Public Library; Brockes, "I Refuse to Cater to the Bullshit of Innocence."

11. More specifically, Philip's father contested his son's valuing of romantic passion above familial obligation and his dismissal of grander career prospects for work as a tailor in America, which some traditionalists deemed a godless country. Philip's father would only send his son letters or presents via other relatives, avoiding direct contact with Philip. Brockes, "I Refuse to Cater to the Bullshit of Innocence."

12. Selma G. Lanes, interview transcript, June 22, 1989.

13. Zarin, "Not Nice."

14. John Burningham, "His Stories and Illustrations Captivate Children, but Maurice Sendak—the Author of Where the Wild Things Are—Explains Why for Him They Are a Means of Exorcising a Painful Past," *The Telegraph*, January 12, 2005.

15. Dressing a child in white, like the shrouds of a corpse, is a *zgule*, a folk remedy, which is used to fool the Angel of Death, believed to snatch children away from the world of the living. Calling a boy "alter" or a girl "alte" (meaning "old person") is a similar means of fooling the Angel of Death. Author's conversation with Ellen Kellman, Brandeis University, March 13, 2017.

16. *There's a Mystery There: Sendak on Sendak*, The Rosenbach Museum & Library, retrospective of Sendak interviews, Portia Productions, 2008, DVD.

17. Harris, "Impressions of Sendak," 38.

18. Kushner, *Art of Maurice Sendak*, 24.

19. Sendak, February 8, 1989, Public Education Program sound recordings.

20. Moyers, "Maurice Sendak."

21. Selma G. Lanes, interview transcript, June 22, 1989.

22. Mariana Cook, "Postscript: Wild Things," *The New Yorker*, May 21, 2012, 58.

23. Lanes, *Art of Maurice Sendak*, 16.

24. See Scott McCloud, *Understanding Comics* (New York: HarperCollins, 1993).

25. Cott, "Maurice Sendak, King of All Wild Things."

26. Selma G. Lanes, interview transcript, June 22, 1989.

27. Chinn, *Inventing Modern Adolescence*, 81.

28. Gary Groth, Interview with Maurice Sendak, *The Comics Journal* 302 (2013): 82.

29. Irving Howe, *World of Our Fathers* (New York: Harcourt Brace Jovanovich, 1976).

30. Alice Miller, *Drama of the Gifted Child* (New York: Basic Books, 1981).

31. Quoted in Howe, *World of Our Fathers*, 254–255.

32. Miller, *Drama of the Gifted Child*, 35.

33. Brockes, "I Refuse to Cater to the Bullshit of Innocence."

34. Lanes, *Art of Maurice Sendak*, 18–19.

35. Moyers, "Maurice Sendak."

36. Teeman, "Maurice Sendak: I'm Ready to Die."

37. Zarin, "Not Nice."

38. Moyers, "Maurice Sendak."

39. Maurice Sendak, "Moby Dick, Creativity, and Other Wild Things," commencement address, *Vassar Quarterly* 92, No. 4 (September 1, 1996): 11. See also Mark Swed, "'Wild Things' in Operaland: Maurice Sendak Moves from Children's Books to Stage Designer and Librettist," *Los Angeles Times*, June 3, 1990.

40. Brockes, "I Refuse to Cater to the Bullshit of Innocence."

41. However, it is important to note that comparing immigrants or other minority groups to children has been a way to exclude them from civil rights. Karen Sanchez-Eppler, *Dependent States: The Child's Part in Nineteenth-Century American Culture* (Chicago and London: University of Chicago Press, 2005), xxiv, cited in Chinn, *Inventing Modern Adolescence*, 34.

42. "Maurice Sendak on Being a Kid," animated video by Andrew Romano and Ramin Setoodeh, produced by David Gerlach, PBS Digital Studios, based on *Newsweek* interview, September 9, 2009.

43. *Writers Talk: Maurice Sendak with Paul Vaughan*, video, 1985, Institute of Contemporary Arts, London, Roland Collection of Films and Videos on Art.

44. Sendak, September 14, 1993, Public Education Program sound recordings.

45. Rachel Federman, *Drawing the Curtain: Maurice Sendak's Designs for Opera and Ballet* (New York, Munich, and London: Morgan Library & Museum and DelMonico Books, 2019), 51.

46. *Tell Them Anything You Want: A Portrait of Maurice Sendak*, directed by Spike Jonze and Lance Bangs, featuring Maurice Sendak, Lynn Caponera, and Catherine Keener, Oscilloscope Laboratories, 2010.

47. A. Bergman, "Yiddish oder Yiddishkayt," quoted in Young, "'A Language Is Like a Garden,'" 160n21.

48. Cott, "Maurice Sendak, King of All Wild Things."

49. Philip and Maurice Sendak, typescript, no date, *In Grandpa's House*, Maurice Sendak Collection, The Rosenbach Museum & Library, Philadelphia.

50. Kushner, *Art of Maurice Sendak*, 43.

51. Philip and Maurice Sendak, typescript for *In Grandpa's House*, 49.

52. Kushner, *Art of Maurice Sendak*, 161.

53. Young, "'A Language Is Like a Garden,'" 160–161.

54. See Kadar, *Raising Secular Jews*, 178.

55. See Leora Batnitzky, *How Judaism Became a Religion* (Princeton, NJ: Princeton University Press, 2011); and Deborah D. Moore, *At Home in America* (New York: Columbia University Press, 1983), 124.

56. Benjamin Ross assured me that the Sendaks would not have attended a Reform synagogue. Benjamin Ross (grandson of Philip Sendak's second cousin Jacob Ross [Rzodkiewicz]), in discussion with the author, July 9, 2014.

57. The Hearst Corporation, "Maurice Sendak: Stories My Father Told Me," 1995, box 32, folder 9: Maurice Sendak: In His Own Words and Pictures—The William Breman Jewish Heritage Museum (no. 393), Benjamin Hirsch and Associates, Inc. Records (DM009), Georgia Institute of Technology Archives, Atlanta.

58. Brockes, "I Refuse to Cater to the Bullshit of Innocence."

59. Irving Howe, "Memoir of the Thirties," in *Steady Work: Essays in the Politics of Democratic Radicalism, 1953–1966* (New York: Harcourt, Brace & World, 1966), 305–351, cited in Moore, *At Home in America*, 86.

60. Sendak, September 14, 1993, Public Education Program sound recordings.

61. Sendak later told an interviewer that it was he who had thrown the ball, admitting, "I didn't see the body and his mother didn't blame me, which was such a relief." Teeman, "Maurice Sendak: I'm Ready to Die."

62. Sendak, February 8, 1989, Public Education Program sound recordings.

63. Moyers, "Maurice Sendak."

64. Kushner, *Art of Maurice Sendak*, 24.

65. Evans, "Wild World of Maurice Sendak."

66. Sendak, "Sources of Inspiration," 10.

67. Teeman, "Maurice Sendak: I'm Ready to Die." See also Cech, *Angels and Wild Things*, 231.

68. *There's a Mystery There: Sendak on Sendak*.

69. Sendak, "Enamored of the Mystery," 363, 362–374.

70. Sendak, September 14, 1993, Public Education Program sound recordings.

71. Maurice Sendak in *When We Were Young*, ed. John Burningham (Bloomsbury: London, 2004), 124.

72. Seth Lerer, "Wild Thing: Maurice Sendak and the Worlds of Children's Literature," lecture at the Contemporary Jewish Museum, published on YouTube September 29, 2009.

73. Until its amendment in 1952, the Johnson-Reed Act of 1924 enforced the strictest American barring of Eastern and Southern European immigrants by instating quotas based on country of origin that allowed entry to only 2 percent of each national population as reflected in the American census of 1890. Jonathan D. Sarna, *American Judaism: A History* (New Haven, CT, and London: Yale University Press, 2004), 215; see also Matthew Frye Jacobson, *Whiteness of a Different*

Color: European Immigrants and the Alchemy of Race (Cambridge, MA: Harvard University Press, 1998); Lucy S. Dawidowicz, *On Equal Terms: Jews in America, 1881–1981* (New York: Holt, Rinehart and Winston, 1982).

74. Sigmund C. Taft, "A Study and Evaluation of the Jewish Community of Bensonhurst, Borough Park, Flatbush and Williamsburg, Neighborhoods in the Borough of Brooklyn in New York City," master's thesis, New York School of Social Work, Columbia University, 1943, YIVO, Center for Jewish History, New York.

75. Jacobson, *Whiteness of a Different Color*, Chapter 2.

76. Matthew Baigell, *Jewish Art in America: An Introduction* (Lanham, MD: Rowman & Littlefield, 2007), 71.

77. Eric L. Goldstein, *The Price of Whiteness: Jews, Race, and American Identity* (Princeton, NJ: Princeton University Press, 2006), 189, 191.

78. Amos Vogel, *How Little Lori Visited Times Square* (New York: Harper & Row, 1963).

79. Illick, *American Childhoods*, 108.

80. Maurice Sendak to Laurie Deval, June 13, 1969, box 2, Muir mss. II, 1892–1981, LMC 2286, Manuscripts Department, Indiana University Lilly Library, Bloomington.

81. Antonia Saxon, "A Loving Tribute: Maurice Sendak on 'My Brother's Book,'" *Publishers Weekly*, February 22, 2013.

82. Chinn, *Inventing Modern Adolescence*, 39; Sammond, *Babes in Tomorrowland*, 7; Stearns, *Anxious Parents*, 179.

83. Stephen S. Wise, *Child Versus Parent: Some Chapters on the Irrepressible Conflict in the Home* (New York: Macmillan Company, 1922), 35.

84. Jacob Kohn, *Modern Problems of Jewish Parents: A Study in Parental Attitudes* (New York: The Women's League of the United Synagogue of America, 1932), 31.

85. Chinn, *Inventing Modern Adolescence*, 102. See also Kathy Peiss, *Cheap Amusements: Working Women and Leisure in Turn-of-the-Century New York* (Philadelphia: Temple University Press, 1986).

86. Nicholas Sammond, "*Dumbo*, Disney, and Difference: Walt Disney Productions and Film as Children's Literature," in *The Oxford Handbook of Children's Literature*, ed. Lynne Vallone and Julia Mickenberg (New York: Oxford University Press, 2011), 149–150; Cook, "Postscript: Wild Things," 58; Allison Flood, "Maurice Sendak Tells Parents Worried by Wild Things to 'Go to Hell,'" *The Guardian*, October 20, 2009.

87. Sammond, *Babes in Tomorrowland*, 6, 14.

88. Sendak, February 8, 1989, Public Education Program sound recordings.

89. Reesa Sheryl Malca Sorin, "The Fears of Early Childhood: Writing in

Response to a Study of Maurice Sendak," master's thesis, School of Journalism and Creative Writing, University of Wollongong, 1994, 235.

90. Illick, *American Childhoods*, 110–111.

91. See Stearns, *Anxious Parents*.

92. Ibid.; Sammond, *Babes in Tomorrowland*, 6; Henry Jenkins, ed., *The Children's Culture Reader* (New York: New York University Press, 1998), 458; Peter N. Stearns and Jan Lewis, eds., *An Emotional History of the United States* (New York: New York University Press, 1998), 396–401.

93. Sammond, *"Dumbo*, Disney, and Difference," 151.

94. Joyce Antler, *You Never Call! You Never Write!: A History of the Jewish Mother* (Oxford, UK: Oxford University Press, 2008); Lawrence Fuchs, *Beyond Patriarchy: Jewish Fathers and Families* (Hanover, NH: Brandeis University Press, 2000); Prell, "Family Economy/Family Relations."

95. Prell, "Family Economy/Family Relations," 185.

96. Wise, *Child Versus Parent*, 142.

97. Ibid., 103–104.

98. Agnieszka Bedingfield, "Trans-Memory and Diaspora: Memories of Europe and Asia in American Immigrant Narratives," in *Sites of Ethnicity: Europe and the Americas*, ed. William Boelhower et al. (Heidelberg: Universitätsverlag Winter, 2004), 333–346, 345.

99. "Selling Food to Children: *The Mother's Own Book* (1928)," in *The Children's Culture Reader*, ed. Henry Jenkins (New York: New York University Press, 1998), 463–464 (New York: New York University Press).

100. Quoted in Nathalie Op de Beeck, *Suspended Animation: Children's Picture Books and the Fairy Tale of Modernity* (Minneapolis: University of Minnesota Press, 2010), 121.

101. Jess H. Wilson, "Does Your 'Research' Embrace the Boy of Today?" *Printers Ink* 118 (March 16, 1922), rpt. in *The Children's Culture Reader*, ed. Henry Jenkins (New York: New York University Press, 1998), 462.

102. Girls' fashion in the 1930s, however, remained diminutive and child-like, dominated by simple dresses, pinafores, sunsuits, playsuits, and bloomers. Bob Batchelor, *American Pop: Popular Culture Decade by Decade* [4 volumes], vol. 2 (Westport, CT: Greenwood, 2009), 78–79.

103. Batchelor, *American Pop*, vol. 2, 44.

104. Maurice Sendak to I. B. Singer, September 4, 1968, Isaac Bashevis Singer Papers, Harry Ransom Center, University of Texas at Austin.

105. Brockes, "I Refuse to Cater to the Bullshit of Innocence."

106. Wise, *Child Versus Parent*, 33

107. Rochman, "The Booklist Interview," 1849.

108. Sendak, February 8, 1989, Public Education Program sound recordings.

109. Selma G. Lanes, interview transcript, June 22, 1989.

110. Sendak, February 8, 1989, Public Education Program sound recordings.

111. Sholem Aleichem, "The 'Four Questions' of An American Boy," in *Yiddish Literature in America: 1870–2000*, ed. Emanuel S. Goldsmith, trans. Barnett Zumoff (Jersey City, NJ: Ktav, 2009), 50–52.

112. Maurice Sendak to Harry Ford, August 5, 1975, Non-Book-Related Correspondence, Manuscript Series, Maurice Sendak Collection, The Rosenbach Museum & Library, Philadelphia.

113. See Danny Fingeroth, *Disguised as Clark Kent* (New York and London: Continuum, 2007); Arie Kaplan, *From Krakow to Krypton: Jews and Comic Books* (Philadelphia: Jewish Publication Society, 2008); Samantha Baskind and Ranen Omer-Sherman, eds., *The Jewish Graphic Novel: Critical Approaches* (New Brunswick, NJ: Rutgers University Press, 2008).

114. Maurice Sendak, Introduction to *The Maxfield Parrish Poster Book* (New York: Harmony Books, 1974), 5.

115. George Chauncey, *Gay New York: Gender, Urban Culture, and the Makings of the Gay Male World 1890–1940* (New York: Basic Books, 1994), 325.

116. Steven Heller, Interview with Maurice Sendak, in *Innovators of American Illustration*, ed. Steven Heller (New York: Van Nostrand Reinhold, 1986), 70–81, rpt. in *Conversations with Maurice Sendak*, edited by Peter C. Kunze (Jackson: University Press of Mississippi, 2016), 104.

117. Lanes, *Art of Maurice Sendak*, 182.

118. Op de Beeck, *Suspended Animation*, x, 1–2, 14.

119. Cech, *Angels and Wild Things*, 49.

120. Sendak, February 8, 1989, Public Education Program sound recordings. Full text available in *Worlds of Childhood: The Art and Craft of Writing for Children*, ed. William Knowlton Zinsser et al. (Boston: Houghton Mifflin, 1998).

121. Walter Clemons, "Sendak's Enchanted Land," *Newsweek*, May 18, 1981, 102, Blaine Pennington Papers, series 3, box 1, folder 21, University of Missouri-Kansas City Special Collections.

122. Kidd, *Freud in Oz*, 98.

123. Sammond, *Babes in Tomorrowland*, 9–10, 18.

124. Sammond, "*Dumbo*, Disney, and Difference," 150.

125. Howe, *World of Our Fathers*, 254.

126. Moore, *At Home in America*, 90–91, 105, 111.

127. Illick, *American Childhoods*, 108–110.

128. Moore, *At Home in America*, 14, 89.

129. Sendak attended P.S. 205, 177, Boody Jr. High, and Lafayette High. Harris, "Impressions of Sendak," 38.

130. Saul Braun, "Sendak Raises the Shade on Childhood," *New York Times*

Magazine, June 7, 1970, Francelia Butler Papers, series 2, box 9, folder: "Sendak, Maurice (Author)," University of Connecticut Archives & Special Collections, Thomas J. Dodd Research Center, Storrs, CT.

131. Nat Hentoff, "Among the Wild Things," *New Yorker*, January 15, 1966, 54.

132. Sendak, "Enamored of the Mystery," 362–374.

133. Maurice Sendak, typescript, for *Kenny's Window*, folder 1, Maurice Sendak Papers, Kerlan Collection, Elmer Andersen Library, University of Minnesota Archives and Special Collections.

134. Zarin, "Not Nice."

135. Hearst Corporation, "Maurice Sendak: Stories My Father Told Me."

136. Harris, "Impressions of Sendak," 38.

137. The Hearst Corporation, "Maurice Sendak: Getting Kids to Read," 1995, Maurice Sendak: In His Own Words and Pictures—The William Breman Jewish Heritage Museum (no. 393), Benjamin Hirsch and Associates, Inc. Records (DM009), Georgia Institute of Technology Archives, Atlanta.

138. Jonathan Cott, *There's a Mystery There: The Primal Vision of Maurice Sendak*. New York: Doubleday, 2017, 5.

139. Anne Commire, "Maurice Sendak," in *Something About the Author: Facts and Pictures About Authors and Illustrators of Books for Young People* 27 (Detroit: Gale Research Company, Book Tower, 1982), 198. See also Randall Jarrell, *Fly by Night*, pictures by Maurice Sendak (New York: Farrar, Straus & Giroux, 1976), 26–27.

140. Sonheim, *Maurice Sendak*, 78, 110.

141. Lanes, *Art of Maurice Sendak*, 175.

142. Ibid., 182–183.

143. Sendak would later claim, "I drew Oliver Hardy, not Hitler. But I can see it that way. The Holocaust became the subject of so much of my later work that I have to allow that it was there." Burningham, "His Stories and Illustrations Captivate Children."

144. Maurice Sendak, Stephen Greenblatt, et al., *Changelings: Children's Stories Lost and Found* (Berkeley: Doreen B. Townsend Center for the Humanities, University of California, 1996), 50–51.

145. Berlant, *Cruel Optimism*.

Chapter 2

1. Mitzel, "Approach to the Gay Sensibility," 46.

2. Groth, Interview with Maurice Sendak, 41.

3. Maguire, *Making Mischief*, 8–9.

4. Maurice Sendak, sound recording, 1999, box 32, folder 9: Maurice Sendak: In His Own Words and Pictures—The William Breman Jewish Heritage Museum

(no. 393), Benjamin Hirsch and Associates, Inc. Records (DM009), Georgia Institute of Technology Archives, Atlanta.

5. Philip Sendak, *In Grandpa's House*, pictures by Maurice Sendak (New York: Harper & Row, 1985), 4.

6. Kushner, *Art of Maurice Sendak*, 190.

7. See Eichler-Levine, "Maurice Sendak's Jewish Mother(s)," 3.

8. Burningham, "His Stories and Illustrations Captivate Children."

9. Brockes, "I Refuse to Cater to the Bullshit of Innocence."

10. Lenore J. Weitzman describes the phenomena of role reversals and "role sharing" between romantic partners, as well as between parents and children, in the Jewish ghettos of World War II. Weitzman, "Resistance in Everyday Life: Family Strategies, Role Reversals, and Role Sharing in the Holocaust," in *Jewish Families in Europe, 1939–Present*, ed. Joanna Beata Michlic, (Waltham, MA: UPNE/Brandeis University Press, 2017), 46–47.

11. Bedingfield, "Trans-Memory and Diaspora," 341; See also Weitzman, "Resistance in Everyday Life" and Dalia Ofer, "Parenthood in the Shadow of the Holocaust," in *Jewish Families in Europe, 1939–Present*, ed. Joanna Beata Michlic (Waltham, MA: UPNE/Brandeis University Press, 2017).

12. Brockes, "I Refuse to Cater to the Bullshit of Innocence."

13. "Zambrow," *The Encyclopedia of Jewish Life Before and During the Holocaust*, Vol. 3, ed. Shmuel Spector (New York: New York University Press, 2001), 1487, Center for Jewish History Reading Room Library, New York.

14. *Sefer Zambrov: zikaron li-ḳehilat ha-ḳodesh she-hushmedah h. y. d.*, ed. Yom-Tow Lewinski, 1899 (Tel Aviv: ha-Irgunim shel yots'e ha-'ir be-'Artsot ha-Berit Argentinah ye-Yiśra'el, 1963), 120, YIVO, Center for Jewish History, New York.

15. "Zambrow," *The Encyclopedia of Jewish Life Before and During the Holocaust*, Vol. 3, 1487.

16. Zakroczym developed from a small community in the fifteenth century, constructing its first synagogue in the 1820s. By 1897, Jews constituted about half of the town's population of 4,218. "Zakrocym," *The Encyclopedia of Jewish Life Before and During the Holocaust*, Vol. 3, ed. Shmuel Spector (New York: New York University Press, 2001), 1484–1485.

17. Cook, "Postscript: Wild Things," 58.

18. Deborah Walike, "Every Witch Way: The Opera 'Hansel and Gretel' Is a Majestic Piece of Music with Chilling Insight," *Baltimore Jewish Times* 257, no. 2 (December 8, 2000): 53.

19. Bedingfield, "Trans-Memory and Diaspora."

20. Hirsch developed the theory of postmemory in her analysis of Art Spiegelman's graphic novel *Maus* (1980–91). Marianne Hirsch, "The Generation of Postmemory," *Poetics Today* 29, no. 1 (2008): 103–128.

21. Bedingfield, "Trans-Memory and Diaspora," 334–335.

22. Ibid., 343, 349.

23. Cech, *Angels and Wild Things*, 31; Andrew Wheeler, "R.I.P. 'Where the Wild Things Are' Creator Maurice Sendak (1928–2012)," *Comics Alliance*, May 8, 2012.

24. See, for example, Naomi Seidman, "The Ghost of Queer Loves Past: Ansky's 'Dybbuk' and the Sexual Transformation of Ashkenaz," in *Queer Theory and the Jewish Question*, ed. Daniel Boyarin, Daniel Itzkovitz, and Ann Pellegrini (Columbia University Press, 2004), 228–245. For a striking historical example, see Ḥayyim Vital Describes Male Souls in Female Bodies" (Tsfat, Mid-Sixteenth Century) in *A Rainbow Thread: An Anthology of Queer Jewish Texts from the First Century to 1969*, ed. Noam Sienna (Philadelphia: Print-O-Craft Press, 2019).

25. Eli Somer, "Trance Possession Disorder in Judaism: Sixteenth-Century Dybbuks in the Near East," *Journal of Trauma & Dissociation* 5, no. 2 (2004): 143; and Rachel Elior, *Dybbuks and Jewish Women in Social History, Mysticism and Folklore* (Jerusalem: Urim Publications, 2008), both cited in Justin Almquist, "Confronting Terezín: A Production History of Maurice Sendak and Tony Kushner's *Brundibar*" (master's thesis, Central Washington University, 2014), 40.

26. Kushner, *Art of Maurice Sendak*, 192–193.

27. Brockes, "I Refuse to Cater to the Bullshit of Innocence."

28. Sutton, "An Interview with Maurice Sendak," 695.

29. Selma G. Lanes, interview transcript, June 22, 1989. This story was likely based on the classic narrative template of the "Clothing Caught in Graveyard" supernatural tale, labeled "1676B" in Ernest W. Baughman, *Type and Motif-Index of the Folktales of England and North America* (The Hague: Mouton & Co., 1966), 43. I thank Noam Sienna for making this connection.

30. Philip and Maurice Sendak, typescript for *In Grandpa's House.*

31. Sendak in Burningham, *When We Were Young*, 122.

32. Harris, "Impressions of Sendak," 41.

33. Philip and Maurice Sendak, typescript for *In Grandpa's House*, 49.

34. Kadar, *Raising Secular Jews*, 222.

35. Mantovan, "Reading Soviet-Yiddish Poetry," 104; Mikhail Krutikov, "An End to Fairy Tales," 114–115.

36. Krutikov, "An End to Fairy Tales," 120.

37. "Nayes fun der velt" (world news), *Kinder Zhurnal* (April 1942). Reproduced from microfilm, Kinder Zhurnal/Farlag Matones, 1924–63, YIVO Library, New York.

38. Ibid., (August-September 1942), 3–6.

39. Kadar, *Raising Secular Jews*, 158.

40. Quoted in Diane K. Roskies, *Teaching the Holocaust to Children* (Brooklyn: Ktav, 1975), 18.

41. Richard M. Gottlieb, "Maurice Sendak's Trilogy," in *Psychoanalytic Study of the Child*, Vol. 63, ed. Robert A. King and Samuel Abrams (New Haven: Yale University Press, 2009), 199.

42. "Maurice Sendak on Being a Kid."

43. Peter Dobrin, "Rosenbach Reels in Rare Sendak Trove," *Philadelphia Inquirer*, January 29, 2017; Selma G. Lanes, interview transcript, June 22, 1989.

44. Selma G. Lanes, interview transcript, June 22, 1989.

45. Moyers, "Maurice Sendak"; See also Zarin, "Not Nice."

46. "'Fresh Air' Remembers Author Maurice Sendak," *NPR.org*, May 8, 2012.

47. Lanes, *Art of Maurice Sendak*, 12; Zarin, "Not Nice."

48. Groth, Interview with Maurice Sendak, 68.

49. Selma Lanes, interview transcript, 1989, Farrar, Straus & Giroux, Inc. records.

50. David G. Roskies and Naomi Diamant, *Holocaust Literature: A History and Guide* (Hanover, NH: Brandeis University Press, 2012), 49.

51. Congregation Sons of Israel Yearbook, 1947, "The Days of Our Years," 3, BM225.N5 B46, American Jewish Historical Society, Center for Jewish History, New York.

52. Ibid., 4.

53. Brockes, "I Refuse to Cater to the Bullshit of Innocence."

54. Clifton Fadiman, "A Meditation on Children and Their Literature," afterword to *Sharing Literature with Children: A Thematic Anthology*, by Francelia Butler (New York: David McKay, 1977), 477.

55. Nel, "Wild Things, Children and Art," 14.

56. Cech, *Angels and Wild Things*, 126.

57. Almquist, "Confronting Terezín," 40.

58. Sendak, "Sources of Inspiration."

59. Roland Barthes, *The Rustle of Language*, trans. Richard Howard (New York: Farrar, Straus & Giroux, 1986), 49.

60. "Questions to an Artist Who Is Also an Author," 274.

61. Groth, Interview with Maurice Sendak, 63.

62. Selma G. Lanes, interview transcript, June 22, 1989. Selma Lanes's records from an interview with Sendak state that Philip's parents both died natural deaths and all other relatives remaining in Poland were killed in the Holocaust. Peter Crane, letter to the editor, *New York Times*, April 10, 2016.

63. Lanes, *Art of Maurice Sendak*, 23.

64. Brockes, "I Refuse to Cater to the Bullshit of Innocence."

65. Stearns, *Anxious Parents*, 63.

66. Glenn Edward Sadler, "A Conversation with Maurice Sendak and Dr. Seuss," 1982, rpt. in *Conversations with Maurice Sendak*, ed. by Peter C. Kunze (Jackson: University Press of Mississippi, 2016), 67.

67. Hillel Italie, "Maurice Sendak with the Wild Things, Now," Associated Press, *Christian Science Monitor*, May 8, 2012.

68. See, for example, David Grossman, *See Under—Love*, trans. Betsy Rosenberg (New York: Picador USA/Farrar, Straus and Giroux, 1989).

69. Isaac Bashevis Singer, *Zlateh the Goat and Other Stories*, pictures by Maurice Sendak, trans. I. B. Singer and Elizabeth Shub (New York: Harper & Row, 1966), xi.

70. Researcher's notes, box 32, folder 9: Maurice Sendak: In His Own Words and Pictures—The William Breman Jewish Heritage Museum (no. 393), Benjamin Hirsch and Associates, Inc. Records (DM009), Georgia Institute of Technology Archives, Atlanta; Brockes, "I Refuse to Cater to the Bullshit of Innocence."

71. Brockes, "I Refuse to Cater to the Bullshit of Innocence."

72. Maurice Sendak to Mrs. Kane, June 23, 1966, Kane Family Letters, Maurice Sendak Collection, The Rosenbach Museum & Library, Philadelphia; Maurice Sendak to I. B. Singer, n.d., series 2, Isaac Bashevis Singer Papers.

73. Glynn, "Desperate Necessity," 147.

74. Evans, "Wild World of Maurice Sendak."

75. Sendak, February 8, 1989, Public Education Program sound recordings. Full text available in Zinsser et al., *Worlds of Childhood*.

76. Rochman, "The Booklist Interview," 1848.

77. Donald Haase, "Children, War, and the Imaginative Space of Fairy Tales," *The Lion and the Unicorn* 24, no. 3 (2000): 363–364.

78. Maurice Sendak to Selma Lanes, July 16, 1969, MS 292, Smith College Library Special Collections; Cech, *Angels and Wild Things*, 20; Kidd, *Freud in Oz*, 126.

79. Lanes, *Art of Maurice*, 227.

80. From Bernard Holland, "The Paternal Pride of Maurice Sendak," *New York Times*, November 8, 1987, 44, quoted in Sonheim, *Maurice Sendak*, 12.

81. Eichler-Levine, "Maurice Sendak's Jewish Mother(s)," 149.

82. Maguire, *Making Mischief*, 62.

83. Katie Roiphe, "The Wildest Rumpus: Maurice Sendak and the Art of Death," *The Atlantic*, March 7, 2016.

84. Sendak, "Enamored of the Mystery," 364.

85. "Questions to an Artist Who Is Also an Author," 278.

86. Eve Kosofsky Sedgwick, "Shame, Theatricality, and Queer Performativity: Henry James's *The Art of the Novel*," in *Gay Shame*, ed. David M. Halperin and Valerie Traub (Chicago and London: University of Chicago Press, 2009), 54.

87. Ibid.

88. Author's conversation with Eric Pederson, August 8, 2019.

89. Lisa Hammel, "Maurice Sendak: Thriving on Quiet," *New York Times*, January 5, 1973, Maurice Sendak, Art & Artist Files, Smithsonian American Art Museum/ National Portrait Gallery Library, Washington DC, consulted November 7, 2015.

90. Maurice Sendak to Mrs. Kane, August 16, 1965, Kane Family Letters, Maurice Sendak Collection, The Rosenbach Museum & Library, Philadelphia.

91. Maurice Sendak to I. B. Singer, December 23, 1968, series 2, Isaac Bashevis Singer Papers.

92. Sonheim, *Maurice Sendak*, 12.

93. Maurice Sendak to I. B. Singer, September 4, 1968, Isaac Bashevis Singer Papers.

94. *Writers Talk: Maurice Sendak with Paul Vaughan*, video interview, 1985, Institute of Contemporary Arts, London, Roland Collection of Films and Videos on Art; Justin G. Schiller, "Recollections for an Exhibition," in *Maurice Sendak: A Celebration of the Artist and His Work*, ed. Leonard S. Marcus, curated by Justin G. Schiller and Dennis M. V. David (New York: Abrams, 2013), 8–13.

95. Maurice Sendak to I. B. Singer, December 29, 1968, Isaac Bashevis Singer Papers.

96. Maurice Sendak to Minnie Kane, September 3, 1968, Kane Family Letters, Maurice Sendak Collection, The Rosenbach Museum & Library, Philadelphia.

97. Maurice Sendak to Mrs. Kane, July 21, 1969, Kane Family Letters, Maurice Sendak Collection, The Rosenbach Museum & Library, Philadelphia; Maurice Sendak to Coleman Dowell, May 13, 1969, Coleman Dowell Papers, MSS 36, Fales Library & Special Collections, New York University.

98. These Yiddish transcriptions would later offer the basis of the picture book *In Grandpa's House* (1985). Harper hired Seymour Barofsky to do the translation from Yiddish, because Sendak's Yiddish was not quite fluent enough. Kushner, *Art of Maurice Sendak*, 41.

99. *Writers Talk: Maurice Sendak with Paul Vaughan*.

100. Marcus, *Dear Genius*, 315, 313.

101. Harris, "Impressions of Sendak," 41.

102. Hammel, "Maurice Sendak: Thriving on Quiet."

103. Burningham, "His Stories and illustrations Captivate Children."

104. *There's a Mystery There: Sendak on Sendak*.

105. Brockes, "I Refuse to Cater to the Bullshit of Innocence"; see also Cott, "Maurice Sendak, King of All Wild Things."

106. Brockes, "I Refuse to Cater to the Bullshit of Innocence."

107. Cott, "Maurice Sendak, King of All Wild Things."

108. Sendak, September 14, 1993, Public Education Program sound recordings; Pamela Warrick, "Facing the Frightful Things These Days, Maurice Send-

ak's Wild Creatures Are Homelessness, AIDS and Violence—Big Issues for Small Kids," *Los Angeles Times*, October 11, 1993.

109. Cook, "Postscript: Wild Things," 58.

110. Ibid.

111. Cott, "Maurice Sendak, King of All Wild Things."

112. Brockes, "I Refuse to Cater to the Bullshit of Innocence."

113. Teeman, "Maurice Sendak: I'm Ready to Die."

114. Sendak, "Moby Dick, Creativity, and Other Wild Things," 11.

115. Avi Steinberg, "'We Are Inseparable!': On Maurice Sendak's Last Book," *The New Yorker*, March 12, 2013.

116. Zarin, "Not Nice"; Lanes, *Art of Maurice Sendak*, 23; Sendak, February 8, 1989, Public Education sound recordings.

117. Robert Everett-Green, "Maurice Sendak Draws on His Passions and Past," *The Globe and Mail*, January 23, 1998, University of Guelph Archival & Special Collections, Guelph, ON, Canada.

118. Hyman and Alice Chanover, *Happy Hanukah Everybody*, pictures by Maurice Sendak (New York: United Synagogue Commission on Jewish Education, 1954).

119. Robert Garvey, *Good Shabbos, Everybody*, pictures by Maurice Sendak (New York: United Synagogue Commission on Jewish Education, 1951).

120. Meindert DeJong, *House of Sixty Fathers*, pictures by Maurice Sendak (New York and Evanston, IL: Harper & Row, 1956).

121. Maurice Sendak, pencil draft, for *House of Sixty Fathers*, Maurice Sendak Papers, MC 1175, Kerlan Collection, Elmer Andersen Library, University of Minnesota Archives and Special Collections, Minneapolis.

122. Eugene Glynn, "To Express a Serious Sorrow," review of *Vincent van Gogh: A Psychological Study* by Humberto Nagera and *Stranger on the Earth: A Psychological Biography of Vincent van Gogh* by Albert J. Lubin, *The Print Collector's Newsletter* 4, no. 4 (September-October 1973): 88–90, rpt. in *Desperate Necessity: Writings on Art and Psychoanalysis*, by Eugene Glynn, edited by Jonathan Weinberg. Pittsburgh: Periscope, 2008, 90.

123. Ibid., 88–89.

124. Eichler-Levine, "Maurice Sendak's Jewish Mother(s)," 9.

125. Cott, "Maurice Sendak, King of All Wild Things."

126. Helen Epstein, *Children of the Holocaust* (New York: Penguin Books, 1979); Alan L. Berger, *Children of Job: American Second-Generation Witnesses to the Holocaust* (Albany: State University of New York Press, 1997); Dina Wardi, *Memorial Candles: Children of the Holocaust* (London and New York: Tavistock/Routledge, 1992).

127. Herman Melville, *Pierre; or, The Ambiguities* (1852), Kraken edition, ed. Hershel Parker, pictures by Maurice Sendak (New York: HarperCollins, 1995).

128. Moyers, "Maurice Sendak."

129. *There's a Mystery There: Sendak on Sendak.*

130. Saxon, "A Loving Tribute."

131. Stephen Greenblatt, foreword to *My Brother's Book*, by Maurice Sendak (New York: Michael di Capua Books/HarperCollins, 2013), 6.

132. *There's a Mystery There: Sendak on Sendak.*

133. Spitz, "Maurice Sendak's Sexuality."

134. Tony Kushner, endorsement for Maurice Sendak, *My Brother's Book* (New York: Michael di Capua Books/HarperCollins, 2013), back cover.

135. Brockes, "I Refuse to Cater to the Bullshit of Innocence."

136. Flood, "Maurice Sendak Tells Parents Worried by Wild Things to 'Go to Hell.'"

137. Glynn, "Desperate Necessity," 147.

138. Ibid.

139. Art Spiegelman and Maurice Sendak, "In the Dumps," *The New Yorker*, September 27, 1993, 80.

140. Maurice Sendak to Coleman Dowell, February 2, 1969, Coleman Dowell Papers.

Chapter 3

Portions of this chapter appeared in an earlier form in Moskowitz, "Before *Wild Things*."

1. Illick, *American Childhoods*, 115.

2. Teeman, "Maurice Sendak: I'm Ready to Die."

3. Eve Kosofsky Sedgwick, *Epistemology of the Closet* (Berkeley and Los Angeles: University of California Press, 1990), 81.

4. Lee Edelman, *No Future: Queer Theory and the Death Drive* (Durham, NC: Duke University Press, 2004), 13.

5. Chauncey, *Gay New York*, 356.

6. Midge Decter, "The Boys on the Beach," *Commentary*, September 1, 1980.

7. "'Fresh Air' Remembers."

8. *Tell Them Anything You Want.*

9. Cohen, "Concerns Beyond Just Where the Wild Things Are."

10. In the early 1920s, Stephen S. Wise referred to the "evil of solitariness," a message taught to and internalized by children. Wise, *Child Versus Parent*, 36.

11. Kohn, *Modern Problems of Jewish Parents*, 75.

12. Michael J. Sweet, "Talking About *Feygelekh*: A Queer Male Representation in Jewish American Speech," in *Queerly Phrased: Language, Gender, and Sexuality*, ed. Anna Livia and Kira Hall (Oxford, UK, and New York: Oxford University Press, 1997), 116–117.

13. Warren Hoffman, *The Passing Game: Queering Jewish American Culture* (Syracuse, NY: Syracuse University Press, 2009), 89. For an additional account of gay Jewish youth at midcentury, see "A Homosexual Jewish College Student Writes His Life Story (New York, ca. 1958)," in *A Rainbow Thread: An Anthology of Queer Jewish Texts from the First Century to 1969*, ed. Noam Sienna (Philadelphia: Print-O-Craft Press, 2019), 346–350.

14. Selma G. Lanes, interview transcript, June 22, 1989.

15. David Herszenson, "Of Fags, Flags, Faggots and Feygeles," *The Jewish Daily Forward*, April 21, 2010; David M. Lugowski, "Queering the (New) Deal: Lesbian and Gay Representation and the Depression-Era Cultural Politics of Hollywood's Production Code," *Cinema Journal* 38, no. 2 (Winter 1999): 3–35; Chauncey, *Gay New York*, 353.

16. Cott, "Maurice Sendak, King of All Wild Things." These pictures were copyrighted but not published. Sendak, February 8, 1989, Public Education sound recordings.

17. Braun, "Sendak Raises the Shade on Childhood."

18. Langlois, "The Influence of Maurice Sendak," 165.

19. Lanes, *Art of Maurice Sendak*, 24–25.

20. Author's conversation with Eric Pederson, August 8, 2019.

21. Groth, Interview with Maurice Sendak, 57.

22. Stearns, *Anxious Parents*, 108.

23. Groth, Interview with Maurice Sendak, 53.

24. Ibid., 47.

25. Jonathan Weinberg mentioned that Sendak signed his name "Mark" when writing to Eugene Glynn in the 1950s. Edmund Newman, Glynn's nephew, recalls that, outside of work, Sendak was "Mark" well into the 1970s, even at family gatherings on Glynn's side. Author's conversations with Jonathan Weinberg, October 28, 2017, and Edmund Newman, April 12, 2020.

26. *Tell Them Anything You Want*.

27. Chauncey, *Gay New York*, 159.

28. The term "wolf" was used primarily in the 1920s and 1930s but would likely still have been known to urban queer people in the 1940s and 1950s. Chauncey, *Gay New York*, 86–90.

29. Lanes, *Art of Maurice Sendak*, 29.

30. Maxwell Eidinoff, *Atomics for the Millions* (New York: Whittlesey House, McGraw-Hill, 1947).

31. Maurice Sendak, ink drawing, "Atomics for the Millions," Maurice Sendak Collection, The Rosenbach Museum & Library, Philadelphia.

32. Sutton, "An Interview with Maurice Sendak," 694.

33. Lanes, *Art of Maurice Sendak*, 33.

34. Teeman, "Maurice Sendak: I'm Ready to Die."

35. "'Fresh Air' Remembers," 2012.

36. Teeman, "Maurice Sendak: I'm Ready to Die."

37. Cott, "Maurice Sendak, King of All Wild Things."

38. Teeman, "Maurice Sendak: I'm Ready to Die." Slaff was co-founder of the New York Society for Adolescent Psychiatry in 1958 and was at one point a president of the American Society for Adolescent Psychiatry. He would also take on a leadership role in the Association of Gay and Lesbian Psychiatrists. Slaff had experience as a captain in the Army Medical Corps (1946–48) before beginning private practice in 1949, during which time he also became Associate Clinical Professor of Psychiatry at the Child-Adolescent Division of the Mt. Sinai Department of Psychiatry. A person of literary sensitivities, he joined the board of directors of the nonprofit Dalkey Archive Press, as well as served as a "first reader" of Dowell's work. *Association of Gay and Lesbian Psychiatrists Newsletter* 30, no. 2 (April 2004): 5; Louise Schneider, "A Personal Remembrance of My Uncle, Bert Slaff," and Gregory P. Barclay, "Bertram Slaff, M.D.," *American Society for Adolescent Psychiatry Newsletter*, "In Memoriam" section (Winter 2013): 13; Kushner, *Art of Maurice Sendak*, 192.

39. Eugene Hayworth, introduction to *Fever Vision: The Life and Works of Coleman Dowell* (Champaign, IL, and London: Dalkey Archive Press, 2007), xvi–xviii.

40. Richard Canning describes Dowell's subject matter as "the vicissitudes, thrills, and agonies of the human mind as it struggles to make sense of the body's impulses, vexations, and pleasures." Richard Canning, "Something Unforgettable, Forgotten," *The Gay & Lesbian Review Worldwide* 14, no. 6 (November-December 2007): 19–21. See also Edmund White, preface to *Fever Vision: The Life and Works of Coleman Dowell*, by Eugene Hayworth (Champaign, IL, and London: Dalkey Archive Press, 2007), xiii.

41. Associations between "artistic" men and homosexuality may stem from popular stereotypes associating theater, music, and visual art with gay men, as well as early twentieth-century psychological studies of "inverts," such as those by Havelock Ellis. See, for example, Havelock Ellis, *Studies in the Psychology of Sex*, Volume 1: *Sexual Inversion* (Watford, London, and Leipzig: University Press, 1900), 122-124.

42. *Writers Talk: Maurice Sendak with Paul Vaughan.*

43. Bertram Slaff, "Creativity: Blessing or Burden?" *Adolescent Psychiatry* (1981): 86.

44. Ibid.

45. Maurice Sendak to Mrs. Kane, November 6, 1961, Kane Family Letters, Maurice Sendak Collection, The Rosenbach Museum & Library, Philadelphia.

46. Cott, "Maurice Sendak, King of All Wild Things."

47. Ibid.

48. Cech, *Angels and Wild Things*, 79; Evans, "Wild World of Maurice Sendak."

49. Maurice Sendak, "Really Rosie," *Rolling Stone* 229 (December 30, 1976): 52. This was a short piece that was included within Cott, "Maurice Sendak, King of All Wild Things," in the print version of the article but not in the later online version cited elsewhere.

50. Maurice Sendak to Mrs. Kane, November 6, 1961, Kane Family Letters, Maurice Sendak Collection, The Rosenbach Museum & Library, Philadelphia.

51. Cott, "Maurice Sendak, King of All Wild Things."

52. "Questions to an Artist Who Is Also an Author," 264.

53. Hammel, "Maurice Sendak: Thriving on Quiet."

54. David Rosen, *Sin, Sex & Subversion: How What Was Taboo in 1950s New York Became America's New Normal* (New York: Carrel Books, 2016); Hayworth, *Fever Vision*, 36.

55. Hayworth, *Fever Vision*, 36. For further writing on Bernstein's sexuality and artistic career, see Billy J. Harbin et al., eds., *The Gay & Lesbian Theatrical Legacy: A Biographical Dictionary of Major Figures in American Stage History in the Pre-Stonewall Era* (Ann Arbor: University of Michigan Press, 2007), 59–62; and Leonard Bernstein, *The Leonard Bernstein Letters*, ed. Nigel Simeone (New Haven, CT: Yale University Press, 2013).

56. Kirstein's social circle also included Bernard Perlin, a painter and gay son of Russian Jewish immigrants. Like Sendak, he created figurative images that sometimes featured undertones of a queer boyhood and Holocaust-infused notions of Jewish endangerment. Rosen, "Bernard Perlin"; Leddick, *Intimate Companions*, 93.

57. Teeman, "Maurice Sendak: I'm Ready to Die."

58. Meryle Secrest, "Sendak Hasn't Lost That Direct Link with Childhood," Francelia Butler Papers, Series 2, box 9, folder: "Sendak, Maurice (Author)," University of Connecticut Archives & Special Collections, Thomas J. Dodd Research Center, Storrs, CT; Sendak, foreword to *R.O. Blechman*, 7.

59. *Moby-Dick* describes, for example, two men intertwined in bed, in their "hearts' honeymoon." Herman Melville, *Moby-Dick* (New York: Bantam Classics, 1981), 69. See Erik Hage, *The Melville-Hawthorne Connection: A Study of the Literary Friendship* (Jefferson, NC, and London: McFarland, 2014), 22; Peter C. Kunze, ed. *Conversations with Maurice Sendak* (Jackson: University Press of Mississippi, 2016), 88; John Bryant, "Pierre and Pierre: Editing and Illustrating Melville," review of *Pierre; or, the Ambiguities*, the Kraken Edition, by Herman Melville, ed. Hershel Parker, pictures by Maurice Sendak, *College English* 60, no. 3 (March 1998): 336–341.

60. Author's conversation with Eric Pederson, August 8, 2019.

61. Marcus, "Chapter I: The Artist and His Work," 15; Op de Beeck, *Suspended Animation*, xix.

62. Sendak, "Moby Dick, Creativity, and Other Wild Things," 10.

63. Minutes, National Social Welfare Assembly Comics Committee, February 1950, box 48, folder 20, Comics Project Files, Social Welfare History Archives, University of Minnesota Archives and Special Collections, Minneapolis.

64. Sammond, *Babes in Tomorrowland*; Jacqueline Rose, *The Case of Peter Pan, or the Impossibility of Children's Fiction* (New York: Macmillan, 1984); Edelman, *No Future*.

65. Lanes, *Art of Maurice Sendak*, 247.

66. Edna Edwards interviews Maurice Sendak, 1973.

67. Sammond, *Babes in Tomorrowland*, 2–6.

68. Goldstein, *Price of Whiteness*, 191.

69. This figure is according to a 1957 study. A December 1951 report showed that readership of the comic inserts was slightly higher among adults over twenty-one than among children. Sendak was about twenty-three at the time. Report, December 1951, box 48, folder 32, Comics Project Files, Social Welfare History Archives, University of Minnesota Archives and Special Collections, Minneapolis.

70. *Kinder Zhurnal* (April 1946), Kinder Zhurnal/Farlag Matones. Reproduced from microfilm.

71. Fanny Goldstein, "The Jewish Child in Bookland," 84–85.

72. June Cummins, "Becoming an 'All-of-a-Kind' American: Sydney Taylor and Strategies of Assimilation," *The Lion and the Unicorn* 27, no. 3 (2003): 324–343.

73. For more on the literary and cultural afterlife of Anne Frank, see Barbara Kirshenblatt-Gimblett and Jeffrey Shandler, eds., *Anne Frank Unbound* (Bloomington: Indiana University Press, 2012).

74. Mark M. Anderson, "The Child Victim as Witness to the Holocaust: An American Story?" *Jewish Social Studies* 14, no. 1 (2007); Sylvia Barack Fishman, *Negotiating Both Sides of the Hyphen: Coalescence, Compartmentalization, and American Jewish Values* (Cincinnati: Judaic Studies Program, University of Cincinnati, 1996).

75. Gladys Baker Bond, *Seven Little Stories on Big Subjects*, pictures by Maurice Sendak (New York: Anti-Defamation League of B'nai B'rith, 1955).

76. Marcus, "Chapter I: The Artist and His Work," 20.

77. Edna Edwards interviews Maurice Sendak, 1973.

78. Dummy for *Where the Wild Things Are*, Series 26: Box 9. Maurice Sendak Collection. University of Connecticut Archives & Special Collections, Thomas J. Dodd Research Center, Storrs, CT.

79. Maria Popova, "How Ursula Nordstrom, the Greatest Patron Saint of

Modern Childhood, Stood Up for Creativity Against Commercial Cowardice,"
Brain Pickings, February 2, 2015. See also Blewett, "Ursula Nordstrom and the
Queer History of the Children's Book."

80. Marcus, "Chapter I: The Artist and His Work," 16–17.

81. Nordstrom was the daughter of actors Henry E. Dixie and Marie Ursula
Nordstrom and completed boarding school at Long Island's Winnwood School,
largely attended by children of theater professionals. Marcus, *Dear Genius*, xix–xx.

82. Marcus, introduction to *Dear Genius*, xxxvi–xxxvii.

83. Marcus, "Chapter I: The Artist and His Work," 17.

84. Marcus, *Dear Genius*, 224.

85. Ibid., 223.

86. Sarah Lyall, "Maurice Sendak Sheds Moonlight on a Dark Tale," *New York
Times*, September 20, 1993.

87. Marcus, *Dear Genius*, 41.

88. Lanes, *Art of Maurice Sendak*, 35.

89. Ibid.; Marcel Aymé, *The Wonderful Farm*, pictures by Maurice Sendak
(New York: Harper, 1951).

90. Groth, Interview with Maurice Sendak, 58.

91. Marcus, "Chapter I: The Artist and His Work," 17.

92. Marcus, *Dear Genius*, 81, 165.

93. Ibid., 147–148.

94. Ibid., 99–100.

95. Maurice Sendak, Eulogy for Ruth Krauss, 1993, GEN MSS 1199, box 1, Lillian Hoban Papers, General Collection, Beinecke Rare Book and Manuscript Library, Yale University, New Haven, CT, 2–3; Philip Nel, *Crockett Johnson and Ruth
Krauss: How an Unlikely Couple Found Love, Dodged the FBI, and Transformed
Children's Literature* (Jackson: University Press of Mississippi, 2012), 123.

96. Marcus, "Chapter I: The Artist and His Work," 18.

97. Ibid., 131.

98. Sendak, Eulogy for Ruth Krauss.

99. Nel, "In or Out?"

100. "'Don't Assume Anything': A Conversation with Maurice Sendak and
Philip Nel," from interviewer's private collection, June 28, 2001, rpt. in *Conversations with Maurice Sendak*, ed. Peter C. Kunze (Jackson: University Press of Mississippi, 2016), 133.

101. Edna Edwards interviews Maurice Sendak, 1973.

102. Sendak contrasted this aspect of midcentury American children's publishing with that of Europe. Jennifer M. Brown, "The Rumpus Goes On: Max,
Maurice Sendak and a Clan of Bears Pay Tribute to a Lifelong Mentorship," *Publishers Weekly* April 18, 2005, 19.

103. "Don't Assume Anything," 133.

104. Marcus, "Chapter I: The Artist and His Work," 18; Nel, *Crockett Johnson and Ruth Krauss*, 166.

105. Sendak, Eulogy for Ruth Krauss.

106. *Sendak at the Rosenbach*, 8; Marcus, "Chapter I: The Artist and His Work," 18.

107. Lanes, *Art of Maurice Sendak*, 40–42.

108. Sendak, Eulogy for Ruth Krauss.

109. Marcus, "Chapter I: The Artist and His Work," 18.

110. Hentoff, "Among the Wild Things."

111. Lanes, *Art of Maurice Sendak*, 26.

112. Selma G. Lanes, interview transcript, June 22, 1989.

113. Hayworth, *Fever Vision*, 43.

114. Ruth Krauss, *I'll Be You and You Be Me*, pictures by Maurice Sendak (New York: HarperCollins, 1954).

115. Lanes, *Art of Maurice Sendak*, 27.

116. Ruth Krauss. *I Want to Paint My Bathroom Blue*, pictures by Maurice Sendak (New York: Harper & Brothers, 1956).

117. Dummy for *I Want to Paint My Bathroom Blue*, 1955, Series 14: Box 4, Maurice Sendak Collection, University of Connecticut Archives & Special Collections, Thomas J. Dodd Research Center, Storrs, CT.

118. "Questions to an Artist Who Is Also an Author," 34.

119. Lanes, *Art of Maurice Sendak*, 260.

120. *Far Out Isn't Far Enough: The Tomi Ungerer Story*, dir. Brad Bernstein, Far Out Films, 2013.

121. Jack Sendak, *Circus Girl*, pictures by Maurice Sendak (New York: Harper & Brothers, 1957).

122. Else Holmelund Minarik, *Little Bear*, pictures by Maurice Sendak (New York: Harper & Row, 1957).

123. Else Holmelund Minarik, *No Fighting, No Biting!*, pictures by Maurice Sendak (New York: Harper, 1958).

124. Maurice Sendak, ink study, for *Wheel on the School*, Maurice Sendak Archive, The Rosenbach Museum & Library, Philadelphia.

125. Krauss, *I'll Be You and You Be Me*, pictures by Sendak.

126. Maurice Sendak, pencil study for *Let's Be Enemies*, Maurice Sendak Papers, Kerlan Collection, Elmer Andersen Library, University of Minnesota Archives and Special Collections.

127. Nordstrom also worked on a sequel titled *The Secret Choice*, but she could not find a way to finish it, so she burned the manuscript. Blewett, "Ursula Nordstrom and the Queer History of the Children's Book."

128. Else Holmelund Minarik, *A Kiss for Little Bear*, pictures by Maurice Sendak (New York: HarperCollins, 1968).

129. Sendak, Eulogy for Ruth Krauss.

130. Maurice Sendak, pencil sketch, Ruth Krauss Papers, series 2, box 8, folder 270, University of Connecticut Archives & Special Collections, Thomas J. Dodd Research Center, Storrs, CT.

131. Maurice Sendak, pencil study for *I'll Be You and You Be Me*, Maurice Sendak Papers, Kerlan Collection, Elmer Andersen Library, University of Minnesota Archives and Special Collections.

132. Maurice Sendak, pencil study for *Kenny's Window*, Maurice Sendak Papers, Kerlan Collection, Elmer Andersen Library, University of Minnesota Archives and Special Collections.

133. Patrick Rodgers, "Selected Sendak: Interviews by the Rosenbach," Rosenbach Museum Archives, 2007–8, rpt. in *Conversations with Maurice Sendak*, ed. Peter C. Kunze (Jackson: University Press of Mississippi, 2016), 165.

134. Dorothy W. Baruch, *One Little Boy* (New York: Julian Press, 1952).

135. Zarin, "Not Nice"; Kidd, "Wild Things and Wolf Dreams," 213.

136. Maurice Sendak, corrected typescripts for *Kenny's Window*, folder 1, pp. 4–6, Maurice Sendak Papers, Kerlan Collection, Elmer Andersen Library, University of Minnesota Archives and Special Collections.

137. Sendak, typescript for *Kenny's Window*, folder 1.

138. Ibid., folder 3.

139. Ibid.

140. Ibid., folder 1.

141. Sendak, typescript draft for *Kenny's Window*.

142. Cott, "Maurice Sendak, King of All Wild Things."

143. Author's conversation with Edmund Newman, April 12, 2020.

144. Weinberg, introduction to *Desperate Necessity*, 11, 13; Kunze, *Conversations*, 10.

145. Author's conversation with Edmund Newman, April 12, 2020.

146. Author's conversation with Judith Goldman, July 23, 2019, and subsequent correspondence on January 11, 2020.

147. Brockes, "I Refuse to Cater to the Bullshit of Innocence."

148. Teeman, "Maurice Sendak: I'm Ready to Die."

149. Brockes, "I Refuse to Cater to the Bullshit of Innocence."

150. Cohen, "Concerns Beyond Just Where the Wild Things Are."

151. Teeman, "Maurice Sendak: I'm Ready to Die."

Chapter 4

1. Rochman, "The Booklist Interview," 1849.

2. "Camp: Notes on Fashion," May 9–September 8, 2019, Metropolitan Museum of Art, New York.

3. Susan Sontag, "Notes on Camp" (1964), in *Against Interpretation: And Other Essays* (New York: Picador, 2001), 291.

4. Ibid., 280.

5. Ibid., 283, 287.

6. Maurice Sendak, book jacket study for *The Sign on Rosie's Door*, Maurice Sendak Papers MC 1174, Kerlan Collection, Elmer Andersen Library, University of Minnesota Archives and Special Collections.

7. Sendak, "Sources of Inspiration"; Maurice Sendak to Mrs. Kane, September 24, 1962, Kane Family Letters, Maurice Sendak Collection, The Rosenbach Museum & Library, Philadelphia.

8. Commire, "Maurice Sendak," 192.

9. Sontag, "Notes on Camp," 289.

10. Hammel, "Maurice Sendak: Thriving on Quiet."

11. *Really Rosie*, directed by Maurice Sendak, produced by Sheldon Riss (CBS, February 19, 1975).

12. Cech, *Angels and Wild Things*, 68–69.

13. Scott Long, "The Loneliness of Camp," in *Camp Grounds: Style and Homosexuality*, ed. David Bergman (Amherst: University of Massachusetts Press, 1993), 79, cited in Jonathan Weinberg, "Ray Johnson Fan Club," in *Ray Johnson: Correspondences*, ed. Donna M. De Salvo and Catherine Gudis (Columbus, OH: Wexner Center for the Arts, 1999), 106.

14. Jason Vondersmith, "Magical Mozart," *Portland Tribune*, May 3, 2016; Author's conversation with Christopher Mattaliano, September 7, 2016.

15. *Writers Talk: Maurice Sendak with Paul Vaughan*.

16. Hayworth, *Fever Vision*, xvi, xii.

17. Maurice Sendak, "A Tribute to a Friend," *American Book Collectors of Children's Literature* 14, no. 2 (Fall 2002): 6.

18. Schneider, "A Personal Remembrance of My Uncle, Bert Slaff," 14.

19. Maurice Sendak to Coleman Dowell, April 7, 1969, Coleman Dowell Papers.

20. Maurice Sendak to Coleman Dowell, n.d., Coleman Dowell Papers.

21. Coleman Dowell Papers; Edmund White, preface to Hayworth, *Fever Vision*, xiii.

22. Maurice Sendak to Coleman Dowell, March 1971, Coleman Dowell Papers.

23. Maurice Sendak to Coleman Dowell, February 12, 1971, Coleman Dowell Papers; Maurice Sendak to Coleman Dowell, March 1971, Coleman Dowell Papers.

24. Maurice Sendak to Coleman Dowell, March 1971, Coleman Dowell Papers.

25. Maurice Sendak to Coleman Dowell, May 9, 1975, Coleman Dowell Papers; Maurice Sendak to Coleman Dowell, January 4, 1978, Coleman Dowell Papers.

26. Hammel, "Maurice Sendak: Thriving on Quiet."

27. Tali Berner, "Children and Rituals in Early Modern Ashkenaz," *The Journal of the History of Childhood and Youth* 7, no. 1 (2014): 75; Harvey E. Goldberg, *Jewish Passages: Cycles of Jewish Life* (Berkeley: University of California Press, 2003), 45; Lawrence A. Hoffman, *Covenant of Blood: Circumcision and Gender in Rabbinic Judaism* (Chicago: University of Chicago Press, 1996), 200; Evans, "Wild World of Maurice Sendak," 583.

28. Weinberg, introduction to *Desperate Necessity*, 11, 13.

29. Marcus, *Dear Genius*, 147.

30. Edna Edwards interviews Maurice Sendak, 1973.

31. Patrick Rodgers, "Chapter X: Where the Wild Things Are," 196.

32. Author's e-mail correspondence with Deborah Belford de Furia, August 29, 2015.

33. Author's e-mail correspondence with Loring Vogel, August 19, 2019, December 22, 2019, and January 5, 2019.

34. Thomas McGann, "Wild Things: Maurice Sendak on Fire Island," *Fire Island News* 63, no. 5 (July 19, 2019): 47.

35. Author's conversation with Eric Pederson, August 8, 2019.

36. Jas Chana, "Herman Wouk's Fire Island Synagogue," *Tablet*, May 28, 2015.

37. As Kenneth Kidd has noted, wolves in folklore signify creatures that flourish beyond the bounds of an existing civilization. Kidd, *Making American Boys*, 150.

38. Marc Michael Epstein draws a comparison between Max's wolf suit and the medieval fool's costume, a visual trope apparent even in medieval talmudic commentary. Marc Michael Epstein, ed., *Skies of Parchment, Seas of Ink: Jewish Illuminated Manuscripts* (Princeton, NJ, and Oxford: Princeton University Press, 2015), 16.

39. Sendak, "Moby Dick, Creativity, and Other Wild Things."

40. "Grim Colberty Tales with Maurice Sendak," *The Colbert Report*, Part One, January 24, 2012.

41. Avi Steinberg, "Maurice Sendak on 'Bumble-Ardy,'" *The Paris Review*, December 27, 2011.

42. Maurice Sendak to Mrs. Kane, June 21, 1964, Kane Family Letters, The Rosenbach Museum & Library, Philadelphia; Maurice Sendak to Mrs. Kane, August 16, 1965, Kane Family Letters, The Rosenbach Museum & Library, Philadelphia; Maurice Sendak to Laurie E. Deval, Sept. 16, 1966; Autograph File, S, Harvard University Houghton Library, Cambridge, MA; Maurice Sendak to Mrs. Kane, July 8, 1964, Kane Family Letters, The Rosenbach Museum & Library, Philadelphia.

43. Hayworth, *Fever Vision*, 106.

44. Maurice Sendak to Selma Lanes, March 25, 1968, MS 292, Smith College Library Special Collections.

45. Maurice Sendak to Mary Jarrell, May 6, 1968, Randall Jarrell Collection 1914–1969, The Henry W. and Albert A. Berg Collection of English and American Literature, The New York Public Library, Astor, Lenox and Tilden Foundations, New York.

46. Maurice Sendak to Leroy Richmond, August 7, 1966, The Maurice Sendak and Leroy Richmond Collection of Correspondence, 1965–2007, Irvin Department of Rare Books and Special Collections, University of South Carolina Libraries, Columbia, SC.

47. Marcus, *Dear Genius*, 255. Silverstein worked as a columnist for *Playboy* for over forty years. Andrew Belonsky, "Shel Silverstein Covered Fire Island for 'Playboy,'" *Out* magazine, May 22, 2013.

48. Belonsky, "Shel Silverstein Covered Fire Island For 'Playboy.'"

49. Ibid.

50. Decter, "The Boys on the Beach." See also Lee Bennett Hopkins, *Books Are by People: Interviews with 104 Authors and Illustrators of Books for Young Children* (New York: Citation Press, 1969), 254.

51. Sontag, "Notes on Camp," 291.

52. See Kathryn Bond Stockton's *The Queer Child*.

53. Decter, "The Boys on the Beach." For more on Fire Island's early gay communities and social politics around ethnicity and race within them, see Esther Newton, *Cherry Grove, Fire Island: Sixty Years in America's First Gay and Lesbian Town* (Boston: Beacon Press, 1993).

54. Ellis, *Studies in the Psychology of Sex*, 123–124.

55. Alisa Solomon, "Performance: Queerly Jewish/Jewishly Queer in the American Theater," in *The Cambridge History of Jewish American Literature*, ed. Hana Wirth-Nesher (New York and Cambridge, UK: Cambridge University Press, 2016), 548.

56. Sedgwick, *Epistemology of the Closet*, 70–71.

57. Kidd, "Wild Things and Wolf Dreams," 212–213.

58. Ibid., 216.

59. See, for example, Heather K. Love, *Feeling Backward: Loss and the Politics of Queer History* (Cambridge, MA: Harvard University Press, 2007).

60. George Chauncey, "The Trouble with Shame," in *Gay Shame*, ed. David M. Halperin and Valerie Traub (Chicago and London: University of Chicago Press, 2009), 281.

61. Erving Goffman, *Stigma: Notes on the Management of Spoiled Identity* (Englewood Cliffs, NJ: Prentice-Hall), 1963, 81.

62. Ibid., 87.

63. George Steiner, "In Lieu of a Preface," *Salmagundi* 58–59: Homosexuality: Sacrilege, Vision, Politics (Fall 1982–Winter 1983), 8; Israel Goldstein, *American Jewry Comes of Age: Tercentenary Addresses* (n.c.: Block, 1955), 104.

64. Maurice Sendak interview in Wintle, *The Pied Pipers*, 29.

65. Edna Edwards interviews Maurice Sendak, 1973.

66. Goffman, *Stigma*, 88.

67. Kushner, *Art of Maurice Sendak*, 77.

68. Marcus, "Chapter I: The Artist and His Work," 18–19.

69. Heller, Interview with Maurice Sendak, 102.

70. Author's conversation with Ellen Kellman, March 13, 2017, Brandeis University.

71. Sylvia Barack Fishman, ed., *Follow My Footprints: Changing Images of Women in American Jewish Fiction* (Hanover, NH, and London: Brandeis University Press and the University Press of New England, 1992), 88.

72. Judy Taylor, "Chapter II: Influences on Book Illustration: Some Influences on the Work of Maurice Sendak," in *Maurice Sendak: A Celebration of the Artist and His Work*, ed. Leonard S. Marcus (New York: Abrams, 2013), 28–31; Maurice Sendak, *Higglety Pigglety Pop! or There Must Be More to Life* (New York: Harper & Row, 1967), 10, 12.

73. Jonathan Cott, *Pipers at the Gates of Dawn: The Wisdom of Children's Literature* (New York: Random House, 1981), 59.

74. Dobrin, "Rosenbach Reels in Rare Sendak Trove."

75. Kushner, *Art of Maurice Sendak*, 85.

76. Andrea Most, *Making Americans: Jews and the Broadway Musical* (Cambridge, MA: Harvard University Press, 2004).

77. Marcus, *Dear Genius*, 313, 315.

78. Leslie Tannenbaum, "Betrayed by Chicken Soup: Judaism, Gender and Performance in Maurice Sendak's *Really Rosie*," *The Lion and the Unicorn* 27, no. 3 (2003): 362–364, 368.

79. Cott, "Maurice Sendak, King of All Wild Things."

80. Kushner, *Art of Maurice Sendak*, 45.

81. Marcus, *Maurice Sendak: A Celebration*, 111.

82. Singer, *Zlateh the Goat and Other Stories*, pictures by Sendak, 21–23.

83. Federman, *Drawing the Curtain*, 171–176.

84. Ibid., 175–188.

85. Mark Greif, *The Age of the Crisis of Man: Thought and Fiction in America, 1933–1973* (Princeton, NJ: Princeton University Press, 2015), 118.

86. Edna Edwards interviews Maurice Sendak, 1973.

87. Francelia Butler interviews Maurice Sendak, typescript, April 1976, 19, box 9, folder: "Sendak, Maurice—Children's Literature," series 2, Francelia Butler Papers, University of Connecticut Archives & Special Collections, Thomas J. Dodd Research Center, Storrs, CT.

88. Lanes, *Art of Maurice Sendak*, 183.

89. Maurice Sendak to Coleman Dowell, April 7, 1969, Coleman Dowell Papers.

90. Dummy for *In the Night Kitchen*, July 10, 1969, Series 56: Box 16, Maurice Sendak Collection, University of Connecticut Archives & Special Collections, Thomas J. Dodd Research Center, Storrs, CT.

91. Lanes, *Art of Maurice Sendak*, 174.

92. Clemons, "Sendak's Enchanted Land."

93. Cited in Sonheim, *Maurice Sendak*, 14.

94. Author's conversation with Eric Pederson, August 8, 2019.

95. Marcus, *Maurice Sendak: A Celebration*, 15–27, 24.

96. Marcus, *Dear Genius*, 326, 333–335.

97. Bill Morgan and Nancy J. Peters, eds., *Howl on Trial: The Battle for Free Expression* (San Francisco: City Lights Books, 2006), 12.

98. Lyall, "Maurice Sendak Sheds Moonlight on a Dark Tale."

99. "From Kids' Books to Erotica, Tomi Ungerer's 'Far Out' Life," Terry Gross interviews Tomi Ungerer, *Fresh Air*, National Public Radio, July 1, 2013.

100. Joanna Carey, "Tomi Ungerer, Rennaisance Man of Children's Book Illustration," *The Guardian*, February 24, 2012. See also Sarah Cowan, "All in One: An Interview with Tomi Ungerer," *The Paris Review*, January 30, 2015.

101. Groth, Interview with Maurice Sendak, 58–59.

102. Cott, "Maurice Sendak, King of All Wild Things."

103. John Updike, "Randall Jarrell Writing Stories for Children," *New York Times*, November 14, 1976.

104. Maurice Sendak to Coleman Dowell, April 19, 1971 and March 1971, Coleman Dowell Papers.

105. Author's conversation with Eric Pederson, August 8, 2019.

106. May, "Envisioning the Jewish Community in Children's Literature," 147.

107. Bernard Malamud, *A Malamud Reader* (New York: Farrar, Straus and Giroux, 1967).

108. Iona and Peter Opie, *I Saw Esau: The Schoolchild's Pocket Book*, pictures by Maurice Sendak (Somerville, MA: Candlewick Press, 1992).

109. Sendak in Burningham, *When We Were Young*.

110. Cott, "Maurice Sendak, King of All Wild Things."

111. Exodus 19:4, Sefaria.org. I thank Jonathan D. Sarna for suggesting this connection.

112. Maurice Sendak, *Fantasy Sketches* (Philadelphia: Philip H. & A.S.W. Rosenbach Foundation, 1970).

113. Tony Kushner, *Brundibar*, pictures by Maurice Sendak (New York: Michael di Capua Books/Hyperion Books for Children, 2003).

114. Stockton, *The Queer Child*.

115. Rose, *The Case of Peter Pan*, 25.

116. Cited in J. Jack Halberstam, "Queer Temporality and Postmodern Geographies," in *In a Queer Time and Place* (New York: New York University Press, 2005), rpt. in *Reading Feminist Theory: From Modernity to Postmodernity*, ed. Susan Archer Mann and Ashly Suzanne Patterson (New York and Oxford, UK: Oxford University Press, 2015), 346.

117. Commire, "Maurice Sendak," 187.

118. Slaff, "Creativity: Blessing or Burden?," 81.

119. Derick Dreher, "Maurice Sendak; or, What the Nineteenth Century Can Mean to the Twenty-First," *PMLA* 126, no. 1 (2014): 106.

120. Marcus, *Dear Genius*, 154.

121. Hopkins, *Books Are by People*, 250.

122. Harris, "Impressions of Sendak," 36–37.

123. Stephanie Nettell, "Maurice Sendak obituary," *The Guardian*, May 8, 2012.

124. Stockton, *The Queer Child*, 11, 3.

125. Steinberg, "Maurice Sendak on 'Bumble-Ardy.'"

126. Sendak, "Moby Dick, Creativity, and Other Wild Things," 12.

127. Ibid., 11.

128. Rochman, "The Booklist Interview," 1848.

129. Maurice Sendak to Mrs. Kane, September 24, 1962, Kane Family Letters, The Rosenbach Museum & Library, Philadelphia.

130. Ibid.

131. Selma G. Lanes, interview transcript, June 22, 1989.

132. Maurice Sendak to Mrs. Kane, November 6, 1961, Kane Family Letters, The Rosenbach Museum & Library, Philadelphia.

133. Hentoff, "Among the Wild Things."

134. *Writers Talk: Maurice Sendak with Paul Vaughan*.

135. Maurice Sendak to Coleman Dowell, May 1, 1975, Coleman Dowell Papers.

136. Hayworth, *Fever Vision*, xii, 155.

137. Heller, Interview with Maurice Sendak, 102.

138. *Tell Them Anything You Want*.

139. Glynn, *Desperate Necessity*, 15.

140. Maurice Sendak to Mrs. Kane, June 23, 1966, Kane Family Letters, The Rosenbach Museum & Library, Philadelphia.

141. Maurice Sendak to Mrs. Kane, April 14, 1962, Kane Family Letters, The Rosenbach Museum & Library, Philadelphia.

142. Maurice Sendak to Coleman Dowell, May 9, 1975, Coleman Dowell Papers.

Chapter 5

1. Cook, "Postscript: Wild Things," 58.

2. Roiphe, "The Wildest Rumpus."

3. Robert Rosenblum, *The Romantic Child* (London: Thames and Hudson, 1988), 24.

4. Ellen Handler Spitz, "Ethos in Steig's and Sendak's Picture Books: The Connected and the Lonely Child," *Journal of Aesthetic Education* 43, no. 2, (Summer 2009): 74.

5. Ibid., 70, 72, 74.

6. Jean Perrot, "Deconstructing Maurice Sendak's Postmodern Palimpsest," *Children's Literature Association Quarterly* 16, no. 4 (Winter 1991–92): 262, cited in Sorin, "The Fears of Early Childhood," 18.

7. "'Don't Assume Anything,'" 146.

8. Braun, "Sendak Raises the Shade on Childhood."

9. Stix, "Sendak Draws on Childhood Truths."

10. James Bohlman, "Truly Wealthy!" *Journey2Kona2019* (blog), May 16, 2002.

11. Kushner, *Art of Maurice Sendak*, 193.

12. *Tell Them Anything You Want.*

13. Sonheim, *Maurice Sendak*, 20.

14. Brockes, "I Refuse to Cater to the Bullshit of Innocence."

15. Sophia M. Fischer, "Grimm's Tale Used to Depict Holocaust," *Jewish Journal*, Deerfield Beach, Florida, April 2, 1992, 3A.

16. Moyers, "Maurice Sendak."

17. Sendak, "Enamored of the Mystery," 369.

18. Sendak, Eulogy for Ruth Krauss.

19. Sendak also turned three of his theater designs into picture books: *The Love for Three Oranges* (1984), *The Cunning Little Vixen* (1985), and *The Nutcracker* (1984). Kushner, *Art of Maurice Sendak*.

20. Nel, "Wild Things, Children and Art," 27.

21. Judith Rosen, "Two NYC Kids' Stores Celebrate 70 Years—Combined," *Publishers Weekly*, November 15, 2010.

22. Joe Fassler, "For 'Hugo' Author Brian Selznick, Life (Thankfully) Imitates Art," *The Atlantic*, February 7, 2012.

23. Walt Whitman, *Live Oak, with Moss*, ill. Brian Selznick (New York: Abrams, 2019), 2–3.

24. Groth, Interview with Maurice Sendak, 68.

25. Teeman, "Maurice Sendak: I'm Ready to Die."

26. Zarin, "Not Nice."

27. Katie Roiphe, *The Violet Hour* (New York: Dial Press, 2016), 212.

28. *Tell Them Anything You Want.*

29. Roiphe, *Violet Hour*, 214.

30. Herbert J. Gans, "Symbolic Ethnicity: The Future of Ethnic Groups and Cultures in America," *Ethnic and Racial Studies* 2, no. 1 (2010): 1–20; Mary C. Waters, *Ethnic Options: Choosing Identities in America* (Berkeley: University of California Press, 1990).

31. Goldstein, *Price of Whiteness*, 211.

32. Ibid., 211, 213.

33. Kushner, *Art of Maurice Sendak*, 190.

34. Lanes, interview transcript, 1989.

35. Federman, *Drawing the Curtain*, 188.

36. See Sonheim, *Maurice Sendak*, 239; Researcher's notes, box 32, folder 9: Maurice Sendak: In His Own Words and Pictures—The William Breman Jewish Heritage Museum (no. 393), Benjamin Hirsch and Associates, Inc. Records, Georgia Tech Library Archives, Atlanta. For further study of Sendak's use of Holocaust memory in *Dear Mili*, see Bettina Kümmerling-Meibauer, "Romantic and Jewish Images of Childhood in Maurice Sendak's *Dear Mili*," *European Judaism* 42, no. 1 (Spring 2009): 5–16; Hamida Bosmajian, "Hidden Grief: Maurice Sendak's *Dear Mili* and the Limitations of Holocaust Picture Books," in *Sparing the Child: Grief and the Unspeakable in Youth Literature About Nazism and the Holocaust* (New York and London: Routledge, 2002), 215–240; and Bosmajian, "Memory and Desire in the Landscapes of Sendak's *Dear Mili*."

37. Charlotte Delbo, *La mémoire et les jours* (Paris: Berg International, 1985), 13.

38. Lanes, interview transcript, 1989.

39. Author's correspondence with Justin Cammy, who owns the watercolor and lent it to Sendak, January 9, 2020.

40. Glenn Dickson, "Our Afternoon with Maurice: Klezmer Band Leader Recalls Recording with Sendak," *Jewish Advocate*, June 1, 2012, 13; Author's conversation with Glenn Dickson, January 2, 2019.

41. Robert Gluck, "For Sendak, Menorahs Burn with Memories," *Jewish Advocate*, December 23, 2011, 17.

42. Maurice Sendak interview in Wintle, *The Pied Pipers*, 25.

43. Harper & Row catalog, c.1971, box 1, folder 21, Blaine Pennington Papers, University of Missouri-Kansas City Archives, Kansas City, MO.

44. "Questions to an Artist Who Is Also an Author," 30.

45. Maurice Sendak, ink study for *Kenny's Window*, folder 1, Maurice Sendak Papers, Kerlan Collection, Elmer Andersen Library, University of Minnesota Archives and Special Collections. His later works *Outside Over There* and *Dear Mili* would draw most from German Romanticism.

46. Selma G. Lanes, interview transcript, June 22, 1989.

47. Hammel, "Maurice Sendak: Thriving on Quiet"; Selma G. Lanes, interview transcript, June 22, 1989; Sendak, "Enamored of the Mystery," 362–374.

48. Cott, "Maurice Sendak, King of All Wild Things."

49. *Writers Talk: Maurice Sendak with Paul Vaughan.*

50. Groth, Interview with Maurice Sendak, 37–38.

51. Rosenblum, *The Romantic Child*, 24. After his Sealyham terrier, Jennie, died in the late 1960s, Sendak's dogs, in order, were Erda (a German shepherd), Io (a golden retriever drawn in his *Some Swell Pup* and *Dear Mili*), and Aggie and Runge (both German shepherds). All three German shepherds feature in *Outside Over There* and *Dear Mili*. Monks of New Skete, *Art of Raising a Puppy* (New York: Little, Brown, 1991), 245.

52. In the 1860s through the 1880s, with increasing contact between *maskilim* (proponents of the Haskalah) and traditional Jews via individual travel and the growth of Eastern European Jewish presses, depictions of Germans in Eastern European literature reflected ambivalent and satirical attitudes about the influences of German secularism. Amy Blau, "Afterlives: Translations of German Weltliteratur into Yiddish," Dissertation, University of Illinois at Urbana, 2005, 55, YIVO, Center for Jewish History, New York.

53. Rosenblum, *The Romantic Child*, 24.

54. Ibid., 51.

55. Glynn, "Desperate Necessity," 149.

56. See Kümmerling-Meibauer, "Romantic and Jewish Images of Childhood in Maurice Sendak's *Dear Mili*," 6.

57. Rosenblum, *The Romantic Child*, 50.

58. Kushner, *Art of Maurice Sendak*, 9–10.

59. "Questions to an Artist Who Is Also an Author," 265.

60. Edna Edwards interviews Maurice Sendak, 1973.

61. Ibid.

62. Heather K. Love, "Emotional Rescue," in *Gay Shame*, ed. David M. Halperin and Valerie Traub (Chicago and London: University of Chicago Press, 2009), 258.

63. Sendak, "Enamored of the Mystery," 363.

64. Kushner, *Art of Maurice Sendak*, 210.

65. Edna Edwards interviews Maurice Sendak, 1973.]

66. Hammel, "Maurice Sendak: Thriving on Quiet."

67. Edna Edwards interviews Maurice Sendak, 1973.

68. Hammel, "Maurice Sendak: Thriving on Quiet."

69. Edna Edwards interviews Maurice Sendak, 1973.

70. Maurice Sendak to Coleman Dowell, March 1971, Coleman Dowell Papers.

71. Kushner, *Art of Maurice Sendak*, 11.

72. Glynn, "Desperate Necessity," 137–138.

73. Monks of New Skete, *Art of Raising a Puppy*, 253.

74. Ibid., 248–249.

75. Ibid., 249–250.

76. Heller, Interview with Maurice Sendak, 70–81.

77. Sutton, "An Interview with Maurice Sendak," 690.

78. Ibid., 689.

79. Mercier, "Sendak on Sendak," 45–46.

80. Braun, "Sendak Raises the Shade on Childhood."

81. Marcus, *Maurice Sendak: A Celebration*, 26.

82. Rosenblum, *The Romantic Child*, 54.

83. James Marshall inscription to Maurice Sendak in Sendak's copy of Marshall's *The Stupids Die* (1981), Maurice Sendak Collection of James Marshall, box 1, University of Connecticut Archives & Special Collections, Thomas J. Dodd Research Center, Storrs, CT.

84. Stephen Hayward and Sarah Lefanu, *God: An Anthology of Fiction* (London and New York: Serpent's Tail, 1992), 128.

85. Kushner, *Art of Maurice Sendak*, 24.

86. Author's conversation with Eric Pederson, August 8, 2019.

87. Melville, *Moby-Dick*, 69.

88. Heller, Interview with Maurice Sendak, 104.

89. Sendak in Burningham, *When We Were Young*, 123.

90. Burningham, "His Stories and Illustrations Captivate Children."

91. Sendak, February 8, 1989, Public Education Program sound recordings.

92. Selma G. Lanes, interview transcript, June 22, 1989.

93. Evans, "Wild World of Maurice Sendak"; Nettell, "Maurice Sendak obituary."

94. "Maurice Sendak: On Life, Death and Children's Lit," Terry Gross interviews Maurice Sendak, *Fresh Air*, National Public Radio, December 29, 2011 (originally broadcast September 20, 2011).

95. Ibid.

96. Groth, Interview with Maurice Sendak, 83–84.

97. Teeman, "Maurice Sendak: I'm Ready to Die."

98. "Maurice Sendak: On Life, Death and Children's Lit."

99. Mercier, "Sendak on Sendak."

100. Color study for *Outside Over There*, series 62: box 14, Maurice Sendak Collection, University of Connecticut Archives & Special Collections, Thomas J. Dodd Research Center, Storrs, CT.

101. Quoted in Chauncey, *Gay New York*, 179–180. See also Leddick, *Intimate Companions*, 48.

102. Haase, "Children, War, and the Imaginative Space of Fairy Tales," 363.

103. Kümmerling-Meibauer, "Romantic and Jewish Images of Childhood in Maurice Sendak's *Dear Mili*," 7–8.

104. Justin G. Schiller, "Recollections for an Exhibition," 8, 11.

105. Lanes, interview transcript, 1989; Maurice Sendak, "Descent into Limbo: The Creative Process," lecture, Bennington College, April 18, 1989; Bosmajian, "Memory and Desire in the Landscapes of Sendak's *Dear Mili*," 187.

106. Wilhelm Grimm, *Dear Mili*, trans. Ralph Manheim, pictures by Maurice Sendak (New York: Farrar, Straus and Giroux, 1988).

107. Sedgwick, *Epistemology of the Closet*, 74.

108. Specifically, the decision upheld a Georgia sodomy law that criminalized oral and anal sex in private between consenting adults, particularly with respect to homosexuals. *Bowers v. Hardwick*, Supreme Court, decided June 30, 1986, Legal Information Institute, Cornell Law School.

109. Neta Alexander, "How AIDS Forced the LGBT Community to Redefine 'Home,'" *Haaretz*, September 27, 2017.

110. Drake, "Born to be Wild," 87–88; Weinberg, introduction to *Desperate Necessity*, 13.

111. Teeman, "Maurice Sendak: I'm Ready to Die."

112. C. W. Henderson, "$25,000 Funding Received for Pediatric AIDS Care," *AIDS Weekly Plus*, June 8, 1998, 2–a7, a8.

113. Caroline Bermudez, "How a Social-Service Fund Raiser Lured a $1-Million Gift," *Chronicle of Philanthropy* 22, no. 16 (August 2010): 19.

114. Kushner, *Art of Maurice Sendak*, 141.

115. Maurice Sendak to Selma Lanes, July 24, 1980, MS 292, Smith College Library Special Collections.

116. Maurice Sendak to James Bohlman, February 3, 1988, Maurice Sendak Collection, The Rosenbach Museum & Library, Philadelphia.

117. After Marshall's death, Sendak helped facilitate the publication of Marshall's *The Owl and the Pussycat* (1998), and he would also illustrate Marshall's *Swine Lake* (New York: HarperCollins, 1999). Norman D. Stevens, "Celebrating

the Life and Work of James Marshall (1942–1992)," *American Book Collectors of Children's Literature* 14, no. 2 (Fall 2002): 5.

118. Sendak, "Moby Dick, Creativity, and Other Wild Things," 12.

119. Drake, "Born to be Wild," 89.

120. "Maurice Sendak Talks About *We Are All in the Dumps with Jack and Guy*," promotional literature for *We Are All in the Dumps* (New York: HarperCollins, July 1993), 2.

121. Sasha Weiss, "Art Spiegelman Discusses Maurice Sendak," *New Yorker*, May 9, 2012.

122. Heinrich von Kleist, *Penthesilea*, trans. Joel Agee, pictures by Maurice Sendak (New York: Michael di Capua Books/HarperCollins, 1998), 89.

123. Cott, *Pipers at the Gates of Dawn*, 64–65; Bryant, "Pierre and Pierre."

124. Kushner, *Art of Maurice Sendak*, 70.

125. Bryant, "Pierre and Pierre," 340.

126. Kushner, *Art of Maurice Sendak*, 65, 69.

127. Teeman, "Maurice Sendak: I'm Ready to Die"; see aso Zarin, "Not Nice"; Groth, Interview with Maurice Sendak, 73.

128. Drake, "Born to be Wild," 88.

129. Naomi Pfefferman, "'Dance's' Conflict Is Center Stage," *Jewish Journal*, April 17, 2003.

130. *Last Dance*, dir. Mirra Bank, featuring Robby Bernett, Maurice Sendak, Michael Tracy, Jonathan Wolken, and Arthur Yorinks, First Run Features, 2002.

131. Roiphe, *Violet Hour*, 204–205.

132. Edelman, *No Future*, 13.

133. Tony Kushner, *Angels in America: A Gay Fantasia on National Themes* (New York: Theatre Communications Group, 1995), 16.

134. Cohen, "Concerns Beyond Just Where the Wild Things Are."

135. Author's correspondence with Philip Nel, January 14, 2020.

Conclusion

1. Robin Bernstein, *Racial Innocence: Performing American Childhood from Slavery to Civil Rights* (New York: New York University Press, 2011).

2. See Robin Bernstein, "Let Black Kids Just Be Kids," *New York Times*, July 26, 2017.

3. Brockes, "I Refuse to Cater to the Bullshit of Innocence."

4. Cohen, "Concerns Beyond Just Where the Wild Things Are."

5. Quoted in Hentoff, "Among the Wild Things."

6. James Bohlman, "THE Maurice Sendak?!!!" *Journey2Kona2019* (blog), July 14, 2015.

7. Nettell, "Maurice Sendak obituary."

8. John Cech, "Maurice Sendak and *Where the Wild Things Are*: A Legacy of Transformation," *PMLA* 129, no.1 (2014): 105.

9. Joyce Antler, *Jewish Radical Feminism: Voices from the Women's Liberation Movement* (New York: New York University Press, 2018), 278–279.

10. Sorin, "Fears of Early Childhood"; Mark Bixler and Mariano Castillo, "Author of 'Where the Wild Things Are' Dies," *CNN.com*, May 8, 2012.

11. Concepción de León, "The 10 Most Checked-Out Books in N.Y. Public Library History," *New York Times*, January 13, 2020.

12. Cech, *Angels and Wild Things*, 112; Kidd, "Wild Things and Wolf Dreams," 223.

13. Author's conversation with Eric Pederson, August 8, 2019.

14. Weiss, "Art Spiegelman Discusses Maurice Sendak."

15. Sendak, "Moby Dick, Creativity, and Other Wild Things," 11.

16. Evans, "Wild World of Maurice Sendak."

BIBLIOGRAPHY

Archival Collections

Arne Nixon Papers. Arne Nixon Center for the Study of Children's Literature. California State University. Fresno, CA.

Art & Artist Files. Smithsonian American Art Museum/National Portrait Gallery Library. Smithsonian Libraries. Washington, DC.

Autograph File, S. Harvard University Houghton Library. Cambridge, MA.

Benjamin Hirsch and Associates, Inc. Records (DM009). Georgia Institute of Technology Archives. Atlanta, http://finding-aids.library.gatech.edu/repositories/2/resources/436.

Beulah Campbell Papers. A. B. Colvin Collection and Archives. Montgomery Library. Campbellsville University. Campbellsville, KY.

Blaine Pennington Papers. University of Missouri-Kansas City Archives. Kansas City, MO.

Coleman Dowell Papers. MSS 36. Series I. Boxes 1, 3, 4. Fales Library & Special Collections. New York University. New York.

Comics Project Files. Social Welfare History Archives. University of Minnesota Archives and Special Collections. Minneapolis.

De Grummond Children's Literature Collection. McCain Library & Archives University of Southern Mississippi. Hattiesburg, MS.

Edna Edwards Interviews with Children's Authors and Illustrators. MS 101. Loyola Marymount University Archives & Special Collections. Los Angeles, CA.

Farrar, Straus & Giroux, Inc. records. Manuscripts and Archives Division. The New York Public Library. Astor, Lenox, and Tilden Foundations New York, NY.

Francelia Butler Papers. University of Connecticut Archives & Special Collections. Thomas J. Dodd Research Center. Storrs, CT.

Isaac Bashevis Singer Papers. Harry Ransom Center, The University of Texas at Austin.

Joanna Foster Dougherty Papers. Special Collections & University Archives. University of Oregon. Eugene.

Jules Feiffer Papers, 1919–95. Library of Congress. Washington, DC.

Kinder Zhurnal/Farlag Matones, 1924–63. YIVO. New York, NY.

Lillian Hoban Papers. Beinecke Rare Book and Manuscript Library. Yale University. New Haven, CT.

The Maurice Sendak and Leroy Richmond Collection of Correspondence, 1965–2007. Irvin Department of Rare Books and Special Collections. University of South Carolina Libraries. Columbia, SC.

Maurice Sendak Collection. The Rosenbach Museum & Library. Philadelphia, PA.

Maurice Sendak Collection of James Marshall. University of Connecticut Archives & Special Collections. Thomas J. Dodd Research Center. Storrs, CT.

Maurice Sendak Papers. Kerlan Collection. Elmer Andersen Library. University of Minnesota Archives and Special Collections. Minneapolis.

Morton E. Wise Collection of Maurice Sendak. Dartmouth Rauner Library. Hanover, NH.

Muir mss. II, 1892–1981. Manuscripts Department. Indiana University Lilly Library. Bloomington.

Oral History Collection. American Jewish Committee. New York Public Library. New York.

Phillip Applebaum Collection. American Jewish Historical Society. Center for Jewish History. New York, NY.

Public Education Program sound recordings. New York Public Library Archives. The New York Public Library. New York.

Randall Jarrell Collection 1914–69. The Henry W. and Albert A. Berg Collection of English and American Literature. The New York Public Library, Astor, Lenox and Tilden Foundations. New York.

Ruth Krauss Papers. University of Connecticut Archives & Special Collections. Thomas J. Dodd Research Center. Storrs, CT.

Smith College Library Special Collections. Northampton, MA.

Stuart Wright Collection: Randall Jarrell Papers, Collection No. 1169-005. East Carolina Manuscript Collection, J.Y. Joyner Library, East Carolina University, Greenville, NC.

Truman A. Warner Papers. Western Connecticut State University Archives. Danbury, CT.

University of Guelph Archival & Special Collections. Guelph, ON, Canada.

Zena Bailey Sutherland Papers. Special Collections Research Center, University of Chicago Library. Chicago, IL.

Pictures by Sendak

Aymé, Marcel. *The Wonderful Farm*. New York: Harper, 1951.

Bond, Gladys Baker. *Seven Little Stories on Big Subjects*. New York: Anti-Defamation League of B'nai B'rith, 1955.

Chanover, Hyman and Alice. *Happy Hanukah Everybody*. New York: United Synagogue Commission on Jewish Education, 1954.

DeJong, Meindert. *Wheel on the School*. New York: Harper, 1954.

——. *House of Sixty Fathers*. New York and Evanston, IL: Harper & Row, 1956.

Eidinoff, Maxwell. *Atomics for the Millions*. New York: Whittlesey House, McGraw-Hill, 1947.

Engvick, William, ed., music by Alec Wilder. *Lullabies and Night Songs*. New York: Harper & Row, 1965.

Garvey, Robert. *Good Shabbos, Everybody*. New York: United Synagogue Commission on Jewish Education, 1951.

Grimm, Wilhelm. *Dear Mili*. Translated by Ralph Manheim. New York: Michael di Capua Books/Farrar, Straus and Giroux, 1988.

Jarrell, Randall. *The Animal Family*. New York: Pantheon, 1965.

——. *Fly by Night*. New York: Farrar, Straus & Giroux, 1976.

Kleist, Heinrich von. *Penthesilea*. Translated by Joel Agee. New York: Michael di Capua Books/HarperCollins, 1998.

Krauss, Ruth. *A Hole Is to Dig*. New York: HarperCollins, 1952.

——. *A Very Special House*. New York: Harper & Brothers, 1953.

——. *I'll Be You and You Be Me*. New York: HarperCollins, 1954.

——. *I Want to Paint My Bathroom Blue*. New York: Harper & Brothers, 1956.

——. *Open House for Butterflies*. New York: Harper & Brothers, 1960.

Kushner, Tony. *Brundibar*. New York: Michael di Capua Books/Hyperion Books for Children, 2003.

MacDonald, George. *The Golden Key*. New York: Farrar, Straus & Giroux, 1967.

Marshall, James. *Swine Lake*. New York: HarperCollins, 1999.

Melville, Herman. *Pierre; or, The Ambiguities* (1852). Kraken edition, edited by Hershel Parker. New York: HarperCollins, 1995.

Minarik, Else Holmelund. *Father Bear Comes Home*. New York: Harper & Row, 1959.

——. *A Kiss for Little Bear*. New York: HarperCollins, 1968.

——. *Little Bear*. New York: Harper & Row, 1957.

——. *Little Bear's Friend*. New York: Harper & Brothers, 1960.

——. *Little Bear's Visit*. New York: Harper, 1961.

——. *No Fighting, No Biting!* New York: Harper, 1958.

Opie, Iona and Peter. *I Saw Esau: The Schoolchild's Pocket Book*. Somerville, MA: Candlewick Press, 1992.

Segal, Lore, and Randall Jarrell, trans. *The Juniper Tree and Other Tales by Grimm*. New York: Farrar, Strauss & Giroux, 1973.

Sendak, Jack. *Circus Girl*. New York: Harper & Brothers, 1957.

——. *The Happy Rain*. New York: Harper Collins, 1956.

Sendak, Philip. *In Grandpa's House*. New York: Harper & Row, 1985.

Singer, Isaac Bashevis. *Zlateh the Goat and Other Stories*. Translated by I. B. Singer and Elizabeth Shub. New York: Harper & Row, 1966.

Udry, Janice May. *Let's Be Enemies*. New York: Harper & Row, 1961.

Vogel, Amos. *How Little Lori Visited Times Square*. New York: Harper & Row, 1963.

We Are All in the Dumps with Jack and Guy. New York: Michael di Capua Books/ HarperCollins, 1993.

Yorinks, Arthur, and Maurice Sendak, *Presto and Zesto in Limboland*. New York: Michael di Capua Books, 2018.

Text and Pictures by Sendak

Bumble-Ardy. New York: Michael di Capua Books/HarperCollins, 2011.

Fantasy Sketches. Philadelphia: Philip H. & A.S.W. Rosenbach Foundation, 1970.

Hector Protector and As I Went Over the Water: Two Nursery Rhymes with Pictures. New York: Harper & Row, 1965.

Higglety Pigglety Pop! or There Must Be More to Life. New York: Harper & Row, 1967.

In the Night Kitchen. New York: Harper & Row, 1970.

Kenny's Window. New York: Harper & Row, 1956.

Mommy? Scenario by Arthur Yorinks, paper engineering by Matthew Reinhart. New York: Michael di Capua Books/Scholastic, 2006.

My Brother's Book. New York: Michael di Capua Books/HarperCollins, 2013.

Nutshell Library (*Alligators All Around, One Was Johnny, Chicken Soup with Rice*, and *Pierre*). New York: Harper & Row, 1962.

Outside Over There. New York: Harper & Row, 1981.

The Sign on Rosie's Door. New York: Harper & Brothers, 1960.

Some Swell Pup or Are You Sure You Want a Dog? New York: Farrar, Straus & Giroux, 1976.

Very Far Away. New York: Harper & Brothers, 1957.

Where the Wild Things Are. New York: Harper & Row, 1963.

Prose and Public Speaking by Sendak

Caldecott & Co.: Notes on Books and Pictures. New York: Michael di Capua Books/Farrar, Straus & Giroux, 1988.

Changelings: Children's Stories Lost and Found, with Stephen Greenblatt, Herbert A. Schreier, and Wye Jamison Allanbrook. Berkeley: Doreen B. Townsend Center for the Humanities, University of California, 1996.

"Descent into Limbo: The Creative Process." Lecture. Bennington College, April 18, 1989, https://vimeo.com/143889683.

"Dreamer of Beauty." In *Little Nemo*, by Winsor McCay. New York: Nostalgia Press, 1976.

"Enamored of the Mystery." In *Innocence and Experience: Essays & Conversations on Children's Literature*, edited by Barbara Harrison and Gregory Maguire, 362–374. New York: Lothrop, Lee & Shepard, 1987.

Foreword to *R.O. Blechman: Between the Lines*, edited by Bea Feitler. New York: Hudson Hills Press, 1980.

Introduction to *The Maxfield Parrish Poster Book*. New York: Harmony Books, 1974.

"Moby Dick, Creativity, and Other Wild Things." *Vassar Quarterly* 92, no. 4 (September 1, 1996).

Sound cassette (2 sound files), February 8, 1989, and September 14, 1993, Public Education Program sound recordings, Manuscripts and Archives Division, The New York Public Library.

"Sources of Inspiration." Inaugural Zena Sutherland Lecture, May 20, 1983. Zena Bailey Sutherland Papers, box 7, folder 4. Special Collections Research Center, University of Chicago Library. Chicago.

"A Tribute to a Friend," *American Book Collectors of Children's Literature* 14, no. 2 (Fall 2002).

Exhibitions and Catalogs

The ABC of It. New York Public Library exhibit. Curated by Leonard S. Marcus. June 21, 2013–March 23, 2014. Stephen A. Schwarzman Building, New York.

Anderson, Brian. Catalogue for an Exhibition of Pictures by Maurice Sendak. December 16–February 29, 1975–76. Ashmolean Museum, Oxford, UK. London: Bodley Head, 1975.

Camp: Notes on Fashion. May 9–September, 2019. Metropolitan Museum of Art, New York.

Collecting Inspiration: Contemporary Illustrators and Their Heroes. Curated by Tony DiTerlizzi and Mo Willems. May 23–November 26, 2017. The Eric Carle Museum of Picture Book Art, Amherst, MA.

Federman, Rachel. *Drawing the Curtain: Maurice Sendak's Designs for Opera and Ballet*. New York, Munich, and London: Morgan Library & Museum and DelMonico Books, 2019.

Hanrahan, Joyce Y. *Works of Maurice Sendak: Revised and Expanded to 2001*. Saco, Maine: Custom Communications, 2001.

Harper & Row catalog, c.1971. Box 1, folder 21. Blaine Pennington Papers. University of Missouri-Kansas City Archives. Kansas City, MO.

Maguire, Gregory. *Making Mischief: A Maurice Sendak Appreciation*. New York: Harper-Collins, 2009.

Marcus, Leonard S. *The Art of Maurice Sendak: A Conversation with Maurice Sendak Conducted by Leonard S. Marcus*. November 22, 2002–January 12, 2003. The Eric Carle Museum of Picture Book Art. Amherst, MA.

Schiller, Justin G. "Recollections for an Exhibition." In *Maurice Sendak: A Celebration of the Artist and His Work*, edited by Leonard S. Marcus, curated by Justin G. Schiller and Dennis M. V. David. New York: Abrams, 2013.

Sendak at The Rosenbach. Exhibition catalog. Curated by Vincent Giroud and Maurice Sendak. April 28–October 30, 1995. The Rosenbach Museum & Library, Philadelphia, PA.

Wild Things: The Art of Maurice Sendak: A Selling Exhibition. Maurice Sendak Foundation. November 14–December 18, 2015. Sotheby's Gallery, New York.

Historical Documents

Beth Sholem Peoples Temple Yearbook, 1928. American Jewish Historical Society, Center for Jewish History, New York.

Bowers v. Hardwick, Supreme Court, decided June 30, 1986. Legal Information Institute, Cornell Law School, https://www.law.cornell.edu/supremecourt/text/478/186.

Congregation Sons of Israel Yearbook, 1947. American Jewish Historical Society. Center for Jewish History. New York.

Goldstein, Israel. *American Jewry Comes of Age: Tercentenary Addresses*. n.c.: Block, 1955.

Hartshorne, E. Y. *German Youth and the Nazi Dream of Victory by America in a World at War* 12. New York and Toronto: Farrar & Rinehart, 1941.

Kohn, Jacob. *Modern Problems of Jewish Parents: A Study in Parental Attitudes*. New York: The Women's League of the United Synagogue of America, 1932.

Levine, Hillel. "To Share a Vision." In *Jewish Radicalism: A Selected Anthology*, edited by J. N. Porter and P. Dreier. New York: Grove Press, 1973.

McNally, Evalyn Grumbine. *Reaching Juvenile Markets: How to Advertise, Sell, and Merchandise Through Boys and Girls*. New York and London:

McGraw-Hill, 1938. Reprinted in *The Children's Culture Reader*, edited by Henry Jenkins. New York: New York University Press, 1997.

Proceedings of the White House Conference on Children in a Democracy. Washington, DC: U.S. Government Printing Office, 1940. Digitized by the Boston Public Library, https://archive.org/details/proceedingsofwhi00whit.

Roskies, Diane K. *Teaching the Holocaust to Children*. Brooklyn: Ktav, 1975.

"Selling Food to Children: *The Mother's Own Book* (1928)." Reprinted in *The Children's Culture Reader*, edited by Henry Jenkins, 463–467. New York: New York University Press, 1998.

Sienna, Noam, ed. *A Rainbow Thread: An Anthology of Queer Jewish Texts from the First Century to 1969*. Philadelphia: Print-O-Craft Press, 2019.

Wilson, Jess H. "Does Your 'Research' Embrace the Boy of Today?" *Printers Ink* 118 (March 16, 1922). Reprinted in *The Children's Culture Reader*, edited by Henry Jenkins. New York: New York University Press, 1997.

Wise, Stephen S. *Child Versus Parent: Some Chapters on the Irrepressible Conflict in the Home*. New York: Macmillan Company, 1922.

Books

Abate, Michelle Ann, and Kenneth B. Kidd, eds. *Over the Rainbow: Queer Children's and Young Adult Literature*. Ann Arbor: University of Michigan Press, 2011.

Adler, Eliyana R. *In Her Hands: The Education of Jewish Girls in Tsarist Russia*. Detroit: Wayne State University Press, 2011.

Ahmed, Sara. *The Promise of Happiness*. Durham, NC: Duke University Press, 2010.

Antler, Joyce. *You Never Call! You Never Write!: A History of the Jewish Mother*. Oxford, UK: Oxford University Press, 2008.

——. *Jewish Radical Feminism: Voices from the Women's Liberation Movement*. New York: New York University Press, 2018.

Bader, Barbara. *American Picture Books from Noah's Ark to the Beast Within*. New York: Macmillan, 1976.

Baigell, Matthew. *Jewish Art in America: An Introduction*. Lanham, MD: Rowman & Littlefield, 2007.

Barthes, Roland. *The Rustle of Language*. Translated by Richard Howard. New York: Farrar, Straus & Giroux, 1986.

Baruch, Dorothy W. *One Little Boy*. New York: Julian Press, 1952.

Baskind, Samantha, and Ranen Omer-Sherman, eds. *The Jewish Graphic Novel: Critical Approaches*. New Brunswick, NJ: Rutgers University Press, 2008.

Batchelor, Bob. *American Pop: Popular Culture Decade by Decade* 2. Westport, CT: Greenwood, 2009.

Batnitzky, Leora. *How Judaism Became a Religion*. Princeton, NJ: Princeton University Press, 2011.

Baughman, Ernest G. *Type and Motif-Index of the Folktales of England and North America*. The Hague: Mouton & Co., 1966.

Bausum, Ann. *Stonewall: Breaking Out in the Fight for Gay Rights*. New York: Penguin, 2016.

Beeck, Nathalie Op de. *Suspended Animation: Children's Picture Books and the Fairy Tale of Modernity*. Minneapolis: University of Minnesota Press, 2010.

Berger, Alan L. *Children of Job: American Second-Generation Witnesses to the Holocaust*. Albany: State University of New York Press, 1997.

Berlant, Lauren. *Cruel Optimism*. Durham, NC: Duke University Press, 2011.

Bernstein, Leonard. *The Leonard Bernstein Letters*. Edited by Nigel Simeone. New Haven, CT: Yale University Press, 2013.

Bernstein, Robin. *Racial Innocence: Performing American Childhood from Slavery to Civil Rights*. New York: New York University Press, 2011.

Bettelheim, Bruno. *The Uses of Enchantment: The Meaning and Importance of Fairy Tales*. New York: Knopf, Distributed by Random House, 1976.

Biale, David. *Eros and the Jews*. Berkeley: University of California Press, 1997.

Body, N. O. *Memoirs of a Man's Maiden Years*. Philadelphia: University of Pennsylvania Press, 2006.

Brown, Stuart. *Play: How It Shapes the Brain, Opens the Imagination, and Invigorates the Soul*. New York: Avery, 2009.

Bruhm, Steven, and Natasha Hurley, eds. *Curiouser: On The Queerness Of Children*. Minneapolis: University of Minnesota Press, 2004.

Burningham, John, ed. *When We Were Young*. London: Bloomsbury, 2004.

Butler, Francelia. *Sharing Literature with Children: A Thematic Anthology*. New York: David McKay, 1977.

Caruth, Cathy. *Unclaimed Experience: Trauma, Narrative and History*. Baltimore: Johns Hopkins University Press, 1996.

Cech, John. *Angels and Wild Things: The Archetypal Poetics of Maurice Sendak*. University Park: Pennsylvania State University Press, 1995.

Chauncey, George. *Gay New York: Gender, Urban Culture, and the Makings of the Gay Male World, 1890–1940*. New York: Basic Books, 1994.

Chinn, Sarah E. *Inventing Modern Adolescence: The Children of Immigrants in Turn-of-the-Century America*. New Brunswick, NJ: Rutgers University Press, 2009.

Cohen, Beth B. *Case Closed: Holocaust Survivors in Postwar America*. New Brunswick: Rutgers University Press, 2007.

Cohen, Naomi W. *What the Rabbis Said: The Public Discourse of Nineteenth-Century American Rabbis*. New York: New York University, 2008.

Cott, Jonathan. *Pipers at the Gates of Dawn: The Wisdom of Children's Litera-ture*. New York: Random House, 1981.

——. *There's a Mystery There: The Primal Vision of Maurice Sendak*. New York: Doubleday, 2017.

Cvetkovich, Ann. *Depression: A Public Feeling*. Durham, NC: Duke University Press, 2012.

Dawidowicz, Lucy S. *On Equal Terms: Jews in America, 1881–1981*. New York: Holt, Rinehart and Winston, 1982.

Delbo, Charlotte. *La mémoire et les jours*. Paris: Berg International, 1985.

Diner, Hasia. *Lower East Side Memories: A Jewish Place in America*. Princeton, NJ: Princeton University Press, 2000.

——. *We Remember with Reverence and Love: American Jews and the Myth of Silence After the Holocaust, 1945–1962*. New York: New York University Press, 2009.

Edelman, Lee. *No Future: Queer Theory and the Death Drive*. Durham, NC: Duke University Press, 2004.

Egan, R. Danielle, and Gail Hawkes. *Theorizing the Sexual Child in Modernity*. New York: Palgrave Macmillan, 2010.

Elior, Rachel. *Dybbuks and Jewish Women in Social History, Mysticism and Folk-lore*. Jerusalem: Urim Publications, 2008.

Epstein, Helen. *Children of the Holocaust*. New York: Penguin Books, 1979.

Epstein, Marc Michael, ed. *Skies of Parchment, Seas of Ink: Jewish Illuminated Manuscripts*. Princeton, NJ, and Oxford, UK: Princeton University Press, 2015.

Ficowski, Jerzy, ed. *Letters and Drawings of Bruno Schulz*. Translated by Walter Arndt with Victoria Nelson. New York: Harper & Row, 1988.

Fingeroth, Danny. *Disguised as Clark Kent*. New York and London: Continuum, 2007.

Fishman, Sylvia Barack, ed. *Follow My Footprints: Changing Images of Women in American Jewish Fiction*. Hanover, NH, and London: Brandeis University Press and the University Press of New England, 1992.

Fishman, Sylvia Barack. *Negotiating Both Sides of the Hyphen: Coalescence, Compartmentalization, and American Jewish Values*. Cincinnati: Judaic Studies Program, University of Cincinnati, 1996.

Flanzbaum, Hilene, ed. *Americanization of the Holocaust*. Baltimore: Johns Hopkins University Press, 1999.

Freeze, ChaeRan Y. *Jewish Marriage and Divorce in Imperial Russia*. Hanover. NH, and London: Brandeis University Press and University Press of New England, 2002.

Fricker, Miranda. *Epistemic Injustice: Power and the Ethics of Knowing*. Oxford, UK: Oxford University Press, 2007.

Fuchs, Lawrence. *Beyond Patriarchy: Jewish Fathers and Families*. Hanover, NH: Brandeis University Press, 2000.

Goffman, Erving. *Stigma: Notes on the Management of Spoiled Identity*. Englewood Cliffs, NJ: Prentice-Hall, 1963.

Goldberg, Harvey E. *Jewish Passages: Cycles of Jewish Life*. Berkeley: University of California Press, 2003.

Goldstein, Eric L. *The Price of Whiteness: Jews, Race, and American Identity*. Princeton, NJ: Princeton University Press, 2006.

Greif, Mark. *The Age of the Crisis of Man: Thought and Fiction in America, 1933–1973*. Princeton, NJ: Princeton University Press, 2015.

Grossman, David. *See Under—Love*. Translated from the Hebrew by Betsy Rosenberg. New York: Picador USA/Farrar, Straus and Giroux, 1989.

——. *Writing in the Dark*. Translated by Jessica Cohen. New York: Farrar, Straus & Giroux, 2008.

Hage, Erik. *The Melville-Hawthorne Connection: A Study of the Literary Friendship*. Jefferson, NC, and London: McFarland, 2014.

Halperin, David M., and Valerie Traub, eds. *Gay Shame*. Chicago and London: University of Chicago Press, 2009.

Harbin, Billy J., et al., eds. *The Gay & Lesbian Theatrical Legacy: A Biographical Dictionary of Major Figures in American Stage History in the Pre-Stonewall Era*. Ann Arbor: University of Michigan Press, 2007.

Hayward, Stephen, and Sarah Lefanu. *God: An Anthology of Fiction*. London and New York: Serpent's Tail, 1992.

Hayworth, Eugene. *Fever Vision: The Life and Works of Coleman Dowell*. Champaign, IL, and London: Dalkey Archive Press, 2007.

Hirsch, Marianne. *Family Frames: Photography, Narrative, and Postmemory*. Cambridge, MA: Harvard University Press, 1997.

Hoffman, Lawrence A. *Covenant of Blood: Circumcision and Gender in Rabbinic Judaism*. Chicago: University of Chicago Press, 1996.

Hoffman, Warren. *The Passing Game: Queering Jewish American Culture*. Syracuse, NY: Syracuse University Press, 2009.

Hopkins, Lee Bennett. *Books Are by People: Interviews with 104 Authors and Illustrators of Books for Young Children*. New York: Citation Press, 1969.

Howe, Irving. *World of Our Fathers*. New York: Harcourt Brace Jovanovich, 1976.

Illick, Joseph E. *American Childhoods*. Philadelphia: University of Pennsylvania Press, 2002.

Jacobson, Matthew Frye. *Whiteness of a Different Color: European Immigrants and the Alchemy of Race*. Cambridge, MA: Harvard University Press, 1998.

Jenkins, Henry, ed. *The Children's Culture Reader*. New York: New York University Press, 1998.

Kadar, Naomi Prawer. *Raising Secular Jews: Yiddish Schools and Their Periodicals for American Children, 1917–1950*. Waltham, MA: Brandeis University Press, 2017.

Kaplan, Arie. *From Krakow to Krypton: Jews and Comic Books*. Philadelphia: Jewish Publication Society, 2008.

Kazin, Alfred. *New York Jew*. New York: Alfred A. Knopf, 1978.

Kidd, Kenneth. *Freud in Oz: At the Intersections of Psychoanalysis and Children's Literature*. Minneapolis: University of Minnesota Press, 2011.

———. *Making American Boys: Boyology and the Feral Tale*. Minneapolis: University of Minnesota Press, 2004.

Kirshenblatt-Gimblett, Barbara, and Jeffrey Shandler, eds. *Anne Frank Unbound*. Bloomington: Indiana University Press, 2012.

Klapper, John. *Nonconformist Writing in Nazi Germany: The Literature of Inner Emigration*. Rochester, NY: Camden House, 2015.

Krasner, Jonathan B. *The Benderly Boys and American Jewish Education*. Waltham, MA: Brandeis University Press, 2011.

Kristeva, Julia. *Desire in Language: A Semiotic Approach to Literature and Art*. Edited by Leon S. Roudiez. Translated by Thomas Gora, Alice Jardine, and Leon S. Roudiez. New York: Columbia University Press, 1980.

Kunze, Peter C., ed. *Conversations with Maurice Sendak*. Jackson: University Press of Mississippi, 2016.

Kushner, Tony. *Angels in America: A Gay Fantasia on National Themes*. New York: Theatre Communications Group, 1995.

———. *A Dybbuk and Other Tales of the Supernatural*. Adapted from translation of S. Ansky by Joachim Neugrochel. New York: Theatre Communications Group, 1997.

———. *The Art of Maurice Sendak: 1980 to the Present*. New York: Abrams, 2003.

Lambert, Joshua. *Unclean Lips: Jews, Obscenity, and American Culture*. New York: New York University Press, 2013.

Lanes, Selma G. *The Art of Maurice Sendak*. New York: Harry N. Abrams, 1980.

Leddick, David. *Intimate Companions: A Triography of George Platt Lynes, Paul Cadmus, Lincoln Kirstein, and Their Circle*. New York: St. Martin's Press, 2000.

Lerer, Seth. *Children's Literature: A Reader's History, from Aesop to Harry Potter*. Chicago: University of Chicago Press, 2009.

Love, Heather K. *Feeling Backward: Loss and the Politics of Queer History*. Cambridge, MA: Harvard University Press, 2007.

Malamud, Bernard. *A Malamud Reader*. New York: Farrar, Straus & Giroux, 1967.

Marcus, Ivan G. *Rituals of Childhood: Jewish Acculturation in Medieval Europe*. New Haven, CT: Yale University Press, 1998.

Marcus, Leonard S., ed. *Dear Genius: The Letters of Ursula Nordstrom*. New York: HarperCollins, 1998.

McCarthy, Dennis, ed. *Deep Play—Exploring the Use of Depth in Psychotherapy with Children*. London and Philadelphia: Jessica Kingsley, 2015.

McCay, Winsor. *Little Nemo*. New York: Nostalgia Press, 1976.

McCloud, Scott. *Understanding Comics*. New York: HarperCollins, 1993.

Melville, Herman. *Moby-Dick*. New York: Bantam Classics, 1981 (originally published 1851).

Miller, Alice. *Drama of the Gifted Child*. New York: Basic Books, 1981.

Monks of New Skete, *Art of Raising a Puppy*. New York: Little, Brown, 1991.

Moore, Deborah D. *At Home in America*. New York: Columbia University Press, 1983.

Morgan, Bill, and Nancy J. Peters, eds. *Howl on Trial: The Battle for Free Expression*. San Francisco: City Lights Books, 2006.

Mosse, George. *The Image of Man: The Creation of Modern Masculinity*. New York: Oxford University Press, 1996.

Most, Andrea. *Making Americans: Jews and the Broadway Musical*. Cambridge, MA: Harvard University Press, 2004.

Nel, Philip. *Crockett Johnson and Ruth Krauss: How an Unlikely Couple Found Love, Dodged the FBI, and Transformed Children's Literature*. Jackson: University Press of Mississippi, 2012.

Newton, Esther. *Cherry Grove, Fire Island: Sixty Years in America's First Gay and Lesbian Town*. Boston: Beacon Press, 1993.

Peiss, Kathy. *Cheap Amusements: Working Women and Leisure in Turn-of-the-Century New York*. Philadelphia: Temple University Press, 1986.

Poole, L. M. *Maurice Sendak and the Art of Children's Book Illustration*. Maidstone, Kent, UK: Crescent Moon, 1996.

Reddy, William M. *The Navigation of Feeling*. Cambridge, UK: Cambridge University Press, 2001.

Roiphe, Katie. *The Violet Hour*. New York: Dial Press, 2016.

Rose, Jacqueline. *The Case of Peter Pan, or the Impossibility of Children's Fiction*. New York: Macmillan, 1984.

Rosen, David. *Sin, Sex & Subversion: How What Was Taboo in 1950s New York Became America's New Normal*. New York: Carrel Books, 2016.

Rosenblum, Robert. *The Romantic Child*. London: Thames and Hudson, 1988.

Roskies, David G., and Naomi Diamant. *Holocaust Literature: A History and Guide*. Hanover, NH: Brandeis University Press, 2012.

Roth, Henry. *Call It Sleep*. New York: Robert O. Ballou, 1934.

Sadler, Glenn Edward. "A Conversation with Maurice Sendak and Dr. Seuss." 1982. Reprinted in *Conversations with Maurice Sendak*, edited by Peter C. Kunze. Jackson: University Press of Mississippi, 2016.

Sammond, Nicholas. *Babes in Tomorrowland: Walt Disney and the Making of the American Child, 1930–1960*. Durham, NC: Duke University Press, 2005.

Sanchez-Eppler, Karen. *Dependent States: The Child's Part in Nineteenth-Century American Culture*. Chicago and London: University of Chicago Press, 2005.

Sarna, Jonathan D. *American Judaism: A History*. New Haven, CT, and London: Yale University Press, 2004.

——. *JPS: The Americanization of Jewish Culture, 1888–1988*. Philadelphia: Jewish Publication Society, 1989.

Sedgwick, Eve Kosofsky. *Epistemology of the Closet*. Berkeley and Los Angeles: University of California Press, 1990.

Seidman, Naomi. *The Marriage Plot: Or, How Jews Fell in Love with Love, and with Literature*. Stanford, CA: Stanford University Press, 2016.

Sonheim, Amy. *Maurice Sendak*. New York: Twayne, 1991.

Spiegelman, Art. *Metamaus*. New York: Pantheon, 2011.

Stampfer, Shaul. *Families, Rabbis, and Education: Traditional Jewish Society in Nineteenth-Century Eastern Europe*. Oxford, UK: Littman Library of Jewish Civilization, 2010.

Stearns, Peter N. *Anxious Parents*. New York and London: New York University Press, 2003.

Stearns, Peter N., and Jan Lewis, eds. *An Emotional History of the United States*. New York: New York University Press, 1998.

Sternlicht, Sanford. *The Tenement Saga: The Lower East Side and Early Jewish American Writers*. Madison: University of Wisconsin Press, 2004.

Stockton, Kathryn Bond. *The Queer Child*. Durham, NC: Duke University Press, 2009.

Wallach, Kerry. *Passing Illusions: Jewish Visibility in Weimar Germany*. Ann Arbor: University of Michigan Press, 2017.

Wardi, Dina. *Memorial Candles: Children of the Holocaust*. London and New York: Tavistock/Routledge, 1992.

Waters, Mary C. *Ethnic Options: Choosing Identities in America*. Berkeley: University of California Press, 1990.

Wenger, Beth S. *New York Jews and the Great Depression: Uncertain Promise*. New Haven, CT: Yale University Press, 1996.

Whitfield, Stephen J. *In Search of American Jewish Culture*. Hanover, NH: Brandeis University Press, 1999.

Whitman, Walt. *Live Oak, with Moss.* Illustrated by Brian Selznick. New York: Abrams, 2019.

Winnicott, D. W. *Playing and Reality.* London and New York: Routledge, 2005.

Wintle, Justin. *The Pied Pipers: Interviews with the Influential Creators of Children's Literature.* New York: Paddington Press, 1975.

Yahil, Leni. *The Holocaust: The Fate of European Jewry, 1932–1945.* Oxford, UK: Oxford University Press, 1987.

Zelizer, Viviana. *Pricing the Priceless Child.* Princeton, NJ: Princeton University Press, 1985.

Zinsser, William et al. *Worlds of Childhood: The Art and Craft of Writing for Children.* Boston: Houghton Mifflin, 1998.

Articles and Book Chapters

Anderson, Mark M. "The Child Victim as Witness to the Holocaust: An American Story?" *Jewish Social Studies* 14, no. 1 (2007): 1–22.

Angelides, Steven. "Feminism, Child Sexual Abuse, and the Erasure of Child Sexuality." *GLQ: A Journal of Lesbian and Gay Studies* 10, no. 2 (2004): 141–177.

Arakelian, Paul G. "Text and Illustration: A Stylistic Analysis of Books by Sendak and Mayer," *Children's Literature Association Quarterly* 10, no. 3 (1985): 122–127.

Bedingfield, Agnieszka. "Trans-Memory and Diaspora: Memories of Europe and Asia in American Immigrant Narratives." In *Sites of Ethnicity: Europe and the Americas,* edited by William Boelhower et al. Heidelberg: Universitätsverlag, Winter 2004.

Berner, Tali. "Children and Rituals in Early Modern Ashkenaz." *The Journal of the History of Childhood and Youth* 7, no. 1 (2014): 65–86.

Bilge, Sirma. "Intersectionality Undone: Saving Intersectionality from Feminist Intersectionality Studies." *Du Bois Review: Social Science Research on Race* 10, no. 2 (2013): 405–424.

Bosmajian, Hamida. "Hidden Grief: Maurice Sendak's *Dear Mili* and the Limitations of Holocaust Picture Books." In *Sparing the Child: Grief and the Unspeakable in Youth Literature About Nazism and the Holocaust,* 215–240. New York and London: Routledge.

——. "Memory and Desire in the Landscapes of Sendak's *Dear Mili.*" *The Lion and the Unicorn* 19, no. 2 (1995): 186–210.

Bryant, John. "Pierre and Pierre: Editing and Illustrating Melville." Review of *Pierre; or, the Ambiguities. The Kraken Edition,* by Herman Melville, edited by Hershel Parker, pictures by Maurice Sendak. *College English* 60, no. 3 (March 1998): 336–341.

Cech, John. "Maurice Sendak and *Where the Wild Things Are*: A Legacy of Transformation." *PMLA* 129, no. 1 (2014).

Cederbaum, Sophie N. "American Jewish Juvenile Literature During the Last Twenty-Five Years." *Jewish Book Annual* (1967–68): 192–203.

Chauncey, George. "The Trouble with Shame." In *Gay Shame*, edited by David M. Halperin and Valerie Traub, 277–282. Chicago and London: University of Chicago Press, 2009.

Commire, Anne. "Maurice Sendak." In *Something About the Author: Facts and Pictures About Authors and Illustrators of Books for Young People* 27. Detroit: Gale Research Company, Book Tower, 1982.

Corsaro, Frank. "Chapter VI: On Stage: Theater, Opera, and Ballet: M&M (Maurice and Me)." In *Maurice Sendak: A Celebration of the Artist and His Work*, edited by Leonard S. Marcus, curated by Justin G. Schiller and Dennis M. V. David, 133–136. New York: Abrams, 2013.

Crenshaw, Kimberlé. "Intersectionality and Identity Politics: Learning from Violence Against Women of Color." In *Reconstructing Political Theory: Feminist Perspectives*, edited by Mary Lyndon Shanley and Uma Narayan, 178–193. University Park: Pennsylvania State University Press, 1997.

Cummins, June. "Becoming an 'All-of-a-Kind' American: Sydney Taylor and Strategies of Assimilation." *The Lion and the Unicorn* 27, no. 3 (2003): 324–343.

Dashefsky, Arnold, and Irving M. Levine. "The Jewish Family: Continuity and Change." In *Families and Religions: Conflict and Change in Modern Society*, edited by William V. D'Antonio and Joan Aldous. Beverly Hills, CA: Sage, 1985.

Dreher, Derick. "Maurice Sendak; or, What the Nineteenth Century Can Mean to the Twenty-First." *PMLA* 126, no. 1 (2014): 106.

Eichler-Levine, Jodi. "Maurice Sendak's Jewish Mother(s)." In *Mothers in the Jewish Cultural Imagination*, edited by Marjorie Lehman, Jane Kanarek, and Simon J. Bronner. Oxford, UK, and Portland, OR: The Littman Library of Jewish Civilization, 2017.

Ellis, Havelock. *Studies in the Psychology of Sex*, Vol. 1: *Sexual Inversion*. Watford, London, and Leipzig: University Press, 1900.

Eustace, Nicole. "AHR Conversation: The Historical Study of Emotions." *American Historical Review* 117, no. 5 (2012): 1487–1531.

Fadiman, Clifton. "A Meditation on Children and Their Literature." Afterword to *Sharing Literature with Children: A Thematic Anthology*, by Francelia Butler. New York: David McKay, 1977.

Fischer, Sophia M. "Grimm's Tale Used to Depict Holocaust." *Jewish Journal*, Deerfield Beach, Florida, April 2, 1992, 3A.

Gans, Herbert J. "Symbolic Ethnicity: The Future of Ethnic Groups and Cultures in America." *Ethnic and Racial Studies* 2, no. 1 (2010): 1–20.

Glynn, Eugene. "Desperate Necessity: Art and Creativity in Recent Psychoanalytic Theory." *The Print Collector's Newsletter* 8, no. 2 (May-June 1977): 29–36. Reprinted in Eugene Glynn, *Desperate Necessity: Writings on Art and Psychoanalysis*, edited by Jonathan Weinberg. Pittsburgh: Periscope, 2008.

———. Review of *Egon Schiele's Portraits* and *Schiele in Prison*, both by Alessandra Comini. *The Print Collector's Newsletter* 6, no. 3 (July-August 1975): 77–79. Reprinted in Eugene Glynn, *Desperate Necessity: Writings on Art and Psychoanalysis*, edited by Jonathan Weinberg. Pittsburgh: Periscope, 2008.

———. "Television and the American Character." 1956. Reprinted in Eugene Glynn, *Desperate Necessity: Writings on Art and Psychoanalysis*, edited by Jonathan Weinberg. Pittsburgh: Periscope, 2008.

———. "To Express a Serious Sorrow." Review of *Vincent van Gogh: A Psychological Study*, by Humberto Nagera, and *Stranger on the Earth: A Psychological Biography of Vincent van Gogh*, by Albert J. Lubin. *The Print Collector's Newsletter* 4, no. 4 (September-October 1973): 88–90. Reprinted in Eugene Glynn, *Desperate Necessity: Writings on Art and Psychoanalysis*, edited by Jonathan Weinberg. Pittsburgh: Periscope, 2008.

Goldstein, Fanny. "The Jewish Child in Bookland." *The Jewish Book Annual* 5 (1946–47): 84–100.

Goren, Arthur. "A 'Golden Decade' for American Jews: 1945–1955." In *American Jewish Experience*, edited by Jonathan Sarna. New York and London: Holmes and Meier, 1986.

Gottlieb, Richard M. "Maurice Sendak's Trilogy." In *Psychoanalytic Study of the Child*, Vol. 63, edited by Robert A. King and Samuel Abrams. New Haven, CT: Yale University Press, 2009.

Greenbaum, Avraham. "The Girls' Heder and the Girls in the Boys' Heder in Eastern Europe Before World War I." *East/West Education* 18, no. 1 (1997): 55–62.

Greenblatt, Stephen. Foreword to *My Brother's Book*, by Maurice Sendak. New York: Michael di Capua Books/HarperCollins, 2013.

———. "Mozart, Shakespeare and the Art of Maurice Sendak." In *Changelings: Children's Stories Lost and Found*, edited by Christina M. Gillis. Berkeley: Doreen B. Townsend Center for the Humanities, University of California, 1996.

Greenspan, Henry. "Imagining Survivors: Testimony and the Rise of Holocaust Consciousness." In *Americanization of the Holocaust*, edited by Hilene Flanzbaum. Baltimore: Johns Hopkins University Press, 1999.

Haase, Donald. "Children, War, and the Imaginative Space of Fairy Tales." *The Lion and the Unicorn* 24, no. 3 (2000): 360–377.

Halberstam, J. Jack. "Queer Temporality and Postmodern Geographies." In *In a Queer Time and Place*. New York: New York University Press, 2005. Reprinted in *Reading Feminist Theory: From Modernity to Postmodernity*, edited by Susan Archer Mann and Ashly Suzanne Patterson. New York and Oxford, UK: Oxford University Press, 2015.

"Ḥayyim Vital Describes Male Souls in Female Bodies" (Tsfat, Mid-Sixteenth Century). In *A Rainbow Thread: An Anthology of Queer Jewish Texts from the First Century to 1969*, edited by Noam Sienna. Philadelphia: Print-O-Craft Press, 2019.

Hirsch, Marianne. "The Generation of Postmemory." *Poetics Today* 29, no. 1 (2008): 103–128.

Hyman, Paula E. "The Jewish Family: Looking for a Usable Past." In *On Being a Jewish Feminist*, edited by Susannah Heschel, 19–26. New York: Schocken Books, 1995.

Kidd, Kenneth. "'A' is for Auschwitz: Psychoanalysis, Trauma Theory, and the Children's Literature of Atrocity." *Children's Literature* 33 (2005): 120–149.

——. "Wild Things and Wolf Dreams: Maurice Sendak, Picture-Book Psychologist." In *The Oxford Handbook of Children's Literature*, edited by Lynne Vallone and Julia Mickenberg, 211–230. New York: Oxford University Press, 2011.

Krasner, Jonathan B. "A Recipe for American Jewish Integration: *The Adventures of K'tonton* and *Hillel's Happy Holidays*." *The Lion and the Unicorn* 27, no. 3 (September 2003): 344–361.

Krutikov, Mikhail. "An End to Fairy Tales: The 1930s in the *Mayselekh* of Der Nister and Leyb Kvitko." In *Children and Yiddish Literature: From Early Modernity to Post-Modernity*, edited by Gennady Estraikh, Kristin Hoge, and Mikhail Krutikov. Cambridge, UK, and New York: Legenda, 2016.

Kümmerling-Meibauer, Bettina. "Romantic and Jewish Images of Childhood in Maurice Sendak's *Dear Mili*." *European Judaism* 42, no. 1 (Spring 2009): 5–16.

Lederhendler, Eli. "Orphans and Prodigies: Rediscovering Young Jewish Immigrant 'Marginals'." *American Jewish History* 95, no. 2 (June 2009): 135–155.

Lipstadt, Deborah E. "America and Memory of the Holocaust, 1950–1965." *Modern Judaism* 16, no. 3 (October 1996): 195–214.

Love, Heather K. "Emotional Rescue." In *Gay Shame*, edited by David M. Halperin and Valerie Traub. Chicago and London: University of Chicago Press, 2009.

Lugowski, David M. "Queering the (New) Deal: Lesbian and Gay Representation and the Depression-Era Cultural Politics of Hollywood's Production Code." *Cinema Journal* 38, no. 2 (Winter 1999): 3–35.

Mantovan, Daniela. "Reading Soviet-Yiddish Poetry for Children: Der Nister's *Mayselekh in Ferzn* 1917–39." In *Children and Yiddish Literature: From Early Modernity to Post-Modernity*, edited by Gennady Estraikh, Kristin Hoge, and Mikhail Krutikov. Cambridge, UK, and New York: Legenda, 2016.

Marcus, Leonard S. "Chapter I: The Artist and His Work: Fearful Symmetries: Maurice Sendak's Picture Book Trilogy and the Making of an Artist." In *Maurice Sendak: A Celebration of the Artist and His Work*, edited by Leonard S. Marcus, curated by Justin G. Schiller and Dennis M. V. David, 15–27. New York: Abrams, 2013.

May, Jill P. "Envisioning the Jewish Community in Children's Literature: Maurice Sendak and Isaac Singer." *Journal of the Midwest Modern Language Association* 33, no. 3 / 34, no. 1 (Autumn 2000–Winter 2001): 137–151.

Mickenberg, Julia. "The Pedagogy of the Popular Front: 'Progressive Parenting' for a New Generation, 1918–1945." In *The American Child: A Cultural Studies Reader*, edited by Caroline Field Levander. New Brunswick, NJ: Rutgers University Press, 2003.

Moskowitz, Golan. "Before *Wild Things*: Maurice Sendak and the Postwar Jewish American Child as Queer Insider-Outsider." *Images: A Journal of Jewish Art and Visual Culture* (2019): 85–94.

Nel, Philip. "Wild Things, Children and Art: The Life and Work of Maurice Sendak." *The Comics Journal* 302 (2013): 12–29.

Ofer, Dalia. "Parenthood in the Shadow of the Holocaust." In *Jewish Families in Europe, 1939–Present*, edited by Joanna Beata Michlic. Waltham, MA: UPNE/Brandeis University Press, 2017.

Perrot, Jean. "Deconstructing Maurice Sendak's Postmodern Palimpsest." *Children's Literature Association Quarterly* 16, no. 4 (Winter 1991–92): 259–263.

——. "Maurice Sendak's Ritual Cooking of the Child in Three Tableaux: The Moon, Mother, and Music." *Children's Literature* 18 (1990): 68–86.

Plamper, Jan. "The History of Emotions: An Interview with William Reddy, Barbara Rosenwein, and Peter Stearns." *History and Theory* 49, no. 2 (May 2010): 237–265.

Prell, Riv-Ellen. "Family Economy/Family Relations: The Development of American Jewish Ethnicity in the Early Twentieth Century." In *National Variations in Jewish Identity*, edited by Steven M. Cohen and Gabriel Horenczyk, 177–198. Albany: State University of New York Press, 1999.

"Questions to an Artist Who Is Also an Author: A Conversation Between Maurice Sendak and Virginia Haviland." *Quarterly Journal of the Library of Congress* 28, no. 4 (October 1971): 262–280. Reprinted in *Conversations with Maurice Sendak*, edited by Peter C. Kunze. Jackson: University Press of Mississippi, 2016.

Rodgers, Patrick. "Chapter X: Where the Wild Things Are: Mad Max: On Three Preliminary Drawings for *Where the Wild Things Are*." In *Maurice Sendak: A Celebration of the Artist and His Work*, edited by Leonard S. Marcus, curated by Justin G. Schiller and Dennis M. V. David, 195–201. New York: Abrams, 2013.

———. "Selected Sendak: Interviews by the Rosenbach." Rosenbach Museum Archives, 2007–8. Reprinted in *Conversations with Maurice Sendak*, edited by Peter C. Kunze. Jackson: University Press of Mississippi, 2016.

Rosen, Aaron. "Bernard Perlin: Europe's American." In *In Focus: Orthodox Boys 1948 by Bernard Perlin*, edited by Aaron Rosen. Tate Research Publication, 2016. Accessed November 4, 2016, http://www.tate.org.uk /research/publications/in-focus/orthodox-boys-bernard-perlin/europes -american.

Ryan, Caitlin L., and Jill M. Hermann-Wilmarth. "Already on the Shelf: Queer Readings of Award-Winning Children's Literature." *Journal of Literacy Research* 45, no. 2 (2013): 142–172.

Salvato, Nick. "Queer Structure, Animated Form, and *Really Rosie*." *Camera Obscura* 33, no. 2 (2018): 139–159.

Sammond, Nicholas. "*Dumbo*, Disney, and Difference: Walt Disney Productions and Film as Children's Literature." In *The Oxford Handbook of Children's Literature*, edited by Lynne Vallone and Julia Mickenberg. New York: Oxford University Press, 2011.

Sarna, Jonathan. "From K'tonton to the Torah." *Moment Magazine* (October 1990): 44–47.

Sedgwick, Eve Kosofsky. "How to Bring Your Kids Up Gay." *Social Text* 29 (1991): 18–27.

———. "Shame, Theatricality, and Queer Performativity: Henry James's *The Art of the Novel*." In *Gay Shame*, edited by David M. Halperin and Valerie Traub, 49–62. Chicago and London: University of Chicago Press, 2009.

Seidman, Naomi. "The Ghost of Queer Loves Past: Ansky's 'Dybbuk' and the Sexual Transformation of Ashkenaz." In *Queer Theory and the Jewish Question*, edited by Daniel Boyarin, Daniel Itzkovitz, and Ann Pellegrini, 228–245. New York: Columbia University Press.

Shneer, David. "Queer Is the New Pink: How Queer Jews Moved to the Forefront of Jewish Culture." *Journal of Men, Masculinities and Spirituality* 1, no. 1 (January 2007): 55–64.

Sholem Aleichem. "The 'Four Questions' of An American Boy" (n.d.). In *Yiddish Literature in America: 1870–2000*, edited by Emanuel S. Goldsmith, translated by Barnett Zumoff. Jersey City, NJ: Ktav, 2009.

Sholokhova, Lyudmila. "Soviet Propaganda in Illustrated Yiddish Children's

Books: From the Collections of the YIVO Library, New York." In *Children and Yiddish Literature: From Early Modernity to Post-Modernity*, edited by Gennady Estraikh, Kristin Hoge, and Mikhail Krutikov. Cambridge, UK, and New York: Legenda, 2016.

Singer, Rachel. "Maurice Sendak's *Where the Wild Things Are*: An Exploration of the Personal and the Collective." *Ars Judaica* 7 (2011): 17–32.

Slaff, Bertram. "Creativity: Blessing or Burden?" *Adolescent Psychiatry* (1981): 78–87.

Solomon, Alisa. "Performance: Queerly Jewish/Jewishly Queer in the American Theater." In *The Cambridge History of Jewish American Literature*, edited by Hana Wirth-Nesher. New York and Cambridge, UK: Cambridge University Press, 2016.

Somer, Eli. "Trance Possession Disorder in Judaism: Sixteenth-Century Dybbuks in the Near East." *Journal of Trauma & Dissociation* 5, no. 2 (2004): 131–146.

Sontag, Susan. "Notes on Camp" (1964). In *Against Interpretation: And Other Essays*. New York: Picador, 2001.

Spigel, Lynn. "Seducing the Innocent: Childhood and Television in Postwar America." In *The Children's Culture Reader*, edited by Henry Jenkins, 110–135. New York: New York University Press, 1997.

Spitz, Ellen Handler. "Ethos in Steig's and Sendak's Picture Books: The Connected and the Lonely Child." *Journal of Aesthetic Education* 43, no. 2 (Summer 2009): 64–76.

Stearns, Peter N., and Carol Z. Stearns. "Emotionology: Clarifying the History of Emotions and Emotional Standards." *American Historical Review* 90, no. 4 (1985): 813–836.

Steiner, George. "In Lieu of a Preface." *Salmagundi* 58–59: Homosexuality: Sacrilege, Vision, Politics (Fall 1982–Winter 1983).

Stimpson, Catherine R. "The Beat Generation and the Trials of Homosexual Liberation." In *Salmagundi* 58–59: Homosexuality: Sacrilege, Vision, Politics (Fall 1982–Winter 1983).

Sutton, Roger. "An Interview with Maurice Sendak." *The Horn Book Magazine* (November-December 2003): 687–699. Reprinted in *Conversations with Maurice Sendak*, edited by Peter C. Kunze. Jackson: University Press of Mississippi, 2016.

Sweet, Michael J. "Talking About *Feygelekh*: A Queer Male Representation in Jewish American Speech." In *Queerly Phrased: Language, Gender, and Sexuality*, edited by Anna Livia and Kira Hall. Oxford, UK, and New York: Oxford University Press, 1997.

Tannenbaum, Leslie. "Betrayed by Chicken Soup: Judaism, Gender and Performance in Maurice Sendak's *Really Rosie*." *The Lion and the Unicorn* 27, no. 3 (2003): 362–376.

Taylor, Judy. "Chapter II: Influences on Book Illustration: Some Influences on the Work of Maurice Sendak." In *Maurice Sendak: A Celebration of the Artist and His Work*, edited by Leonard S. Marcus. New York: Abrams, 2013.

Udel, Miriam. "The Sabbath Tale and Jewish Cultural Renewal." In *Children and Yiddish Literature: From Early Modernity to Post-Modernity*, edited by Gennady Estraikh, Kristin Hoge, and Mikhail Krutikov. Cambridge, UK, and New York: Legenda, 2016.

Weber, Donald. "Accents of the Future: Jewish American Popular Culture." In *The Cambridge Companion to Jewish American Literature*, edited by Hana Wirth-Nesher and Michael P. Kramer, 129–148. Cambridge, UK: Cambridge University Press, 2003.

Weinberg, Jonathan. Introduction to *Desperate Necessity: Writings on Art and Psychoanalysis*, by Eugene Glynn, edited by Jonathan Weinberg. New York: Periscope, 2008.

———. "Ray Johnson Fan Club." In *Ray Johnson: Correspondences*, edited by Donna M. De Salvo and Catherine Gudis. Columbus, OH: Wexner Center for the Arts, 1999.

Weitzman, Lenore J. "Resistance in Everyday Life: Family Strategies, Role Reversals, and Role Sharing in the Holocaust." In *Jewish Families in Europe, 1939–Present*, edited by Joanna Beata Michlic. Waltham, MA: UPNE/Brandeis University Press, 2017.

White, Edmund. Preface to *Fever Vision: The Life and Works of Coleman Dowell*, by Eugene Hayworth. Champaign, IL, and London: Dalkey Archive Press, 2007.

Young, Jennifer. "'A Language Is Like a Garden': Shloyme Davidman and the Yiddish Communist School Movement in the United States." In *Children and Yiddish Literature: From Early Modernity to Post-Modernity*, edited by Gennady Estraikh, Kristin Hoge, and Mikhail Krutikov. Cambridge, UK, and New York: Legenda, 2016.

Zipperstein, Steven J. "Transforming the Heder: Maskilic Politics in Imperial Russia." In *Jewish History: Essays in Honor of Chimen Abramsky*, edited by Ada Rapoport-Albert and Steven J. Zipperstein, 87–109. London: Halban, 1988.

Film, Web Content, and Radio

Bohlman, James. "THE Maurice Sendak?!!!" *Journey2Kona2019* (blog), July 14, 2015, https://journey2kona2019.wordpress.com/2015/07/14/the-maurice -sendak.

———. "Truly Wealthy!" *Journey2Kona2019* (blog), May 16, 2002, https://journey2kona2019.wordpress.com/2012/05/16/truly-wealthy.

Far Out Isn't Far Enough: The Tomi Ungerer Story. Directed by Brad Bernstein. Far Out Films, 2013.

"'Fresh Air' Remembers Author Maurice Sendak." *NPR.org*. May 8, 2012, http://www.npr.org/2012/05/08/152248901/fresh-air-remembers-author-maurice-sendak.

"From Kids' Books to Erotica, Tomi Ungerer's 'Far Out' Life" (radio transcript). Terry Gross interviews Tomi Ungerer. *Fresh Air*, National Public Radio, broadcast July 1, 2013, https://www.npr.org/2013/07/01/196335794/from-kids-books-to-erotica-tomi-ungerers-far-out-life.

Glass, Ira. "204: 81 Words" (radio show transcript). *This American Life*, January 18, 2002. Accessed November 3, 2016, http://www.thisamericanlife.org/radio-archives/episode/204/transcript.

"Grim Colberty Tales with Maurice Sendak," *The Colbert Report*, Part One, January 24, 2012, www.cc.com/video-clips/gzi3ec/the-colbert-report-grim-colberty-tales-with-maurice-sendak-pt–1.

Last Dance. Directed by Mirra Bank, featuring Robby Bernett, Maurice Sendak, Michael Tracy, Jonathan Wolken, and Arthur Yorinks. First Run Features, 2002.

Lerer, Seth. "Wild Thing: Maurice Sendak and the Worlds of Children's Literature." Lecture at the Contemporary Jewish Museum. Published on YouTube September 29, 2009, https://www.youtube.com/watch?v=lducj5nUkrI.

Marcus, Leonard S. "The Resilience of Children in Maurice Sendak's Books." Interview by NYU Child Study Center Grand Rounds. Published on YouTube by NYU Langone Medical Center. October 28, 2013, https://www.youtube.com/watch?v=9Q9UgR3Zyxs.

"Maurice Sendak on Being a Kid." Animated video created by Andrew Romano and Ramin Setoodeh, produced by David Gerlach. PBS Digital Studios (based on *Newsweek* interview, September 9, 2009).

"Maurice Sendak: On Life, Death and Children's Lit" (radio transcript). Terry Gross interviews Maurice Sendak. *Fresh Air*, National Public Radio, December 29, 2011 (originally broadcast September 20, 2011), www.npr.org/2011/12/29/144077273/maurice-sendak-on-life-death-and-childrens-lit.

Nel, Philip. "In or Out? Crockett Johnson, Ruth Krauss, Sexuality, Biography." *Nine Kinds of Pie* (blog), February 17, 2011. http://www.philnel.com/2011/02/17/in-or-out.

Popova, Maria. "How Ursula Nordstrom, the Greatest Patron Saint of Modern

Childhood, Stood Up for Creativity Against Commercial Cowardice." *Brain Pickings*, February 2, 2015.

——. "Peanuts and the Quiet Pain of Childhood: How Charles Schulz Made an Art of Difficult Emotions." *Brain Pickings*, January 20, 2015.

Tell Them Anything You Want: A Portrait of Maurice Sendak. Directed by Spike Jonze and Lance Bangs, featuring Maurice Sendak, Lynn Caponera, and Catherine Keener. Oscilloscope Laboratories, 2010.

There's a Mystery There: Sendak on Sendak. The Rosenbach Museum & Library, Philadelphia. Retrospective of Sendak Interviews. Portia Productions, 2008. DVD.

"This Pig Wants to Party: Maurice Sendak's Latest" (radio transcript). Terry Gross interviews Maurice Sendak. *Fresh Air*, National Public Radio, broadcast September 20, 2011. Reprinted in *Conversations with Maurice Sendak*, edited by Peter C. Kunze, 195–203. Jackson: University Press of Mississippi, 2016.

Where the Wild Things Are (film), directed by Spike Jonze, produced by Tom Hanks, Gary Goetzman, Maurice Sendak, John Carls, and Vincent Landay, screenplay by Spike Jonze and Dave Eggers. Warner Bros. Pictures, 2009.

Writers Talk: Maurice Sendak with Paul Vaughan (video interview, 1985). Institute of Contemporary Arts, London. Roland Collection of Films and Videos on Art. San Francisco: Kanopy Streaming, 2014. Accessed through University of Massachusetts Amherst Library, June 18, 2016.

Press and Obituaries

Alexander, Neta. "How AIDS Forced the LGBT Community to Redefine 'Home.'" *Haaretz*, September 27, 2017.

Alverson, Brigid, and Eva Volin. "Comics Censorship, from 'Gay Batman to Sendak's Mickey." *School Library Journal*, September 23, 2014.

Association of Gay and Lesbian Psychiatrists Newsletter 30, no. 2 (April 2004).

Bader, Barbara. "Five Gay Picture-Book Prodigies and the Difference They've Made." *The Horn Book Magazine*, March 5, 2015.

Belonsky, Andrew. "Shel Silverstein Covered Fire Island for 'Playboy.'" *Out* magazine, May 22, 2013.

Bermudez, Caroline. "How a Social-Service Fund Raiser Lured a $1-Million Gift." *Chronicle of Philanthropy* 22, no. 16 (August 2010): 19.

Bernheimer, Martin. "Sendak's Picturesque 'Zauberflote.'" *Los Angeles Times*, April 16, 1990.

Bernstein, Robin. "Let Black Kids Just Be Kids." *New York Times*, July 26, 2017.

Bixler, Mark, and Mariano Castillo. "Author of 'Where the Wild Things Are' Dies." *CNN.com*, May 8, 2012.

Blewett, Kelly. "Ursula Nordstrom and the Queer History of the Children's Book." *Los Angeles Review of Books*, August 28, 2016.

Braun, Saul. "Sendak Raises the Shade on Childhood." *New York Times Magazine*, June 7, 1970. Francelia Butler Papers, series 2, box 9, folder: "Sendak, Maurice (Author)." University of Connecticut Archives & Special Collections. Thomas J. Dodd Research Center. Storrs, CT.

Brigada, Gerry, and Warren Taylor. "Sendak's Childrens Books Come from Personal Life." *The Connecticut Daily Campus*, April 29, 1981.

Brockes, Emma. "I Refuse to Cater to the Bullshit of Innocence." *The Believer* (November-December 2012).

Brown, Jennifer M. "The Rumpus Goes On: Max, Maurice Sendak and a Clan of Bears Pay Tribute to a Lifelong Mentorship." *Publishers Weekly*, April 18, 2005.

Burningham, John. "His Stories and Illustrations Captivate Children, but Maurice Sendak—the Author of Where the Wild Things Are—Explains Why for Him They Are a Means of Exorcising a Painful Past." *The Telegraph*, January 12, 2005.

Cahalan, Susannah. "'Goodnight Moon' Author Was a Bisexual Rebel Who Didn't Like Kids." *New York Post*, January 7, 2017.

Canning, Richard. "Something Unforgettable, Forgotten." *The Gay & Lesbian Review Worldwide* 14, no. 6 (November-December 2007): 19–21.

Carey, Joanna. "Tomi Ungerer, Rennaisance Man of Children's Book Illustration." *The Guardian*, February 24, 2012.

Chana, Jas. "Herman Wouk's Fire Island Synagogue." *Tablet*, May 28, 2015.

Clemons, Walter. "Sendak's Enchanted Land." *Newsweek*, May 18, 1981. Blaine Pennington Papers, series 3, box 1, folder 21. University of Missouri-Kansas City Archives. Kansas City, MO.

Cohen, Patricia. "Concerns Beyond Just Where the Wild Things Are." *New York Times*, September 9, 2008.

Cook, Mariana. "Postscript: Wild Things." *The New Yorker*, May 21, 2012.

Cott, Jonathan. "Maurice Sendak, King of All Wild Things." *Rolling Stone*, December 30, 1976, https://www.rollingstone.com/culture/culture-news/maurice-sendak-king-of-all-wild-things-235862.

Cowan, Sarah. "All in One: An Interview with Tomi Ungerer." *The Paris Review*, January 30, 2015.

Crane, Peter. Letter to the editor. *New York Times*, April 10, 2016. Accessed April 11, 2016, http://www.nytimes.com/2016/04/10/books/review/letters-every-college-girls-dream.html?_r=0.

Debnam, Betty. "Meet the Author and Artist of 'The Monster Book.'" *The Mini Page*, March 31, 1974.

Decter, Midge. "The Boys on the Beach," *Commentary*, September 1, 1980.

Dickson, Glenn. "Our Afternoon with Maurice: Klezmer Band Leader Recalls Recording with Sendak." *Jewish Advocate*, June 1, 2012.

Dobrin, Peter. "Bulk of Sendak Collection Leaving Rosenbach." *Philadelphia Inquirer*, September 14, 2014.

——. "Rosenbach Reels in Rare Sendak Trove." *Philadelphia Inquirer*, January 29, 2017.

"'Don't Assume Anything': A Conversation with Maurice Sendak and Philip Nel" (2001). Reprinted in *Conversations with Maurice Sendak*, edited by Peter C. Kunze. Jackson: University Press of Mississippi, 2016.

Drake, David. "Born to Be Wild: Interview by David Drake." *Poz* (September 1999): 87–89. ONE Archives Foundation, Los Angeles.

Evans, Sara. "The Wild World of Maurice Sendak: A Visit with the Most Celebrated Children's Author of Our Time." *Parents* (November 1992). Phillip Applebaum Collection, box 6, folder 67. American Jewish Historical Society. Center for Jewish History.

Everett-Green, Robert. "Maurice Sendak Draws on His Passions and Past." *The Globe and Mail*, January 23, 1998. University of Guelph Archival & Special Collections, Guelph, ON, Canada.

Fassler, Joe. "For 'Hugo' Author Brian Selznick, Life (Thankfully) Imitates Art." *The Atlantic*. February 7, 2012. Ferst, Devra. "The Twisty History of Jewish Kid Lit." *The Jewish Daily Forward*, November 24, 2010.

Flood, Allison. "Maurice Sendak Tells Parents Worried by Wild Things to 'Go to Hell.'" *The Guardian*, October 20, 2009.

Fox, Margalit. "Maurice Sendak, Author of Splendid Nightmares, Dies at 83." *New York Times*, May 8, 2012.

Gluck, Robert. "For Sendak, Menorahs Burn with Memories." *Jewish Advocate*, December 23, 2011.

Green, Jesse. "The Gay History of America's Classic Children's Books." *New York Times*, February 7, 2019.

——. "Review: Reviving a 'Really Rosie' That's Hard-Candy Cute." *New York Times*, August 3, 2017.

Griswold, Jerry. "Outside Over There and Gay Pride." *The Horn Book Magazine*, June 28, 2017.

Groth, Gary. Interview with Maurice Sendak. *The Comics Journal* 302 (2013): 30–109.

Haddock, Robert. "Sendak Doesn't Kid 'Kids.'" *News-Times*, January 26, 1975. Truman A. Warner Papers, MS 026, box 3, folder 28. Western Connecticut State University Archives.

Hammel, Lisa. "Maurice Sendak: Thriving on Quiet." *New York Times*, January

5, 1973. Maurice Sendak Art & Artist Files, Smithsonian American Art Museum/National Portrait Gallery Library, Smithsonian Libraries, Washington DC, consulted November 7, 2015.

Harris, Muriel. "Impressions of Sendak" (1970). Reprinted in *Conversations with Maurice Sendak*, edited by Peter C. Kunze. Jackson: University Press of Mississippi, 2016.

Heller, Steven. Interview with Maurice Sendak. In *Innovators of American Illustration*, ed. Steven Heller, 70–81. New York: Van Nostrand Reinhold, 1986. Reprinted in *Conversations with Maurice Sendak*, edited by Peter C. Kunze. Jackson: University Press of Mississippi, 2016.

Henderson, C. W. "$25,000 Funding Received for Pediatric AIDS Care." *AIDS Weekly Plus*, June 8, 1998. ProQuest. Accessed through University of Toronto Libraries, Toronto, ON, Canada.

Hentoff, Nat. "Among the Wild Things." *New Yorker*, January 15, 1966.

Herszenson, David. "Of Fags, Flags, Faggots and Feygeles." *The Jewish Daily Forward*, April 21, 2010.

Italie, Hillel. "Maurice Sendak with the Wild Things, Now." Associated Press, *Christian Science Monitor*, May 8, 2012.

Kakutani, Michiko. "Digging to the Roots of Maurice Sendak's Vision." *New York Times*, May 15, 2017.

Lahr, John. "The Playful Art of Maurice Sendak." *New York Times Magazine*, October 12, 1980.

León, Concepción de. "The 10 Most Checked-Out Books in N.Y. Public Library History." *New York Times*, January 13, 2020.

Lyall, Sarah. "Maurice Sendak Sheds Moonlight on a Dark Tale." *New York Times*, September 20, 1993.

McGann, Thomas, "Wild Things: Maurice Sendak on Fire Island," *Fire Island News* 63, no. 5 (July 19, 2019).

Mercier, Jean. "Sendak on Sendak." *Publishers Weekly*, April 10, 1981.

Mitzel, John. "An Approach to the Gay Sensibility in Literature." *The Gay Alternative* 11 (Spring 1976): 4–7 and 43–46. Archive.org. Accessed February 6, 2018, https://archive.org/details/TheGayAlternative11Spring1976.

Moyers, Bill. "Maurice Sendak: 'Where the Wild Things Are.'" *PBS NOW*. March 12, 2004.

Nettell, Stephanie. "Maurice Sendak obituary." *The Guardian*, May 8, 2012.

Pfefferman, Naomi. "'Dance's' Conflict Is Center Stage." *Jewish Journal*, April 17, 2003.

Poole, Buzz. "The Wisdom of Sendak: Children Are Wild, Honest, Immoral Beings." *Literary Hub*, May 22, 2017.

Rochman, Hazel. "The Booklist Interview: Maurice Sendak." *Booklist*, June 15, 1992.

Roiphe, Katie. "The Wildest Rumpus: Maurice Sendak and the Art of Death." *The Atlantic*, March 7, 2016.

Rosen, Judith. "Two NYC Kids' Stores Celebrate 70 Years—Combined." *Publishers Weekly*, November 15, 2010.

Rosenblum, Ira. "SIGNOFF; A Fairy Tale, but Hold the Gingerbread." *New York Times*, December 14, 1997.

Russell, John. "Art: Sendak and Friends at the Morgan Library." *New York Times*, September 4, 1981. Maurice Sendak Art & Artist Files, Smithsonian National Portrait Gallery Library, Washington DC, consulted November 7, 2015.

Saxon, Antonia. "A Loving Tribute: Maurice Sendak on 'My Brother's Book.'" *Publishers Weekly*, February 22, 2013.

Schneider, Louise. "A Personal Remembrance of My Uncle, Bert Slaff," *American Society for Adolescent Psychiatry Newsletter*, "In Memoriam" section (Winter 2013).

Spiegelman, Art, and Maurice Sendak. "In the Dumps." *The New Yorker*, September 27, 1993.

Spitz, Ellen Handler. "Maurice Sendak's Sexuality." *New Republic*, February 21, 2013.

Steinberg, Avi. "Maurice Sendak on 'Bumble-Ardy.'" *The Paris Review*, December 27, 2011.

——. "'We Are Inseparable!': On Maurice Sendak's Last Book." *The New Yorker*, March 12, 2013.

Stevens, Norman D. "Celebrating the Life and Work of James Marshall (1942–1992)." *American Book Collectors of Children's Literature* 14, no. 2 (Fall 2002).

Stix, Harriet. "Sendak Draws on Childhood Truths." *Los Angeles Times*, December 7, 1984. Arne Nixon Papers, box 1, folder 103. Arne Nixon Center for the Study of Children's Literature.

Stokes, Colin. "'Frog and Toad': An Amphibious Celebration of Same-Sex Love." *New Yorker Magazine*, May 31, 2016.

Swed, Mark. "'Wild Things' in Operaland: Maurice Sendak Moves from Children's Books to Stage Designer and Librettist." *Los Angeles Times*, June 3, 1990.

Teeman, Tim. "Maurice Sendak: I'm Ready to Die." *The Times*, September 24, 2011.

Updike, John. "Randall Jarrell Writing Stories for Children." *New York Times*, November 14, 1976.

Vondersmith, Jason. "Magical Mozart." *Portland Tribune*, May 3, 2016.

Walike, Deborah. "Every Witch Way: The Opera 'Hansel and Gretel' Is a Majestic Piece of Music with Chilling Insight." *Baltimore Jewish Times* 257, no. 2 (December 8, 2000).

Warrick, Pamela. "Facing the Frightful Things These Days, Maurice Sendak's Wild Creatures Are Homelessness, AIDS and Violence—Big Issues for Small Kids." *Los Angeles Times*, October 11, 1993.

Weiss, Sasha. "Art Spiegelman Discusses Maurice Sendak." *New Yorker*, May 9, 2012.

Wheeler, Andrew. "R.I.P. 'Where the Wild Things Are' Creator Maurice Sendak (1928–2012)." *Comics Alliance*, May 8, 2012.

Zarin, Cynthia. "Not Nice: Maurice Sendak and the Perils of Childhood." *The New Yorker*, April 17, 2006.

Dissertations and Theses

Almquist, Justin. "Confronting Terezín: A Production History of Maurice Sendak and Tony Kushner's *Brundibar*." Master's thesis, Central Washington University, 2014.

Blau, Amy. "Afterlives: Translations of German Weltliteratur into Yiddish." Dissertation, University of Illinois at Urbana, 2005. YIVO, Center for Jewish History, New York.

Langlois, Dagmar. "The Influence of Maurice Sendak, Leo and Diane Dillon, and Chris Van Allsburgh on Contemporary American Children's Book Illustration." Master's thesis, Syracuse University, 1991.

Sorin, Reesa Sheryl Malca. "The Fears of Early Childhood: Writing in Response to a Study of Maurice Sendak." Master's thesis, School of Journalism and Creative Writing, University of Wollongong, 1994.

Taft, Sigmund C. "A Study and Evaluation of the Jewish Community of Bensonhurst, Borough Park, Flatbush and Williamsburg, Neighborhoods in the Borough of Brooklyn in New York City." Master's thesis, New York School of Social Work, Columbia University, 1943. YIVO, Center for Jewish History, New York.

Reference

The Encyclopedia of Jewish Life Before and During the Holocaust, Vol. 3. Edited by Shmuel Spector. New York: New York University Press, 2001. Center for Jewish History Reading Room Library, New York.

Sefer Zambrov: zikaron li-ḳehilat ha-ḳodesh she-hushmedah h. y. d. Edited by Yom-Tow Lewinski (1899). Tel Aviv: ha-Irgunim shel yots'e ha-'ir be-'Artsot ha-Berit Argenṭinah ye-Yiśra'el, 1963. YIVO, Center for Jewish History, New York.

INDEX

Devi Mays, *Forging Ties, Forging Passports: Migration and the Modern Sephardi Diaspora*
2020

Clémence Boulouque, *Another Modernity: Elia Benamozegh's Jewish Universalism*
2020

Dalia Kandiyoti, *The Converso's Return: Conversion and Sephardi History in Contemporary Literature and Culture*
2020

Marc Volovici, *German as a Jewish Problem: The Language Politics of Jewish Nationalism*
2020